Systematic Interviewing

Communication Skills
for Professional Effectiveness

Edited by

John M. Dillard
Texas A & M University

Robert R. Reilly
Texas A & M University

Systematic Interviewing

Communication Skills
for Professional Effectiveness

Merrill Publishing Company
A Bell & Howell Information Company
Columbus • Toronto • London • Melbourne

To our children

Brian Milton and Scott Maurice

and

Robert R., Terence T., John J.,
Ann A., Kelly K., and Steven S.

Published by Merrill Publishing Company
A Bell & Howell Information Company
Columbus, Ohio 43216

This book was set in Garamond.
Administrative Editor: Vicki Knight
Production Coordinator: Anne Daly
Art Coordinator: Lorraine Woost
Cover Designer: Cathy Watterson

Library of Congress Catalog Card Number: 87–62848
International Standard Book Number: 0–675–20824–6
Printed in the United States of America
1 2 3 4 5 6 7 8 9—92 91 90 89 88

Preface

Systematic Interviewing: Communication Skills for Professional Effectiveness addresses the topics significant to the development of interviewing skills for persons trained in professions that involve working with people. Lawyers, teachers, health-care professionals, social-agency personnel, employment interviewers, reporters, survey conductors, supervisors, and many others fall into this category. These individuals are often called upon to interview, yet their preparation or training may not be adequate to perform this task. Frequently, they have excellent capacity to work effectively with people but need assistance in gaining effective skills in and useful knowledge about interviewing. These objectives are best achieved through a combination of instruction and illustration. Accordingly, a considerable amount of case study and other illustrative material is included with the more traditional instruction found in this text.

This book presents basic interviewing skills first, then applies them to specific groups and issues. This format allows the reader to progress from theory to practice.

Chapters are grouped into three parts. Part One (comprising Chapters 1–4) introduces basic concepts and skills of interviewing, the theory and techniques fundamental to all following chapters. Chapter 1 discusses the nature, characteristics, and uses of the interview. A first step in becoming competent in interviewing is to gain an understanding of the elements involved in the interview. Chapter 2 is directed toward the interviewer achieving an awareness and understanding of himself and the interviewee. Interviewing, the human encounter, relies heavily on communication between two or more individuals. The interviewer and the interviewee engage in a reciprocal encounter regarding a variety of significant concerns. Understanding the interview requires awareness and understanding of these participants, their needs, goals, and, particularly, their roles in the interviewing process.

Chapter 3 is a detailed description of the interviewing approach or model that forms the central theme of this text. Its major focus centers on interviewing skills, and it provides a detailed discussion of these skills and their application in the interview along with practical examples. Interviewing is presented as a communicative process with goals, stages, skills, and similar characteristics.

Chapter 4 organizes the detailed and wide-ranging communicative skills–process model of Chapter 3 into stages. A step-by-step procedure for planning and executing the interview is discussed. Goals and techniques appropriate to each stage are presented to integrate the materials discussed in the previous chapters.

Part Two concerns interviewing specific groups of individuals. The basic interviewing skills and concepts of Part One are applied to specific populations: children, adolescents, adults, and older adults.

Interviews with children are the focus of Chapter 5. The reader is provided an overview of the child's cognitive development, language usage, and psychosocial characteristics. Other ideas essential to interviewing a child are discussed. Much of the chapter is devoted to descriptions and examples of interviewing techniques appropriate to various stages of child development.

Developmental issues also represent a major topic in Chapter 6, which deals with the special problems of interviewing adolescents. Physical development, cognitive functioning, and identity formation are among the characteristics integrated into the interviewing model to make it appropriate for use with the adolescent. Specific problems of adolescence, including drug abuse and academic difficulties, are addressed in this chapter.

Chapter 7 addresses concerns common during the adult years. Interviewing in this chapter concerns two major groups: young adults and middle-aged adults. Career and family issues, divorce, and midlife crisis are among the content areas. Techniques and approaches particularly appropriate for working with the mature individual are presented.

Older adults have recently begun receiving some of the attention they deserve. Chapter 8 provides guidance in working with this increasingly important group and begins with a discussion of changing popular perceptions and changing realities relative to older Americans. It concludes with a series of concrete guidelines for the interviewer working with older persons. Again, the liberal use of examples illustrates the application of this interviewing perspective.

Part Three concludes the text by drawing close attention to some vital and pervasive issues: the family, health, and employment.

Chapter 9 addresses the difficult topic of interviewing applied to marriage, family, and sexual issues. The tendency to maintain privacy about such issues makes this type of interviewing particularly challenging, as do the special conditions when family members are interviewed together. Basic principles and techniques of family interviewing are presented in Chapter 9. Human sexuality interviews are dealt with as a special type of family or couple interviewing.

Interviewing in health-care settings is discussed in Chapter 10. Health-care interviews vary widely in locale and topic, but they share a common focus on issues of vital, personal involvement. Most persons care about their personal health. Purposes, techniques, and other distinctive characteristics of the health interview are discussed in this chapter. Guidelines for each stage of the health-care interview are presented in the chapter summary.

Perhaps more has been written regarding interviewing in business and industry than any other interviewing topic. Chapter 11 addresses this application of the interviewing model. Historical and legal influences on business interviewing are discussed, as are likely future trends. While the employment or hiring interview is stressed, other purposes of business and industry communication are included. Underlying concepts, strategies, issues, and effective skills are presented.

Each chapter concludes with a summary and a list of suggested readings. Complete references follow the text. Additionally, an appendix provides statements of ethical principles from representative groups of professional organizations (National Association of Social Workers, American Association for Counseling and Development, and American Psychological Association) whose members are concerned with the interviewing process.

ACKNOWLEDGMENTS

We would like to acknowledge and thank several individuals who have made significant contributions to the creation of this text. Certainly, the chapter contributors are foremost among those meriting acknowledgment. Each has provided a special perspective and necessary element to this project. Their patience through revisions has been particularly appreciated. Thanks go to Jan Hughes, Frances Worchel, Ronn Johnson, Michael Duffy, Arthur Roach, and Ann McDonald.

We wish to thank Jim Montross, who came to our aid when needed; and Doris Gutcher, Kim Shultz, Rebecca Kocurek, who went beyond the call of duty in preparing this manuscript. Their expertise and cooperation added materially to the completion of this project. Vicki Knight, Administrative Editor at Merrill Publishing, provided just the correct mix of carrot and stick to keep editors and contributors working productively. Thank you, Vicki.

Finally, we wish to acknowledge the professional contribution of the individuals who reviewed early versions of this text: Pam Wise, Ohio State University; Arthur M. Horne, Indiana State University; Dan Romero, University of California at Irvine; Kenneth Dimick, Ball State University; Elaine I. Johnson, Pennsylvania State University; Lawrence Beymer, Indiana State University; John H. Childers, Jr., University of Arkansas; and Stephen G. Weinrach, Villanova University.

John M. Dillard
Robert R. Reilly

Contents

Part Three / Interviewing Applied to Specific Issues

PART ONE

Basic Concepts and Interviewing Skills

Successful interviewing is built on a foundation of skills and knowledge. The interviewer learns these skills and knowledge through systematic training that includes self-assessment, awareness and understanding of others, interview skills and style, and evaluations. Chapters 1–4 introduce the techniques, skills, and concepts basic to all types of professional interviewing. They present and define the types of interviews, they discuss significant factors relating to the interviewer and the interviewee, and they provide a systematic model, an approach to interviewing, incorporating appropriate skills and techniques. Finally, the text systematically integrates these concepts, skills, and models into a set of four interview stages.

1

Introduction: A Perspective on Interviewing

John M. Dillard
Robert R. Reilly
Texas A & M University

Interviewing is an activity common to many, if not most, professions. Physicians, lawyers, accountants, social workers, and others interview their clients or patients. Interviewing is a commonly used tool of reporters, police officers, and personnel workers, among others. Professional assistance and interpersonal encounters typically begin with an interview. This form of communication can be considered a necessary skill in the preparation of a wide array of professionals. Fortunately, research in interviewing has progressed to the point that reliable aid is available to individuals who want to acquire the skill.

This chapter details how individuals acquire that skill and explores the meaning and nature of professional interviewing. It discusses types, characteristics, and uses of interviews to provide a foundation for the chapters that follow. Interviewing as presented is more than the verbal exchange of information. It is a relationship deeply rooted in nonverbal and verbal communication and aimed at specific goals.

STEPS TOWARD ACHIEVING COMPETENCE IN PROFESSIONAL INTERVIEWING

Professionals usually have extensive training in at least one professional field (social work, teacher education); however, they may not be proficient in interviewing persons they are to assist. To become competent in interviewing, the professional must acquire awareness and understanding of self, potential interviewees, cultural factors including verbal and nonverbal communication, interviewing techniques, and interviewing stages (see Figure 1–1).

Self-appraisal

When asked, "Who are you?" we generally respond by stating our name and a few personal, observable features of ourselves. This typical response expresses little about who we really are internally or physically.

Figure 1–1   Sequential Steps to Achieve Effective Interviewing

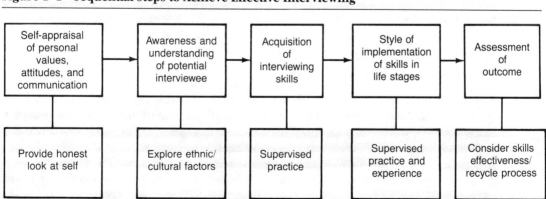

3

Self-awareness is a crucial first step toward helping others. Knowing who you are requires an examination of the total self. You learn about who you are and how to feel about yourself through communication with other individuals. Ultimately, how you perceive yourself is the result of how you perceive others seeing you (Myers & Myers, 1980).

In building a full self-image, you build emotions concerning who you believe you are. Typically, you look to others for confirmation of these feelings. This confirmation, when received, makes you feel entitled to have a certain image of yourself. At times you might conceal parts of your self-image from others, fearing that if they knew these parts of you, they would not accept you.

The more the professional knows about himself, the better he can understand, evaluate, and control his behavior and the better he can understand and appreciate the behavior of potential interviewees. As the professional becomes more aware of himself, he can feel less threatened by what he finds. He might even get to the point that he genuinely likes some things he thought he disliked. Hence, as long as he continues to assess and explore himself, he will probably develop professionally and personally. Self-awareness makes the professional more comfortable with himself and therefore able to put interviewees more at ease with themselves and with him. Additionally, since the professional is personally at ease, his discomfort will be less likely to interfere with his understanding of the interviewee during the interview.

Communication

The most essential ingredient in interviewing is communication. Whether the interview is conducted in person or via telephone, it requires communication between an interviewer and an interviewee. Communication during this joint venture means verbal participation by both. Effective interviews are characterized by effective professional interaction between interviewer and interviewee.

The professional interviewer has an awareness and understanding of communicating across ethnic and cultural lines. She realizes that potential interviewees can have many cultural and ethnic experiences and these experiences can affect how they communicate during the interview. Thus, serious preinterview conditions are focused on eye contact, rate of speech, tone of voice, spatial distance, and language. Each of these factors may influence interviewees' verbal and nonverbal behavior according to their ethnic and cultural experiences. The interviewer's consideration of these factors before the interview can help ensure effective communication with interviewees.

Interview Skills

Communication and interview skills are virtually inseparable. Skills applied in the interview are communication skills designed specifically for use in that setting. Most professional interviewers have learned the basic interviewing skills of communication, including skills in listening. They listen not only with their ears but also with their feelings and emotions. That is, they listen to nonverbal as well as verbal messages. Communication skills include mirroring the interviewee's messages as well as informing her on issues. It requires the interviewer to be aware as well as to understand his biases and projections.

Communication means the sharing of talking time. In the interview situation, the proper balance of communication ranges from about 15% for the professional interviewer to 85% for the interviewee. Obviously, the extent to which the two parties engage in sharing the communication in the interview process will vary according to the type of relationship between the interviewee and interviewer.

Sequence of the Interview Skills

The next step in achieving interviewing competence involves applying communication skills in a sequential order. The competent interviewer learns that effective interviewing depends on applying skills at appropriate times throughout the entire interview. An interview generally has four stages: preparation, initiation, direction, and conclusion. While many skills apply across the four stages, others are most appropriate in certain stages. Through training and supervised practice, the interviewer learns when to apply various skills. As the professional learns and practices, she develops and broadens her skills repertoire. This enhanced awareness and understanding permits her to respond accurately and spontaneously to the interviewee's messages.

In summary, the more aware the interviewer is of her own values, the less need she has to impose them on the interviewee, and the greater her ability to assist him in becoming aware of himself and achieving desired goals. The competent interviewer is aware of and understands her own motivations, beliefs, values, emotions, and assumptions that influence personal behavior and decisions (Eisenberg & Delaney, 1977). The interviewer's self-awareness can also lead to better understanding of interviewees, which involves communication. Professional interviewing skills hinge on effective communication that enables the interviewee to feel comfortable. Through supervised practice and assessment, the interviewer's ability to implement these skills within appropriate stages matures.

DEFINING THE INTERVIEW

An interview can be defined as a sequence of purposeful and serious communication between the interviewee(s) and the professional interviewer engaging in a reciprocal relationship designed to provide and/or receive information. Participants in the interview have goals or purposes; communication, the interchange of information, is seen as the means to achieve these goals. The dimensions of this communication involve both *what,* is being transmitted and how it is transmitted (Epstein, 1985), both of which influence meaning.

The term "professional interviewer" is used here to designate an individual with particular expertise, knowledge, skill, or responsibility regarding the topic being discussed and/or the other participant. The interviewer is a professional in some field (police work, journalism, education) but usually not simply in interviewing. Both participants bring to the interview characteristics that influence the course of the session and affect the communicative behavior of the other.

The common characteristic of all interviews is the communication of information. Information is given, obtained, and often used in decision making during the interview.

Information is not limited to objective facts; it frequently includes opinions, wishes, desires, or emotions of one of the participants. Note these examples:

Employer: So, I gather you don't like working on weekends.

Lawyer: Do you really feel determined to take this matter to court?

Physician: You seem upset now. Let's call it a day and continue our discussion at our next visit.

Interviewing, as used in this text, can better be defined through the variables of purpose, duration, and participants. As noted previously, interview participants have serious purposes for their communication. These purposes demand the exchange of information and are more pressing than the goals of casual conversation. While a series of interviews could last over an extended period, duration is usually one session of less than an hour. The interviewer is trained and experienced in some profession and relies on interviewing skills to lead the discussion. Interviewing as we see it is not synonymous with psychotherapy. Rather, interviewing is more limited in scope and usually different in purpose. Psychotherapy or counseling, as conducted by professionally trained therapists, aims to identify and remediate psychological problems, often through major change in personality or behavior, and frequently extends over a number of sessions. Interviewing involves communication of information over a brief period and does not include a therapeutic relationship between participants.

CHARACTERISTICS OF THE INTERVIEW

While diverse, interviews do share significant qualities. Interviews involve purposeful communication regarding personally important topics; participants have goals to be achieved in the session; certain interviewing techniques and communication skills are likely to aid in reaching these goals; interviews involve a process and a plan of action with discernible stages; and the interview's outcomes can be subjected to assessment. These common elements provide some cohesiveness to what may first appear to be a set of unrelated events. They help the professional in studying, understanding, preparing for, and conducting the interview logically and scientifically. Effective interviewing can be learned; to assist in that learning is the purpose of this text.

All interviews share three significant dimensions: (a) purpose, (b) plan of action, and (c) communication. (Other commonalities are discussed later in the chapter.)

Purpose

Unlike social conversations among friends, the interview functions with a goal or purpose in mind. At least one of the participants enters the interview with a goal, which can be either general or specific. Broad or general goals may include learning more about a particular topic, becoming familiar with employees' concerns, or teaching a subordinate about management's policies and objectives. We meet these general objectives when we share background information. No immediate action may result from the interview.

Specific purposes, however, are much narrower in scope and often have more immediate results. Examples include obtaining information about an applicant's training or experience so that a hiring decision can be made, determining the effectiveness of a treatment that can be continued or terminated, and providing a client alternatives so that an insurance policy can be purchased.

Several purposes, both general and specific, often exist for the same interview. An employer may wish some specific information from an employee but at the same time may hope to make a general evaluation of the employee's competence. The employee's goal for the same interview may be to impress the employer.

As events progress within the interview, both the specific and general goals in initiating the session may be modified, substituted, or eliminated. Donaghy (1984) offers some examples of these changing goals.

> In a hiring or selection interview, for example, interviewers often plan to seek information from applicants at the beginning of the interview and then give information about the organization toward the end of the interview. In other situations, information can come up which will modify, change, or add to the interview purpose. For example, in a work performance interview, the respondent might bring up a policy inconsistency which was not anticipated, thus modifying the interview purposes. (p. 3)

Plan of Action

Following goal setting, a plan of action is developed to achieve the goal. Rarely do professional interviewers begin an interview before they first consider procedure. Many human service organizations have already gathered some information regarding the potential interviewee. For example, data are gathered before the individual sees the interviewer in such settings as a physician's office, a child-guidance clinic, or employment office. A professional studies the information and develops an initial plan of action for working with the interviewee. The plan, however, is usually tentative, subject to modification as additional information is obtained.

The plan of action is not necessarily a formal, written document. More likely, the experienced interviewer quickly draws up a mental image of the plan based on the information and the purposes of the particular interview, but a plan guides the action.

Communication

Communication, or the exchange of objective and subjective information, is a third characteristic of an interview. Often, this communication is termed a *dyadic interaction* (Donaghy, 1984). The term *dyad* refers to the interview as a close or even intimate interchange between two parties, each influencing the other. Note that more than two persons may be involved in an interview (for example, two company executives interviewing a job applicant, a journalist interviewing three members of a winning team), but they represent two parties—an interviewer party and an interviewee party (Stewart & Cash, 1978).

Most interviews are conducted in person with face-to-face contact; some interviews are conducted via telephone, television, or other technical means. These remote interviews tend to lose part of the information the face-to-face meeting usually affords. The phone interview, for example, focuses attention strictly on verbal communication. The face-to-face interview involves not only the spoken word but also observable nonverbal communication—the messages transmitted by facial expression, body movement, gestures, and the like (Manos, 1979). The core of any interview is the exchange of communication between the involved parties. While much of this communication appears to be conveyed through questions and answers, the verbal and nonverbal behavior of one party triggers behavior and influences the understanding of the other party. A face-to-face meeting enhances this interchange.

The quality and outcome of the interview depend greatly on the professional's ability to recognize appropriate purposes, develop a useful plan of action, and communicate effectively through a set of well-developed interviewing skills. These vital characteristics each help move the session along to a successful conclusion. Because of their key roles in the interviewing process, this text devotes considerable attention to them.

TYPES OF INTERVIEWS

Because of their wide application and flexibility, interviews are not easily classified or assigned to distinct categories. Consider Table 1–1, a sample of interview types. These interviews are classified under several headings: (a) interviewer, the person who does the interviewing; (b) setting, the physical location of the session; (c) interviewee, the person being interviewed; and (d) topic, the subject matter discussed. Other headings, such as length, outcome, and purpose, could be equally appropriate. Note that Table 1–1 only hints at the varieties of interviews possible. No attempt will be made to discuss all possible classifications, but it is instructive to look at them in terms of professional use and purpose.

Table 1–1   A Sample of Interview Types

Interviewer	Settings	Interviewee	Topic
Employer	Business office	Applicant	Requirements and qualifications
Reporter	City hall	Mayor	Mayor's political plans
Insurance adjuster	Policy holder's home	Policy holder	Nature and extent of loss
Nurse	Hospital	Patient	Symptoms
Social worker	Welfare office	Mother of dependent children	Financial situation
Teacher	School	Student	Career plans

Professionals Who Use the Interview

The interview is an invaluable tool applied by numerous professionals in a variety of settings. Table 1–2 illustrates examples of these professionals. Generally, the goals of the interview for any professional are similar: to meet the needs of the interviewee and/or the organization for which he or she works. But specific goals and the plans of action developed by different professionals may vary widely. For example, a teacher interviewing a 10-year-old child about inappropriate classroom behavior, a physician obtaining a new patient's medical history, and a personnel manager meeting with a job applicant differ in their specific goals and plans of action. However, the outcomes or results associated with this wide spectrum of professional-client or interviewer-interviewee encounters depend largely on the communication skills of each professional. Chapters 2–4 of this text describe the application of communication skills.

Interview Purposes

Perhaps the most fruitful classification of interviews is by purpose, or the general goals to be achieved. Several authors (Cormier, Cormier, & Weisser, 1984; Donaghy, 1984; Stewart & Cash, 1978) have discussed types of interviews in terms of purposes or goals. Some of these types of interviews are limited to a particular field or line of work, for example, a public opinion poll or consumer survey. Other types have wider application. Seven broad categories of interviews occur in most professions. These categories can be described by their purposes: (a) information providing, (b) information collecting, (c) selection, (d) performance evaluation, (e) complaint receiving, (f) decision making, and (g) persuasion (Donaghy, 1984; Stewart & Cash, 1978).

Information Providing

Many interview situations require professionals to give information. Providing information to others can include the physician explaining to the patient procedures for taking a prescribed medication, the social worker giving instructions to a mother about the steps to take in securing additional financial support, a personnel manager informing a new

---

Table 1–2   Examples of Professionals Who Conduct Interviews

Corrections officer	Minister	Psychologist
Dentist	News correspondent	Rehabilitation counselor
Health counselor	Nurse	Salesperson
Gerontologist	Occupational therapist	School counselor
Insurance claims adjuster	Personnel manager	Social science researcher
Journalist	Physical therapist	Social worker
Lawyer	Physician	Sports reporter
Marriage and family therapist	Police officer	Teacher
Mental health counselor	Probation officer	

employee about the company's insurance program, or the dentist explaining to the patient the condition of her teeth and what needs to be done to correct an existing problem. Some work situations call for professionals to inform each other about present conditions. For instance, supervisors in hospitals and industrial plants provide other workers with information about present conditions before changes in work shifts.

Information Collecting

The second type of interview involves the professional gathering information. For example, the school counselor interviewing an adolescent regarding academic concerns often gathers information about the adolescent's background and problems prior to taking any steps toward improvement. The lawyer interviews a prospective defendant to gather pertinent information before defending a case in court. Investigative interviews are used by a number of professionals, including lawyers, journalists, police officers, social workers, researchers, or insurance agents, to obtain information they need to perform their work. Exit interviews are not uncommon for personnel workers. These interviews often help personnel obtain information about working conditions or other aspects of employment. In other situations, the information may lead to a diagnosis or insight into a problem.

Selection

The selection interview is frequently, but not exclusively, used in employment situations. For example, most job applicants are interviewed to aid in screening, hiring, or placement (Stewart & Cash, 1978). Such an interview might eliminate unqualified candidates who apply to an organization or determine whether an individual should be transferred or promoted. Donaghy (1984) points out that often the selection interview is a process of mutual assessment by both the interviewer and the interviewee: The college applicant is judging the college at the same time the admissions officer is evaluating the potential student.

Performance Evaluation

"Every day of our lives, we evaluate the performance or behavior of others, and we are evaluated by others" (Donaghy, 1984, p. 317). The performance evaluation as a professional responsibility involves not only judging another person's behavior but also communicating with the individual regarding performance. The supervisor, teacher, probation officer, and coach all frequently engage in this type of interview. The performance evaluation interview may result in praise, counseling, discipline, or even termination.

Complaint Receiving

This type of interview recognizes that not everyone is always satisfied with the treatment, service, or product received. Complaints and grievances are a reality and the interview provides a forum for their expression. Formal union grievances, informal employee complaints, gripes from taxpayers, customer complaints, and client objections to their bills allow virtually every professional ample opportunity to experience this type of interview (Stewart and Cash, 1978).

Decision Making

The sixth type of interview, one used for decision making, concerns problem solving for the interviewee or the interviewer. This type of interview focuses on specific problems and works toward reaching a decision. For example, problem solving and decision making are common procedures in marriage and family interviews. This type of interview presents, analyzes, and applies information toward solving a specific problem. The professional usually takes the lead in moving the session through the decision-making process.

Persuasion

The final category, persuasion, focuses on influencing an interviewing party regarding an idea, event, policy, or product. Persuasion is commonly used in business transactions, for example, in selling products or conducting negotiations. Its use certainly is not limited to these areas, though. In most professional endeavors, people have many opportunities to persuade others to accept their proposals, their products, their ideas, or even themselves. Business and professional endeavors are not static; rather, they grow and change to address new circumstances. One of the professional's responsibilities is to persuade others to make changes to meet new challenges.

INTERVIEWING RESEARCH

The scientific method, which helped advance the physical and social sciences, promotes a tandem view of research and theory. We develop a testable theory to explain a phenomenon, perform research to determine the viability of the theory, and use the research results to confirm or alter the theory, which in turn promotes additional research. However, research and theory in interviewing do not always follow this classic design. Some examples can help illustrate this point.

People who use interviewing are often quite practical, and their approaches tend to be rooted in a specific field or discipline that uses interviewing as a tool. The resulting research, therefore, usually depends on the interview's usefulness as a tool in that field. Arvey and Campion (1982) present the personnel psychologist's view of the employment interview. Paget (1984) reviews the use of structured interviews in assessing psychopathology in children. Foley and Sharf (1981) discuss interviewing techniques for physicians.

A different perspective on interviewing research comes from authors who begin with a communication-oriented approach. This is more likely to focus on communication skills in the interview rather than on the interview as a tool to reach a more general objective. Jablin and McComb (1984) review the empirical research on the employment screening interview with a communication perspective.

Several specific aspects or applications of the interview have drawn researchers attention. A few examples include the effects of different types of questions (Tengler &

Jablin, 1983), nonverbal communication (Malandro & Barker, 1983), and the teaching of interviewing skills (Stillman & Burpeu-Di Gregorio, 1984; Uhlemann, Hearn, & Evans, 1980).

Each of these approaches has provided useful data both for specific applications of the interview and for developing a more general theory of interviewing. Yet, not all approaches are equally fruitful or have the potential for guiding research likely to produce results with broad applicability. The classic research-theory tandem may be most effectively employed within the communications-theory approach. Accordingly, several authors have called for more communications-oriented research (Jablin & McComb, 1984; Goodall & Goodall, 1982).

SUMMARY

Chapter 1 has introduced the interview in terms of its definition, characteristics, and common types. Purpose, plan, and communication—the significant characteristics of interviewing—characterize the seven types of professional interviews discussed. Just as there are various types of interviews, so there are many different professionals who conduct interviews in their daily work.

SUGGESTED READINGS

Beatty, R. H. (1986). *The five-minute interview.* Somerset, NJ: John Wiley & Sons.

Benjamin, A. (1981). *The helping interview.* Boston: Houghton Mifflin.

Gorden, R. L. (1980). *Interviewing: Strategy, techniques, and tactics* (3rd ed.). Homewood, IL: The Dorsey Press.

Marshall, E., Charping, J. W., & Bell, W. J. (1979). Interpersonal skills training: A review of research. *Social Work Research and Abstracts, 15,* 10–16.

Okun, B. F. (1987). *Effective helping—Interviewing and counseling techniques* (3rd ed.). Monterey, CA: Brooks/Cole.

2

The Professional: An Introspection of Self

John M. Dillard
Robert R. Reilly
Texas A & M University

At the heart of the interviewing process is the encounter between the professional interviewer and the interviewee. The interviewing encounter relies on verbal and nonverbal communication by both parties—the professional and the interviewee. The quality of this communication influences the interpersonal exchange in the interview.

Few competent and successful professionals engage in the interviewing process without thorough knowledge of themselves and how their interpersonal communication can affect others. Coupled with self-understanding is awareness of the interviewee's communication patterns and behaviors. Therefore, the first step toward successful interviewing includes introspection and how one interacts with others. Additionally, professionals can increase their skill in interviewing by becoming aware of and understanding the interviewee's patterns of communication and character traits.

This chapter discusses common characteristics of an interpersonal encounter between an effective professional interviewer and the interviewee. The focus of this chapter includes factors that influence the verbal and nonverbal behavior of the interviewer and the interviewee. The need to consider potential differences between the two persons involved in the interview is discussed. Suggestions to facilitate cultural differences toward positive interview outcomes are also presented.

THE INTERVIEWER'S NEEDS AND CHARACTERISTICS

The many needs and characteristics of effective interviewers vary from one interviewer to the next. Professional interviewers for human-services organizations share some of these needs and characteristics. What are some factors that seem to set competent professionals apart from others? Are they learned or inherent? What kind of actions might the interviewers engage in that appear different from those of their counterparts? Answers to these and similar questions will provide only partial understanding of the interviewer. More important, what is it about the *effective* interviewer that leads to the achievement of desired interview outcomes? What are the needs of the professional interviewer?

Interviewer's Personal Needs

It is not uncommon for persons to want to assist others. Individuals' purposes and rationales for this desire are many and often not clear even to them. Many say something like "It makes me feel good to see that I have helped someone else," or "It tends to add something to my life once I know that I have helped to unlock the potential of another person." Sincere caring for others' welfare is a great human motivation, and many of us engage in helping relationships for this very reason. Brammer (1977) presents other possible reasons for professionals to want to engage in a human-services profession requiring interviewing:

> Feeling worthwhile as a person underlies much [interviewing] behavior. "If I can contribute productively to another's growth, I grow, too," seems to be the rationale. Seeing another person achieve greater life potential by moving from the misery of self-depreciation to joyful confidence, or from dependence to independence, for example, brings much satisfaction to a [professional], especially when the behavioral outcomes match the [professional's] choice of the values. (p. 304)

While caring for the interviewee is often shaped by a need to provide service, the critical question is: "How much am I attempting to meet or satisfy my own personal needs through aiding others?" A number of professionals who are compelled by their needs work to assist others. According to Brammer (1977), some professionals are motivated to "keep them [interviewees] dependent, or make them conform to the [professional's] conception of social behavior" (p. 304). Professionals must go beyond these personal needs and the limited satisfaction of controlling and maintaining power over others.

The professional achieves the need for high self-esteem primarily by being perceived by clients as a clever, wise expert. This perception often surfaces from the total confidence placed on the professional with credentials. Occasionally, the professional rationalizes her attempts to affect the interviewee with some degree of reference to her own projected view of social improvement (Brammer, 1977). In this case, the professional's efforts toward meeting needs do not consider the interviewee or the organization. Whose needs are to be met? The interviewer's, interviewee's, or organization's? Conflict in needs attainment can lead to subpar criterion outcomes.

Occasionally, the professional seems compelled by a curious desire to experience vicariously the interviewee's intimate life experiences. The manner and type of queries the professional applies during an interview may illustrate clearly her most important motivations in seeking information. According to Brammer (1977):

> Some [professionals] meet their needs for intimacy and giving compassion and love safely and ethically through a helping relationship. It seems that many people who come to helpers are emotionally starved. This relationship provides a convenient vehicle for the [professional] to use . . . her compassion and loving concern in [helping] ways without an investment in intimate behavior or long-term commitment. (p. 304)

Frequently the interviewee becomes dependent on this kind of empathetic relationship. Often, the interviewee's reluctance to withdraw from this emotional climate creates ongoing problems for the professional and the interviewee as well. The professional's efforts to meet her own needs by attempting to assist the interviewee are inappropriate and not conducive to positive outcomes. Furthermore, the inability to recognize her own professional behavior and its affect on the interviewee is a barrier to achieving professional maturity.

Characteristics of the Interviewer

The qualities that characterize the professional interviewer are both speculative and empirical (Shertzer & Stone, 1981); however, some common characteristics distinguish the effective professional interviewer from others. Gazda, Asbury, Balzer, Childers, and Walters (1984) advocate that characteristics of effective interviewing professionals are separate from characteristics of effective professionals in general. No one type of personality trait or quality represents the professional interviewer type, but the consensus seems to be that the prospective interviewer have a preexisting set of potential characteristics that promise full professional development. Gazda et al. argue: "Without these prerequisites it is doubtful that any amount of training will enable one to be truly effective in helping a relationship" (p. 7). What are some of these prerequisites to becoming an effective interviewer? They hinge on the concept of the "fully functioning individual" (Gazda et al., 1984; Eisenberg & Delaney, 1977).

Gazda et al. (1984) outline the prerequisite cluster of effective professional interviewing characteristics: values, motives, strengths, weaknesses, feelings, purpose in life, and current level of functioning. They maintain that the potential professional interviewer's awareness of his own characteristics will enable him to better utilize individual interviewing skills (delineated in Chapters 3 and 4) to achieve desired outcomes. Serious awareness and consideration of these prerequisite characteristics, while learning interviewing skills, will produce to some degree, a "fully functioning" individual.

Awareness of Personal Values

Complete awareness of one's own values and needs and how they may affect others is critical to the interviewing process. Being aware of her values enables the interview participant to avoid imposing them on others. Equally important to achieving interview goals is accepting the interviewee and his values. That is, the interviewer suspends conditions and value judgments toward the interviewee. The interviewee's values may differ from the interviewer's, but this should not influence any assessment of the interviewee. The fully functioning interviewer avoids placing conditions on the interviewee—for example: "If you refrain from drinking alcohol the next few weeks, I will give you a weekend pass." Suspending conditions during the interview helps encourage the interviewee to feel accepted. The fully functioning interviewer is aware of and understands how her belief system can affect the interviewee. Also, the interviewer deals with the interviewee unconditionally without placing a value on him as a person, and permits him to be himself.

Awareness of Personal Goals and Motives

Professionals' motives and goals are strongly interwoven into their values. What they are seeking and their motivations usually can indicate their personal biases. Fully functioning professional interviewers are readily aware that their goals may be incongruent with the interviewee; thus, they avoid allowing their personal goals to direct their behavior as they attempt to assist the interviewee. The ability to separate personal motives from the interview's goals is essential for fully functioning professionals.

Awareness of Personal Emotions

How the interviewer feels about certain situations and persons is related to aspects of his value system and motives. Recognizing and understanding those feelings can help to identify values that may either block or facilitate the interpersonal exchange. Even the "best" professional can have certain preferences and dislikes for certain types of interviewees. These feelings or emotions may be expressed through attitudes such as caring, acceptance of myths and stereotypes, empathy, sympathy, fear, anger, happiness, and sadness. The fully functioning professional knows the impact that his feelings can have on an interpersonal exchange; thus, he separates his personal emotions from the interview, particularly those that would hinder the interviewing process. In cases where feelings are too strong toward a particular interviewee, however, the professional avoids imposing his feelings by referring the interviewee to another professional or agency. In many human-services organizations, the professional cannot refer the interviewee to a colleague or another agency. For example, a social worker may find it difficult, if not impossible, to refer a potential interviewee when her colleagues have more cases than they can handle. In any event, the professional must be fully aware of his feelings or emotions to interview effectively. The professional interviewer's effectiveness can be determined by his awareness and understanding of personal attitudes about other persons.

Strengths and Weaknesses

Another group of characteristics require the interviewer's awareness and understanding of her strengths and weaknesses. The fully functioning professional has identified and understands her abilities. She probably will be unable to resolve all situations or assist in achieving all the goals of an organization and interviewee. However, honest awareness of personal limitations will spur the professional either to acquire the skills necessary to provide sufficient assistance or to refer the interviewee to another colleague or human-services agency. The fully functioning professional is not a "superhuman," but rather an individual who knows and acts according to her strengths and weaknesses in professional interviewing situations.

Plan or Aim in Life

The final prerequisite personal characteristic of the fully functioning professional focuses on the individual's life plan or aim. Dillard (1985) offers these questions: "Where are you going? How do you plan to get there? If you get there, how will you know that you have arrived?" (p. 1). The point here is the professional understands where she wants to go and what she needs to get there, and she will know when she has achieved her purpose. This is not a short-term plan but one that is continually expressed through the professional's personality, attitude, and behavior. This feeling of a worthy plan or purpose sustains and motivates the individual in most of her professional and nonprofessional activities. The fully functioning professional's shared purpose in life provides a foundation of hope and a motivation for interpersonal exchange.

Awareness of personal characteristics and which of them the professional can control may determine whether he can become a competent professional interviewer. It is important for a prospective professional to build on his strengths and learn the skills to correct and/or strengthen his weaknesses.

THE PROFESSIONAL: INCREASING SELF-KNOWLEDGE

Some of the psychological and social makeup of the interviewer is a function of her attitudes, values, expectations, and language. Examining these personal factors can help in understanding how they influence the professional's behavior and interpersonal exchange. Let us examine these four related characteristics of the professional interviewer.

It was mentioned earlier that the professional interviewer's behavior can affect the interviewing relationship as well as the results. We stress, however, that the professional's actual behavior during the interview can mirror the interviewee's attitudes. Baruth and Huber (1985) and Carkhuff, Pierce, and Cannon (1977) suggest such terms as caring, liking, interest, and respect to identify the professional's attitudes. The extent to which the professional can adequately provide a nonthreatening, warm atmosphere that encourages the interviewee to communicate concerns depends on how well the professional can convey positive attitudes toward the interviewee.

Some authors, such as Baruth and Huber (1985) and Schulman (1982), maintain that the professional interviewer should focus his attention on his attitudes to facilitate assistance to the interviewee. Pietrofesa, Leonard, and Van Hoose (1978) suggest that the following attitudes characterize the professional during the interviewing exchange:

Highly Characteristic
— The professional is capable of engaging in the interviewee's communication.

Very Characteristic
— The professional's responses are usually consistent with what the interviewee is attempting to communicate.
— The professional views the interviewee as a partner who focuses on a common concern.
— The professional views the interviewee as a counterpart.
— The professional is capable of internalizing the interviewee's emotions.
— The professional follows the interviewee's train of thought.
— The professional's tone of voice communicates complete ability to share the interviewee's emotions.

The situation of Ms. Meese, in her first interview session, may help to illustrate these points. Ms. Meese has been experiencing problems managing her two children. She was referred to a social-welfare agency by her probation officer. She cancelled the first three appointments because she had difficulty scheduling the appointments around her work hours or the children were ill. She manages to keep her fourth appointment.

Once Ms. Meese meets the social worker for the first time, she hastily conveys her frustration. The following excerpt is from the initial interview.

Social worker: I'm pleased that we are able to meet. I want you to feel that you can talk freely with me.
Ms. Meese: Okay. (Silence.) I'm not sure what to say or where to start . . . I really feel a little uptight right now. I'm . . . I'm. . . .
Social worker: You're not sure why you are here. (Silence.) You're feeling uncomfortable about this situation.
Ms. Meese: Well, I don't know what information was given to you. Ah, I realize I have some concerns that need attention, yet . . . I . . . I just don't know anything about you. But, I'm here only because Mrs. Jones, my probation officer, felt that you could help.
Social worker: Yes, Mrs. Jones told me very little about you. It's rather difficult to be expected to talk about your concerns with me when you know very little about me. I don't know you either, but I would like to get to know you. I do want to help you.

Ms. Meese: Well . . . uh. . . . (Silence.) It's unbelievable . . . it's unbelievable. I used to be able to handle my children well before I became incarcerated. But now, things just seem to go haywire. I know it's me, but I'm not sure I can discuss it.

Social worker: It's not always easy to talk about yourself and those things very close to you. I would like for you to feel free to share with me whatever you think is important that will enable me to help you.

Ms. Meese: Oh, maybe my situation isn't so terrible, but Mrs. Jones feels that I need to talk with you. She seems to be the only person who has an interest in me. I don't really have anyone to talk to about my problems with the children.

Social worker: This is our first meeting and I am interested in your and your concerns. I'm willing to talk with you about your concerns.

Regardless of what the professional social worker was experiencing, in her initial statements to the interviewee or in the repetition of her statements, she sincerely tried to convey a positive attitude toward Ms. Meese. The professional's behavior and other personal factors—such as anxiousness—may have affected the early interpersonal exchange.

The Professional's Values and World Views

Values or beliefs grow out of the professional's attitudes concerning the interviewee. These attitudes are the professional's world views, or perceptions of his life experiences with others that make up his values and beliefs. D'Augelli, D'Augelli, and Danish (1981) state: "Our beliefs and values, both of which are a set of attitudes, affect our [interviewing] and so must be considered" (p. 26.). Beliefs and values must be viewed synonomously with the professional's world views. Sue (1978) defines a world view as

> . . . the way in which people perceive their relationship to nature, institutions, other people, and things. World view constitutes our psychological orientation in life and can determine how we think, behave, make decisions, and define events. Our cultural upbringing and life experiences frequently determine or influence our world view. (p. 458)

The professional often holds world views or values contrary to the interviewee's. The professional may be unaware of the sources for these value differences and most likely will ascribe negative traits to interviewee. Further, value or world view differences between the professional and the interviewee can lead to conflict that hinders the reciprocal relationship. D'Augelli et al. (1981) state that

> . . . [professionals] . . . have values about specific current controversial issues like abortion, suicide, homosexuality, political activism, women's liberation, [ethical/racial relations], and a variety of other subjects. These values will also enter the [interviewing] relationship. When a [professional] sees [an interviewee] experiencing a problem relating to the [professional's] values, the [professional] is in conflict. Should the [professional] avoid influencing the [interviewee] toward . . . her own position? Is it possible not to influence [an interviewee]? Should the [professional] specifically try to influence the decision without the [interviewee] knowing, or should . . . she indicate a position on the subject? (p. 26)

It is not always easy for the professional to function in a reciprocal relationship and be consciously aware of how she communicates her values through her behavior. Lack of such an awareness can certainly have a nonproductive influence on this reciprocal interaction. Examine the following illustration.

Mrs. Scott, a 28-year-old college graduate with an MBA, has worked three years for Fields Manufacturing Company as an administrative assistant to the general plant manager, Mr. Green. Recently, an in-house position as manager of accounts and purchases became available, and the company wants to fill the position from within. Mrs. Scott has expressed her interest and strong desire to Mr. Green about applying for the position. However, Mr. Green has tried to persuade her not to pursue the position simply because few people, particularly men, would not want to work under direction of a woman. Not applying for the position would be for the good of the company and she would have fewer headaches, he thinks. He also considers business management a "man's job." Mrs. Scott adamantly opposes Mr. Green's argument.

Apparently Mrs. Scott is not consciously aware of Mr. Green's values or beliefs. His sexist attitude advocates giving women a position subordinate to men, and such stereotyping and prejudice offend Mrs. Scott.

In summary, the professional interviewer's conscious awareness of his attitudes, values, and beliefs is critical to achieving positive outcomes. The degree to which his values can influence the interviewee depends upon his awareness of and ability to control them during the reciprocal relationship. Occasionally it may be necessary to be frank about certain values or beliefs with the interviewee. The interviewee may not support those views, and she has the opportunity to agree or disagree with them. Self-introspection that occurs through growing awareness of one's world view and values will enable the interviewer to maximize his effectiveness when assisting the interviewee whose values are contrary to his own.

The Professional's Expectations

Like values, attitudes, and world views, expectations can affect the professional-interviewee encounter. The professional interviewer begins with implicit and explicit expectations; these develop further as interviewing progresses (Marsella & Pedersen, 1981). The interviewer's ideas about what he wants to occur in the interview often depend on his personal values and professional goals and the goals of the human-services organization. Additionally, his preference of interviewee case selection (if given a choice of interviewee) can influence the interviewing variables (Garfield & Bergin, 1978).

Interviewing variables may be the interviewee's appearance, sex, social status, or values systems as judged by the professional (Dillard, 1983). The professional's emotions toward the interviewee color these variables. Some professionals may avoid anyone of another ethnic and/or cultural group. The acronym YAVIS (young, attractive, verbal, intelligent, and successful) describes the type of interviewee most middle-class professionals prefer to assist (Ridley, 1978; Dillard, 1983). In short, the professional interviewer's subjective behavior, professional and personal value systems, attitudes, and expectations are interrelated and communicated in numerous ways.

A LOOK AT THE INTERVIEWEE

Not unlike the professional interviewer, the interviewee brings several personal factors— attitudes, values, world views, expectations, language—to the interview that affect the reciprocal enterprise. How these personal factors specifically influence the interview will vary across interviewee-professional relationship. Awareness of the interviewee's characteristics can affect an interview and can be important for her self-assessment and achievement of positive outcomes.

The Interviewee's Attitudes

Attitudes that enter into the interview may have been shaped by a number of external factors, such as previous experiences with family members, neighbors, friends, co-workers, supervisors, and past events. Bennett (1986) calls attitudes "a relatively stable organization of interrelated beliefs that describe, evaluate, and advocate action with respect to a person, object, or situation" (p. 137). They not only affect the interviewee's overt behaviors, but they can also cause him to distort his perceptions—that is, to interpret events so they agree with his predispositions. (This is also true for the professional interviewer.) Thus, he may view things as he wants them to be rather than as they really are. These attitudes heavily influence communication between members of diverse cultures; they might be labeled absolute values, myths, stereotypes, or prejudices.

The interviewee may convey his likes or dislikes about aspects of the interview. For example, refusal or resistance to share information indicates his attitude. Frequent tardiness or failure to make appointments on time could mean that the individual does not want to be interviewed. Disapproval of the interviewer or professional are communicated verbally and nonverbally. Verbal expressions of disagreement can be obvious to the professional, but nonverbal expressions are not always easily recognized. It should be emphasized, however, that most interviewees express positive attitudes. They usually help facilitate the reciprocal enterprise.

The Interviewee's Values

Bennett (1986) defines values as "beliefs about how one ought or ought not to behave, or about some end state of existence worth or not worth attaining" (p. 137). The interviewee and the professional use their values to guide their actions, beliefs, comparisons, assessments, and justifications of others and themselves.

Similarities and differences between the interviewer's and the interviewee's values should be expected. Considering the broad range of possible cultural experiences, education, belief systems, and socioeconomic levels, it is little wonder that problems do happen. Extreme differences in values often lead to conflict.

To what extent should the interviewer accept the interviewee's values? Gibson and Mitchell (1986) cite Gilbert Wrenn's argument:

This difference between the values of the [interviewee] and those of the [interviewer] is often a difference between generations or between cultures. Always, of course, the values of the [interviewee] are the product of his life experience, unique to him and often markedly different from the experience of the [interviewer]. The 30-year-old, middle-class, socially accepted, college-educated [interviewer] cannot be expected to understand in all cases the values of a 16-year-old, ghetto-reared, socially rejected [male] or [female] or those of an affluent, socially amoral, parentally rejected youth. In fact, experiential understanding of another is rare. What is most important, however, is that the [interviewer] accept the [interviewee's] values as being as real and as right for him as the [interviewer's] values are for the [interviewer]. There is too frequently a tendency to protest inwardly, 'He can't really *mean* that,' when the value expressed by the [interviewee] is in sharp contrast to a related value held by the [interviewer]. The point is that the [interviewee] does mean that; his value assumption is as justifiable to him as yours is to you.

So far I have said nothing about the [interviewer's] responsibility for helping the [interviewee] to examine a given value assumption, particularly if the value is likely to result in behavior harmful to another or to society. He has such a responsibility differing widely from [interviewee] to [interviewee] and varying often with the [interviewee's] psychological readiness to examine values. Basic to the success of any such confrontation, however, is the [interviewer's] acceptance of the 'right' of the [interviewee] to have different values. If [an interviewer] enters into a discussion of another point of view with the assumption that he is 'right' and the other is 'wrong,' failure is assured. (pp. 188–189)

In summary, the professional interviewer's conscious awareness of his attitudes, values, and beliefs is critical to achieving positive outcomes. The degree to which his values can influence the interviewee depends upon his awareness of and ability to control them during the reciprocal relationship.

The Interviewee's Expectations and Preferences

Another area of concern is the interviewee's expectancy about various aspects of the interview, such as its length. The interviewee may have many expectations about being assisted or about what will occur during the interview. Garfield and Bergin (1978) contend that if the actual interview is inconsistent with the interviewee's expectations, the interviewee will probably be dissatisfied and more inclined to withdraw.

Hansen, Stevic, and Warner (1986) state that both the professional and the interviewee approaching a new experience develop certain preconceptions of the interview, their role, and the role of the other in the interview. These preconceptions, along with their preferences, influence their behavior. Each party has apprehensions and anticipations concerning the upcoming encounter.

The professional must be aware of and understand her own points of view as well as the interviewee's. Awareness and understanding of the interviewee's expectations and preferences can assist the professional in addressing them within her own expectations.

It has been reported that some interviewees were dissatisfied only when they derived no benefits from the interview (Hansen et al., 1986). They were satisfied if they obtained some type of assistance, regardless of whether their perceived expectations were satisfied. Interviewees usually enter the interview equipped with a number of expectations and generally feel satisfied if only some of those expectations are satisfied. Thus, the interviewer must be fully alert to the interviewee's multiple expectations.

The interviewee's preferences for the interview are also noteworthy. During the first interview, for example, the interviewee who speaks with the type of professional she prefers can perceive having more favorable outcomes than will the interviewee who was assigned to a less-preferred professional. While interviewee preferences appear significant, the interviewee tends to prefer the more professional-looking and acting type, whether her expectations and actual interview experiences agree or disagree. That is, interviewee expectations and preferences can be altered to provide an effective and satisfying encounter (Hansen et al., 1986).

The relationship between the interviewee's preference and the professional's physical attractiveness should also be noted. For instance, the interviewee has been reported (Shertzer & Stone, 1981) to regard the physically attractive female professional more highly than her unattractive counterpart in terms of competence, professionalism, assertiveness, interest, and ability to assist with personal concerns. Further, the physically attractive male professional, compared to the unattractive male professional, was viewed by the female interviewee as more effective than the physically unattractive male professional. Again, while interviewee preferences are important to note, attitudes toward physical unattractiveness can be subordinated through competent, effective interviewing.

In short, the professional's physical attractiveness may affect some interviewees' opinion of the professional's competence. Being aware of the interviewee's expectations and preferences is critical to maximizing the chances of attaining the interview goals. This awareness enables the professional to move in a progressive rather than a cyclical fashion during the interview.

DEALING WITH INTERVIEWEE-PROFESSIONAL CULTURAL DIFFERENCES AND SIMILARITIES

While self-introspection and awareness of the interviewee are critical aspects of a reciprocal encounter, awareness and understanding of communication across cultures are equally critical. The fully functioning interviewer understands many aspects of both verbal and nonverbal communication and how communication is culturally different and therefore influenced. The interviewee can have a variety of cultural experiences, but the following discussion will focus on five areas: (a) preinterview considerations, (b) nonverbal communication, (c) situational cues, (d) environmental cues, and (e) interactive cues.

Some Preinterview Considerations

The interviewee brings personal characteristics and experiences to the interview, and the competent interviewer gives serious consideration to these preinterviewing factors to develop a positive alliance. Awareness of how personal characteristics can vary among individuals as well as across cultures can facilitate the interviewer's efforts in forming such an alliance. These factors include eye contact, rate of speech, tone of voice, proxemics, and language.

Eye Contact

Cross-cultural differences in eye contact are many. Many Western societies regard the individual as slightly suspicious or "shifty" should she not maintain a certain amount of culturally prescribed eye contact when communicating face-to-face.

We typically focus our eyes on the face more than on any other part of the body, and facial expressions are quickly and readily interpreted. Sathré, Olson, and Whitney (1977) maintain that

> . . . Our eye contact seems to be maintained more as we listen than when we are talking. It is not uncommon for us to avoid eye contact when we are asked questions that can cause us to feel uncomfortable or guilty. When reacting in a defensive or aggressive manner we may increase eye contact dramatically, and our pupils often dilate when we are emotionally aroused and excited. In an "eyeball-to-eyeball" confrontation, both individuals attempt to maintain eye contact. During such confrontations the concentration is usually very intense. Intense eye contact is awkward, and it is generally considered impolite, suggestive, or hostile to stare too long at others. This basic rule in our culture sometimes presents problems, because it is also impolite to ignore and avoid looking at those with whom we are speaking. It is acceptable, however, to stare at animals and objects, and, under certain conditions, to stare at some people, as in a long, intimate look between lovers. (p. 146)

Various cultures assign different meanings to eye contact. Ivey (1983) found the following:

> Direct eye contact is considered a sign of interest in White middle-class culture. However, even there a person often gives you more eye contact while listening and somewhat less while talking. Research indicates, moreover, that some Blacks in the United States may have reverse patterns; that is, they may look more when talking and slightly less when listening. Among some Hispanic groups, eye contact by the young is a sign of disrespect. Imagine the problems this may cause the [interviewer] who tells a youth "look at me!" when this directly contradicts basic cultural values. Some other cultural groups (for instance, certain native American, Eskimo, or aboriginal Australian groups) generally avoid eye contact, especially when talking about serious subjects. (p. 22)

The interviewing skills (including eye contact) delineated in Chapter 3 are general and based on middle-class American experiences. These skills should be adapted to accommodate other cultural situations where needed.

Rate of Speech

Like eye contact, the beginning professional should give special consideration to rate of speech. It is well known that individuals' rates of speech differ; these differences may be at least partly attributed to ethnic and cultural variations, as well as to regional differences (Dillard, 1983). For instance, some lower-class Black interviewees from parts of Mississippi speak slowly, but many Black and Puerto Rican interviewees reared in Harlem, New York, or Boston speak quickly. Additionally, urban northeastern Whites are likely to speak faster than many southern Appalachian Whites. More importantly, however, the interviewee whose rate of speech appears slow does not necessarily listen effectively only to slow speech. The professional should carefully observe the interviewee to see if she needs to adjust her speech rate to facilitate verbal interaction. As the professional begins to talk or respond to the interviewee, she can look for facial expressions, such as a frown, a yawn, eyes closed, or other behaviors (such as the Japanese interviewee scratching behind his ear) that might suggest lack of understanding (Dillard, 1983). Should the interviewee's responses contain fragmented statements or concepts different from those made by the professional, this, too, may indicate a need to alter the rate of speech. Dillard (1983) suggests that a moderate rate may be most appropriate, at least in the first interview meeting. In any event, any adjustment in the professional's speech rate should happen because of necessity, not to mimic the interviewee's speech pattern.

Tone of Voice

The professional interviewer's tone of voice is another significant factor for preinterview consideration. While the meanings attached to the professional's words influence communication, the underlying message of her communication can be more important. The interviewee is often more perceptive to the tone of voice than to the words. Therefore, the professional "must avoid sounding harassed, condescending, disinterested, or unpleasant" (Dillard, 1983, p. 287). One way to achieve this is to project and maintain a positive tone of voice.

Proxemics

The professional communicates nonverbally through the inflections of her voice, tone, and pitch. Proxemics, or spatial distance, is an important feature of the communication system the professional uses with the interviewee. Proxemics is the language of social space concerning physical distance between the professional and the interviewee. Gollnick and Chinn (1986) state that cultural factors influence proxemics.

> The normal conversational distance between white Americans, for example, is about 21 inches. A distance much greater than this may make the individual feel too far apart for normal conversation and a normal voice level. Individuals of other cultural groups, such as Arabs, Latin-Americans, and southern Europeans are accustomed to standing considerably closer when they talk.
> ... in the natural positioning of people, blacks tended to stand farthest apart. Whites maintained an intermediate distance, and Mexican-Americans stood the closest together.
> When a person from a cultural group that tends to stand close in conversation speaks with a white American, the latter individual often backs up while the other individual continually moves in closer. (p. 152)

Finally, it may be necessary to give the interviewee latitude concerning seating by offering several options. This will allow the interviewee flexibility so that she feels most comfortable and sets the limits of her "personal space" (Dillard, 1983).

Language

One of the most obvious differences in culture—and one of the most obvious barriers to communication—is language. But many professionals naively feel that a competent interviewer is all that setting persons of different cultures to communicate requires. This notion fails to consider the relationship between culture and language. Language is largely the result of culture. What we think about and how we think about it are direct functions of our language.

A major barrier in language differences is the part words play in perception. When the professional communicates interculturally, he is likely to find that cultural differences in word meaning and connotations sometimes influence his ability to communicate. Often, these difficulties will occur when least expected.

For example, a Puerto Rican or Mexican American interviewee for whom English is a second language has problems that work not only against the goals of the interview but also against attempts to adopt or translate terms. (A single translation across various geographic locations would not likely render effective communication simply because of variations in dialect. Differences exist among Spanish-speaking groups as well. There are several translations for the term "kite"—*papalote, cometa, valantin, chiringa,* or *huila*—depending on the country of origin. Regional differences further complicate communication. To a Puerto Rican, the term *tastone* means a squashed section of a banana that was fried, but it may signify a half dollar to a Chicano.

Dillard (1983) states that the professional interviewer is often culturally unfamiliar with or intolerant of linguistic patterns found among the many people in rural mountain areas of the southern Appalachians. Additional barriers of dialect, vocabulary, and expression may be present. For example, "I don't care to" to an Appalachian often really means "Yes, I would be delighted to" (p. 247).

Communication interactions between the interviewee and the professional are important considerations, particularly when the interviewee is Black. Effective communication between the two participants depends on linguistic compatibility. Many of the goals conveyed in interviewing are focused on the interviewing process—for example, empathy and genuineness—rather than the goals of the interviewee. Thus, many professionals work under the assumption that the interviewee, no matter what his socioeconomic level, is a member of the middle class and communicates in middle-class terms.

The professional should be aware of within-group variations in language and usage among cultural and ethnic groups. While many Blacks may use Ebonics or Black English outside the interview with friends and family members, they will probably use standard English in the interview setting.

Many verbal expressions may be limited to a geographical location, socioeconomic class, and education. For example, some slang expressions that Blacks in one regional area use may be unknown or not used by Blacks in another area. These expressions can be further limited even within a single regional area. That is, some expressions spoken by some lower social–status and less-educated persons may be nonexistent or spoken less among many educated persons of middle and upper status. Therefore, the communication styles and patterns can vary within, as well as across, cultures.

Another consideration is the nature of change within language. Gollnick and Chinn (1986) state that aspirations and needs of cultural groups are reflected in the forms of communication. They further argue that:

In some areas language changes are so gradual that they go unnoticed. In other circumstances changes are more easily noticed. There are expressions and words that tend to be identified with a particular period. Sometimes the language is related to particular microcultures for certain periods. For example, words and phrases such as "outasight," "far out," and "groovy" are a part of our language for a time and are then replaced by other expressions. (p. 143)

Finally, the professional must recognize that language usage and word meanings can vary from one interviewee to the next, simply because of the latter's life experiences and cultural affiliation. Few interviewees will enter the interviewing process with a style and pattern of language compatible to the professional's. Therefore, the professional may need to make some adjustments in his interview communication. Other factors, such as nonverbal cues, also demand special attention to ensure positive goal attainment.

INTERPERSONAL CUES

Gazda et al. (1984) categorized nonverbal behaviors into four modalities. (See Table 2-1.) Note that nonverbal behaviors are highly idiosyncratic; interpretation of these clues must be tentative and based on the context in which they are transmitted.

Several factors can influence interpersonal behaviors of the professional and the interviewee. How nonverbal cues such as touch and body movement are handled determines the direction of the interview.

Touching

According to Myers and Myers (1980), touching is a powerful communicative tool that serves to convey a broad range of emotions, such as fear, love, anxiety, warmth, or coldness. Yet touching between the professional and interviewee can be a risky venture, since both the professional and interviewee bring a broad range of attitudes and reactions to the interview (Gazda et al., 1984). The norms and standards that govern touching behavior in interpersonal relations can differ from culture to culture. For this reason, the professional must use touch with caution. For touching to be effective in the interview depends on the extent to which the interviewee is comfortable with it. Gazda et al. (1984) state that when they are under emotional stress, most interviewees not only welcome but *need* the strong bond that touch, more effectively than verbal statements, can transmit.

Gazda et al. also suggest two significant factors to consider when attempting to communicate through touching: "(1) the level of trust between the two persons and (2) whether or not the touch is perceived as sexual; and it is the other person's perception, not your intent, that determines this" (p. 111). The total context influences the degree of trust and perceptions. Several contextual factors are involved; for example, the interviewee's attitudes and experiences, the professional-interviewee relationship, and the quality of both present and past communication.

The professional must recognize the interaction of touching and must moderate it with caution. Touching may need to be applied sparingly or not at all with some interviewees. If the professional is not comfortable with touching, she might consider ways to enhance her communication through touching behavior (D'Augelli et al., 1981).

Kinesics (Body Language)

Like other forms of nonverbal communication, body movements can have an impact on the reciprocal enterprise. *Kinesics* refers to body language that includes facial expressions, posture, gestures, and other movements that can transmit a message (Gollnick & Chinn, 1986). Movements and gestures of the body (including the eyes, as discussed earlier) exhibit emotions and attitudes. The interviewee's body language might cue the professional that a statement has been accepted or rejected by the interviewee. The professional sitting in her chair and leaning slightly toward the interviewee may indicate willingness to work or acceptance, while looking at her watch, the floor, or out the window might suggest boredom or rejection (Bull, 1983).

Occasionally, body movements or language unintentionally transmit messages. For example, the interviewee's rhythmically tapping his fingers on top of the desk or on the side of his chair communicates anxiousness. Often, he is unaware of this behavior. The professional's very rigid posture can unintentionally convey a noncaring attitude to the interviewee. Conversely, a slouching posture may indicate a lack of interest and attention (D'Augelli et al., 1981). In addition, the professional or the interviewee positioned with his arms across the chest could unintentionally send a defensive message. Nodding the head can be a useful interviewing tool for the professional, and the ability to moderate such nodding will determine, to some degree, the effectiveness of the professional-interviewee relationship. Occasional and appropriate head nodding is generally recommended. Some view excessive head nods as annoying and intolerable (D'Augelli et al., 1981).

Facial Expressions

Interview participants are seldom motionless or expressionless. Their faces and bodies move, communicating a lot about their emotions and reactions. Occasionally, these movements are conscious and intentional; for instance, when the participants deliberately smile at each other, frown to convey dissatisfaction, or raise an eyebrow to express surprise (Myers & Myers, 1980). Facial expressions can also suggest some degree of happiness, sadness, fear, disgust/contempt, love, or anger. Frequently, however, these behaviors are so much a part of these emotions that they seem to happen unintentionally and unconsciously.

Visual examination of the interviewee can convey a great deal. A professional sensitive to facial expressions may identify a resistive, belligerent, challenging interviewee prior to the latter uttering a single word. An interpretation comes from subtle facial cues, transmitted by the interviewee's posture and manner of looking at the professional (Myers & Myers, 1980).

Gollnick and Chinn (1986) suggest that more than expressing emotions, the face mirrors interpersonal attitudes and gives feedback on statements of each participant. Since facial expressions show several emotions, however, interpretation is not simple. The professional's "ability to accurately interpret a facial expression may be a function of how well acquainted . . . [she] is with the emotional and social context in which the emotion occurs and the familiarity with the [interviewee] being observed" (p. 154).

CULTURAL CUES

The way we use and organize our spatial distance and time are other cultural factors the beginning professional must consider. Different cultures often attach different meanings

Table 2–1 Categories of Nonverbal Communication Behaviors

Nonverbal Communication Behaviors Using Time

— Recognition
— Promptness or delay in recognizing the presence of another or in responding to his or her communication
— Priorities
— Amount of time another is willing to spend communicating with a person
— Relative amounts of time spent on various topics

Nonverbal Communication Behaviors Using the Body

Eye contact (important in regulating the relationship)

— Looking at a specific object
— Looking down
— Steadily looking at the helper
— Defiantly looking at helper ("hard" eyes), glaring
— Shifting eyes from object to object
— Looking at helper but looking away when looked at
— Covering eyes with hand(s)
— Frequency of looking at another

Posture (often indicative of physical alertness or tiredness)

— "Eager," as if ready for activity
— Slouching, slovenly, tired looking, slumping
— Arms crossed in front as if to protect self
— Crossing legs
— Sits facing the other person rather than sideways or away from
— Hanging head, looking at floor, head down
— Body positioned to exclude others from joining a group or dyad

Hand and arm gestures

— Symbolic hand and arm gestures
— Literal hand and arm gestures to indicate size of shape
— Demonstration of how something happened or how to do something

Self-inflicting behaviors

— Nail biting
— Scratching
— Cracking knuckles
— Tugging at hair
— Rubbing or stroking

Repetitive behaviors (often interpreted as signs of nervousness or restlessness but may be organic in origin):

Signals or commands

— Snapping fingers
— Holding finger to lips for silence
— Pointing
— Staring directly to indicate disapproval
— Shrugging shoulders
— Waving
— Nodding in recognition
— Winking
— Nodding in agreement, shaking head in disagreement

Touching

— To get attention, such as tapping on shoulder
— Affectionate, tender
— Sexual

Eyes
— "Sparking"
— Tears
— "Wild-eyed"
— Position of eyelids

Skin
— Pallor
— Perspiration
— Blushing
— "Goose bumps"

Facial expression (primary site for display of affects; thought by researchers to be subject to involuntary responses)
— No change
— Wrinkled forehead (lines of worry), frown
— Wrinkled nose
— Smiling, laughing
— "Sad" mouth
— Biting lip

— Tapping foot, drumming or thumping with fingers
— Fidgeting, squirming
— Trembling
— Playing with button, hair, or clothing

— Challenging, such as poking finger into chest
— Symbols of camaraderie, such as slapping on back
— Belittling, such as a pat on top of head

Nonverbal Communication Behaviors Using Vocal Media

Tone of voice
— Flat, monotone, absence of feelings
— Bright, vivid changes of inflection
— Strong, confident, firm
— Weak, hesitant, shaky
— Broken, faltering

Rate of speech
— Fast
— Medium
— Slow

Loudness of voice
— Loud
— Medium
— Soft

Diction
— Precise versus careless
— Regional (colloquial) differences
— Consistency of diction

Table 2–1 Categories of Nonverbal Communication Behaviors, *continued*

Nonverbal Communication Behaviors Using the Environment

Distance	*Arrangement of the physical setting*	*Clothing* (often used to indicate what a person wants others to believe about him/her)	*Position in the room*
— Moves away when the other moves toward	— Neat, well-ordered, organized	— Bold versus unobtrusive	— Protects or fortifies self in position by having objects such as desk or table between self and other person
— Moves toward when the other moves away	— Untidy; haphazard, careless	— Stylish versus nondescript	— Takes an open or vulnerable position, such as in the center of the room, side by side on a sofa, or in a simple chair
— Takes initiative in moving toward or away from	— Casual versus formal		— Nothing between self and other person
— Distance widens gradually	— Warm versus cold colors		— Takes an attacking or dominating position—may block exit from area or may maneuver other person into boxed-in position
— Distance narrows gradually	— Soft versus hard materials		— Moves about the room
	— Slick versus varied textures		— Moves in and out of other person's territory
	— Cheerful and lively versus dull and drab		— Stands when other person sits, or gets in higher position than other person
	— "Discriminating" taste versus tawdry		
	— Expensive or luxurious versus shabby or Spartan		

Source: From *Human relations: A manual for educators* (3rd ed., pp. 62–65) by G. M. Gazda, F. S. Asbury, F. J. Balzer, W. C. Childers, and R. P. Walters, 1984, Boston: Allyn & Bacon.

to the same or similar interpersonal distance and time. We unconsciously design space and time as a function of our culture, and they often serve as a nonverbal means of communication. Social distance has been discussed earlier in this chapter; this section focuses more on the interpersonal use of time.

Time is a form of interpersonal communication. How time is organized and used can vary across cultures. Our culture generally views time as a precious, rare commodity (Myers & Myers, 1980). We value punctuality and frown upon tardiness, especially in middle-class, urban cultures. Professionals and many interviewees share this time concept and make a conscious effort to make scheduled appointments on time.

What happens to the interviewee when she arrives early or makes the appointment as scheduled? D'Augelli et al. (1981) state that middle-class American culture permits the professional who has high social status to be late. On many occasions, however, the client must wait for assistance despite her early arrival—because the professional was either late for the interview or failed to complete his earlier appointment. The interviewee's waiting for the professional is irritating and annoying. Being left unattended for a scheduled appointment can generate feelings that the professional is noncaring or that the interviewee is not important.

The interviewee's tardiness for the interview can elicit negative emotions that indicate his behavior is not acceptable. However, many professionals fail to consider differences in time conception. That is, some interviewees are guided by their cultural influences, which define time differently from the middle-class, educated professional concerned with punctuality and efficiency. Being punctual may not be a particularly strong consideration, especially for the first interview. In some situations, the interviewee is fully aware of her appointed time, but believes that family matters have priority. Such a matter may make her tardy but not embarrassed by her apparent lack of responsibility for the appointment.

Prudent use of time is a significant factor in most professional situations; however, the professional who is sensitive to cultural differences in time usage will approach this situation with an open attitude and a flexible schedule when possible.

RESEARCH ON DECODING NONVERBAL CUES

Researchers have dealt with a number of interpersonal behavior issues that are important to the interview. One major issue is the extent to which men and women interviewers differ in interpersonal sensitivity or accuracy decoding (interpreting) nonverbal cues. Some findings (Kirouac & Doré, 1983) suggest that women tend to interpret nonverbal cues more quickly than men do. Hall (1984) reports that research supports the status-nonverbal-awareness hypothesis that less-dominant individuals in a group glance more frequently at others than do more-dominant individuals. Hall argues that whether low status in women is the basis of their heightened ability to perceive nonverbal cues warrants additional research.

Hall's (1984) and Bull's (1983) research literature on sex differences in nonverbal cues indicate that women are better decoders of nonverbal expressions than men. The same results remain over various ages and the sex of those being observed (Hall, p. 27).

Although women are reliably better than men in decoding nonverbal cues, women's advantage is greater for facial cues, less pronounced for body cues, least pronounced for vocal cues.

Hall (1984) states that evidence from other studies on nonverbal communication suggests that the face and voice are "special" in the content of their messages. This evidence stems from five studies conducted by DePaulo and Rosenthal (1979). The face seems to be a more reliable source of information regarding the type of emotion, positive or negative.

Research indicates, according to Hall (1984), that although people in general pay more attention to the face than the voice when presented with a choice, women prefer the face more than men do (DePaulo, Rosenthal, Eisenstat, Rogers, & Finkelstein, 1978). Facial cues may have special relevance to women; this is consistent with their gaze patterns. Research has also shown that the amount of attention one allocates to the face and body is correlated with accuracy in decoding cues from them (i.e., people who attend more to the face are better decoders of the face). According to Hall (1984), furthermore, research shows women have more expressive faces and they smile and laugh more than men.

In conclusion, although women may be better at interpreting nonverbal cues, the accuracy of their interpretation is a learned behavior. This process then seems to suggest that both men and women interviewers who lack accuracy in interpreting nonverbal cues can eventually acquire that skill through practice.

SUMMARY

Self-introspection is critical for the professional or prospective professional to learn who he is, how his behavior may affect the interviewee, and how to avoid unintended negative outcomes. It is also important to develop ideas about what a potential interviewee will bring into a reciprocal encounter. Being aware of and understanding the verbal and nonverbal communication in the professional-interviewee relationship can help you achieve the interviewee's and human-service organization's goals.

SUGGESTED READINGS

Axelson, J. A. (1985). *Counseling and development in a multicultural society.* Monterey, CA: Brooks/Cole.

Eakins, B. W., & Eakins, R. G. (1978). *Sex differences in human communication.* Boston: Houghton Mifflin.

Galassi, M. D., & Galassi, J. P. (1977). *Assert yourself! How to be your own person.* New York: Human Sciences.

Harper, R. G., Wiens, A. N., & Matarazzo, J. D. (1978). *Nonverbal communication: The state of the art.* New York: Wiley.

Hayakawa, S. I. (1979). *Through the communication barrier: On speaking, listening, and understanding.* New York: Harper and Row.

Knapp, M. L., & Miller, G. R. (1985). *Handbook of interpersonal communication.* Beverly Hills, CA: Sage.

McGann, M. (1980). *Coping with language: Talk your way to success.* New York: Richards Rosen Press.

Samovar, L. A., Porter, R. E., & Jain, N. C. (1981). *Understanding intercultural communication: A reader.* Belmont, CA: Wadsworth.

3

Communicative Skills Process Approach to Interviewing

John M. Dillard
Robert R. Reilly
Texas A & M University

The first steps toward effective interviewing are understanding and awareness of oneself and the interviewee. Understanding and awareness are important for establishing a positive interpersonal exchange that will help achieve successful outcomes. Once the relationship is developed, a set of prescribed skills and techniques must be employed to influence the process within the interview (Dillard, 1983; Ivey & Gluckstern, 1974; Egan, 1975). The interviewer must acquire effective communication skills to attain any interview goals.

Application of these skills is also important. The type of interview and the setting may determine which skills are appropriate. Any general model for interviewing should then be flexible enough to fit a variety of human-services settings as well as the diverse interviewees being served.

The ability to obtain complete, accurate reports (for example, automobile accident reports from drivers, law enforcement reports for defendants and plaintiffs, social case studies from families, and medical histories from patients) is the cornerstone of information seeking and evaluation. The interaction between the skilled interviewer and interviewee provides information for making certain decisions and develops the interviewer-interviewee relationship that is critical for assistance, service, or compliance (Epstein, 1985).

Professionals who obtain substandard outcomes may ask themselves the following types of questions:

— How can I obtain the necessary information from this driver to complete an accident or a policy report?
— What kind of responses should I make in this interview that would provide informative data for the television viewers?
— What are the best techniques to use for eliciting the most accurate, detailed information from my patients to make a clinical diagnosis?
— As an attorney, how can I best obtain needed information regarding an individual's social case history?

Obviously, these represent only a few of the professions that engage in the interview process.

Some investigations (Tapia, 1972; Stillman, Burpeu-Di Gregorio, Nicholson, Sabers, & Stillman, 1983) that followed the performance of student interviewers indicate several limitations in their interviewing skills. These potential interviewers often failed to focus on pertinent issues, failed to respond to relevant verbal and nonverbal cues, and avoided discussing important social and psychological issues (Stillman et al, 1983, p. 941). Hence, they may have been unable to uncover the real condition of the interviewee's situation.

Some studies have assigned neophyte interviewers to interviewees and asked them to gather and record information regarding these persons. These cases, according to Stillman et al. (1983), provide little, if any, systematic monitoring of the interviewer's skills and techniques to determine their success. Often, the unskilled interviewer has received only a list of readings or attended a workshop or seminar on the topic. For many, however, the only assistance in conducting an interview is an outline of a series of questions and/or major components of a case study. The recorded report of an incident or case history usually does not reflect the interviewer's communication skills, deficient interpersonal skills, or wrong or inappropriate techniques; nor can we assume that the information actually recorded is accurate and complete. Thus any skill requires repeated practice by the beginning interviewer and continuous, constructive criticism by skilled professional interviewers.

This chapter describes a model of basic communicative skills for interview development. These skills are presented to help you develop strategies needed for effective interviewing as you formulate and perfect your personal style of communicating. Steps and techniques for gathering information and effectively assisting the interviewee are discussed.

COMMUNICATIVE SKILLS PROCESS MODEL

Analysis of the Model

The interview process includes systematic steps involving verbal and nonverbal exchanges in dyads or groups. This process can consist of one or more interviews to achieve certain goals (see Figure 3–1). It allows for enhanced awareness and understanding of communicative behaviors as they happen. A sequence of communicative steps or procedures only succeeds as far as it works toward attaining the goals stated at the outset of the interview process. The procedures used should address those goals.

The major goal of most helping procedures ultimately is to meet the interviewee's needs. Unlike these procedures, however, interviewing is aimed toward the goals of both the interviewee and the human-services organization, such as hospitals, social-work agencies, employment and law-enforcement agencies, and educational and penal institutions. Epstein (1985) maintains that:

> Organizational goals chart a direction for administration, stating what a whole program intends to accomplish. Organizational goals do not translate readily into [interviewee] case goals. However, it is unlikely that any individual case goal would contradict the general intention of the program's operation. Organization goals are put forward in broad terms, such as strengthening family life, reducing mental illness, educating children and youth, educating and training adults, rehabilitating the physically handicapped, and enhancing productive patient use of medical care. (pp. 68–69)

The interviewee's goals are also important to consider in the interview. According to Epstein (1985), the interviewee's goals:

> represent what changes the [interviewee] perceives as necessary, desirable, and wanted, and what he is willing and able to work on. Dissonance or lack of congruence between practitioner and client goals may set up conflict and possible struggle that will dispose a case to failure. Many [interviewees] are willing to seriously consider and often adopt professional suggestions about advisable goals. (p. 69)

Successful achievement of goals depends upon interviewing skills and techniques, that is, the practitioner's attempts to elicit information from the interviewee. Techniques are viewed as the planning process phases of the interview process wherein the skilled interviewer considers the interviewee's characteristics, interviewing goals, and process goals and decides how best to approach them.

Figure 3–1 Interviewing Process Model

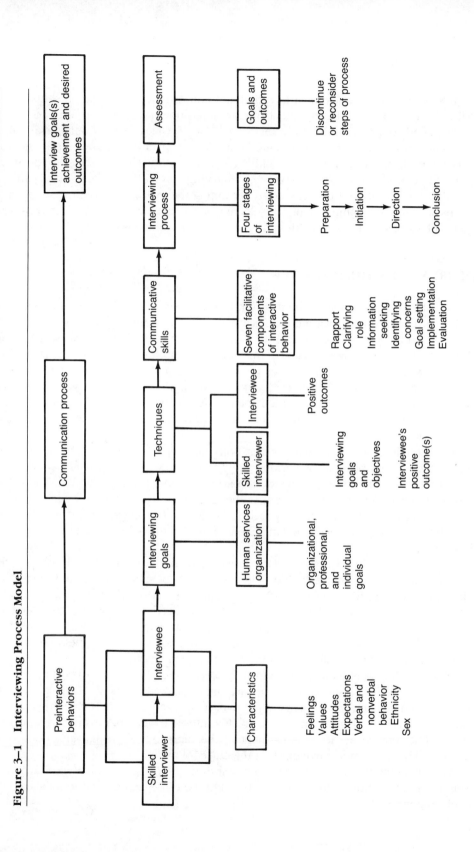

39

Interviewing techniques include verbal and nonverbal communication skills. Nonverbal behavior is a critical component of communication; it constitutes approximately 80%–90% of all communication (Mehrabian, 1972; Ivey & Gluckstern, 1974; Dillard, 1983).

Facilitating components of interview communication include seven major dimensions comprising both verbal and nonverbal skills (see Table 3–1). These are (a) establishing rapport to convey acceptance, (b) communicating professional role involvement, (c) inquiring to initiate the process, (d) determining the major and possible secondary concerns and attaining commitment, (e) selecting goals on which to work, (f) implementing plans of actions, and (g) evaluating the interviewee's applied action.

RAPPORT WITHIN THE INTERVIEW

Rapport building requires setting the stage for the interview to foster a positive interviewer-interviewee relationship. Providing such a warm, nonthreatening environment demands much effort on the part of the interviewer. The skilled interviewer recognizes that many interviewees lack interview experience; this condition can limit or hinder the interview process. How the interviewee perceives the interviewer and the interview environment will undoubtedly influence the interviewee's behavior. The interviewee's readiness for interviewing is also critical. The skilled interviewer recognizes that the interviewee's showing up for the interview does not necessarily mean that she is prepared to participate in the interview.

In most human-services organizations, both the interviewee and interviewer understand that the primary purpose of working together is to attain stated goals. Readiness and ability to communicate on the interviewee's part allow work toward that goal. The interviewee should have positive expectations of the practitioner that can develop into a sense of a significant other. The interview process should direct sufficient need gratification toward the interviewee to foster the latter's perception of the interviewer as a competent professional.

Most often, the interviewee and professional begin as strangers, with all of the attendant ambiguities and uncertainties. One factor that contributes to the uniqueness of the interview relationship, however, is its potential for success. While in most instances the interviewee presents herself for help, this indicates a need for information or direction, distress or discomfort, or perceived concern. More than likely, she wants to resolve her concern; to do this, however means sharing and working with a stranger, the professional. Thus, the interviewee may enter the interview with mixed emotions.

Understanding of and compassion for the interviewee's beginning expectations and emotions are critical to a successful reciprocal interpersonal exchange. During the first contact, or even the first few minutes of the interview, creating a nonthreatening climate is essential. Some general guidelines often produce effective outcomes from this exchange. Rules are fine, but an accurate assessment of the interviewee's verbal and nonverbal behavior will be important, particularly at the outset of the interview.

When meeting the interviewee for the first time, the professional should introduce herself and politely direct him—for example, into the office and a comfortable seat. An example might be:

Table 3–1   Anatomy of the Interview

Components	Techinques	Specific Skills
Rapport	Exchange greetings, make introductions, put the interviewee at ease, create a nonthreatening environment for interview productivity	Using polite and pleasant greetings in a professional manner, handshakes, pleasant facial gestures, good eye contact, suggesting where to sit, identifying who you are, "small talk" or brief talk about nonessentials, and other amenities
Role clarification	Convey how you might assist the interviewee, what the interviewee will do	Sharing information with the interviewee about your role and function in her case
Information seeking	Starting the interview, inquiry is initiated either by the practitioner or interviewee	Using open- and closed-ended questions, observing the interviewee and his surroundings, good eye contact, active listening, clarifying issues
Identifying concerns	Seek information by helping the interviewee sort out the facts, identify real concerns, capture relevant facts, explore alternatives	Employ open- and closed-ended questions, probing, clarifying, paraphrasing, confronting, mirroring statements, pulling common themes together, focusing on relevant data
Goal setting	Identify things to work on; reach agreement between interviewer and interviewee to carry out plan	Supporting, contracting, encouraging, promoting, giving advice, considering alternative courses of action
Implementation	Assess the interviewee's implementation of plan, identify any road blocks, or make suggestions for improvement	Advice giving, informing, inquiring, approving, encouraging interviewee to implement plan of action(s)
Evaluation	Determine what level at which the interviewee succeeds; end the interview	Contacting resources, assessing, encouraging, and supporting the interviewee

Interviewer: "Good morning, Mr. Anderson. How are you? I'm Mrs. Jones, a social worker here at Mt. Helena Hospital. Would you come with me to my office?"

Although the interviewer wants the interviewee to feel comfortable, it is also important to avoid behaving superficially from the start. An artifical climate can permeate the interview. As some authors (Dyer & Vriend, 1975) suggest, often statements about the weather, last night's ballgame, or something about the local public transportation can be perceived as a superficial opening. While such comments or discussions are quite familiar in the general public as social "ice-breakers" or informal small talk, they contribute little to the interview process. Furthermore, if prolonged, the "chit chat" can detract from rather than enhance the relationship (Dyer & Vriend, 1975).

A warm beginning, however, also conveys a sense of acceptance and hospitality to the interviewee. Other techniques can help the interviewer convey an accepting attitude. Personal introductions to other staff members help. In many human-services organizations, the interviewee first sees a receptionist or secretary, then the interviewer. In this case, it is essential that the receptionist or secretary greets the interviewee in a friendly manner and presents her by name to the interviewer as illustrated in the following example.

Secretary: Good afternoon.
Interviewee: Good afternoon. I'm Ms. Alvarez and I have an appointment to see Mr. Hall.
Secretary: Hi, Ms. Alvarez. I'm Mrs. Thomas, Mr. Hall's secretary. Let me see if he is off the phone . . . I'll take you down the corridor to his office. (Walking down the corridor.) The snow was really falling while I was out for lunch. What was it doing outside on your way in?
Interviewee: It seems that the snow has now changed into a light drizzle of rain.
Secretary: Okay. Here we are. Mr. Hall, this is Ms. Alvarez. Ms. Alvarez, this is Mr. Hall.
Interviewer: Good afternoon, Ms. Alvarez. How are you?
Interviewee: Hello. I'm fine.

Adhering to the scheduled time of the interviewee's appointment is important. Most of us dislike waiting, particularly when we have made a special effort to be on time. The interviewee may perceive waiting for the interviewer as a disregard for and a lack of acceptance of her. An interview setting that is neatly arranged, has comfortable chairs, and is free from distractions (such as phone calls and personal interruptions) will contribute to a warm, accepting environment. Other courtesies, such as adjusting the volume on the radio or closing out the bright sunlight shining on the interviewee through the window can communicate a sense of concern. Although these factors may appear trivial, they can influence the interviewee's perception of the setting, the interviewer, and the interview.

Generally, most beginning statements communicate the central objective of the visit to the interviewing office. In a businesslike manner, the professional conveys an absorbing personal interest in assisting the interviewee. Although no opening is more appropriate than another, it may be helpful to offer some examples: "What has brought you here, Mrs. Thomas?" "This is a rehabilitation office, Mr. Smith. How might I help you?" "I see Mrs. Frazier has suggested that you come here. Would you tell me how that occurred?"

The professional should begin without nervousness and be as direct as possible regarding interviewing expectations. The overly polite, friendly professional may be disappointing to the interviewee who prefers a person who is knowledgeable and confident. A genuine, businesslike opening encourages the interviewee to start working on her concerns.

EXPLAINING THE PROFESSIONAL ROLE

Describing the professional's role, the second skills component, is also an important task that can be done in the initial phase of the interview. The professional probably need not share all the details of her profession or professional background with the client. An interviewee may be concerned about the interviewer's function within the agency or operation. He might only be trying to determine whether he has come to the right person. To answer his question requires only that you identify yourself and convey in simple terms your role in the agency or setting. The interviewer should describe her role or function in terms of what she can or cannot do. The following are examples of this procedure:

— "I'm Ms. Basham, an attorney appointed by the municipal court. You may discuss with me anything you like about the incident that occurred last evening."

— "I understand that we would both want a medical opinion regarding this condition. We don't have a radiology department in our unit, but we work with St. Mary's Hospital. I would like to arrange for you to be examined there."

INFORMATION SEEKING

The third component involving inquiry follows creation of a nonthreatening atmosphere and conveyance of the professional's role. The interview really begins with a question, initiated by either the professional or the interviewee: Why is the interviewee in the interview? The professional may initiate the interview by asking, "How may I help you?" or "What seems to be the problem?"

Some types of questions are obviously better than others. Some allow the interviewee to respond more fully, helping the interviewer to facilitate the interview process. In some professional settings, direct questions often result in more positive outcomes for the interviewer, if not for the interviewee. The types and uses of questions are important considerations for effective interview outcomes. Often, the novice or inexperienced interviewer asks too many, often meaningless questions (Charles, Fleetwood-Walker, & Luck, 1985). Sometimes, questions are asked in such a manner that the interviewee is unable to respond. More importantly, other occasions establish a pattern of repeated questions and answers shifting back and forth between the interviewer and interviewee. This line of questioning does not provide the interviewee with other alternatives for responding. Questions should be tailored to the level of the interviewee's knowledge. It makes little sense to ask questions about something about which the interviewee has limited or no knowledge.

As stated earlier, some types of questions are more appropriate than others during certain intervals of the interview. Timing will determine appropriateness. That is, the interviewer must be perceptive enough to read the interviewee's nonverbal and verbal cues accurately and pose appropriate questions. Competency in questioning can be attained through skill and knowledge of the many forms of questions.

Open and Closed Questions

Many situations encourage use of open questions, which involve more than brief, factual answers. Open questions tend to focus less on one-word answers. Some examples of open questions include:

— "What are your thoughts about receiving food stamps?"
— "How might we work toward achieving this goal?"
— "What were your reasons for seeking assistance from this office?"
— "How have you planned to support the three children and yourself?"

Open questions can produce facilitative responses and reduce the need for additional questions. They contribute to the interviewee's self-disclosure and exploration.

Unlike open questions, closed questions are often less effective and usually require only a single "yes," "no," or "don't know" response. Closed questions have a more factual, focused purpose. Some typical closed questions include following examples:

— "Do you like school?"
— "Did having V.D. make you feel guilty?"
— "Would you care to investigate your chances for employment at the new J.B. Smith plant?"

Both types of questions have their places in the interview. Some interviewees may feel more at ease answering a series of closed questions in the beginning of the interview and take more responsibility by responding to more open questions later in the interview.

The professional most often will integrate open and closed questions. He may begin with an open question, such as "How might I help you, Anthony?" Since Anthony appears a little unsure of himself and ill at ease, the professional may ask closed questions at certain intervals until Anthony becomes more relaxed. He avoids losing Anthony by just asking a series of closed questions.

Direct and Indirect Questions

Direct questions are appropriate when the professional needs immediate information or the interviewee is rambling or seems uncomfortable (Schulman, 1982). In some organizational settings, such as emergency health-care centers and radio and television stations with strict time schedules, use of open or indirect questions is limited.

Open questions can be made even more open by stating them indirectly. The indirect question generally has no question mark following it, but it is an obvious question. Notice the distinction between the direct and indirect queries in the following examples.

Direct questions might include:

— "What do you think about the incident with your girlfriend?"
— "Do you find it tough working during the day and studying at night?"

Indirect questions sound like these:

— "I wonder how the new job seems to you."
— "You've had a lot of work experiences in this area over the past five years. There must be a lot you want to talk about."

Many prefer indirect queries over direct ones simply because they allow the interviewee to take control of the response. Some experienced professionals use a combination of direct and indirect queries at appropriate intervals to help facilitate the interview. Others avoid using questions as much as possible. This probably depends on individual style and personal choice.

Employing "What" Rather Than "Why" Questions

Generally, "why" questions should be avoided simply because they often put the interviewee on the spot (Brammer, 1985; Schulman, 1982). For example, the individual may not know why she needs assistance. She may only know that her condition or situation is uncomfortable. Therefore, asking her why she is in the interview is not productive. Questions using "why" also may suggest that the interviewer is prying, consequently leaving a feeling of guilt.

Multiple Queries

The next type of question is one that does little to encourage positive interview outcomes. It is a compound question, when two or more questions are asked at the same time. Such a format confuses the subject (Benjamin, 1981; Schulman, 1982). The interviewee will probably respond to the least threatening question, attempt to ignore the others, and assume that she is excused from answering the others. Multiple questions can confuse both participants. The interviewee may wonder, "Which question should I respond to first?" or "I understand the first question, but I'm not really sure the second one is clear to me." Consider the following examples:

> **Interviewer:** What kind of skills do you have for this job? Or, have you thought about some other type work or going into business for yourself?
> **Interviewer:** What plans have you made for recuperating at home after leaving the hospital? Have you informed your children and insurance agent about your accident?

Asking the interviewee well-thought-out questions one at a time can help facilitate the interview process. By carefully listening to what is said and how it is conveyed, the professional can ask appropriate questions that move the interview toward its goals. This approach avoids attempting to resolve the interviewee's concern to quickly.

Active Listening

Active listening skills provide an important link to appropriate uses of questions to obtain information. Active listening demands that the professional not be preoccupied, but free to attend fully to the conversation. It includes hearing the way the interviewee communicates, her tone, and her verbal expressions and nonverbal gestures. Also, listening requires an effort to hear what is not stated, what is only alluded to, what is being avoided, and what lies beneath or beyond the surface of the issues involved. We listen with our ears, but we also listen with what Reik (1972) calls our "third ear"—our eyes and mind. Nonverbal behavior communicates certain messages not present in verbal statements. An ability to tie together verbal and nonverbal messages allows the interviewer to hear more accurately what the interviewee means.

The objective is to hear the interviewee with empathic understanding. Many individuals believe they already know how to listen, but active listening must be learned and practiced. Awareness of the active listening tool and understanding of how it operates will help make its use most efficient. How can we determine whether a professional is learning to listen? She is actively listening if she can express to the interviewee in her own words what he has said, including emotions, and if he then agrees with this account. This is also an indication that the interviewer has heard the interviewee with empathic understanding.

Here are some examples of accurate listening that can occur in the interviewing process. These are illustrations of the interviewee sending messages that are cues of problems.

> **Interviewee:** My husband destroyed my contract with a prospective female business partner. (Sobs.)
> **Interviewer:** You're disappointed at losing your contract and angry at your husband for destroying it.
> **Interviewee:** Yeah! Now I'll have to go through the process of getting another contract drawn up!

> **Interviewee:** This nursing home certainly isn't as good as my last one. The nurses and doctors were friendly.
> **Interviewer:** You feel rather left out here.
> **Interviewee:** I honestly do feel that way.

In each of these examples, the interviewer accurately decoded the message and learned what was going on inside the interviewee. In each example, the interviewer also checked out the accuracy of his decoding and elicited verification. Furthermore, in each case the interviewer focused on how the interviewee was feeling about the internal situation, not on the external situation itself. For example, in the first situation, the interviewer focuses on how the interviewee feels about the situation. He does not place the focus on the husband by saying, "Your husband is really a bad guy, huh?"

Requirements for Effective Active Listening

For active listening to be effective, the professional must have certain positive attitudes or mindsets. Without these, he can come across as insincere, patronizing, or manipulative. Even active listening can seem mechanical and unnatural to the interviewee.

Active listening is one powerful tool for facilitating communication. Other tools include using clarifying statements; promoting inquiry; and developing a nonthreatening climate in which the interviewee feels free to think, talk, question, and explore. Professionals trained in effective interviewing skills to promote communication processes grasp and appreciate the importance of active listening and apply it regularly to enhance their own interviewing performance.

Clarifying Issues

Clarifying, in a way, is an extension of active listening. It involves responding to sometimes confusing and unclear aspects of statements by centering on underlying issues and facilitating the interviewee's efforts in sorting out conflicting perceptions. The interviewee may indicate that she is not certain what her views are regarding a particular concern; for example, she has mixed emotions about her husband's abandoning her and their children.

> **Interviewee:** I don't know what I feel right now about James leaving us. (Silence.) I do know that the kids and I will need some kind of public assistance to get necessary food and maintain the apartment.
>
> **Interviewer:** You have mixed feelings about your husband, but you do understand that you must get help with the apartment and food for the family.

Clarification can aid the interviewee in sorting out her thoughts or feelings so that she can focus more sharply on what she is actually experiencing (Cormier & Cormier, 1985). The interviewer remains within the interviewee's frame of reference and helps her put matters into perspective. Ultimately, this method can yield a slightly deeper level of self-examination by the interviewee.

Uncovering the interviewee's real concern may take some time and patience. Understandably, prior to developing sufficient trust in the interviewer, the interviewee may not want to convey information about her true concerns. For instance, an unmarried female patient in a hospital told the nurse that she was worried about her mother, an 80-year-old widow, with whom she lived. As the patient and nurse developed rapport, it became clear to the nurse that the patient was very upset about the hysterectomy she was about to undergo and really concerned that it would discourage a man from ever marrying her. Her mother was a less painful focus of concern and actually allowed her to avoid looking at and dealing with her real fears. Active listening and responding to the interviewee must be done carefully to avoid being misled by superficial problems and issues.

In some instances, the interviewee will raise several concerns at once. Responsive listening skills can help the interviewee sort out the different concerns and prioritize them. It is important to get to the real concern and not rush too quickly into problem identification. Failure to identify clearly the concern means wasted time in interviewing.

An example of clarifying an interviewee's concerns follows:

> **Interviewee:** I will be unable to report to work next Monday. I realize that this is a bad time since the inventory will be done on that day; but I just won't be able to come.
>
> **Interviewer:** Something seems to be troubling you right now.
>
> **Interviewee:** No, not exactly. My wife and I have to seriously search for another place to live beginning Monday.
>
> **Interviewer:** You're having problems where you presently live.
>
> **Interviewee:** Absolutely! The landlord of the apartment where we live is verbally abusive about the way we care for the lawn. He's on our back all the time. We must have an apartment where there is peace and quiet, although I'm not sure how I'll manage it.
>
> **Interviewer:** You sound frightened and unsure of the financial obligations and, at the same time, you're unsure where to turn now—cope with a difficult situation or get another apartment.
>
> **Interviewee:** You're correct. We haven't strongly considered moving into a better apartment in another part of town. I'm not sure that I can manage the cost of a better apartment. Anything without the hassle we're experiencing and a cleaner apartment would probably cost a bundle.
>
> **Interviewer:** Let's see if I can assist you in planning what your expenses might be.

This example, too, illustrates that taking the time simply to listen to the interviewee's messages allowed the interviewer to uncover the subject's underlying fear and uncertainty as opposed to interpreting his experiences with his landlord as the chief concern.

HELPING THE INTERVIEWEE IDENTIFY CONCERNS

Helping the interviewee to identify and define his concerns, the fourth skill, is a major portion of the interview process. Without this, the remainder of the interview will likely become a futile exercise (Egan, 1986). Information about concerns can come from the interviewee and sometimes others who are involved in the situation.

The professional applies the skills discussed in the previous section of this chapter to understand the interviewee's behavior and the relationships between that behavior and the interviewee's concerns, especially in the early stages of the interview. Frequently, skills such as paraphrasing, targeting, summarizing, and confronting help the interviewee define his concerns that warrant special attention and/or assistance.

Paraphrasing the Interviewee's Statements

While most interviewees are quite capable of expressing their concerns, others convey their thoughts less well. To help the interviewee to be more specific in her statements and their meaning, the professional may intervene by paraphrasing. The professional's paraphrase is a response that captures the essentials of the interviewee's message by restating it in fewer words. Blackham (1977) identifies three major purposes for paraphrasing: (a) to communicate to the interviewee that the professional is trying to understand what is being conveyed, (b) to clarify the professional's understanding of the interviewee's message, and (c) to underscore a specific issue or theme or communicate more precisely what the interviewee is attempting to convey. The professional restates the interviewee's message without adding anything to it.

Paraphrasing is a basic listening skill. It tells the interviewee that you are actively hearing what she is saying. It is a direct response to the interviewee's last statement, as the following illustrations show.

> **Interviewee:** I'm so mad at my supervisor, I could hit him. He won't say kind things to me or others. I just don't want to be with him anymore.
> **Interviewer:** You're quite angry with your supervisor.
> **Interviewee:** I really want to work outside the house like many other women, but my husband and mother think I should stay home, take care of the house, and have his supper ready when he gets home. (Sobs.)
> **Interviewer:** It appears that you are upset with your husband and mother for wanting you to live up to their expectations.

In short, the interviewer's paraphrasing helps the interviewee clarify certain aspects of what she has stated; it therefore helps her better understand her concerns (Dillard, 1983). "Paraphrasing and occasionally checking out perceptions and understandings are important to [interviewees] of various ethnic groups where a concrete structure of the [interview] process is being provided" (p. 274). This skill enables interviewees, particularly those lacking interview experience, to conceptualize the interview relationship and sharpen their own communication.

Targeting Concerns

The professional's ability to focus on the essentials of the interviewee's concerns is necessary to uncover the real issues. Using culturally appropriate eye contact in the interview, particularly during the initial stages, helps communicate that the professional is listening to and interested in what is important to the interviewee. Eye contact should continue while the interviewer identifies the interviewee's concerns. Rather than appear to be haphazardly listening, the professional demonstrates her desire to attend and respond to the messages stated by the interviewee.

Verbally following the interviewee's message is also essential (Evans, Hearn, Uhlemann, & Ivey, 1984). This means that the professional selectively listens to particular elements of the interviewee's communication. Ivey (1983) maintains that there are several vital components to targeting the interviewee: central concern, interviewee, interviewer, other persons, groups, subjects, and culture or environment. The following example shows several possible ways of targeting:

Interviewee: How can I perform my work effectively? You're always on my back complaining that I'm not keeping up with the rest of the line. Ever since you have become supervisor these last three weeks, you have not taken the time to see what my previous work was like before you got your new assignment. My work is just as good as the others working on this production line.

The interviewer can target either the central concern or the interviewee.

Targeting the interviewee's major concern encourages her to discuss what occurred with her supervisor and other pertinent information. Targeting the interviewee encourages her to disclose her emotional concerns. Either approach has merit, depending on the interviewee's purpose and/or types of information needed. Often a mixture can help facilitate sorting out and clarifying the concerns involved.

Four other types of focusing or targeting areas that Ivey (1983) proposed can help identify concerns: targeting the interviewer, other persons, interviewer-interviewee or group, and cultural-social context.

An examination of part of an interview transcript will help demonstrate the different interviewer responses employed to determine the major concerns. (These are the interviewee's initial statements.)

Elenore: Okay, I feel that my situation isn't too bad. My husband is in the hospital. He appears to be doing well. And I'm managing to deal with my situation, although I'm having a slightly different experience now that I'm a hospital volunteer. Earlier, I was working on the men's orthopedic ward passing out magazines and serving lunch trays to patients. I'm no longer on that ward. I don't know what he was thinking with all those men up there.

Interviewer as the target: I once did volunteer work, too, in a hospital. My experience was good at the time.

Other persons as the target: Elenore, your husband is still in the hospital. What does he think about your being a hospital volunteer?

Interviewer-interviewee or group as the target: Both of us seem to be saying the same things. But I wonder if we could talk a little more about which of these situations would benefit our interview for today.

Subject as the target: What seem to be your concerns right now? What kinds of things are you doing at the hospital as a volunteer now? How are the duties different from your earlier work?

Culture or surroundings as the target: You mean that you don't want to be around a lot of men on the orthopedic ward because you feel your husband may get the wrong idea about the volunteer work. Many women work on men's wards. Is it a question of your husband being jealous, or is it that you're most comfortable working around women?

It is apparent that each of the interviewer's responses directs the interviewee to different aspects of a discussion. When the interviewer attempts to identify the subject's concerns, he must be able to target the interviewee's communications that seem most relevant. Targeting helps make these concerns less confusing.

In summary, the way a professional listens to the interviewee can determine how well she identifies and understands the interviewee's concern or problem. Passive listening can waste time and effort for both parties. Therefore, selective listening to the interviewee's messages and responses that provide clarity and understanding of the concerns can lead to positive interviewing results for all concerned—interviewee, interviewer, and organization. An analysis of the interviewee's concerns may depend on the professional's ability to apply targeting skills effectively. Finally, a mixture of targeting categories can help identify concerns more effectively than a single category (Dillard, 1983, p. 295).

Tying Main Concerns Together

At various intervals within the interview process, the professional summarizes or ties together several main ideas and emotions stated by the interviewee. This facilitates the interviewee's ability to clarify incongruities in her communication and encourages her to discuss her concern further. Summarizing also helps the professional verify his perceptions of what is being said (Blackham, 1977). In summarizing, the professional tries not to add any new material to what the interviewee has said. He makes no effort to identify how events affect each other. A summary is tentative and communicated so that the interviewee may alter, add to, or provide more detail.

The professional usually applies a summary (a) when the interviewee has conveyed ideas or emotions that sound vague or rambling, (b) to emphasize or tie together at the close of a discussion interval or interview, and (c) to give some interview guidelines at a first session. While the interviewer usually summarizes, sometimes it can be beneficial for the interviewee to summarize. The following examples illustrate summaries:

Interviewer summarization: You're unsure why your production quota has dropped; yet you know that you constantly experience throbbing pain in your head and upper back and have difficulty sleeping nights. I'm wondering whether or not your pain and lack of sleep are caused by your strain to meet the production quotas.

Interviewer's request for summarization: Mrs. Thomas, for the past 30 minutes we have talked about the things that you can do to improve your grades. Would you tell me what you can do?

Obviously, each of these summaries has a different purpose. The interviewer's summarization response may either link the main ideas together or identify similar themes or patterns in what the interviewee is attempting to convey. A summarization also provides a useful feedback response to enable the interviewee to better understand his own unclear and often complex communication (Cormier & Cormier, 1985). The interviewer could request that the interviewee summarize an interval or session to determine how well the interviewee understands the main points or to clarify any of his misconceptions of material covered.

Interviewer summaries generally highlight two major areas of the interviewee's comments: emotion and content (Ivey & Gluckstern, 1974). Summarization of emotion is quite similar to mirroring emotions: it identifies different emotional areas of the interviewee's talk and conveys understanding of those emotions by the interviewer. The major difference between mirroring and summarization is identity. Mirroring is a recapitulation of several emotional areas of the interviewee's comments. Summarizing emotion is actually an extension of mirroring the interviewee's emotional messages—the interviewer in his own words mirrors the interviewee's emotions. To reiterate, it includes tying emotions into important thematic patterns. For example:

Interviewee: The last four weeks I haven't felt like looking for a job at all . . . I'm not exactly certain why I feel this way. . . it just doesn't "turn me on" . . . yesterday I almost had to force myself to go downtown to the employment office . . . I used to go to all job interviews the employment office would give me when I was first paroled, but now I couldn't care less.
Interviewer: You feel that even though you were initially interested in finding a job, now you feel less and less interested . . . you're not certain why this occurs. . . .

The second major area of summarization is the interviewer's content responses to the interviewee's comments. The central purpose of summarizing content or cognitive material is to help tie the interviewee's ideas together. It is not uncommon for the interviewee to ramble. To assist her in organizing the cognitive elements of her concerns, the professional summarizes them. Evans, Hearn, Uhlemann, and Ivey (1984) maintain that these responses should be "concise, accurate, and timely summaries" (p. 68). You should note that summarizing content response accurately mirrors the nonemotional or cognitive elements of a message, whereas summarization of emotional response mirrors a series of feelings. The following is an example of the interviewer summarizing content response to an interviewee's comments:

Interviewee: Well, after learning that many of my employees have problems, I've put in a great deal of time and effort trying to do some of their jobs . . . moving different workers around from job to job and putting in a lot of late hours. Because of this, I can't spend sufficient time with my wife and kids, so she's angry at me. There're many times that I just don't want to be a supervisor.
Interviewer: Your difficulties with your workers have been interfering with your family relationship.

By mirroring the content of the interviewee's statements, the interviewer clears up her own understanding of these statements. If the interviewer's understanding is inaccurate, the interviewee will provide her with more relevant information. Let us examine another example of an interviewer summarizing the content of the interviewee's comments:

Interviewer: (Starting a subsequent interview.) Ms. Alvarez, the last time we met, you were concerned for the safety of your children being home alone evenings from 4:00 p.m. to about 11:00 p.m. while you worked. Being the sole breadwinner in your family, you're not able to be with them during the evenings. There were two things that you were going to do to secure your children. You were going to ask your mother to come and live with you and the children. If that didn't work out, you would ask your sister's oldest daughter to sit with the children each evening while you're working. Is that a fairly accurate summary? Where would you like to start today?

Interviewer: (15 minutes into the interview.) For the past few minutes, you've stated that you have been attending a Weight Watchers club once a week to assist you in your weight reduction. You're also involved in lifting weights three days a week and a daily three-mile brisk walk in the neighborhood. Yet you find none of these activities really benefit you in losing weight. Since these haven't worked, let's consider another plan that might be helpful to you.

Interviewer: (During the close of a session.) Mr. Wagner, since our time is nearly up for today, I'll highlight some of the important things we've discussed. You believe your qualifications for the supervisory position meet our requirements. You made three specific points about these qualifications: you have several years of management supervisory experience with Bell Lab Industries, you have three years of experience as an industrial management troubleshooter, and you have a master's degree in industrial management. Would you care to add anything that I may have left out?

These three examples occur at three different places in the interview. The interview itself may require separate summaries of nonemotional and emotional material in the interviewee's comments. Generally, however, a summary response that includes both emotional and nonemotional material will allow the interviewee to clarify and better understand his concerns. Summarizing both content and emotion can communicate to the interviewee that you are attending to the total person. The next example integrates emotional and nonemotional material in a single summary response.

Interviewer: (Midway into the interview.) Billy, let's see if I'm following you correctly. You're not completely satisfied with your assignment covering news in the field. You feel like you have been passed up with opportunities to substitute as anchor newscaster on weekends. Field work is boring and doesn't seem to be helping you move up the career ladder. Right now, you feel that you deserve a chance to make a better contribution to journalism. Is this about accurate?

The emotions involved focused on the way she felt about the situation—not completely satisfied, passed over, performing boring work, and deserving a change. The non-emotions focused on a chance for a higher-level position and making a contribution to her field of work. The interviewee in this case can perceive the interviewer's attempt to hear her. This summary allows the interviewee to correct the interviewer's perceptions.

In short, summary responses of either emotional or nonemotional material should not be overused. Both elements of summary responses should be employed in a step-by-step process as an effective communication skill. More importantly, integrating summary responses into the interview can help to uncover the interviewee's real concerns.

Confrontation

Confrontation can provide a powerful tool for facilitating understanding of both verbal and nonverbal behavior. Often, the interview process moves in a circular direction, simply because the interviewee is unaware of the inconsistencies conveyed through her verbal and/or nonverbal communication. Confrontation challenges the interviewee to examine herself honestly, with the professional pointing out her specific behaviors or discrepancies between her verbal and nonverbal messages. To help the interviewee identify her concerns, the professional must provide opportunities for the former to become aware of her inconsistent messages during the interview. This involves honest feedback about what he observes. The professional might verbally react to the genuineness of the interviewee's responses by saying, "I really feel that you're trying to avoid discussing this matter" or "It appears that you aren't really serious about discussing what's troubling you" or "I'm not sure about your reason for feeling that you need to punish yourself continually for Billy's failure. How does this benefit you or change the situation?" Dillard (1983) maintains that

> When the [interviewer] applies this skill, he conveys a sense of wholeness of self—he is not a "phony" in the relationship. He is consistent in his feelings and does not hide himself in the transaction with the [interviewee]. He will always deal with an issue when it arises, thus avoiding the chance that something important slip by undealt with. (p. 277)

The professional may focus on confronting the interviewee's inconsistencies. For example, "You say that you and your family need financial assistance to purchase food, but you refuse to accept food stamps." Okun (1976) suggests: "An effective way of using confrontation is to send 'I messages,' to own your responsibility for the confrontation by sharing openly your own genuine feelings with the [interviewee] or by focusing on the [interviewee's] avoidance or resistant behavior" (p. 53).

Finally, the professional's role is to help the interviewee gain awareness and deal with the implications of what she is saying in the interview. By challenging the interviewee with her distortions, inconsistencies, or vague messages, he helps the interviewee communicate her concerns more readily. However, he should approach confrontation with caution. Confronting responses can range from a mild challenge ("How possible is it?") to a strong or direct challenge ("I don't see you really wanting to change your situation. When are you going to do something other than give a lot of talk?"). The point is that one interviewee may be less emotionally ready to handle some types of confronting responses than another. It may be more appropriate to confront the interviewee during, for example, the latter half of the interview than at the beginning.

In summary, the four components of interviewing discussed here are essential for helping the interviewee discuss her concerns clearly. How much the professional uses these skills will vary according to his style and the concerns and behavior brought to the interview. Systematic integration of these skills can lead to productive outcomes. Some of these skills also overlap with the other six components discussed in this chapter.

FACILITATING GOAL SETTING

Once the concerns have been identified, the next step is to establish a possible goal, the fifth skills component. The interviewee's concerns must be translated into workable goals. Krumboltz (1966) provides three general guidelines for developing interviewing goals. The first is tailoring the goal to fit the interviewee. The interviewee is likely to put forth greater effort to attain goals when they are appropriate. Both parties usually agree upon which goals and objectives to pursue. Second, the professional should be willing to assist the interviewee in working to reach the goal. Obviously, few goals will be achieved if the professional does not make an honest, serious effort to help the interviewee meet the stated goals. Third, the goal outcome should be observable. Goals thus take into account the interviewee's abilities and willingness to achieve them.

The interviewee usually has more than one goal. Her concerns can be associated with both present (immediate) and future (long range) goals. For example, Mrs. Smith's goal is to improve economic conditions for her three children and herself. Subgoals might be to attain a paying job now (present goal) and to become a typist by attending a local business school part-time (future goal). When the interviewee has multiple goals, it becomes necessary to encourage him to prioritize or rank these goals by importance. Generally the professional should encourage the interviewee to work on single goals at a time. He can also work toward future subgoals simultaneously, but this will depend on the complexity of the goal, the interviewee, and the situation.

Encouraging the Interviewee to Assume Responsibility

Getting the interviewee to select a workable goal that conforms to his needs is not always easy. On some occasions, the professional must encourage the interviewee to take an active, responsible role in selecting and designing goals that can best resolve his concerns. Often, the interviewee comes to the interview with passive, nonchalant, or defensive attitudes and expects the professional not only to diagnose the concerns but tell him what he needs to work on to achieve success. This style of behavior may stem from a variety of circumstances, such as a lack of previous interview experiences or the learned style of an affiliated culture or ethnic group. With this type of interviewee, it becomes helpful to free the individual of any distorted perception of a threatening environment and/or professional authority and status.

The professional works to encourage the interviewee to engage actively in the goal-setting process. While the professional's attitude is important throughout the interview, she must give specific consideration to directing the interviewee's behavior toward both present and future goals. Pointing out and indirectly suggesting goals can provide an atmosphere that encourages a reciprocal interviewer-interviewee relationship. For example, the interviewer can use appropriate and polite face and hand gestures, such as smiles and an occasional partial extension of the arm with open palm. Obviously, these gestures cannot dominate any portion of the interview. But each can be most effective when applied at times when the interviewee must be influenced or motivated to be comfortable enough to set realistic goals. The interviewer can enhance the interviewee's involvement in goal setting by giving some priority to a concern or element of a concern that is relatively easy to resolve. The interviewee often has some ambivalence about obtaining professional help, and he is uncertain about the interviewer's ability to assist in resolving his concerns. Blackham (1977) suggests: "If [the professional] can help [the interviewee] quickly resolve elements of a highly conflicting problem situation, the motivation of [the interviewee is] enhanced and [his] confidence in the [professional] increases rapidly" (p. 80). Thus, if the interviewee perceives that a particular element of his goal can bring immediate, helpful change to his concerns, he is more likely to feel the need to actively participate in the goal-setting process. This positive change can raise the self-esteem of the interviewee and increase his comfort, confidence, and trust in the professional (Blackham, 1977). Consider the example that follows.

Marie is 30 years old, was divorced two months ago, and now lives with her mother and three children, aged 1, 4, and 13. She completed two years of college, but has never been employed outside the home and does not have marketable work skills.

Interviewee's concern: I have been divorced two months, but my ex-husband's child-support and alimony checks just don't enable me to take care of all of our basic needs. I need a job, but since I don't have job skills, it seems doubtful that I would get one that would allow me to earn enough to make up the difference.

This example illustrates the interviewee's definition of her concerns. It also shows the interviewee taking responsibility for her own behavior in the immediate situation.

At this point, the interviewer helps the interviewee to learn which concern most needs attention. Egan (1975) advocates four criteria for choosing present concerns; (a) provide some priority; (b) deal with easier concerns first; (c) choose a concern that, if acted upon, could improve other concerns; or (d) move from less serious concerns to more serious ones (pp. 207–209).

For example, Marie's concern has two basic elements: (a) lack of sufficient money to support her family and (b) insufficient job skills and experience outside the home. Her present concern is finding work that would help cover expenses; this concern needs top priority, but since Marie lacks job skills and experience, a central concern is also her education. Marie needs to develop some type of marketable skill.

In this case, the professional must assist the interviewee in translating concerns into clear goals (Dillard, 1983). Krumboltz (1966) maintains that goals must be tailored to fit the interviewee, related to the interviewee's personal and cultural values, and stated in observable terms. Helping the interviewee translate her concerns into clear, realistic goal statements promotes or encourages her. For example, nonverbal cues can influence the behavior of the interviewee to take an interest in defining workable goals for herself.

Marie's immediate concern and goal may then be stated as follows:

Immediate concern: I'm not able to fulfill the economic needs of my five-member family with my ex-husband's child support and alimony checks.
Immediate goal: I want to obtain work that will enable me to be financially self-supporting.
Subconcern: I don't have the necessary resources. I don't have enough education or sufficient work skills. I need more education to be able to obtain a good-paying job and become financially independent like many educated women with children.
Subgoal: I will go back to school part-time and complete my college degree within the next four years.

Now that Marie's concerns have been defined, the interviewer might use one or a combination of prompting methods to inspire or encourage her to make goal statements (Cormier & Cormier, 1985)

Interviewer: (Focusing on immediate goal.) Okay, I understand how this can be nagging at you. What exactly would you like to do about your financial situation?

Marie: (Immediate goal statement.) Well, I want to find a job that pays me enough to support my children and me.

Interviewer: (Focusing on subgoal.) You really seem to know what's necessary for you to begin to get a handle on this situation. This is our immediate goal that we want to achieve. Since you already have some college background, and you did well while you were there, what would you want to do to improve your education and economic condition for the future?

Marie: (Subgoal.) I'll ask Mr. Brown, an advisor at Temple University, about setting up a schedule for my going to school on a part-time basis. I believe I can finish my college degree in three and a half years.

The interviewer can also inspire Marie to set her goals by making suggestive statements (Cormier & Cormier, 1985). Observe the following illustration:

Interviewer: (Focusing on immediate goal.) You are really very concerned about making ends meet. Have you thought very much about getting some type of work that would help you supplement your ex-husband's payments to you? You might want to consider securing a job, for example, at St. Matthew's Hospital.

Marie: (Immediate goal.) Yeah! That's a good idea. I want to get a job that will help me support my family.

Interviewer: (Focusing on subgoal.) There's also something else that's not quite as immediate as getting a job. Looking at your educational record, you could have a good future ahead of you. You might want to consider the possibilities of furthering your education. What would you like to do that will help to improve your situation and make you self-supporting?

Marie: I really want to re-enter college and continue my studies in teacher education with a specialization at the elementary level. My aim is to finish my degree within three and a half years.

Each method of prompting can encourage the interviewee to make statements that indicate her desire to achieve something within her control, ability, and available resources. Which of the two types of prompting will be appropriate for the interviewee obviously will depend on her behavior during the interview.

Objective Advice Giving

Not unlike prompting the interviewee to set goals, the professional may need to encourage the interviewee through advice giving. You should note that advice is usually personal, subjective information. While advice giving is useful in interviewing, it must be handled with caution. It should not be overused or dominate the responses. Limiting personal advice will help the interviewee to be independent and take more responsibility in goal setting. The professional should not offer advice to satisfy his own need to dominate or to satisfy the interviewee's need to submit.

Advice giving is a kind of informing activity implemented by the interviewer. In many human services organizations, the interviewee expects the interviewer to provide sound advice about the issues of concern. Occasionally, it is easier to give advice without becoming involved in the concerns of the interviewee. This is true particularly when the interviewer-interviewee contact is short and superficial, and the interviewer feels unable to assist the interviewee in making a change in her situation. Giving advice might seem unavoidable. Unfortunately, some professionals believe they have to give advice on all occasions.

After assessing the interviewee's concern, however, the professional should question herself prior to giving advice. Benjamin (1981) suggests the following questions:

— "Do I know enough about what is involved to give advice?"
— "Do I have enough factual information, as well as adequate knowledge of the conveyed concerns of the interviewee, so that my advice can sound meaningful for her to set goals?"
— "Have we come to the point where my advice might honestly spur her on to set goals?"

Note the following example:

Interviewer: At this point, I feel that we have thoroughly examined this situation of locating employment for you. In recognizing what you have told me and the problems you have encountered, I believe that you might consider getting a job that will help you become financially independent of your ex-husband as one of your immediate goals. You may also want to think about going back to college part-time to complete your degree as one of your future goals. By that time, you will be able to. . . .

Once the interviewer has presented advice, how does the interviewee assess, understand, and respond to it? Benjamin (1981) suggests that the simplest approach for answering this question is to elicit a reaction from the interviewee. For example, "How do you feel about my advice? It would be helpful to know whether this information sounds useful to you," or "I'm curious about your reactions toward my advice." While urging the interviewee to set goals through his advice, the professional must also be able to accept the interviewee's rejection as well as acceptance of that advice. Obviously, the interviewee will not accept advice in all interview situations. The rejected advice may also lead to achieving both the interviewee's and the human-service agency's goals.

Supporting the Interviewee

Not unlike prompting, encouraging, or advice giving, the interviewee can receive motivation for setting goals during the interview through support from the interviewer. As mentioned earlier, the interviewee's interview experiences can vary from limited practice in setting goals to keen awareness of goals. Therefore, the interviewee may need support for the concerns being considered to stimulate goal formulation.

Supportive verbal and nonverbal responses convey attention to the interviewee's comments and expressions and demonstrate that her behavior or emotions are not uncommon. Responding to the interviewee's comments and/or behavior toward goal setting may be necessary. A supportive response may be applied when the interviewee shows feelings of anxiousness or frustration to help reduce those feelings and help her to concentrate her efforts on goal setting. Note the following illustration:

> **Interviewer:** I would like for you to pause for a moment and take a few deep breaths before beginning again. (Silence.) Now, I want you to take your time as you talk.
>
> **Interviewee:** I have so many concerns that need to be dealt with . . . I just find it kind of hard to know what to start focusing on first as a goal. I know what they are, but I feel a little bit uneasy right now. . .
>
> **Interviewer:** You're feeling a little tense and anxious about resolving some of your concerns at the office. It's not always easy to come up with what you need to do. I'm here to help you think through the steps you need to take to resolve the conflict with your supervisor. Let's consider some of the things you might be able to do to improve your relationship with your supervisor. What would you like to achieve in this relationship?

Supportive responses can help spur the interviewee toward formulating personal goals, but these responses may not be limited to only goal setting. That is, supportive responses can be a powerful tool applied in other areas of interviewing. The interviewer, however, should avoid overusing supportive responses to prevent the interviewee's dependency on such responses.

Contracting for Goal Attainment

One method for clarifying expectations of goals is to develop a contract with the interviewee (Epstein, 1985). It can take the form of a written or verbal agreement concerning the goals to be accomplished and their priority. Brammer (1979) maintains that a contract "is an agreement between the [interviewer] and the [interviewee] that they will work toward certain *goals,* that each will carry out specific *responsibilities* to achieve the goals, and specific *outcomes* will be taken as evidence that the help was successful" (p. 59). In some cases, the interviewee performs a specific task and receives a reward in return. For example, the 13-year-old male is rewarded two hours of television viewing three consecutive evenings after dinner for completing his homework three times a week. The formal or written contract is drawn up only when there is a question about whether the interviewee (for instance, a young child) understands her responsibilities in achieving a stated goal. A 30-year-old female factory worker, for example, might sign a contract agreeing to increase the quota on the production line in return for an extended vacation period. A mature interviewee can set goals using informal contracts that both parties verbally accept. The formal contract often involves written statements of (a) responsibilities involved, (b) rewards and support for achieving or not achieving agreed obligations, (c) privileges given, and (d) how the parties will determine when stated conditions are met and the contract is to be terminated.

Used in an interview, formal contracts can help specify the behaviors necessary to attain a particular goal. They clearly state the responsibilities of both parties, and each knows when the agreement has been completed. In most interviews dealing with an adult or a mature interviewee, however, the interviewer may prefer to use an informal or verbal agreement. Usually, this is the case, since an implied assumption exists between both parties once goal setting and prioritizing begin: Each has an obligation to carry out the responsibilities to move toward a plan of action.

IMPLEMENTING THE DECIDED PLAN OF ACTION

Implementation is the sixth component of interviewing. It involves launching a stated plan based on mutually agreed-upon goals and priorities formulated between the interviewer and the interviewee. Implementation of the action program is critical to any attempt to achieve the goals of both the interviewee and the organization. The interviewer should monitor the interviewee's application of a prescribed plan to identify and minimize any unforeseen roadblocks and suggest improvements. Dillard (1983) argues: "If the problem is clearly understood and attempts have been made to rehearse portions of the program to simplify procedures, the [interviewee's] goal may be fairly easily attained" (p. 308).

Informing the Interviewee

Providing valid, unbiased information can be a useful tool as the interviewee considers translating his goals into action. While the interviewee's stated goals may certainly be sound, steps for achieving such goals can be ill-planned, thus resulting in a "hit and miss" approach. Facts about situations that they may encounter can help: procedures for obtaining food stamps, for example, or legal aid; and requirements for vocational programs, nursing homes, private schools, or medical-care facilities. Here is a specific case where the interviewer sees that the interviewee needs additional factual information:

> **Interviewer:** I commend you for your efforts in trying to resolve the conflict and change your parents' perceptions of the kind of career you wanted to pursue in college. However, there are a couple of things that I feel you need to know to help your parents better understand your decision. For example, . . .

The professional, in this illustration, recognizes efforts made toward the interviewee's task before supplying information to make any corrections. Information provided should contain only factual data that would help improve the action taken and the interviewee's understanding.

Approving Actions Taken

The interviewee needs approval or agreement as he implements his plan of action. This approval, also another form of support, can encourage the interviewee to take greater strides toward achieving his stated goals. Approval may be communicated either verbally or nonverbally. Verbal approval can take the form of a statement, such as "I really think you're on the right track, Mr. Elsom. Keep up the good work," or "It seems to me that you have given a lot of thought to what you need to change in your plan to make it work for you. That's great!"

Nonverbal responses conveying approval can include a simple smile or head nods. Both nonverbal and verbal responses of approval are often used simultaneously. This combination can in fact convey greater agreement than a single verbal or a nonverbal response.

EVALUATION AND FOLLOW-UP

Evaluation, the seventh skills component, should not be thought of as a single event occurring at the close of the interview. It is applied continually throughout each session. The interviewer may evaluate certain aspects of the interview at various intervals. Evaluation usually begins prior to the initial interview. For example, the mother and her young child enter a child guidance clinic seeking professional assistance for the child's inappropriate behavior. The clinic worker may meet with her for a short period and gather information through a series of questions, a form of assessment. Data gathered are assessed to determine, for example, who the interviewee is, what the present problem is, or which professional would be suited for this case.

Evaluation may also take place without the physical presence of the interviewer and interviewee. Frequently, the interviewee will telephone the human-services organization and request an appointment for assistance. During the phone conversation, the human-services professional may ask several questions, for example: "How old are you?" "What seems to be the problem?" "How can we assist you?" Key questions at this point help to provide an initial appraisal of the situation and answer the following concerns:

— Who is the potential interviewee?
— What services does the potential interviewee request?
— To what extent can this human-services organization provide these services?
— To what other human-services organizations can the potential interviewee be referred to obtain the requested and/or needed services?
— Which professional is best qualified to work with this type of interviewee, concern, or problem?
— What ethnic, cultural, legal, or ethical concerns need to be considered in this case?

Addressing considerations like these prior to the initial interview can enable the professional to respond effectively to the interviewee's needs. Note, however, that these types of considerations are not limited to prior interview interaction.

Assessment within the Interview Process

Continual assessment or evaluation occurs throughout the interview. The interviewer's ongoing monitoring of her own as well as the interviewee's verbal and nonverbal behavior is instrumental in moving toward attaining goals. That is, both parties are concerned about achieving the goals.

Assessment must consider the interviewer as well as the interviewee. The interviewer makes conscious efforts to observe and sense all factors that may influence the interview process. The following list illustrates some evaluative questions:

— How well am I following what the interviewee is conveying to me?
— Is the relationship firm enough for me to be more confrontational with the interviewee?
— What are the interviewee's immediate and future concerns?
— Which concerns should be dealt with first?
— Does the interviewee fully understand her concerns?
— To what extent does the interviewee have external and/or personal resources to handle her situation?
— How well can I recover from my mistakes and achieve the intended goals of the interview?
— How willing am I to work with the interviewee who is an ethnic minority, woman, homosexual, or feminist?
— How do I see the interviewee in relation to her social environment?
— Am I professionally equipped to assist the interviewee in dealing with her concerns?
— What does the interviewee want from this interview?
— Where is the interviewee in relation to the life stages of the interview?
— How well do I perceive the interviewee's underlying emotions or implicit statements?
— How important are these emotions or implicit statements?
— What other methods can I use that might improve this interviewing process?
— To what extent should the interview be ended?
— To what extent is the interviewee prepared for ending the interview?

This list certainly is not exhaustive. These types of questions can help the interviewer and the interviewee improve or adjust their progress. A series of evaluations throughout the interview are usually better than a single evaluation at the conclusion of the interview. Changes or adjustments depend on unforeseen factors that often interfere with the process. Since corrections occur during the interview, goal attainment will remain a positive outcome.

Following up on the Interviewee

Evaluation can continue between interview sessions as well as after the interviewee has been terminated. The professional may need to determine what the interviewee did after a regular interview. For example, the interviewee who is testing out his job-interviewing skills by applying for work at a local business may have found that his experience in the practice interview session did not help him land a job. Going over that failure at a subsequent session can provide valuable information to help correct his approach:

Interviewer: Mr. White, how did things work out during your job interview?
Mr. White: Well, at first things seemed to be going okay, while Mrs. Thomas was doing most of the talking. But I became a little nervous when she started asking me a lot of questions about why I think I deserve the job, and . . . I wasn't offered the job.
Interviewer: If you agree, I would like for us to take a hard look at what happened in your interview and see how you can improve your skills for other job interviews. We can role play

the interview just as it happened, examine it, and then practice these new skills to increase your chances for getting a job.

Numerous situations would prompt the professional to determine how well the interviewee performed a task he promised to do between interview sessions. Did the interviewee practice the relaxation techniques between sessions as promised? How well did the interviewee stay on his medication? How well is the plant supervisor applying the time management program as agreed in the last session?

Following up the interviewee after termination can also provide valuable information both to the organization and to the interviewee. Implementing a follow-up procedure after the interviewee has been terminated will require the assistance of the interviewee and other professionals. Usually after termination, the professional is outside the realm of relevant information that would enable her to judge fairly the interviewee's progress outside the interview. The best sources for information would be the interviewee and other contacts, such as other professionals, family members, or significant others.

Before beginning to gather follow-up information, the interviewer should inform the interviewee of her purpose and whom she plans to contact. The interviewee must give permission (where possible) for her to contact other individuals about him. This procedure demonstrates respect for the interviewee's rights and helps to maintain a positive relationship.

How can follow-up information be obtained on the interviewee? A follow-up interview may be necessary to evaluate his progress. A personal self-assessment of his progress can be given and, if warranted, corrective measures can be provided. Information from agencies, other professionals, family members, or significant others regarding the interviewee can be obtained by several means, such as telephone calls, letters, questionnaires, or personal visits. Each of these procedures would depend on the circumstances involved in the case being considered.

In short, evaluations are often important before the actual interview starts as well as during the interview process. One-time interview assessments offer little, if any, opportunity for corrective action and mutually desired outcomes.

RESEARCH AND SYSTEMATIC SKILLS TRAINING

Kagan (1973) argues that the issue may not be Does interview assistance work? but rather Does it work consistently? In other words, we can teach prospective professionals to interview potential interviewees, but can we provide a set of skills to ensure that most trainees will become competent interviewers? Egan (1982) believes that systematic interview training programs are needed (p. 6).

Carkhuff and Anthony (1979) contend that the interviewer has much to accomplish by applying responding skills in the interview. For example, they directly influence the degree of personally relevant material the interviewee will convey to the interviewer. Further, interviewers who are trying to teach interviewees certain skills or to follow a certain plan of action will improve their chances if they can respond skillfully to the interviewee's experiences.

One example of this systematic approach is research that attempts to identify communication skills appropriate to certain groups (Berman, 1979). She applied ratings of Black and White graduate students' written responses to videotaped interviewee vignettes. The results showed that Blacks tended to use more active expression skills and Whites more attending skills, such as reflection of emotions. Sex differences were not significant.

Systematic interview training skills have been proven to separate the effective professional from the ineffective professional. Research (Carkhuff, 1972) indicates that many students in helping professions become less capable of assisting because of the training they receive. Programs highly cognitive in nature, often lacking systematic training, are directed by educators who themselves do not possess basic interviewing skills (Egan, 1975, p. 18).

SUMMARY

Becoming a skilled professional interviewer requires knowledge grounded in a set of systematic interviewing skills that facilitate communication with the interviewee. The professional must also be able to practice these skills to the point of developing a reservoir of natural, comfortable communicative responses that foster positive outcomes. That will enable her to selectively respond to the interviewee's messages and maintain a smooth pace during the interview process. Full knowledge of interviewing skills includes the rationale for each skill, how to apply it, and when to apply it during the interview.

Ability to handle an interview will rely a great deal on the professional's willingness to examine her style of communication with others. Becoming proficient in interviewing may require acquisition of new ways of communicating that lead to effective interviewee assistance.

SUGGESTED READINGS

DeRisi, W. J., & Butz, G. (1979). *Writing behavioral contracts: A case simulation practice manual.* Champaign, IL: Research Press.

Goodyear, R. K., & Bradley, F. O. (1980). The helping process as contractual. *Personnel and Guidance Journal, 58,* 512–515.

Hayness, S. N., & Jensen, B. J. (1979). The interview as a behavioral assessment instrument. *Behavioral Assessment, 1,* 97–106.

Hudson, J., & Danish, S. (1980). The acquisition of information: An important life skill. *Personnel and Guidance Journal, 59,* 164–167.

Jahn, D. L., & Lichstein, K. L. (1980). The resistive client. *Behavior Modification, 4,* 303–320.

Johnson, D. W. (1981). *Reaching out: Interpersonal effectiveness and self-actualization.* Englewood Cliffs, NJ: Prentice-Hall.

Keane, T. M., Black, J. L., Collins, F. L., Jr., & Venson, M. C. (1982). A skills training program for teaching the behavior interview. *Behavioral Assessment, 4,* 53–62.

King, M., Novik, L., & Citrenbaum, C. (1983). *Irresistible communication: Creative skills for the health professional.* Philadelphia: Saunders.

Long, L. (1978). *Listening/responding: Human-relations training for teachers.* Monterey, CA: Brooks/Cole.

Ross, R. S., & Ross, M. G. (1979). *Relating and interacting: An introduction to interpersonal communication.* Englewood Cliffs, NJ: Prentice-Hall.

4

Stages of the Interviewing Process

Robert R. Reilly
Texas A & M University

We can conceptualize the effective interview in many ways, but it is particularly instructive to view it as a dynamic, interactive system of relationships in which information is communicated for a purpose. Development and change characterize the interview as it moves along in response to the forces and counterforces that it encompasses. Major elements such as the setting, purpose, and individuals involved not only influence the progress of the interview but also are themselves influenced by it. Certainly humans respond differently to different settings, purposes, and to other humans. In the interview a constantly changing set of relationships develops, seeking balance or equilibrium in pursuing various purposes.

The skilled interviewer not only recognizes these dynamic, interactive qualities of the situation but also can take control and move the interview in an appropriate direction. This chapter helps develop that skill by furnishing both a framework for understanding the usual stages in the interviewing process and a set of objectives to be achieved during each stage. Rather than being carried along in the stream of conversation, then, the skilled interviewer uses this information to anticipate events and develops an agenda of objectives to pursue at each stage.

An analogy may be helpful here. We can compare the interview situation to a card game in which the individual player's behavior is influenced by other factors and in turn helps determine the actions of others. When deciding what card to play next, the player must consider a number of variables, including his or her own cards, previously played cards, the rules of the game, a plan or strategy, perhaps a partner's behavior, and likely the verbal and nonverbal behavior of the other players. Each player in turn makes a decision based on this multitude of influences, and each card played affects the decisions of other players. In this manner, the game progresses along a course that is unique and varied rather than predetermined. The "interview hand" is also played out in a wide variety of ways, responding to an array of influences. But the skilled interviewer, like the skilled card player, can give control and direction to this undertaking.

Many authors use the term "interviewing" in a more generic sense than that intended for this book. A number of texts on counseling and psychotherapy use this term in their title (e.g., Cormier & Cormier, 1985; Evans, Hearn, Uhlemann, & Ivey, 1984); interviewing and psychotherapy are not used in this text to indicate the same process. Interviewing is more limited in scope and different in purpose. Professionally conducted psychotherapy focuses on identifying and remediating personal problems, often through major change in personality, and frequently extends over a number of sessions. Interviewing in this book designates a communications process of limited duration (usually less than one hour) intended to give or obtain information or make decisions. The interview is often conducted by a professional (nurse, minister, personnel officer) but not necessarily one trained in psychotherapy.

While this distinction points up differences in the two processes, it should be stressed that important similarities also exist. In particular, both counseling and interviewing are significantly concerned with sharing important personal concerns with other human beings. For this reason, a review of the stages suggested in several selected models of counseling should provide points of interest in our discussion of stages in interviewing.

Gerard Egan has studied counseling theory extensively. The third edition of his popular text, *The Skilled Helper: A Systematic Approach to Effective Helping* (1986) provides a three-stage model in a problem-management approach to counseling or psychotherapy. Stage 1, identifying and clarifying problem situations and unused opportunities, helps clients identify and understand both their problems and their resources or opportunities. Clients are encouraged to tell about themselves, focus on related issues, and develop new ways to look at their lives. Stage 2, goal setting, emphasizes the development of a picture or scenario of the problem situation as it is desired. Possible goals are evaluated, and choices are made and committed to in this stage. Stage 3 of Egan's model is an action stage during which strategies and a plan of action to reach the goals are determined and implemented.

Hutchins and Cole (1986) present effective helping as a problem-solving process similar to the Egan model. They identify the following steps:

1. summarizing and identifying the client's problem
2. establishing realistic goals
3. designing effective procedures
4. evaluating the helping process

The authors of this text see the problem-solving process as consisting of these steps, but also as integrating a variety of helping techniques. It should be noted, also, that they view evaluation as ongoing throughout the entire helping process.

While some aspects of these two models apply to interviewing, their stress on personality and personality change and the time devoted to enhancing the relationship (as opposed to communicating information) set them apart from interviewing.

Evans et al. (1984) emphasize skill development in interviewing, but they provide four phases of a typical initial interview. They place development of a working relationship and discovery of the client's problems in phase 1. Phase 2 is concerned with improving the relationship and defining problems more clearly. Maintaining the facilitative relationship continues as an objective of the final two phases, but phase 3 stresses a problem priority agreement, and closure with planning for the next session occupies phase 4. This model, of course, appears more directed to a therapeutic endeavor than to interviewing as defined in this text.

Cormier and Cormier (1985) discuss four stages in a helping or therapeutic process. The initial stage (relationship) seeks mainly to develop an effective relationship between helper and client. Cormier and Cormier note the contributions of Rogers' (1951) client-centered therapy and Strong and Claiborn's (1982) social influence theory in the establishment of this relationship.

Stage 2 (assessment and goal setting) involves assessing the client's circumstances and problems. Both client and helper are seen as profiting from this exploration, and the information it produces is vital in the third stage. Goals for desired outcomes are also developed in stage 2.

The third stage in the Cormier and Cormier model (strategy selections and implementation) concerns the development and execution of a plan of action to reach desired outcomes. Client and helper work together in this endeavor. The plan is based on the data and goals developed in the second stage.

The fourth stage in this system (evaluation and termination) includes an assessment of progress toward desired outcomes and a resulting decision on termination. When the client's progress is not satisfactory, the action plan may be revised.

Few authors have suggested essential steps or stages for the interview. This condition is particularly surprising when the related field of counseling or psychotherapy has produced so many models (usually including stages) that Egan (1986) questions whether they represent "richness or clutter" (p. 8).

Cormier, Cormier, and Weisser (1984) present a three-phase model of interviewing for health professionals. While directed specifically to health settings, the phases apply to other fields. Phase 1, beginning the interview, includes rapport building, structuring, and clarifying expectations. Phase 2, managing, is the period during which information is obtained and given and the patient's reactions are acknowledged. Summary and follow-up are major tasks of phase 3, terminating the interview.

Several common themes or issues surface in these models. While some relate more specifically to therapeutic change, others pertain to our more restricted definition of interviewing. These include

1. establishing a working relationship
2. clarifying issues or problems
3. setting goals
4. encouraging client participation
5. selecting strategies and methods
6. evaluating progress
7. solving problems
8. giving and receiving information
9. dealing with feelings
10. planning change

These themes are among the basic considerations for the interviewing stages presented in the next section.

OVERVIEW OF STAGES

Figure 4–1 provides an outline of stages in the interviewing process. This model will be used in several of the following chapters. Four stages are identified—preparation, initiation, direction, and conclusion—each with its own set of objectives. These objectives represent tasks to be accomplished or steps in the process pertinent to the particular stage.

While these stages and objectives are generally appropriate for interviews, every interview does not follow this one pattern. Rather, this outline provides the typical stages for most interviews. Similarly, flexibility is called for in assigning objectives or tasks to the stages of the interview. At times, some objectives may relate more appropriately to another stage or to several stages—or may prove totally inappropriate for a specific situation. Flexibility, professional judgment, and common sense should rule rather than blind adherence to a suggested model.

Figure 4–1   Stages and Objectives in the Interview Process

Stages:	Preparation	Initiation	Direction	Conclusion
	Preinterview considerations	The beginning interviewing stage	The middle interviewing stage	The ending interviewing stage
Objectives:				
	1. Preparing the setting	1. Establishing the alliance	1. Targeting issues	1. Checking communication
	2. Preparing self	2. Structuring the relationship	2. Obtaining information	2. Planning for the future
	3. Learning about the subject	3. Encouraging sharing	3. Giving information	3. Rehearsing for action
	4. Setting tentative goals	4. Sizing up the situation	4. Stimulating and handling responses	4. Terminating the interview
	5. Determining strategies and tactics		5. Solving problems	

The stages presented in Figure 4–1 provide a convenient, logical method of discussing a complicated subject, just as the human body may be studied a system at a time—skeletal system, muscular system, vascular system, and so on. Yet, in reality, like the body, the interview works as a whole.

Stage 1: Preparation

While the interviewer seldom has the luxury of a long period to prepare for a session, a few minutes are usually available. Even the minimal time between clients or while walking to a meeting room can be put to productive use. And even a small amount of preparation can pay handsome dividends in interview effectiveness.

During this preparatory stage, the interviewer may have several tasks or objectives to consider. The nature and circumstances of the particular interview will determine the specific objectives, but the following items are common concerns:

1. preparing the setting—providing a comfortable, confidential, professional environment for the interview
2. preparing self—putting aside inappropriate concerns, attitudes, emotions, or activities that distract from focusing on the task at hand
3. learning about the subject—consulting forms, records, referral slips, notes, or other available data regarding the interviewee and the purpose of the meeting
4. setting tentative goals—deciding (based on available information and subject to change) what is to be achieved in this session
5. determining strategies and tactics—planning an overall approach and specific methods aimed at reaching the tentative goals

Stage 2: Initiation

In this stage, the interviewer and interviewee meet. Both have expectations, preconceptions, and, perhaps, anxieties about the meeting. The interview is full of potential; it can take any one of many directions. But some directions are likely to be more productive, than others.

During the first few minutes, the interviewer must get the interview off to a good start. The skilled professional will seize the initiative and move ahead with confidence in pursuing some of the following objectives:

1. establishing the alliance—developing a constructive working relationship between the participants
2. structuring the relationship—explaining the nature, purpose, and procedures of the meeting
3. encouraging sharing—stimulating the interviewee to disclose and discuss personal concerns that may not usually be appropriate for everyday conversation
4. sizing up the situation—making an evaluation of the current interview situation as a guide in the selection of the best goals, strategy, and tactics in the session

Stage 3: Direction

The main work of the interview is in this stage and it is usually the most time consuming. Here the interviewer "gets down to business" and directs efforts toward accomplishing the goals. While still subject to adjustment, the goals, strategy, and tactics are fairly well set. Ideally, a rapport with the client is established, and the parties agree upon a structure. The interviewer's agenda or set of objectives for stage 3 will necessarily vary with the nature or the interview, but the following are common:

1. targeting issues—determining jointly the topics to be addressed and focusing on these issues
2. obtaining information—gaining appropriate or desired information from the interviewee
3. giving information—providing the interviewee with appropriate facts or explanations
4. stimulating and handling responses—encouraging and handling emotion, defensive behavior, and other reactions
5. solving problems—assisting the interviewee in effective decision making and other aspects of problem resolution

Stage 4: Conclusion

Just as it is important to get off to a good start in the interview, so it is also important to finish well. People remember best—and are therefore most influenced by—the beginning and the end of an event.

The conclusion draws together completed elements and prepares future action. It should ask "What have we accomplished?" and "Where do we go from here?" Objectives in this stage may include

1. checking communication—making certain that all parties have the same understanding of what has transpired

2. planning for the future—developing plans to carry through on decisions made
3. rehearsing for action—practicing any behaviors that have been determined as necessary actions
4. terminating the interview—ending the interview session

A detailed discussion of each of these stages follows, with specific procedures for achieving each objective.

Preinterview Considerations: Preparation

Naturally, complicated professional endeavors profit from careful planning, and planning is part of the preinterview considerations. But interviewing is a very human endeavor that can only be optimally successful if the individuals involved can reach a high degree of trust, acceptance, and communication. Preparation, therefore, involves not only cognitive considerations such as setting goals, but also preparation of the interviewer's emotions, attitudes, and general state of mind.

Preparing the setting. How does the physical environment influence the interview? Research can give some answers to this question, but personal experience is also a useful guide. When we have something important to discuss with someone, we usually try to make the person comfortable first. The life insurance representative prefers the client's home for the discussion. If the boss gives some directions in passing or in a noisy hallway, it seems less important than orders delivered in the quiet and comfort of her office. While the setting may not be the message, it certainly does influence its interpretation.

If people are reasonably comfortable, feel secure, and experience a minimum of distractions, they can attend more fully to the task at hand. In its pamphlet, "Standards for Providers of Psychological Services," the American Psychological Association (1985) calls for a service-delivery setting that promotes optimal human functioning. Along with comfort, it mentions privacy, safety, and health as considerations. The setting may well influence clients' feelings about themselves, their ability to function, and, as the document points out, the effective delivery of services.

Generally, the work environments of most professionals provide safety and health. Federal, state, and local laws usually address these issues. Comfort and privacy are other matters, however. The major concern is that the individual feels comfortable enough to discuss personal matters (Hutchins & Cole, 1986, p. 17).

Both the physical and the social environment can affect an individual's feelings of comfort and privacy. In the interview, people are asked to discuss personal matters, facts and feelings that are private. They have a right to expect that this information will be received and handled in a professional manner. Sensitivity to their feelings and respect for the confidential nature of their statements are reasonable expectations of the interview's social environment.

How do we provide comfort, meet reasonable expectations, and ensure effective interviewing? Where possible, the interview should be conducted in a physically comfortable, reasonably attractive setting. The environment—office, examining room, and so forth—should be appropriate for the serious work at hand. Privacy, at least in terms of what is said, should be provided. Only professionals involved in the case should be present, and distractions must be kept to a minimum. The desired social atmosphere is one of serious-ness, attention, and concern. While the ideal is seldom achieved, every reasonable effort should be made to avoid an interview setting in which loud noise, inadequate seating, unrelated clients, lack of privacy, uninvolved or inattentive staff members, or similar factors distract from the important business being conducted.

Hutchins and Cole (1986) note the manner in which the physical setting—even the arrangement of furniture—can set the tone for interaction. They point out that a more formal, authoritarian situation is suggested when a desk separates the participants. One-way communication is likely to result. In contrast, a less-formal setting of chairs in a conversational arrangement without a barrier between them implies sharing: it promotes two-way interaction.

Preparing the setting for the interview also involves the interviewer's comfort. The interviewer, like the client, will usually function best on his or her "home ground," in a room or favored chair that gives a feeling of security and control. Paperwork on the desk or the presence of certain personnel may be more distracting to the professional than to the client. While these concerns may seem trivial, they could affect the interview's outcome. The professional, therefore, should ensure security and comfort for himself and for the client.

Preparing self. Since the interviewer's feelings and attitudes are an important vari-able in the success of the interview, it helps to make a brief "reading" of these conditions and remediate any difficulties before serious problems develop. Obviously, no one has only perfect days or is always in a good mood. Nor are professionals free of prejudices, negative feelings, and poor attitudes. Just as individuals must expect occasional headaches and colds, so they should expect some undesirable feelings as part of human imperfection. Problems arise only if they allow these feelings to interfere with their proper and produc-tive interviewing behavior.

To prevent negative attitudes and feelings from limiting the success of the interview, the professional must first identify and become aware of these feelings. Next, she must take steps either to eliminate these feelings or to ensure that they do not intrude into the interview. Consciously assigning these concerns to a later time often helps.

Learning about the subject. The longest journey really begins with a look at a road map. The wise interviewer, like the wise traveler, tries to obtain as much information as possible before beginning. Often this information can save much wasted time and prevent costly errors. A major part of many interviews involves the development and testing of hypotheses—about the subject's needs, nature, problem, diagnosis, and so on. Information is essential in this process, as it is in setting tentative goals and determining strategies and tactics.

Before the interview begins, the professional may have several clues about what to expect. Perhaps a referral letter or report has been sent from another agency. Perhaps this client was in the office previously and records are available. Was there an initial contact report or an application form? Even if a phone call was the only contact with this person, perhaps some information was relayed about the purpose of the appointment or the client's status.

This information helps the interviewer tentatively rule out some areas of concern and focus more intently on others. The medical practitioner who knows the patient is concerned about allergy shots can concentrate on this area and play down the significance of another area for the time being. Using this information can facilitate preliminary regarding time, materials, facilities, and personnel.

Setting tentative goals. Often, the interview goals seem determined by the nature of the setting or organization. Certain information must be obtained or given, a form completed, or certain decisions made. Other situations have a variety of possible and acceptable outcomes. In either case, though, room usually exists for some clarification and specification of goals.

Can we merely give or take some information, or are attitudes and understanding also important? Is the client's impression of the agency important or just the accuracy of the completed form? Does the professional wish the client simply to make decisions or also to be committed to them? Goals are often more complicated that they first appear.

Where some information is available about the client and the purposes of the interview, tentative goals can be set. These goals should be considered tentative because events in the interview itself may force changes. These tentative goals, however, do allow for planning in terms of strategies and tactics in the interview.

Determining strategies and tactics. In warfare, strategy is the overall plan for reaching an objective, while tactics are the specific maneuvers a group of soldiers may use to handle a particular situation while in pursuit of the overall goal. In interviewing, we also might well consider both overall plans and specific methods to reach our goals.

Strategy is properly developed within the context of a number of factors—some situational, some professional, some personal. Judgment is called for in providing the type of synthesis required in each individual case and in determining the best approach.

The reader is referred to the "Interviewing Process Model" discussed in the previous chapters for an organized conceptualization of many factors influencing strategy development. On one level, the interview can be viewed as a procedure that uses communication and preinteractive behavior to achieve desired outcomes. On another level, strategy can be seen as the plan to apply the facilitative components of the interview (rapport building, information seeking, etc.) through the four stages of interviewing to obtain the desired goals or outcomes. Chapter 3 addressed the details of transforming strategy into tactics with a discussion of techniques and specific skills.

Application. This application section is intended to provide practical suggestions and examples relating to the material discussed above. It can be considered the "preparation stage in action."

The preparation stage is usually quite brief, often by necessity. A checklist of questions can guide the professional in making necessary arrangements or preparations.

Preparing the setting:

1. Do I have a suitable room or area?
2. Is it comfortable, private, and confidential?
3. Have I arranged to prevent phone calls and other interruptions?

Preparing self:

1. Am I physically and mentally up to this session?
2. How do I feel about this type of interviewee or situation?

Learning about the subject:

1. Have I looked over any available records, notes, applications, and so on?
2. Is there someone I should call or check with about this interviewee?

Setting tentative goals:

1. What do I want to accomplish in this session?

Determining strategies and tactics:

1. What seems to be the best overall approach to this session?
2. What methods may be particularly useful?

Let's use an example. Bill Johnson is an employment counselor at a local office of the state employment commission. He notes on his desk calendar that the receptionist has scheduled him to see a new client, José Garcia, in about 10 minutes.

The setting: His office is free and suitable for the session, but Johnson decides to put away his calculator and a report he has been preparing. They could be distracting and could give Garcia the impression that he is an unwelcome interruption. Johnson asks the receptionist to hold calls during his session with Garcia.

The self: Johnson is feeling fine today. He is a little concerned about finishing the report on time, but reminds himself to worry about it later. His full attention should be on the upcoming session. He has his usual positive feeling about meeting a new client, but recognizes some apprehension sparked by the Mexican-American name. Johnson has not worked with that many Mexican-Americans and feels a bit uncomfortable with them. He decides to overcome his own apprehension by attending more closely to the client's particular needs. He moves chairs a bit closer and reminds himself that the client may appreciate a more formal, gradual introduction to the session.

Learning about the subject: Office routine includes providing a folder for each appointment. Johnson checks the folder on his desk and notes that it is new, with no previous record of contact. A brief summary of Garcia's phone call two days previous is provided. From it Johnson learns that Garcia, a 37-year-old bookkeeper, is seeking employment because he has recently been let go by the largest manufacturing company in town. Since he knows that the company is experiencing substantial growth and has recently hired several people in the clerical and managerial areas, Johnson wonders about the reason for Garcia's termination.

Goals: Johnson's overall goal, his role in the organization, is to help individuals find suitable employment. In addition, he decides it is important in this particular situation to determine what, if any, circumstances may be curtailing Garcia's vocational effectiveness. Possible remediation of the problem is another goal.

Strategies and tactics: Several factors suggest the need for a deliberate, measured, and circumspect overall approach to this session: the fact that Johnson has not met the interviewee previously, unanswered questions regarding his recent termination, and the subject's likely preference for a more formal interaction. Johnson decides that open-ended questions, reflections, and mild probing are appropriate methods for the early stages of the interview. Decisions about other approaches and methods are best put off until he has a chance to size up the situation.

The Beginning Interviewing Stage: Initiation

This stage of the interview occurs when the interviewer and interviewee meet at the start of the session. Time spent initially in purely administrative activities such as finding a room or filling in forms may be considered an interruption; if well handled, it could contribute to the establishment of rapport. The professional's agenda here includes the development of a good working relationship with the interviewee (the alliance), setting out guidelines for the interview (structuring), ensuring that the client considers herself a partner in the interview (sharing), and beginning an ongoing evaluation of the session's progress (sizing up). As with many of the interview tasks, these activities do not usually proceed in any particular order. Rather, they tend to overlap and often occur simultaneously.

This initial stage is often a period of tentative moves and quick changes in tactics as the principals try to find common ground for their discussion and attempt to satisfy their differing objectives within the parameters of the interview. Here is an illustration:

Interviewer: Well, Mr. Jones, there are three or four topics we could discuss today. . . .
Interviewee: Something urgent has come up this morning and I've just got to have some help with it now.
Interviewer: Okay, let's deal with it first and see what time we have left for the other items.

Establishing the alliance. If the interview is to be a joint effort toward meeting some mutually significant goals, a working relationship or alliance is essential. While this relationship has many facets, it is basically a human relationship of trust and confidence, a partnership with mutually desired goals. The professional's task is to foster in the client positive expectations about the interview's goals and methods. The professional must successfully convey to the interviewee that she is truly concerned, empathetic, genuine, and capable of helping. Lazarus (1981) calls this process "inspiring hope" and stresses the role of nonverbal behavior in this essential task.

Egan (1986) stresses the central importance of this working relationship in helping others. Not only must such a relationship be established early in the session, he points out, but it must also be maintained throughout the process. Egan notes that the relationship has several aspects or components, but to a major degree this is a human relationship in which the two parties' ability to be open and give of themselves provides the basis for establishing a helping alliance. Egan lists attention, listening, empathy, challenge, respect, and genuineness as facets of the relationship and notes that a variety of helping relationships must exist because of differing client needs and differing ways of satisfying those needs.

Certainly the establishment of the productive alliance involves more than saying the right words. Evans et al. (1984) point out the importance of tone of voice and rate of speech along with nonverbal communication. Noting that the majority of communication may well be achieved nonverbally, they suggest meaningful gestures, appropriate facial expression, and a relaxed, forward-leaning body position as ways of conveying interest and concern. Reaching out to another human, however, goes beyond behavior, verbal or nonverbal. It involves conveying personal attitudes and feelings to another person. This point is stressed in much of the writing of Rogers (1951; 1961) and Carkhuff (1969).

Structuring the relationship. Structuring is the process by which the participants come to an agreement regarding the significant aspects of the interview. The procedures to be used, the purposes of the interview, and the role of each participant are among the items they agree upon. To a degree, structuring involves comparing expectations and constraints to reconcile differences.

Cormier and Cormier (1985) stress that structuring is an "interactional process" whereby the interviewer and interviewee arrive at similar perceptions regarding the nature of the interviewing process. In addition, these authors point that structuring provides the professional an opportunity to discharge an ethical obligation to inform the subject about any factors that may influence her full participation in the interview. Along with goals and procedures, confidentiality is often a major consideration here. Interviewees may need to know with whom information generated in the interview will be shared. Time limits may be another important consideration and, if so, should be discussed at this point.

Since structuring is essentially an agreement as to where the interview is going and how it will get there, early agreement obviously is helpful. Often this process and the establishment of a working relationship or alliance will overlap. The need for structure, however, may not be completely satisfied in the initial stage. Procedural questions can come up at any point in the interview and will require decisions.

While structuring can be allowed to develop naturally in the course of the interaction, the professional interviewer often will take the initiative in suggesting the "rules of the road." Cormier and Cormier (1985) describe this as direct structuring: The interviewer "actively and directly provides structure" to the subject regarding the significant elements of the interview. Usually direct structuring is a practical procedure for conserving time in a brief interview.

The early minutes of an interview, in which the alliance is established and structure provided, are illustrated here:

Nurse: Hi. Mr. Brown? Pleased to meet you. I'm Miss Jones, one of the nurses you will get to know here on the unit. I hope you had no trouble finding our office.
Patient: No. The directions were good. It just took a while to find a parking place. But I made it on time all right.
Nurse: Good. Are you doing okay today? Any problems or pain?
Patient: No. My back acts up every now and then but right now it's okay.
Nurse: Well I'm glad you're feeling good today, because we want to get this examination under way so that your back problem can be diagnosed and treated. What I would like to do now is to ask you a few questions about your background and history. This should take about 40 minutes. I use this information for a routine form I fill out and send up to your doctor, Dr. Green. He will use it in planning your treatment, and he will explain how some of this information might relate to the problem you have been having with your back. Does all this sound okay to you?

Encouraging sharing. The interview, like any effective human communication, involves give and take, a back and forth of presentation and response. Many individuals find an unresponsive audience not only disconcerting but also uncomfortable or even frightening. Students who stare blankly at the teacher who asks for comments or questions, the "dead" telephone, the empty house that only echoes the ringing bell or knock—these are failures in communication that we feel as well as recognize cognitively.

The interview relationship cannot be complete if it is one-sided. And the interview goes deeper in terms of expected response. It asks for personal, genuine response involving topics that are more than clichés or social amenities. To an extent, it asks the interviewee to take a chance, to risk being hurt, by discussing very personal information or concerns.

Under what conditions would an individual divulge such information? Usually when he feels confident that the interviewer will be interested, concerned, trustworthy, professional, and capable of using the information constructively. And the interviewer should have successfully conveyed the need for such openness.

Sizing up the situation. While plans can be developed before the interview begins, they can only be tentative. After the parties have met and explored their mutual expectations, planning can proceed with greater certainty. Strategies and tactics are most likely to require change as discussions with the interviewee yield new information. At times, even goals may need to be amended.

Sizing up the situation in the initiation stage allows the professional to reaffirm tentative plans or to make changes where needed. While plans may be modified further as the interview progresses into later stages, the need for change should grow less likely.

Egan (1986) notes the need for an ongoing evaluation of the helping process at every stage. He suggests that some part of the interviewer's consciousness should be monitoring all interactions and determining their contribution to interview goals. Periodic opportunities to stop and take stock of progress are recommended.

Application. Often the objectives of the initiation stage are attended to almost simultaneously. Usually, only a few minutes are required to accomplish these important tasks, but, as noted above, the professional may need to return to these tasks later in the interview.

The following points outline the essential steps in this stage, although their order may vary:

1. Greet the subject by name. Attempt to use the name most acceptable to the particular individual. Usually children and young people prefer first names, while older adults may prefer a more formal address (Cormier et al., 1984).
2. Give your name. Also explain your role or position, to the degree that it will help clarify the situation.
3. Make some comment indicating interest in and concern for the subject.
4. Briefly state the purpose of the interview.
5. Ask for the interviewee's general reaction or comment on this purpose.
6. Evaluate the interviewee and decide if tentative plans need alteration.

Returning to the previous example of Bill Johnson, the employment counselor, we can now observe his meeting with José Garcia.

Johnson: Hello, Mr. Garcia. I'm Bill Johnson, your employment counselor. I am sorry you had to wait a few minutes, but a call came in just before our appointment time and I thought it best to settle the matter so that there wouldn't by any interruptions during our meeting. How are you doing today?

Garcia: Just fine, Mr. Johnson. You have a very nice office here. Very comfortable.

Johnson: Thank you. Would you like to sit here? I notice from your phone call that you would like some help in finding new employment. I thought we might talk a little about your work history and experience. Then we can get down to specifics about the kind of help I might provide you. We have a number of positions announcements that we can go over. How does this sound to you?

Garcia: That sounds fine. I have a number of questions—problems—that you may be able to help me with, in addition to just finding another job.

In sizing up the interview to date, Johnson reinforces his earlier suspicion that Garcia's unemployment may be a symptom of some additional problem. He decides to do more listening than talking and to do all he can to encourage Garcia in discussing his concerns.

The Middle Interviewing Stage: Direction

The interview progresses from its beginning into the next phase, the middle interviewing stage. Usually the longest stage, it tends to be more substantive than other stages. Obtaining information, giving information, solving problems, or other goals are to be accomplished during this period.

This stage sometimes requires a firmer hand on the part of the interviewer. Accomplishing the work of the session means making decisions regarding which of several directions to follow. Often the initial stage opens several doors, presenting a number of possible topics for discussion. The professional must now select the most promising direction in terms of the interview's goals. Targeting or focusing on these issues is a first and essential objective of this stage.

A particular session's goals may or may not entail obtaining or giving information or problem solving. However, skill in these facets of interviewing is often required. Since the interview is a two-way communication process, the professional can expect to be called upon to encourage client response and to handle such responses as questions, emotion, reluctance, resistance, and defensive behavior.

Targeting issues. At times, it is interesting to listen to a social conversation and notice how it moves aimlessly from topic to topic, taking off on one tangent after another until someone exclaims, "How did we ever get on this topic?" In everyday discussion one can afford to enjoy this type of variety. The interview, however, has definite goals and a limited time frame and therefore must be kept on track. Targeting or focusing on essential issues directs an interview along its proper path.

The skilled interviewer can keep goals in mind, shift through a welter of distraction, select the appropriate issues, and tactfully guide the discussion back to these topics when it strays. Sensitivity to the client's feelings is essential, since the side issues or distractions may have considerable importance to other aspects of the client's life.

The first step in targeting is to recognize the significant issues in terms of the current interview goals. A second step is to ensure that these issues get sufficient attention. When discussion moves to other topics, these topics must be evaluated in terms of their relevance. When necessary, the interviewer must redirect the discussion to significant items.

Generally, it is helpful to identify and label major issues for the interviewee, whose aid should be enlisted in exploring these topics to their fullest. "Let's get back to . . . ," "How does this relate to . . . ," or "I'm really interested in your comment about . . ." are methods of keeping the interview "on target."

Obtaining information. Frequently, the major goal of the interview is to obtain information. Some of this needed information may be classified as objective or factual (age, address, years of schooling), but often the client's subjective impressions are important (attitudes, desires, symptoms). In these circumstances, interviewer sensitivity is particularly vital. What is said, how it is said, and nonverbal clues are important in gaining understanding of the client. Listening involves more than hearing sounds. It includes interpretation of all meaningful stimuli.

Donaghy (1984) stresses the significance of listening: "In almost every type of interview, you should be doing at least twice as much listening as talking" (p. 151). He goes on to suggest that people listen effectively to only about 25% of what is said to them. They lose much because of such barriers to effective listening as mind wandering, jumping to conclusions, talking too much, and selective listening (Donaghy, 1984).

Preparation and experience help provide the professional with clues as to what to listen for. Because not all communication is pertinent, active listening involves selection and interpretation.

Giving information. Giving information involves more than simply reciting words. Communication theory is quite clear in suggesting that giving information requires two parties, since none is given if none is received. And the information is not merely received onto a blank tape. Attitudes, experiences, and other conditions of the interviewee influence the reception and storage of information. Viewed in this light, giving information is a complex educational process.

Stimulating and handling responses. If the interviewee is truly involved in the communication aspect of interviewing, and if the issues discussed are personal and important to him, then he should respond. The interviewer encourages this response because it is necessary to the subject's processing of the interview content.

Response may take one of several forms. Commonly, people are defensive about their inner life—values, beliefs, and feelings. They guard it from change. Therefore, denial and reluctance to accept information or insights results. Emotion is another common reaction. Here the interviewer must be careful not to close off expressions of feelings before they have run their course.

Solving problems. Much of the interviewer's work may involve problem solving. Some models of interviewing are primarily approaches to problem solving. Most people, as part of their education, have been exposed to the scientific method of problem solving, but we tend to think of it as useful only in objective, scientific problem situations. Actually, however, this proven approach can be successfully adapted for use with problems of a more subjective, personal nature.

Dillard (1983) outlined the following steps in the use of problem solving in a human setting:

— Step one: Defining concerns
— Step two: Selecting immediate concerns
— Step three: Translating concerns into goals
— Step four: Gathering information and listing alternatives
— Step five: Choosing a course of action
— Step six: Taking action
— Step seven: Assessment of action taken
— Step eight: Assessment of the outcome criteria

Chapter 3 provided a detailed discussion of problem-solving techniques.

Application. Because the interview can take any one of a multitude of directions during the middle interviewing stage, the professional must keep objectives clearly in mind and proceed toward their completion. Essential steps often include:

1. Clearly define goals and identify them to the interviewee.
2. Keep the interview on track in terms of the goals.
3. Obtain and provide any necessary information.
4. Make the interviewee part of the process by stimulating and dealing with her responses.
5. Where necessary, lead the interviewee through a problem-solving process.

For an illustration, we will return to Mr. Johnson, the employment counselor, who is continuing his interview with Mr. Garcia. Targeting issues is Johnson's first concern.

Johnson: Certainly helping you find a new position is of critical importance. But perhaps there are some other issues we should discuss also. You mentioned some questions. . . .
Garcia: Yes. Well, I have been wondering for some time now if I am in the right line of work. Bookkeeping has changed. It's so different now. It's all computers.
Johnson: The field has changed and you wonder if you want to or even could change with it.
Garcia: Exactly. I know bookkeeping but I have had no training in this new technology.
Johnson: So I think we have another question or two to focus on: Is bookkeeping still an appropriate field for you? Do you still have interest in it, now that the field has changed so much, and, if so, can you develop the necessary skills?
Garcia: You know, I was reading this book the other day and it brought up the idea that American workers are of two types, those who work to live and those who live to work. I just can't agree too much with that idea.
Johnson: Let's discuss these three or four issues we have come up with and perhaps they will relate back to that theory.

Here, Johnson has targeted the major issues for consideration and labeled them for the interviewee. He redirected attention to the significant issues. Next, Johnson obtains and gives information pertinent to the targeted issues.

Johnson: Perhaps you could give me a rundown on your training and experience in bookkeeping.

Garcia: Well, after I finished high school . . . (he explains his past).

Johnson: So most of your experience and all of your training have been in this one field?

Garcia: That is true. And I have really done well until this last job. I guess you could say the computer got me.

Johnson: Do you mean that your lack of skills in working with a computer resulted in your termination?

Garcia: Yes, it did.

Johnson: There are some good training programs available for people who want to learn these new skills. The community college has several classes, and we support an on-the-job training program in this area.

Garcia: I see.

At this point, Johnson notices Garcia's withdrawal from the conversation. His responses are much shorter, and he sits back and folds his arms in front of him. Garcia is no longer looking at the interviewer. Johnson now attempts to stimulate some response and interaction.

Johnson: But what are your feelings about retraining? Have you given it some thought?

A discussion follows in which Garcia mentions the reasons for his reluctance to enter a training program. He sums up his position:

Garcia: So I ask myself, "What if I spend all this time and money on retraining and it turns out I don't like it or I can't do it? And who is going to support my family?"

Johnson: You feel like you are caught between a rock and a hard place.

Here the interviewer encourages the expression of frustration and other emotions. Only after these concerns are dealt with can the interview move on to the consideration of solving the problems that have been targeted. Johnson employs several problem-solving techniques.

Johnson: What we really need to consider are some ways to help you decide if you should stay in this field. If so, next we need to find some alternative training programs that meet your financial resources. Finally, you will need to find a position—in bookkeeping if you decide to stay with it, or in another field.

Johnson: Let's start with the question about you staying in the field. What would help you decide?

Johnson: Okay. What we are looking for, our goal, is information that would allow you to estimate your chances of success in bookkeeping if you did the retraining. The career tests we have available here could here could be of help in this regard. Also, your own experience should be considered and you could check with some of the instructors doing this type of training.

Goals and alternatives for the other aspects of Garcia's problem could be considered now or at a later session, if he and Johnson believed that Garcia should base future decisions on the outcome of this issue. But they should definitely choose a course of action here. Action and outcome assessment would occur after the interview.

The Ending Interviewing Stage: Conclusion

During the final or ending interviewing stage, attention shifts from the matter at hand to the future. The major goals of the interview, however, are no less important. Rather, energy now goes into making use of the facts or solutions or changes that surfaced in the previous stage. Stage 4 involves implementing or projecting changes into the future. The interviewer also uses this stage to alert the client to the fact that the interview will soon end.

A first step in concluding the interview is to make certain that no major misunderstanding exists, so that everyone has the same meaning. At this point, plans for the future can proceed.

Often, planning requires specific and perhaps complex procedures. Clients may need help in rehearsing these actions before the interview is terminated.

Checking communications. Because individuals come to an interview with differing goals, needs, and experiences, it is not surprising that they interpret what transpires differently. Often we tend to "find" what we are looking for and ignore conflicting evidence. Two individuals arguing about a point can consult an authority and after receiving the new information, cry out in unison, "See, I was right!"

But communication can be considered satisfactory only to the degree that all parties involved agree on its meaning. Sometimes we may prefer to "get something off our chest" even if it didn't "get through" to the audience. But this is an exercise in venting emotion rather than communicating.

Agreement about what has transpired or what decisions have been made must be checked carefully. And the more the parties to the communication differ—in age, race, experience, background, and other variables—the more care this task demands.

A brief listing of the salient points will often satisfy this need. Sometimes asking the subject to state all or part of the findings is beneficial. According to Donaghy (1984), having the interviewee summarize not only helps her clarify issues, but also may result in greater commitment to an agreement. Observe the following discussion for an illustration:

> **Advisor:** Well then, Jack, from our conversation this morning I think we both agree that dropping out of school is not the only solution to your situation.
> **Student:** Yeah, maybe I did push the panic button. If I can get the loan it should keep me going until summer and then I will be able to work a few months and be back on my feet by September.
> **Advisor:** But do you also see how keeping up your grades ties in?
> **Student:** Right. A failing student isn't a very good prospect for a student loan.
> **Advisor:** Right. Now let's plan your next few steps. You have to apply for the loan and you need to do something about that low grade in accounting.

Verifying communications can also serve some of the purposes of the presummary suggested by Cormier et al. (1984). It reminds clients that the interview will end in a few minutes and encourages them to present any question or issue that has not been adequately handled. Some issues are difficult for the client to present and commonly come in a rush at the end of the interview. Realization that time is running out and greater comfort with the interviewer often combine to bring up comments, such as "Well, another thing I should tell you is this condition seems to be affecting my sex life, too."

These additional issues, misunderstandings, and new questions are frequently too important or complex to handle at closure. By checking communications, the interviewer can discover these items while time remains to resolve them. At the same time, the client is prepared for the conclusion of the session.

Planning for the future. The interview is rarely complete and self-contained. Usually we interview to prepare for future events. We obtain information to be used for future decision making; we give information or change attitudes to affect behavior in the future; and we solve problems so that the solutions can influence future happenings. Often the interviewee leaves the session with explicit directions to follow, such as "Do this set of exercises each day for 10 days, then add five repetitions to each set. . . ."

Even where the professional's goals are limited to obtaining information from the interviewee, the client expects (and likely has a right) to know what will happen next. Thus, some planning for the future is implicit or explicit in many interviews. Here the professional guides the individual in taking the next step, which is using the interview's outcome in future circumstances.

Some major planning elements are the current status of the client, his goals and needs in terms of the issue in question, and the particular future events to be faced. Planning involves anticipating events and selecting alternatives that capitalize on the individual's strengths and minimize any limitations. An example follows:

Employment counselor: Mrs. Jones, we can see that you have had considerable training and experience in the secretarial field, but because you have not worked for the last few years your skills need some brushing up and you don't have any experience with computers or word processing. One type of position for you to consider would be a job demanding more in maturity, experience, and supervisory skills, with less emphasis on speed and skill.

Rehearsing for action. Applying for jobs, doing exercises, handling difficult social situations, brushing your teeth, taking medication, wrapping a sprained ankle, working an arithmetic problem, practicing self hypnosis, disciplining children—these are a few of the actions that could be called for in plans resulting from an interview. When the action is complicated or when the subject feels unsure, rehearsal may be beneficial. Certainly, rehearsal also provides an opportunity to see if the directions have been successfully communicated.

Several advantages of rehearsal can be seen: building confidence, correcting errors, practicing. It is usually easy to initiate: "Okay, let me see how you are going to apply this bandage." "I'll be your boss. You ask me for the raise." "Show me how you hold the floss." "So, Johnny says he needs the car tonight and you say. . . ."

Terminating the interview. Once the business of the interview has been completed, the meeting should end quickly and smoothly. Yet, it often drags on. Awkward pauses, rehashing, or repetition often results when the interviewer mishandles this task. He can lose much of the early focus and effectiveness in the final few moments. And the subject may begin to question the professional's ability to be of help.

Three factors often make it difficult to end an interview: the presentation of new issues by the client, the professional's fear of offending the client, and the fact that a close human relationship has developed. Encouraging sharing in the initiation stage, stimulating and handling responses in the directions stage, and checking communication in the conclusion should reduce the likelihood of new issues suddenly appearing at termination. The professional can reduce her fear of offending the client by mentioning time limitations as part of structuring: "We have about 40 minutes before you are due upstairs." In addition, clues to the approaching termination should be given early in the conclusion stage, and more clearly as the time for closure approaches.

The fact that a human relationship has developed should be acknowledged and, where appropriate, the possibility of its continuance should be noted: "Thank you for your cooperation. I've enjoyed working with you. And if something else comes up, please give me a call."

As suggested above, the secrets to a smooth closure are preparation and clear warning. Both verbal and nonverbal signs give warning (see Table 4–1). Summing up, saying thank you, making suggestions for transportation, and saying good-bye are common verbal signs; sitting forward in the chair, glancing at a clock, standing, and shaking hands are nonverbal clues. It is important to end the interview effectively and courteously. Where necessary, the interviewer should practice these skills.

Application. Pacing and timing become significant factors in the conclusion of the interview. The external realities of time and schedule present one set of pressures, while the need to finish the job at hand adequately exerts pressure in the opposite direction. The interviewer usually should

1. Ensure adequate understanding of the major issues in the interview. Asking the interviewee to list these points may be a useful method.
2. Convey to the interviewee that the session will soon be ending.
3. Point out applications or implications of interview results in future events.
4. Role-play or otherwise give practice in necessary behaviors.
5. End the meeting effectively.

Table 4–1   Clues to Termination

	Preliminary	More Direct
Verbal	"To sum up...." "In the time we have left...." "Before we finish...." "We only have a few moments...." "Well, have we covered everything?"	"We will have to conclude now." "I think that about does it." "It has been a pleasure working with you." "Thank you." "Good-bye."
Nonverbal	Changing posture Looking at watch Putting away pen and notes Leaning forward in chair	Preparing to stand Standing Shaking hands Walking to the door

Johnson and Garcia have now developed a plan of action and have reached the conclusion stage of their meeting. Johnson checks their communication:

Johnson: Then in the little time we have left, what would you say we have decided today?

Garcia: First, I'm going to take some interest and aptitude tests here. Next, I phone the computer class instructors and get an idea of what is involved in retraining. Then we will meet again to go over this information.

Johnson: Right. The tests should be scored by Friday so let's meet then. . . . Miss Jones, our receptionist out front, will direct you to the testing officer, and she will have a list of the computer class instructors for you when you finish testing. Can you see how the information from the tests and interviews will help you in coming to some decision?

Garcia: Right. But as you said, I have to do the deciding.

Johnson: Good. Now do you see any problem with calling the instructors? What are you going to say? (As Garcia answers his last questions, Johnson is putting aside his notes and preparing to stand.)

Johnson: I think we have covered a good deal of ground today and I'll be looking forward to our meeting on Friday. (Both stand and shake hands.) Thank you and good luck.

RESEARCH

As noted earlier in this chapter, several authors and researchers have conceptualized their views of interviewing around a series of stages or steps. The interview fits well into this type of process model, which has a flow of activity with a beginning, middle, and end. This model also provides discrete research topics for studying—the separate divisions or stages.

Carl Rogers (1951) provided early encouragement for research on the interview itself, particularly as it related to psychotherapy. Carkhuff (1969) systematized and expanded the early concepts to fit a wide variety of human encounters. Much of the current research on interviewing developed from these foundations with the addition of concepts developed in communications and social psychology (Strong & Claiborn, 1982).

Hutchins and Cole (1986) and several other sources noted in this chapter summarize contemporary research in interviewing. The Donaghy text (1984) is most general, with application to a broad spectrum of interviewing settings. The reader who is primarily interested in reviewing interviewing stages should consider the texts by Egan (1986), Hutchins and Cole (1986), and Cormier and Cormier (1985). Several professional journals may also be consulted, including *Journal of Applied Psychology, Communications Quarterly, Journal of Counseling Psychology, Human Communication Research, Personnel Psychology,* and *Journal of Vocational Behavior.*

SUMMARY

The interview can be seen as a series of verbal and nonverbal exchanges between individuals with each response influenced not only by previous responses but also by the setting and participants' attitudes and purposes. By recognizing the dynamic nature of the interview and anticipating its stages, the professional can take control and direct the session to its appropriate ends.

This chapter presented a model of the stages and objectives in the interview process. While it stressed the need for flexibility, judgment, and common sense, the model can provide a convenient, logical method for understanding the interviewing process. This understanding provides the professional interviewer an opportunity to rely upon planning and skill rather than chance in reaching desired goals.

Preparation or preinterview considerations represent Stage 1 of the interview. Objectives include preparing the setting for the interview, preparing oneself, and learning about the individual to be interviewed, With these items attended to, the interviewer next sets tentative goals and decides upon strategies and tactics to use in the session.

Stage 2 is initiation, or the beginning of the interview. Objectives center around meeting the subject and getting the session off to a productive start. Establishing the alliance, structuring, and encouraging sharing are vital elements. The interviewer should size up the situation once it has begun and decide if changes in strategies or tactics are necessary.

The middle interviewing stage, or Stage 3, is termed *direction* because the professional aims her major efforts at directing the interview process toward reaching the session goals. Targeting issues, obtaining and giving information, stimulating and handling questions, and solving problems are usual objectives at this stage.

Stage 4 is the conclusion, or the ending interview stage. This is usually a brief stage in which the professional checks communication to see that no misunderstanding exists, makes plans with the client, helps her rehearse actions, and terminates the meeting effectively and courteously.

Certain major themes or elements permeate these stage: planning, preparation, and purpose; participation and cooperation; clear communication; and dealing with feelings. These elements are vital in all successful endeavors that involve people working with other people on meaningful issues.

SUGGESTED READINGS

Cormier, W. H., & Cormier, L. S. (1985). *Interviewing strategies for helpers: Fundamental skills and cognitive behavioral interventions* (2nd ed.). Monterey, CA: Brooks/Cole.

Donaghy, W. E. (1984). *The interview: Skills and applications.* Glenview, IL: Scott, Foresman.

Egan, G. (1986). *The skilled helper: A systematic approach to effective helping.* (3rd ed.) Monterey, CA: Brooks/Cole.

Evans, D. R., Hearn, M. T., Uhlemann, M. R., & Ivey, A. E. (1984). *Essential interviewing: A programmed approach to effective communication* (2nd ed.). Monterey, CA: Brooks/Cole.

Fear, A. (1984). *The evaluation interview.* New York: McGraw-Hill.

Hutchins, D. E., & Cole, C. G. (1986). *Helping relationships and strategies.* Monterey, CA: Brooks/Cole.

Sincoff, Z., & Goyer, S. (1984). *Interviewing.* New York: Macmillan.

PART TWO

Interviewing Applied to Special Groups

Flexibility and adaptability are the characteristics of the interview that make it the method of choice in many situations. Chapters 5–8 demonstrate these characteristics as the interview is applied to four specific groups: children, adolescents, adults, and older adults. While these chapters demonstrate applications of basic interviewing skills to specific groups, they also provide a wealth of information, understanding, and strategies appropriate for working with interviewees in each of these special groups.

5

Interviewing Children

Jan N. Hughes
Texas A & M University

The most obvious advantage of interviewing a child is that the child is the expert (the only expert) on his feelings, perceptions, and thoughts. Thus, if knowing the child's point of view is important, the interview is unsurpassed as a technique for obtaining information. If an adult wants to know what or how the child is feeling or thinking, the adult must ask the child. Yarrow (1960) found that "the interview is a technique particularly well adapted to uncovering subjective definitions of experiences, assessing a child's perception of the significant people and events in his environment, and studying how he conceptualizes his life experiences" (p. 561).

The benefits of interviewing children are not automatic, but depend largely on the skill of the interviewer. Furthermore, the way the interviewer asks children questions differs quite a bit from the way the interviewer asks adults questions. Interviewing children requires special skills as well as knowledge of child development. In addition to these teachable skills and knowledge, the interviewer must genuinely respect children's competence and affective experiences. The interviewer who respects children as active problem solvers who are trying to make sense out of their experiences will be much more successful at eliciting meaningful interview information than the interviewer without this respect.

This chapter is based on the assumption that knowledge of the child's cognitive development, language competence, psychosocial development, and social reasoning is essential to conducting a meaningful interview. Even young children can communicate their thoughts, reasoning, attitudes, and feelings to the interviewer if the interviewer recognizes the child's developmental stage and modifies the interview approach to permit the child to demonstrate his competence.

The first section of this chapter presents a rationale for interviewing a child. The second section delineates some important differences between interviewing children and adults. The third and fourth sections provide an overview of developmental processes in cognition (thinking), language, social reasoning, and psychosocial development that characterize early and middle childhood. The next four sections describe techniques for the preparation, initiation, middle, and conclusion stages of the interview. Finally, special techniques for interviewing the resistant child are discussed.

A RATIONALE FOR THE CHILD INTERVIEW

Interviewing is one of several approaches for obtaining information about a child. In deciding whether to interview a child, the interviewer should compare the advantages and the limitations of this approach with other methods of eliciting information. These advantages and limitations will vary, of course, depending on the specific purpose of the interview. For example, if historical facts are desired, interviewing the child's parents will usually yield more useful information. Similarly, if accurate, reliable, and objective behavioral data are desired, behavioral ratings by parents and teachers and behavioral observations are superior to interviewing the child. Although the interviewer can make some very important, useful observations during the interview, these observations may not have much relevance to the child's behavior in other settings, such as home or school. If information about the child's impulsiveness in typical classroom situations is desired, for example, the interview is not a useful data-gathering approach. The impulsive, hyperactive

8-year-old girl may be reflective and calm in the interview situation, where she has the interviewer's undivided attention. Conversely, the child's behavior in the interview situation may provide useful information on such characteristics as the child's reaction to praise, tendency to persevere in the face of frustration, emotional tone, responsiveness to people, and concerns as expressed through doll play or drawings.

Another example may help explain the advantages and limitations of the interview compared to alternative assessment methods. Consider when a child is referred to a school counselor due to poor peer relationships. To determine the child's rate and type of peer interactions, the counselor should unobtrusively observe the child in naturally occurring social situations, such as recess or lunch. Additionally, the counselor could ask the child's parents or teachers to complete a social-skills or other behavior checklist. To determine the extent to which the child is accepted by his peers, the counselor could also ask the child's classmates to rate all the children in the class in terms of how much they like each of their classmates. These three approaches—observation, checklists, and peer ratings—will produce reliable, valid information about the child's social behaviors and popularity.

On the other hand, if the professional wants to know why the child behaves as she does in social situations, he must interview the child. The interview will provide information on the child's knowledge of strategies for solving different social problems, expectations for success in social situations, motivation to interact with peers, perceptions of others' behavior toward her, and other cognitive variables that mediate, or influence, her social behaviors. Thus, a full assessment of the child's social skills requires a combination of data-gathering approaches that include the interview.

A helping professional considers it essential to interview the child at the beginning of the helping relationship. The interview's purpose is to elicit the child's thoughts and feelings about her experience and interpersonal relationships. These thoughts and feelings may become the targets of the helping intervention or may help the professional understand the child's behavior.

Given the importance of knowing the child's thoughts and feelings, it may seem surprising that the interview has had a low priority as a data-gathering approach during most of the the last half-century. The reason for its historical devaluation is the domination of behaviorism in American psychology and education from the 1920s until the mid-1970s. In the behavioral tradition, a person's thoughts, feelings, attitudes, and other cognitions were considered inappropriate for objective study of human behavior. In the behavioral tradition, behavior-rating scales, behavioral observations, and objective tests of a child's abilities were considered more objective, scientific, and acceptable assessment methods.

Since the 1960s, thinking has gained legitimacy as a topic of investigation in psychology. Modern psychological theories of behavior assume a more complex view of human behavior and recognize the reciprocal relationship between thinking and behaving. Today, cognitions are considered important topics of investigation in their own right, and the relationship between cognitions and behavior is studied. Because the interview is a method of investigating a person's thoughts, attitudes, perceptions, and feelings, it has gained importance and legitimacy as a method of investigation.

A second factor contributing to the increased value placed on the interview is research in child development demonstrating that young children are much more competent to report their subjective experiences than researchers had previously thought. Although the thinking of young children, in most cases, is qualitatively different from that of adults, their thinking is rule-governed. Furthermore, the rules change with age, and the thinking of children at similar cognitive-development stages shares certain striking characteristics. Understanding these developmental characteristics is crucial to understanding what children say and do. In the past, when an interviewer did not understand what a child was saying, she concluded that the child had a limited ability to communicate or reason. Today, before the interviewer dismisses a child as not competent to communicate his thoughts or as having very unsophisticated thoughts and undifferentiated emotional feelings, she is more likely to question whether she has appropriately modified her questions so the child can understand them.

DIFFERENCES BETWEEN INTERVIEWING CHILDREN AND ADULTS

Among the differences between interviewing children and adults are the centrality of the relationship, questioning strategies, the initiation stage, and developmental considerations.

The Centrality of the Relationship

Some basic core skills for interviewing adults are also essential for interviewing children. Making the interviewee feel accepted, understood, and secure in the interview is perhaps even more important in interviewing children than in interviewing adults. In interviewing adults, the interviewee has a range of motivations for cooperating with the interviewer. For example, in a survey study of political attitudes, adults' belief that their attitudes count and can influence the survey's outcome will facilitate cooperation. In a diagnostic or helping interview, the adult's expectation of help motivates cooperation, even when the interviewer asks personal and potentially anxiety-provoking questions. Generally, the adult accepts that disclosing personal information is part of the cost of receiving help.

The situation is frequently different with children. This difference may be especially evident in diagnostic and helping interviews. Children do not refer themselves for assistance, and they may see the entire enterprise as coercive. Thus, the interviewer depends on the personal relationship established with the child during the interview to obtain his cooperation. When children feel understood, respected, and secure, they share their rich, deep thoughts and feelings in an open, trusting manner. When these core conditions have not been met, children are often resistant. Too often, the interviewer believes a child's incomplete, superficial answers to her questions result from the child's limited cognitive ability or linguistic skill, when resistance is the real cause.

Question-Asking Strategies

Although the core conditions are the same when interviewing children and adults, techniques for establishing these conditions differ. In interviewing adults, for example, the interviewer might use open-ended questions to communicate a respect for the interviewee's ability to "tell his own story" with minimal direction from the interviewer. Young children find it difficult to answer general, open-ended questions, such as "Tell me how your parents treat you." This type of question is too abstract and requires more organization from the child than he can muster. The child might feel threatened by such a question. The interviewer needs to modify her questioning approach to reduce the question difficulty. (Techniques for reducing the complexity of questions are discussed later in this chapter.)

The Initiation Stage

A third difference is the amount of time adults and children need to adjust to the interview situation. Usually, the child needs more time. Often, an interviewer will have a selection of toys and drawing materials available and gently encourage the child to explore the room and the toys as a way of adjusting to the new situation presented by the interview. The interviewer offers empathic comments on the child's play, such as "I see you picked the frog puppet." These comments are not directive but rather follow the child's lead. After the child relaxes, the interviewer begins his query with factual questions that the child will find easy to answer. Toys may be used during the interview as concrete referents for the interviewer's questions or may be put aside when the more formal interview begins.

Developmental Considerations

Not only do children differ from adults in their interviewing behaviors, children of different developmental levels differ from each other. A 4-year-old and an 8-year-old differ in their use of language, understanding of social relationships, ability to think logically, understanding of the causes of their own and others' emotions, ability to look at a situation from various perspectives, and in many others ways that have implications for the interview. These developmental changes and their implications are discussed in the next section.

INTERVIEWING IN EARLY CHILDHOOD (AGES 3–6)

Cognitive Development

The single most important, comprehensive, and debated theory of children's intellectual development is that of the Swiss scientist Jean Piaget. While even the briefest summary of this theory is not possible within the limits and goals of this chapter, a brief description of his theory of children's thinking in the early and middle childhood years is useful. This summary focuses on aspects of thinking that have implications for interviewing children.

Piaget delineated four stages of cognitive development. The first stage, the sensori-motor intelligence stage, lasts from infancy until the onset of symbolic thought, around the age of 1–2 years. The second stage of cognitive development is the preoperational stage. While the ages at which a child advances from one stage to another vary, the preoperational stage characterizes the thinking of most children between $1\frac{1}{2}$ and 6 or 7 years of age. Therefore, the typical preschool child is in the preoperational stage of cognitive development. Because children younger than age 3 usually do not have the linguistic competence to participate meaningfully in an interview, this discussion of interviewing young children focuses on children between 3 and 6 years of age.

The singular developmental accomplishment of the preoperational child is the ability to engage in symbolic representation, including pretend play and language. The other notable characteristics of the preoperational child's thinking are defined in terms of the child's cognitive limitations. The preoperational child's thinking is self-centered (egocentric), illogical, centered on one aspect of a problem situation at a time, and incapable of distinguishing between appearance and reality.

Symbolic thought makes language and imaginative play possible. The 2-year-old child can mentally represent (i.e., think about) things that are not in her immediate perceptual experience. Language is a system of symbols for representing objects, relationships, needs, intentions, and other experiences. The 2-year-old who pushes a block of wood and says "choo choo" is engaging in symbolic representation (i.e., the wood symbolically represents a train).

Although the preschool child's vocabulary and syntax may limit his ability to verbally communicate his thoughts and feelings, he can communicate a great deal through the medium of play. Symbolic play is the child's attempt to cope with the demands of reality. At a time when reality is making increased demands of the child, he can act out different conflicts and stresses in his play in a gratifying and nonstressful manner. When interviewing preschool children, the interviewer can capitalize on their ability and willingness to act out conflicts and concerns in the context of play. Play is a more natural way for the child to communicate his experiences than is language.

Piaget described the thinking of the preoperational child as egocentric. That is, the child cannot take another person's point of view. The child's inability to see any point of view but his own is demonstrated in Piaget's famous three-mountain problem. Three cardboard mountains of varying sizes are set on a square table. One chair is placed at each side of the table. The child walks around the table, noticing how the view changes. Then, the child is seated in one chair, and a doll is placed on the chair adjacent to the child and then in the chair opposite the child. The child is shown pictures of the view of the mountains from each perspective and asked to point to the picture that shows what the doll is seeing. The young child picks the picture that shows what he sees. It is not until about the age of 9 that the child can consistently pick the picture showing what the doll sees from each location.

The child's egocentrism means that in an interview, the young child will not be able to consider the interviewer's needs as a listener. Consider the following exchange between a 5-year-old boy and his kindergarten teacher. The boy ran into the building during recess and was obviously upset, with tears in his eyes.

Teacher: What happened?
Child: He said if I didn't do it he wouldn't let me be on his team.
Teacher: Who told you that?
Child: Robbie.
Teacher: What did Robbie want you to do?
Child: Jump off the wall.

The task for the interviewer is to obtain the necessary clarification without making the child feel like an inadequate communicator. The interviewer can capitalize on the child's egocentrism by presenting stories that are relevant to the purpose of the interview and asking the child how the story characters feel and what they are thinking. The stories can be presented with pictures or acted out with dolls. The child's answers reflect the child's point of view because he is unable to take any other point of view.

Piaget described the preoperational child's thinking as prelogical. One logical skill the young child does not possess is reversibility, which is critical to successful performance on conservation tasks. Children's difficulty in solving conservation tasks is demonstrated in Piaget's two stick problem. The child is presented with two sticks (or pencils) of equal length, positioned like this:

The experimenter asks if the pencils are the same length or if one is longer. The child responds that they are the same. Next, the experimenter moves one stick, so that it extends farther to the right, like this:

The experimenter says, "Watch what I do" as he moves the sticks. Then, the experimenter repeats the initial question. Typically, 3- to 6-year-olds say the stick that extends farther to the right is longer. The child has not "conserved" the length of the sticks when their placement was changed.

Recent research explains children's failure to answer the conservation question correctly as a result of the weight young children give to the whole situation. The child knows the adult did something. Perhaps the child supposes that what the experimenter did is relevant to the next question the experimenter asks. The child may take the repetition of the question as a cue that he should change his first answer to acknowledge that the experimenter changed something. Consider also that if one of the sticks is moved "accidentally," rather than intentionally, by the experimenter, children as young as 4 years of age answer the second question correctly.

The implication of the stick problem for the interviewer is important. Children do not give language the same weight over situational cues that adults do. Contextual cues carry more meaning than words do. If words and context are inconsistent, children attend to the context. The interviewer thus should rely less on words out of context when interviewing children and should instead use concrete materials to help convey the meaning of questions. Children can give more competent answers to questions when they occur in a natural context and are accompanied by pictures or manipulatives.

What a person knows, or thinks she knows, influences what she remembers about her experiences. Her acquired knowledge powerfully influences what she stores in memory and what she retrieves from memory. What children know differs enormously from what adults know. Thus, children may remember things quite differently from adults. After hearing a story about a girl named Kim getting a baseball bat for her birthday, a boy retold the story, referring to the main character as "he." Several times the story refers to Kim as "she," and her bat as "her" bat. When asked if Kim were a boy or a girl, the boy said, "A boy, of course. 'Cause he got a baseball bat." According to this boy's knowledge of the world, only boys receive baseball bats for birthday presents. His memory of the story is shaped by his prior knowledge.

The difference between children's knowledge and adults' has two implications. First, the interviewer must not assume the child will interpret his questions or statements the same way an adult would. To prevent misunderstandings, the interviewer should be more detailed in his conversation with young children than with adults. Second, the interviewer should capitalize on the reconstructive aspect of children's memory by using incomplete stories, incomplete sentences, and stories told in response to pictures. The child's completions provide a window into what he knows and how he interprets his experiences. For example, if the interviewer wants to know what the child's bedtime routine is, he might begin a story about a girl getting ready to go to bed and ask the child to finish it. The beginning of the story may be acted out with dolls, and the child may be asked to act out the story completion with dolls. The child's story completion will automatically reflect his own bedtime routine. Yet, if the interviewer merely asked the child to describe his bedtime routine, the child might very well state that he could not or would provide a very incomplete account.

Social Cognition

Social cognition refers to thinking about people instead of thinking about objects. Children's developing understanding of their own and others' emotions and their developing perceptions of people are two aspects of social cognition that have implications for interviewing.

Young children about 3–5 years old believe that an event causes the same feelings in different people. Thus, the 4-year-old boy believes his mother feels happy when she receives a sticker in her cereal box and feels sad when a Donald Duck special is not aired on television. This "projection" of their feelings is related to their egocentrism. The interviewer can capitalize on this characteristic of young children's thinking by using indirect questions. For example, the interviewer can use dolls or picture props to tell a story about a child who is unable to tie his shoes, even when he tries very hard. His classmates can already tie their shoes. The interviewer asks the child how the story child feels and what the story child is thinking. The child's answer tells the interviewer how she feels and thinks about similar frustrating experiences.

Young children's reports of their own and others' feelings tend to be global and pure. Feelings are either "good" or "bad." Similarly, people are either good or bad. Young children cannot comprehend mixed feelings. This "all-or-nothing" thinking makes it difficult for young children to recognize and accept their own bad or angry feelings or behavior because it implies that they are all bad. The 6-year-old does not believe that she can both be a good person and feel angry toward her baby sister (a bad feeling). All-or-nothing thinking explains children's vacillations in feeling states. One moment the child feels all happy, and the next moment all sad. The child may feel one parent is all good and that the other parent, who sets limit on the child's behavior, is all bad. If the good parent disciplines the child, the roles may change.

Children's global feelings have several implications in interviewing the young child. First, the interviewer should minimize any threat the child feels from admitting negative emotions. (The later section on interviewing techniques offers suggestions for making it easier for the child to admit negative feelings.) Second, the interviewer should interpret the child's statements like "I hate my brother" as a statement of the child's momentary anger toward the brother rather than as a generalized, stable feeling. Third, the interviewer should not push the child to express negative feelings (like feeling mad) when the child denies feeling that way.

The following excerpt from an interview with a 6-year-old boy illustrates a child's difficulty in expressing negative feelings as well as interviewing techniques that facilitate the child's expression of feelings. The boy and his mother looked tense and angry when the interviewer entered the waiting room. The mother announced to the interviewer that her son, Tommy, had behaved terribly during the last week. When Tommy entered the interview room, he looked dejected and did not explore the play materials.

Interviewer: Would you like to draw?
Child: (No response for a minute. Then he goes to the chalkboard and proceeds to draw, pressing down so hard on the chalk that he breaks two pieces.)
Interviewer: What feeling does your picture tell about?
Child: No feeling.
Interviewer: It gives me a feeling. I feel a little mad, or maybe upset.
Child: Is that how you feel?
Interviewer: Yes. I feel a little mad. But people feel different things when they look at a picture and when they draw. Do you have the same or a different feeling?
Child: Real mad feeling.
Interviewer: A real mad feeling. What kinds of things make a boy feel real mad?
Child: If his mother doesn't want him around anymore, he feels real mad.

Young children's descriptions of people focus on such external characteristics as clothes, possessions, hair color, and size. Children's descriptions of people rarely mention personal traits; if any are mentioned, they are global and highly evaluative (e.g., "she is very nice"). Furthermore, their descriptions are highly egocentric and subjective, based on what the person does for the child (e.g. "she is nice because she gives me candy"). Thus, the interviewer will obtain little meaningful information regarding the young child's perceptions of people's individual characteristics from asking the child "What kind of person is he?" or "What do you like about him?" If the child's perceptions of others are desired, the interviewer might play the "Guess Who?" game with the child. In this game, the interviewer shows the child pictures of the people about whom the interviewer is seeking the child's perceptions. The interviewer asks the child to point to the one who is always grumpy, smiles a lot, reads stories to him, has a bad temper, hugs him a lot, and so forth.

Personality Development

Because preschool children do not possess the cognitive ability to monitor and regulate their emotional expression intentionally, the interviewer is presented with the child's undisguised feelings. Usually, deception is not within the young child's cognitive repertoire, probably because the child cannot take another's perspective. Of course, the young child can be resistant and refuse to cooperate, but he cannot purposefully present himself as something he is not.

The typical 3- to 6-year-old child is eager for adult approval. This desire to please can both help and hinder the interview. It helps because the child is more likely to cooperate with the interviewer's request. It hinders the interview if the interviewer asks leading questions. The child will agree with the interviewer out of a desire for approval. Also, the young child's ego is not well developed, and the child may agree with the interviewer more because of her dependency on the interviewer than because she truly agrees. Therefore, the interviewer must be careful not to present one alternative to a question as more desirable.

Language

Children's vocabulary and syntax develop rapidly during ages 2–6. Nevertheless, even the 5- or 6-year-old child has not mastered all rules of language usage and may have difficulty expressing himself. In this regard, young children's language expression is more competent when it occurs in a meaningful context, as compared with language outside of a meaningful context. This means the interviewer should provide a context for the child's verbal expressions. When play materials, puppets, and stories provide the context around which the interview takes place, the child's language utterances are more complex and richer than they are in a question-and-answer interview format.

INTERVIEWING IN MIDDLE CHILDHOOD (AGES 7–11)

Cognitive Development

Around the age of 6 or 7, the child begins to demonstrate the ability to consider multiple perspectives, to take the role of another, to reason simultaneously about a subclass and the whole class, and to give relatively more weight to language compared to contextual cues. The 7-year-old child is embarrassed at the silliness of conservation problems like the two-pencil problem. In short, the thinking of the 7- to 11-year-old child is more logical and objective than that of the preschool child. Also, the child in middle childhood begins to think deductively. Piaget referred to this third stage of cognitive development as the concrete operational stage. Despite these significant accomplishments, the concrete operational child's thinking is still limited, compared to adults', because it is tied to concrete experiences. She seems able to solve problems only if the objects necessary to solve the problem are immediately present. For example, the concrete operational child can solve the following problem when it is presented with pictures or other visual representations of the girls: Sally is taller than Mary and Mary is taller than Jane; who is the tallest of the three? The same problem presented without the visual aids will be difficult for the concrete operational child to solve. At this stage, then, the interviewer should provide visual aids to help the concrete operational child answer complex questions that require considering several components of a problem.

Social Cognition

Children 6 or older recognize that other people have feelings that may differ from their own. The 6- or 7-year-old child is likely to believe that he is the cause of other people's emotions. As a result, if the child's mother is sad or angry, the 7-year-old may feel responsible for her sadness. It is not until around age 9 or 10 that children believe that events in their parents' and others' lives cause their emotions. The interviewer needs to be aware of the child's tendency to take responsibility for others' feelings.

Children's descriptions of other people become more differentiated, individualized, and detailed during middle childhood. Descriptions of other people include their traits, dispositions, and attitudes. Hence, the child can report meaningfully on his perceptions of other people.

Children in this age period are more willing and able to accept their own and others' mixed feelings. Because the child believes that it is possible to be angry with someone you love, she more readily accepts angry feelings toward important people in her life. This emotional latitude permits her to express a range of feelings, including both positive and negative feelings toward the same person.

Around the age of 9 or 10, the child develops the ability to engage in recursive thought (thinking about one's own or someone else's thoughts). "I think he thinks I like him" is an example of recursive thinking. This ability enables the child to answer questions about what other people might be thinking about him. He can step outside of himself, mentally, and reflect on his own thoughts and actions. "What do you think he thought about you when you did that?" is a question the 9- or 10-year-old child is capable of answering, but younger children are not. Similarly, statements like "I thought you knew I meant X" and "I thought you knew I was joking" can be understood by the child whose thinking has developed this far. The ability to engage in recursive thinking also makes deception possible. Deception requires the ability to think about another person's thoughts. In interviewing the child 9 or older, the interviewer must engage in recursive thinking to figure out whether the child is trying to disguise his real beliefs and attitudes or whether the child is presenting himself honestly.

Personality Development

The concrete operational stage of cognitive development parallels the latency period of psychosocial development. According to psychoanalytic theory, the latency-aged child is interested in competition and mastery. The interviewer can capitalize on these developmentally normal interests and concerns by conducting the interview around or after a game. Checkers, cards, Four Squares, and other games that involve both skill and a rather large amount of luck are preferable to purely chance or predominantly skill games.

The latency-aged child is establishing control of his ego and will not be as easily won over as the younger child. The interviewer must respect the child's autonomy and not try to be too friendly. A quiet acceptance and easy-going questions about such age-appropriate issues as school, sports, and television programs can help to demonstrate to the latency-aged child that the interviewer will respect his identity as a person in his own right. The interviewer can also ask questions about the child's activities outside of the family, recognizing the child's identity as a person apart from his family. At this age, interviewer should also explain the purpose of the interview in more detail, emphasizing the importance of the child's point of view. For example: "No one else can tell me how you think or feel about X, so it is very important that I talk with you, and not just with your parents, or your teachers, or anyone else."

THE PREPARATION STAGE

In the preparation stage, the interviewer learns about the subject, prepares the setting, and determines strategies. The preceding section on developmental issues discussed what the interviewer should know about children. This section discusses the setting and the degree of structure in the interview.

Preparing the Setting

The setting for the interview should tell children that it is a place for them. Colorful pictures of animals, cartoon characters, or other subjects interesting to children; small-sized furniture; play materials; and cheerful paint on the walls and shelves tell children that the room was designed for people just like them. Although the room should be inviting and cheerful, it should not be overstimulating. Some play materials—for example, a rocking horse or finger paints—can overstimulate children. Of course, the selection of play materials will depend on the type and purpose of the interview.

Planning the Amount of Structure

The interview format can vary in the degree of standardization of the questions. The standardized interview uses questions that are completely formulated prior to the interview and are presented to each child identically (Yarrow, 1960). While the standardized interview may be appropriate for some research purposes or to gather simple factual information, it is generally not appropriate for children. The standardized interview does not present a natural context of asking and answering questions, and children are likely to feel inhibited and shy in its artificial, rigid context. If the child's point of view, frame of reference, and interpretation of experiences are desired, the interviewer must be flexible in the way she asks questions, formulates appropriate probes following the child's answers, orders questions, and introduces topics through questions.

The optimal amount of structure depends on the purpose of the interview. In an initial assessment interview, the interviewer will exercise at least moderate control of the content areas by asking questions and redirecting the child's responses to keep within the purposes of the assessment. For example, the psychologist interviewing a child referred for behavioral problems at school will ask questions that address different aspects of the problem. Prior to the interview, the psychologist selects content areas to be covered in the interview. For example, the initial interview may address the child's perception of his academic competence, his problems, his acceptance by his classmates, his responsibility for the problem, perceptions of parental reactions to the problem, and his motivation to work on the problem. In a semistructured interview, the interviewer has a list of areas to address along with questions that address each area. These premeditated probes provide the interview structure. The interviewer follows up the child's answers to these structured probes with open-ended probes. These open-ended probes help the child to clarify his answers to the standardized questions. They also help the interviewer get at the reasoning underlying the child's answers to the standardized question. To the standard question, "What does your mother do that pleases you?" the child might reply, "She reads to me." The interviewer would follow up with an open-ended probe: "What about that pleases you?" The child answers "Because that is when Mom spends time just with me and nobody else."

The interview that uses play materials is much less structured than one without play materials. The former type attempts to help the child gain insight into her problems. The interviewer reacts to the child's expressions, both verbal and nonverbal, and does not introduce interview topics. The interviewer's comments are intended to facilitate the child's movement in the direction she has chosen (Greenspan, 1981).

Advantages of the unstructured, nondirective approach include the opportunity to observe how the child organizes and structures the interview content as well as his associations and sequence of expressions. For example, in play therapy, the child chooses to play with the house and family dolls. The child's play is purposeful and organized for the first few minutes. After the child pretends that the father and mother doll are fighting, the child abruptly leaves the house and goes to the paints where he messily paints, spilling and throwing things. The disintegration in organization apparent between the doll play and the painting suggests the child is frightened and feels insecure when his parent fight. When the child provides his own structures, the professional can observe the level of thematic organization in his play.

Some children introduce new content in a disjointed fashion, while others introduce new content in a logical progression from one theme to the next. An example of an orderly theme development is provided by 11-year-old Scott. Referred for depression and anxiety, Scott played checkers with the interviewer during the first session. While playing, he talked about his desire to win. He stated that he was out of practice. Next, he mentioned how pleased he was at earning better grades than two of his friends and the need to get good grades to get into medical school. The theme of competition resurfaced in the next two topics he introduced, one involving playing basketball and one involving selling charity benefit tickets. Next, he mentioned that he did not always win and that he felt awful when he lost. Finally, he told about a cousin of his who failed a grade and how disappointed his parents were in him. His cousin's parents sent his cousin to a military school. He quickly vowed that he would never disappoint his parents like that. Scott linked one topic to the next in a logical manner and elaborated on a few themes instead of introducing several in a disjointed way. He demonstrated excellent reality testing and organized thinking. He would be a good candidate for verbal counseling.

Scott's behavior is in sharp contrast to that of Sally, a 10-year-old girl referred for counseling for somatic complaints. Sally skipped from drawing, to cards, doll play, and painting. She introduced several topics, but developed none in an orderly fashion, and no link between the topics was evident. This child's disorganized play and poor thematic development suggest either that she has limited capacity for reality testing and organized thinking or that her feelings are so frightening that she does not go "deep" into any thought but keeps her play and conversation on a superficial level.

Because the unstructured interview follows the child's lead, the interviewer cannot control what information the interview yields. When the interviewer wants specific information on a particular topic, a semistructured interview is probably preferable.

THE INITIATION STAGE

Establishing the Alliance

The interviewer wants to establish the core conditions for interviewing: acceptance, warmth, genuineness, empathic understanding, and security. The interviewer must respect children's ability to make sense out of complex experiences. The child must be made to feel at ease in the interview, to feel that his thinking makes a great deal of sense, that the interviewer is interested in his ideas, and that his feelings are accepted. To put the child at ease, the interviewer should smile and engage the child in conversation. The interviewer's first questions and comments should address nonproblem areas. Topics of conversation selected should be likely to engage the interest of children similar in age to the interviewed child. For example, sports and school would be appropriate topics when interviewing a 7- to 11-year-old child (unless school problems are suspected). With younger children, the interviewer might ask the child's parent to have the child bring something he made to the first interview, and this object can be the focal point of this social stage of the interview.

Structuring the Relationship

It is important that the child be capable of answering the first questions asked in the interview. Therefore, the interview starts with easy, factual questions, such as "How old are you?" "Do you have any brothers?" "What school do you attend?" After the child believes that she will be able to perform adequately in the interview, she will attempt the harder questions that she might otherwise have refused to answer. As the child's confidence builds, her willingness to attempt more difficult questions increases.

The child should be told the purpose of the interview. The nature of the explanation and the amount of detail provided will differ according to the child's age and the interview's purpose. But regardless of those criteria, the interviewer should tell the child something about what to expect in the interview and its purpose. Children respond more cooperatively when they are treated as individuals who are capable of understanding what is expected of them. An explanation given to an 8-year-old referred to a child professional for a personality evaluation follows:

> **Interviewer:** Your parents and your teacher told me that you don't seem as happy as other boys, and you keep pretty much to yourself. I want to help you feel happier. Today, we'll talk some. I'll ask you to answer some questions in a booklet about how you feel. Then I'll ask you to make some drawings for me and tell some stories about pictures I will show you. You will have a chance to ask questions as we go along. Do you have any questions right now?

With children over the age of 7, it is important to discuss the issue of the child's confidentiality. Of course, the degree of confidentiality provided to the child depends on her age and the interviewer's purpose. One approach to confidentiality that may be appropriate to the specific interview situation is to tell the child something like the following:

> **Interviewer:** When we are through talking today, I will tell you what I have learned. If I am wrong about something, you will have a chance to tell me that, too. If there is something about what you tell me that you want to keep a secret, I will do my best to keep it a secret. If I cannot keep it a secret, I will tell you before I tell anybody else.

Listening

Of course, listening to the child is an important way to establish the core conditions for interviewing. The successful interviewer depends more on listening skills than on questioning skills. Through listening, the interviewer shows respect for the child and a genuine desire to listen to the child's ideas. Through listening, the interviewer encourages the child to express himself fully and nondefensively. As a result of being listened to, the child develops a clearer understanding of his thoughts and feelings and self-confidence in handling problems.

Empathic listening is different from refraining from speaking. Empathic listening is a communication skill that includes the nonverbal and verbal behaviors discussed above. An empathic response validates and accepts the child's experience. It does not introduce new content or offer advice. It reflects or mirrors the content and the feeling the child expressed. It can be a restating of what the child says, or it can offer a link between seemingly isolated statements made by the child. The important thing is that the child feels understood and is encouraged to share her thoughts and feelings with the interviewer.

Listening is an active task that involves both nonverbal and verbal behaviors. Nonverbal listening behaviors include smiling, appropriately timed nodding, maintaining a relaxed but interested physical posture, matching one's facial expression to the feeling the child expresses, and maintaining frequent (but not constant) eye contact. With children, the interviewer should keep her eyes on the child's level (or close to it). Stooping or sitting in a child's size chair communicates to the child the interviewer's genuine interest in her.

Examples of Reflective Listening

The term "reflective listening" refers to verbal listening behaviors that help a person feel understood and accepted. Consider the following examples of reflective listening.

> **Child:** (Tearing up a drawing he is dissatisfied with.) I'll never get this right.
> **Interviewer:** You weren't pleased with your drawing, and you're feeling discouraged.
>
> **Child:** (After arguing with Johnny.) I hate Johnny. I don't care if I ever play with him again.
> **Interviewer:** I can see you're really mad with Johnny right now.
>
> **Child:** (Near tears.) That mean old Mrs. Jones. She gave me so much homework I'll miss all my favorite television programs.
> **Interviewer:** You have a lot of homework. It must be hard to work all day at school and then to have homework, too.

Child: (Hitting Bobo doll.) Bam. Bam.
Interviewer: You feel like hitting today.

Nine-year-old child with learning problems: The teacher makes me do dumb stuff all the time. The other kids don't do the dumb stuff, and I hate it.
Interviewer: Some of the stuff your teacher gives you to do feels like dumb stuff, and you don't like that a bit. And the fact that the other kids don't have to do it bothers you, too.

Six-year-old: (After talking about parents fighting, the child stops abruptly, in midsentence.)
Interviewer: It's scary when people are angry at each other.

In each of the above examples, the interviewer responded reflectively to the child's statement and behavior. A reflective response does not add anything new to what the child expresses. It rephrases what the child expresses, or it describes what the child is doing in the interviewer's own words. It may rephrase the content of what the child says ("You have a lot of homework"). Or it may reflect the child's feeling, either directly or indirectly expressed by the child ("You're feeling disappointed"), or both. When reflecting a feeling that the child did not directly state, the interviewer should be tentative in suggesting that the child may be expressing a particular feeling. Children do not like to be told in an authoritarian manner how they are feeling, but they do feel accepted and understood when an adult picks up on their feelings and summarizes them in a questioning rather than an "expert" manner.

The child is helped to feel accepted when the interviewer adapts his language to the child's. A pediatric nurse, trying to find out how a 10-year-old who defecates in his pants feels just before he defecates uses the child's language in asking questions. If the boy uses the word "poop," the nurse uses that term: "Right before you poop, does your tummy feel any different than usual?"

The successful interviewer depends more on listening skills than on questioning skills. Through listening, the interviewer shows respect for the child and a genuine desire to listen to the child's ideas. He encourages the child to express herself fully and nondefensively. As a result of being listened to, the child's understanding of her thoughts and feelings and self-confidence in handling problems both grow.

THE DIRECTION STAGE

Getting at the Child's Point of View

The primary advantage of the interview is the opportunity it provides to understand the child's point of view and how she makes sense out of her experience. Its primary advantage is not its ability to get at the truth. Other, more reliable ways of obtaining factual information about a child exist. Therefore, the interviewer should avoid cross-examining the child to get at the truth. Because the child's perceptions are the interview's goal, the interviewer must respect those perceptions and avoid an interrogating style. Direct questions and probes for clarification, such as "What do you mean?" make a child feel as if she is being interrogated or has failed to communicate effectively. A better way to help a child express herself is to ask indirect questions (e.g., "I'm wondering what it is about having a big brother that you don't like") and to make statements such as "I can understand why a girl would enjoy building models."

Reducing the Complexity of the Questions

The difficulty of questions needs to be adjusted to the child's cognitive maturity level and language competence. Questions that an adult readily comprehends may be incomprehensible to a child because they are too long, abstract, or contain unfamiliar words. Several strategies for reducing the complexity and threat of questions follow.

Concrete Referents

The interviewer can introduce concrete referents, such as pictures or manipulatives. For example, if the interviewer is interested in the child's ideas about sex-role typing, he might present pictures of toys and a girl and boy doll and ask the child which toys the girl would choose to play with. A social worker interviewing a friendless, withdrawn child might present pictures of children experiencing different emotions and ask the child to label each emotion. After the child has labeled each emotion, the counselor points to each picture and asks the child to describe one time when she felt that way. Another approach would be for the counselor to tell some stories about different situations and ask the child to point to the picture of how the story child feels. This approach can help the counselor learn how well the child identifies others' feelings and how the child feels in different situations.

A social worker interviewing a child about her reactions to her parents' divorce might present a picture of a mother, father, and a girl and say, "Here is a mother and a father and a girl your age. The mother and father got a divorce. What do you think happened? How do you think the girl feels? Did something like that happen to you?"

A nurse interviewing a child about his reaction to a new baby at home might present a doll play situation involving a mother, father, boy, and baby. "Here is a mother, father, boy your age, and new baby. What will be different at their home, now that the baby has come? How does the boy feel about having a new baby? Have you ever felt that way? What did you do?" The pictures or dolls are used as concrete referents for questions about the child's experiences and perceptions.

Concrete referents can be combined with a pointing response to further reduce the complexity in interviewing children about very sensitive topics. A social worker interviewing a reportedly sexually molested girl might present an anatomically correct girl doll and a man doll and asks the child to point to the places on the girl doll where she was touched, and to point to the places on the man doll where the man touched her.

In interviewing an 11-year-old boy who has trouble controlling his temper, the interviewer might draw an "angry thermometer" with readings marked from 0 to 212 degrees. At the base is written the word "Cool head" and at the top is written "Boiling mad." The child is asked to indicate how angry he feels when different things happen by pointing to a reading on the thermometer between 0 and 212 degrees. The interviewer notes those situations on the thermometer. Knowing those situations that cause the child to feel the angriest will help the counselor, special teacher, or psychologist teach the boy anger-coping responses in those situations.

Incomplete Sentences and Stories

Incomplete sentences can be used to reduce a question's complexity. The child is asked to complete a sentence, such as "Sometimes at night I worry that. . . ." or "The best thing about being me is. . . ." The sentence stems can be read by the child, and she can write her responses, or they can be read aloud by the interviewer, and the child can answer verbally. The incomplete sentence format allows the interviewer to introduce different content. Furthermore, it is easier for the child to complete a sentence than it is for her to formulate her own responses to questions.

The incomplete story is a similar interviewing technique. For example, the professional tells the beginning of a story about a child reading a book after his mother has told him to go to sleep. The mother comes into the child's bedroom and discovers the child reading the book. After this part of the story is presented, the professional asks the child "What does the mother say or do? What does the child say or do? What happens next? Is that what would happen in your family?"

Reducing Threat

Yarrow (1960) described several ways an interviewer can phrase questions to make them less threatening to children. First, she can suggest that other children might feel the same way. For example, "All girls sometimes get mad at their parents. What kinds of things make you feel mad?" Another solution is to present alternatives, all of which appear to be equally acceptable. "Do you think Mom expects too much of you, or do you think she expects about the right amount, or too little?" Choose words that soften an undesirable response or that make it appear more acceptable. Instead of asking the child if he hits, ask him, "If a boy in your class teases you, do you punish him so he stops or do you let the teacher know about it?" This example gives two alternatives that sound about equal in acceptability and phrases negative behavior (tattling) in a more acceptable light (let your teacher know). Another technique is to assume the child engages in negative behaviors instead of requiring her to admit to negative behavior. For example, say: "All children sometimes feel angry with their parents. When you feel angry at your father, how do you let him know you are angry?" If this question is too complex, the interviewer could follow up with: "Some kids tell their parents with words that they are angry, and some kids do something that lets their parents know they are angry. Which way is it with you?" Permitting the child to express positive feelings before negative feelings is sometimes helpful. For example, a child may be asked what she likes about school before she is asked what she dislikes. Similarly, the interviewer would ask her what her mother does that pleases her before asking what her mother does that displeases her.

Phrasing Questions

As discussed in Chapter 3, "why" questions should be avoided. The nurse who asks a child why he avoids using the toilet when he needs to have a bowel movement or a school counselor who asks an 11-year-old why she stole 50 cents from the teacher's desk will receive inadequate answers. Children are often not aware of the motives underlying their behaviors. Furthermore, "why" questions are threatening and increase the child's resistance. Often "why" questions can be rephrased as "what" questions. For example, "What about using the toilet is unpleasant?" "How do you feel when you use the toilet?" "What did you do with the money?" "What do you like most or least about your teacher?" The child's answers to such carefully phrased questions provide the underlying motives.

Gathering Data through Drawings

Drawings can be used several ways in the interview. The interviewer can supply a variety of drawing materials (pencils, felt-tip markers, drawing paper in different colors, chalk, and water colors) and invite the child to draw. The interviewer asks the child to tell about the drawing and makes nonevaluative comments about it.

Julie, aged 10, was referred by her mother for counseling due to her verbal threats to kill herself and her mother's inability to control her. Julie and her mother had had an argument just before arriving for their first counseling session. Julie scowled at her mother during a brief visit with them together. Julie entered the interview situation with an angry expression on her face, plopped down in a chair with her arms crossed, and remained silent. The interviewer had already discussed the purpose of the interview and its confidentiality with her and her mother. After about a minute, he asked Julie if she would like to draw. She selected the markers and white paper and began to draw hearts. The interviewer watched, and then he began to draw, too. He commented, "You seem to like to draw hearts." She did not respond. Then she asked how to spell "valentine." He spelled it for her. After about five more minutes, she put down her markers and said, "I'm going to give this to my Mom." The interviewer responded, "You made a valentine, and you want to give it to your Mom." Julie stated, "I might not." Then she drew a picture of a house with lots of dark clouds and rain. The interviewer commented that her picture looked stormy. She said she would give both pictures to her Mom. He commented that she wanted to give a valentine and a stormy picture to her Mom. Julie had very ambivalent feelings toward her mother. The interviewer later learned that Julie's father had sexually molested Julie, and she felt anger toward her mother for not protecting her from her father. In this first session, Julie had allowed him to see her mixed feelings. Drawings continued to be an important medium for Julie to express her feelings. After she learned that she could trust the interviewer, he began to help her see what her drawings expressed. He used Julie's preference for drawing to help her learn how to express her feelings. One method was to have Julie pick a card with a feeling word written on it and draw a picture of that feeling. They labeled each picture according to the feeling it expressed (i.e., sad, happy, mad, lonely, worried, excited). They then used these pictures during the next three sessions to help Julie understand and express her feelings toward different people and events in her life. For example, she would point to the feeling of a character in a story the interviewer told. Julie selected a feeling to act out in a game of charades. He asked Julie to take the pictures home with her and to write on the back of each picture a time when she experienced that feeling. They discussed what she wrote at the next session.

One interviewing technique that uses drawings is the draw-a-person technique. This technique asks the child to draw a picture of a boy or girl (depending on the child's gender). The interviewer asks the child a series of questions: How old is this boy? What does he like to do for fun? Does he have any brothers? Does he have any sisters? If this boy had three wishes, what would they be? What does this boy sometimes worry about? Is this boy at all like you? How is he like you?

Another drawing technique involves drawing a circle and asking the child to color in the circle with different colors that represent various feelings. The child is provided with a palette of colors. The child who is having a difficult time integrating different feelings may find it easier to express ambivalent feelings when provided with a concrete mode of expression. A slight modification of this technique involves asking the child to divide the circle up into the "parts of me." The child is asked to color the part of her that is dumb one color and the part that is smart another color. Similarly, she colors the part of her that is good one color and the part that is bad another color. The interviewer can ask the child what things are good or bad about her or what are the things about which she is dumb or smart.

Gathering Data through Games

The Talking, Feeling, and Doing Game (Gardner, 1983) is an interview technique that helps children express their feelings, thoughts, and behaviors within the context of a game. The Talking, Feeling, and Doing Game is similar to many board games with which most children are familiar. The interviewer-helper and the child start at a square marked Start. They alternate turns throwing a dice, moving their playing pieces along a path of squares that ends at a square marked Finish. The squares are of different colors, and the color indicates whether the player draws a Talking, Feeling, or Doing card. The Talking cards direct the child to make mostly cognitive and intellectual comments, the Feeling cards focus on emotional issues, and the Doing cards direct the child to engage in some physical activity or play-acting. The cards vary in the degree of threat. Examples of Talking cards are (a) "What do you think of a girl who doesn't take care of her dog?" (b) "What sport are you worst at?" and (c) "A girl was not invited to a birthday party. Why do you think she wasn't invited?" A typical Feeling card is "Tell me something that made you very proud." A Doing card might say, "Make believe that someone grabbed something of yours. Show me what you would do." The interviewer can select the cards that are particularly relevant to the child's problem and the interview's purpose. A child can choose to pass, but if she passes, she does not get to advance her player. The first player to the Finish square receives bonus chips. The player with the most chips wins.

Gathering Data through Puppets

A final interview technique with children is the use of puppets. Sometimes a child will find it easier to answer emotionally sensitive questions if the questions are asked of a puppet and the child answers for the puppet. Many children find answering for a puppet both safe and fun. The interviewer asks the child to select a hand puppet. The interviewer also selects a puppet. The interviewer then has the puppet say, "Hi! My name is Susan (or Billy). I just moved into this neighborhood, and I want to get to know the other kids." The interviewer then asks questions through the puppet, and the child's puppet answers.

Gathering Data through Behavioral Observations

Much of what the interviewer learns about a child comes through observations of the child's behavior during the interview. Some observations depend on the type and purpose of the interview. For example, in a helping interview that employs play materials, the interviewer will observe the child's selection of play materials and note the themes that characterize her play. If a child's play has a common theme, the interviewer hypothesizes that the theme (e.g., dependence, anger control, jealousy, fear of losing a loved one) is an important concern for the child. Play gives children the opportunity to work through conflicts and problems they encounter in their lives. It allows them to master problems in real life. For example, children about to enter a hospital are likelier to choose toys with a hospital theme than children who are not scheduled for hospitalization.

Every interview situation provides opportunities for observing important child behaviors. Behaviors that can be observed during the interview include responsiveness to limit setting, impulsivity, reaction to frustrations, reaction to praise, level of organization in play and conversation, verbal expressive and receptive abilities, responsiveness to the interviewer as a person, emotional reaction to different topics introduced in the interview, distractibility, level of overall activity, nervous mannerisms, ease of separation from the mother, range and appropriateness of affect expressed, reaction to a new situation, cooperativeness, fearfulness, anxiety, general emotional tone, and coordination. These examples do not begin to exhaust the observable possibilities. To assist himself in recording observational data, the interviewer should decide in advance of the interview which behaviors are especially important to observe. Of course, the interviewer should also record unanticipated noteworthy behaviors.

THE CONCLUSION STAGE

After experiencing an interview with an accepting, warm adult, the child may develop erroneous or unrealistic expectations for future contact with the interviewer. If the interview is a one-time contact, the interviewer should make it clear to the child at the beginning of the interview that no future meetings will occur. Otherwise, the child may feel rejected by the interviewer. At the end of the interview, the interviewer should express appreciation to the child for sharing and cooperating and state that she enjoyed the interview or some aspect of it.

With children older than 5 years of age, the interviewer should conclude the interview with a restatement of the interview's purpose. For example, "As I said at the beginning, it is important for me to know what you think and how you feel about living with your daddy. You have helped me very much. Thank you. I will discuss what I've learned with the judge, and she will decide where the best place for you to live is."

When future meetings are expected, the interviewer should tell the child what will happen the next time. To help bridge the time span between meetings, the interviewer might ask the child to bring something from home to the next meeting. For example, "You draw very nice pictures. Will you bring some pictures you draw at home to our next meeting?" With children 7 and older, the interviewer might ask the child to practice something discussed in the interview. For example, "Try acting like a turtle the next time you feel like you're losing your cool, and tell me what happens at our next meeting."

THE RESISTANT CHILD: A SPECIAL CHALLENGE

The interviewer's response to the resistant child depends on the child's age. Resistance is quite common in the 2- to 3-year-old child. The 3-year-old's resistance is probably a result of the young child's emerging sense of self. The interviewer will be most successful with the very young child if he allows the child time to adjust to the interview situation and to explore the room physically. Less-structured interviews, in which the interviewer can adjust the questioning format and sequence to the child's capabilities and inclinations, are preferable at this age. In addition, it is often helpful for the interviewer to talk about his own children, so that the child can identify the interviewer with the familiar role of parent. If the interviewer does not have children, he can let the child know that he has experience with other children, such as nieces or nephews.

Flexibility is a critical asset for the person interviewing the preschool-aged child. The interviewer must permit the child freedom to exert some control in the interview situation; however, the interviewer must be able to enforce behavioral limits. When enforcing limits, it is important to state them as rules rather than just telling the child she cannot do whatever she is doing. For example, if a child begins to poke a leather chair with scissors, the interviewer states: "The scissors are for cutting. It is a rule that we cannot hurt the furniture." If the child begins to hit the interviewer, the interviewer physically restrains the child, if necessary, and states the rule: "There is no hurting people in this room."

When interviewing a child 6 or older, the interviewer can minimize resistance by explaining the purpose of the interview in terms the child can understand. The child is more likely to respond cooperatively if he feels that the interviewer respects his need to know the purpose of the interview. The purpose should be stated to avoid blaming the child and to emphasize the likely benefits of the interview to the child. For example: "I'm told that school is not a very happy place for you now. I want to know how that can be changed to make it happier. You can help me do that by talking to me today." This introduction to the interview is likely to result in better cooperation than the following introduction: "I know that you are having problems at school. I want to know why you are having those problems and what can be done about it."

When interviewing children 7 years old and older, it is important to discuss confidentiality. Of course, the degree of confidentiality provided to the child depends on the interviewer's purpose and the context of the interview. Regardless of the degree of confidentiality provided, the child at this age should be told what will be shared and with whom it will be shared. A preadolescent's resistance in the interview could be the result of her concern that the interviewer will tell her parents or teacher everything she says. She may be reluctant to express feelings or thoughts that are negative toward these people or to admit to behaviors that could be punished.

Because a nondirective approach is less likely to raise resistance than a directive approach, the interviewer might begin with a nondirective approach, following the child's lead. After establishing a trusting relationship, the interviewer can shift to a more directive approach. If the child has a chance to control the content of the interview first, she is more likely to cooperate with the interviewer's agenda.

Humor is helpful in reducing resistance. Because children of different ages think different things are funny, the interviewer needs to know what children of differing ages find humorous. The child under age 6 or 7 probably does not understand riddles, puns, or other plays on words. A child of this age will find unexpected things funny. A polar bear taking a sunbath on the beach or a bus that has its wheels on the top are funny to the young child. They also find stunts and "clowning around" funny. Older children will find riddles and puns funny. In addition, they enjoy inaccurate depictions of concepts they have mastered. For example, when children know the socially approved roles for members of the two sexes, they regard any deviation from these roles as funny. During middle childhood, children become particularly preoccupied with issues of performance and achievement. Humor is one outlet for their concerns, and they find jokes about morons funny (e.g., "Why did the moron take a ladder to school? He wanted to graduate at the top of his class"). Although jokes have a tension-reducing role in the interview, they should be used quite sparingly. The most satisfactory use of humor in the interview is that humor which fits spontaneously into the ongoing interaction with the child.

The interviewer should avoid unintentionally rewarding the resistant child for uncooperative behavior. Although coaxing, urging, and bribery may obtain momentary cooperation, these methods set up an interactional sequence in which the child first resists, then the interviewer coaxes, and the child complies with the initial request. When an interview follows such a sequence, the quality and fullness of the child's answers to the interviewer's questions are unsatisfactory. If a child refuses to answer the interviewer's questions or to talk with the interviewer at all, the interviewer should say something like the following: "I see you don't feel like talking just now. I will wait until you feel like talking or playing the games I have." The interviewer then turns to some work, remaining accessible to the child. After a few minutes, the interviewer might comment on what the child is doing or talk out loud about her own work.

SUMMARY

Three premises have guided the writing of this chapter. First, a child's thoughts and feelings about important people and events in her life determine her behavior, including interpersonal relationships, goal achievement, and mastery. Second, the child is capable of communicating complex affective and intellectual experiences in the context of an interview. Third, to help the child communicate these subjective experiences, the interviewer must modify his questioning approach based on a consideration of the child's cognitive, language, and psychosocial developmental levels. Thus, the interviewer must have a good understanding of child development. This chapter provided an overview of developmental processes with which the child interviewer needs to be familiar. General techniques for conducting the interview were described, as well as specific interview techniques. More important than these techniques, however, is a genuine respect for children as active problem-solvers who are attempting to make sense out of complex experiences. The interviewer should value the child's ideas, accept the child, and respond to the child with genuine warmth and caring.

SUGGESTED READINGS

Dinkmeyer, D., & McKay, G. D. (1982). *Systematic steps for effective parenting: Parent's handbook.* Circle Pines, MN: American Guidance Service.

Ginott, H. G. (1965). *Between parent and child.* New York: MacMillan.

Greenspan, S. (1981). *The clinical interview of the child.* New York: McGraw-Hill.

Irwin, E. C. (1983). The diagnostic and therapeutic use of pretend play. In C. E. Schaefer & K. F. O'Connor (Eds.), *Handbook of play therapy* (pp. 148–173). New York: John Wiley & Sons.

Yarrow, L. J. (1960). Interviewing children. In P. H. Mussen (Ed.), *Handbook of research methods in child development* (pp. 561–602). New York: Wiley.

6

Interviewing Adolescents

Frances F. Worchel
Texas A & M University

Many of the principles in the previous chapter on interviewing children also apply to adolescents; however, additional developmental issues become prominent in the years 12–19. Interviewing the adolescent is a relatively simple task requiring three basic competencies: Solomon's wisdom, Job's patience, and Groucho Marx's sense of humor. Fortunately for both the professional and paraprofessional who consider themselves deficient in these areas, a reasonable substitute is a solid grounding in general interviewing skills, tethered by an understanding of age norms, developmental theory, and the unique concerns and behaviors of the adolescent. Chapter 4 compared the interview situation to a card game in which the interviewer carefully exerts control and direction based on his own hand, previously played cards, the rules of the game, and his partner's strategies. Interviewing the adolescent may follow a similar analogy, with the added complexities that one's partner may not want to play the game, play out of turn, insist on winning, or want to change the rules halfway through the game. Obviously, then, when interviewing an adolescent, the professional must be particularly concerned with developmental issues prompting such idiosyncratic behaviors and maintain the flexibility to adapt to these behaviors. In so doing, you can replace the frustrating experience of attempting to communicate with a stubborn, suspicious, or volatile youth with a challenging, rewarding clinical interview.

This chapter will focus on ways to apply the model of interviewing presented in Chapters 3 and 4 to adolescents. Of course, the same basic techniques apply regardless of age, but the way they are used addresses the adolescent. The first section of the chapter will outline developmental levels to consider, including general characteristics of the adolescent, physical development, cognitive functioning, and identity formation. The second section describes general considerations in interviewing adolescents, followed by a discussion of specific problems often encountered in adolescents, such as drug abuse, anorexia, and academic difficulties. Finally, developmental issues are integrated into the preparation, initiation, direction, and conclusion stages of the interviewing model.

DEVELOPMENTAL CONSIDERATIONS

Adolescence has long been considered a time of turbulence, a time when change and upheaval are the norm. In fact, it is sometimes suggested that diagnosing an adolescent as emotionally disturbed is extremely difficult because many behaviorist that would signify difficulties in an adult (e.g., extreme mood swings, mania, narcissism, delinquent acts) are part of normal behavior for an adolescent. Much of this turbulence is due to the numerous developmental changes that adolescents undergo, particularly since these changes follow directly on the heels of the latency stage, a period of relative calm and stability. Adolescents will typically experience growth in a variety of areas and are expected to master issues of autonomy from parents, sexuality and physical development, cognitive growth and moral development, peer relationships, and identity formation, as well as make a vocational choice and develop an orientation toward the future. Havighurst (1952) described 10 tasks that people must master for healthy passage through adolescence:

1. achieving new and more mature relations with age mates of both sexes
2. achieving a masculine or feminine social role

3. accepting one's physique and using one's body effectively
4. achieving emotional independence of parents and other adults
5. achieving ensurance of economic indepedence
6. selecting and preparing for an occupation
7. preparing for marriage and family life
8. developing intellectual skills and concepts necessary for civic competence
9. desiring and achieving socially responsible behavior
10. acquiring a set of values and an ethical system as a guide to behavior

Clearly, the first step in developing effective skills for interviewing adolescents is understanding these stages of development and the ways that progression throughout these stages will be manifested in adolescent behaviors. As Chapter 5 discussed, it is vital to know age norms associated with normal development. This is important for two reasons: (a) this knowledge will allow the interviewer to structure the dialogue to make it consistent with the adolescent's competencies and current life concerns and (b) the adolescent's adherence to age-appropriate behaviors and topics of conversations can yield much diagnostic information. Often, an adolescent who talks about things one would expect from a younger child may be indicating a fear of entering adolescence. One frequently observes early adolescents lingering in the latency stage; conversations with these youngsters can clarify the degree of their fixation. Rabichow and Sklansky (1980) elaborate on this notion and distinguish among three distinct phases during which adolescents have specific concerns. During the early phase, they appear to regress toward more childlike ways of relating to the world. Often, they may suddenly display a lack of independence and self-assurance. The adolescent suddenly becomes much more demanding, insisting that he is ready for increased responsibilities. However, Rabichow and Sklansky compare this stage to that of a 3-year-old who demands that "I can do it myself!" without the awareness the limitations of reality and the consequences of his behaviors. Adolescents in the early phase want immediate gratification of impulses, yet are unable to perceive adequately the immature nature of their behaviors. Rabichow and Sklansky attribute these activities as an attempt to defend against burgeoning sexual impulses.

In the middle phase, the ever-increasing genital impulses prevent further fixation. The majority of adolescents become gradually more concerned with heterosexual relationships and begin to come to grips with their progression toward adulthood. They acquire an intense concern with grooming, cleanliness, and appearance, and a bit more interest in self-reflection. Adolescents in the middle phase are still quite impulsive, however, and want quick gratification of their needs. During this stage, they develop a great distrust of adults and a heightened perception of the distinction between we (peers) and they (parents and other adults).

Finally, in the late phase, adolescents display an active interest in all things related to the self: identity, vocational aims, future goals, interpersonal relatedness, and the meaning of their own lives. Adolescents in this stage can be very self-motivated and introspective and are much better able to communicate with adults.

As this brief introduction to developmental stages shows, interviewing a 13-year-old is quite different from interviewing an 18-year-old. One might expect the younger adolescent to be more resistant to discussing topics such as sexuality, and the interviewer might at times resort to utilizing techniques discussed in the previous chapter. (e.g., projective storytelling techniques, picture drawings). With the 18-year-old, however, the interviewer would expect a greater capacity for perspective taking and introspection, and thus the interview would more likely focus on topics such as self-identity and future goals.

PHYSICAL DEVELOPMENT

An adolescent can often successfully repress his anxieties about internal thoughts and feelings. However, physical development brings obvious changes that are much more difficult to ignore. To the increasingly peer-conscious adolescent, dealing with changes in his appearance can be quite trying, particularly as these are generally changes over which the adolescent has little or no control. Suddenly, daily life includes such changes as under-arm hair, acne, menstruation, and shaving. What seems to be of critical importance to the adolescent is not so much that these events are occurring, but whether they are occurring at the same time to his close friends. When working with an adolescent, the interviewer should assess whether this youngster is an early or late maturer, as this single aspect of development appears to have important implications for later functioning. In a classic work, Jones and Bayley (1950) asked adults to rate male adolescents on a number of traits. Boys who had matured ahead of their peers were rated as being more masculine, attractive, better groomed, self confident, and curious. Alternately, the late-maturing boys were seen as more childish, tense, attention seeking, bossy, and restless. Early-maturing boys clearly have an advantage in sports, a high-status activity in our society, and are more likely to be chosen as leaders. In addition, the male who attains a positive physical identity is much likelier to have a higher self-concept and self-esteem.

Females' experience differs from males'. The early-maturing girl may be treated as a sex object and thrust prematurely into relationships with the opposite sex. These girls tend to be treated as more mature just because of their physical appearance, and so they often act more mature. Often, however, early-maturing girls are not ready emotionally for such elevated status, and increased sexual and social pressures may result in lower self-esteem.

The skillful interviewer should be aware of the adolescent's physical development. She would want to assess whether obvious physical development is associated with con-comitant emotional, social, and cognitive maturity. The interviewer should remember that appearances can be deceiving and not mistakenly attribute to adolescents the ability to take responsibility or handle interpersonal relationships. The following example may help to illustrate how physical development can be an important consideration in an initial interview.

Brad, a 15-year-old male, was referred to his school guidance counselor for academic underachievement. The counselor was immediately impressed with Brad's appearance: he was quite well-developed for his age; tall, muscular, and well-proportioned. Brad was well-dressed in stylish clothes and physically quite attractive. He appeared charming and open to the conversation, and spoke exuberantly about his exploits as captain of the football team and number one singles player on the tennis team.

Feeling confident that this would be a successful session, the counselor began with a discussion of Brad's school difficulties. She probed very little into Brad's assertions that his poor grades were due to several uncontrollable experiences that were not at all his fault. The counselor was pleased at Brad's immediate acceptance of her recommendations concerning study habits and his enthusiastic assurances that his grades would improve immediately.

In the ensuing weeks, it became apparent that the counselor's recommendations had not worked. After several more in-depth conversations with Brad, it became clear to the counselor that this seemingly mature adolescent was really quite irresponsible, yet often got by without having to accept the consequences of his behaviors. Due to his early physical development, Brad was expected to do well in other areas and often not given adequate instructions or supervision due to the false perception that he was fully capable of handling demands. The counselor wisely realized that she had been deceived by Brad's outward appearance and had failed to probe further to determine Brad's actual abilities.

Brad's case illustrates the importance of assessing whether an adolescent's physical development matches her development in other areas. Physical development is an important consideration in other instances, also. The pubescent teenager who is painfully aware of changes in appearance and secondary sexual development may be so self-absorbed with anxieties about her body that she cannot discuss and consider issues that the interviewer considers paramount. Although the adolescent will probably not be willing to discuss acne in a first meeting, the interviewer should at least be aware that these types of issues will be salient for the adolescent. Thus, the interviewer should understand that the adolescent's self-concept (and thus self-esteem) may be affected by issues related to physical development, that low self-esteem is developmentally normal and probably transient, and that serious emotional disturbance should not be diagnosed on the basis of such concerns alone.

COGNITIVE DEVELOPMENT

Between the ages of 11 and 15, youngsters enter the stage of cognitive development known as formal operations (Piaget, 1972). With the advent of formal operations, adolescents can interact with others on a much more complex level than was previously possible. An understanding of adolescents' different cognitive abilities is vital to conducting a successful interview; awareness of these operations will directly affect the variety of questions, structure of the interview, and complexity of the discussion. One of the major characteristics of this stage is ability to engage in abstract thought, which permits use of problem-solving strategies. The adolescent who has acquired formal-operations ability can manipulate more than two groups of variables at once. When asked to describe himself, for example, a younger child might reply, "I'm tall, I have red hair, I wear glasses, I have green eyes, and my nose it too big." This child can only consider one variable—appearance—at a time. The adolescent, however, should be able to give a response including appearance, status (school, job, clubs), personal characteristics (honest, punctual, stubborn), values (against premarital sex), and relationships (has a boyfriend, dislikes sister). This is particularly helpful when discussing with adolescents the consequences of their actions; they should be able to consider how several different aspects of a problem might affect another person.

In addition, adolescents who have reached this stage are able to separate the real from the possible and recognize a hypothetical problem. Thus, with an adolescent the following conversation could take place.

Interviewer: Lauren, we've been talking about how difficult things have been at home lately, and how you and your parents seem to argue about everything you do. Now let's just suppose you were able to leave home tomorrow and move in with your best friend Beth. How do you think things would be different?

Lauren: Everything would be terrific!

Interviewer: Well, maybe so, but let's see if we can figure out why. Could you be more specific?

Lauren: Oh, let me think . . . I guess I'd have to get a job to support myself and pay my half of the rent, but I could date whoever I wanted to and I wouldn't always be hassled about cleaning my room and getting off the telephone.

Interviewer: I see. Beth doesn't really care about keeping her apartment neat and you think she probably wouldn't mind if you talked on the phone for as long as you wanted?

Lauren: Well, no, not exactly. Beth's a real pill about things looking nice, and she's always on the phone to her boyfriend. I guess maybe we'd just split the phone time in half and I'd keep my own room a mess but the living room neat!

Lauren can consider a circumstance, recognize it as a hypothetical situation, and speculate about the possibilities this might present. Adolescents can also be much more flexible in their thinking, consider a number of alternatives, weigh them, and discard those that do not fit the situation. In the last example, Lauren presented an initial, purely emotional reaction (terrific), proceeded to a more concrete idea (date anyone, never get off the phone or clean room), and finally refined this solution with a more rationally considered one. Of course, it required some prompting by the interviewer. Although adolescents can think about hypotheticals, they are limited by their lack of experience and sometimes reach unrealistic conclusions. Thus, the interviewer will need to facilitate problem solving by challenging solutions and encouraging alternative strategies.

Another problem-solving skill the adolescent should have is the ability to follow a logical sequence of events and solve serialized verbal problems such as the following:

— Aubrey is smarter than Arthur.
— Arthur is smarter than Liz.
— Who is the smartest of the three?

This ability to think sequentially and consider events in relation to one another opens new possibilities in communicating with the adolescent. Thus, the following dialogue could be developed.

Teacher: Gwen, let's brainstorm about how you might pull up your grade in English.

Student: Okay. I just need to hand in my term paper, do my current events report for the class, not talk to Sam so much when I'm supposed to be listening to the week's assignment, and cut down on my TV watching.

Teacher: Those are some excellent suggestions. Now let's see if you can order them in terms of importance, based on what assignments are due first.

Student: Well, I'm not going to accomplish anything if I don't know what I'm supposed to be doing, so I guess I'd first better stop talking to Sam. Then, let's see . . . once I know the assignment, I need to not watch TV so I can actually do the work. Now the first assignment I have due immediately is the current events, so I could go to the library tonight and tomorrow to read periodicals and work on that, and then when that's out of the way I can decide on a topic for my term paper.

Notice that the teacher not only suggested that Gwen order these events, but also helped structure the problem by suggesting she use one variable (which assignments are due) in considering priorities. Gwen was able to order events and also to consider the inter-relationships among them.

Adolescents should be able to separate their own point of view from others', predict their impact on another person, and manipulate that impact toward a specific end (Newman & Newman, 1986). This is particularly important given the adolescents' propensity to become wrapped up in their peer group, with extreme conformity to the standards of the group. The adolescent should be able to state group beliefs, then evaluate these in terms of her own personal adherence to the accepted norms. Thus, in interviewing the adolescent, it often helps to have her distinguish between her best friend's beliefs and her own attitudes and values. Although they would probably be very similar, the adolescent should be able to view herself as a distinct individual, responsible both for her own ideas and the way those ideas affect others.

Other skills associated with formal thought involve detection of inconsistent logic, discussion of ideals and values, understanding of metaphors, and ability to generalize. The use of metaphor is often particularly successful with the adolescent and allows the inter-viewer to develop certain themes throughout the interview. Consider the use of metaphor in the following case where a probation officer is working with Ken, a 16-year-old juvenile offender.

Ken met with his probation officer weekly, and conversations often centered around Ken's near violations of probation. The probation officer recognized that Ken exhibited numerous behaviors designed to help him run away from problems rather than standing up to problems and attempting to solve them. For example, after a particularly bad episode, Ken would "forget" his weekly appointment; during a group therapy session, he would often get angry at the other members and stalk angrily out of the group. The probation officer began pointing out these events and referring to them as Ken's "out-the-door acts." During one talk, the probation officer brought up the subject of grades. Ken quickly changed the subject, then stopped, laughed sheepishly, and said, "Boy, that was a real out-the-door act, wasn't it?"

Although the emergence of formal thought makes the interview with the adolescent much easier in some respects, this stage of reasoning also has some drawbacks. Two characteristics of adolescent thought often lead to a great deal of egocentrism. These are the imaginary audience and the personal fable (Elkind, 1959). The concept of the imaginary audience involves the adolescent's perceptions that he is the focus of everyone's attention, that other people will notice everything about him and see him exactly as he sees himself. Most of you have encountered the teenager who wails with dismay, "I can't wear *socks* to school. What would everyone think? They'd all notice and I'd be the laughing stock of my class!" This perception that "everyone is watching" leads to extreme self-consciousness. Along with the other abilities associated with formal thinking, this can result in self-centeredness and preoccupation with one's own thoughts and behaviors. This type of

thinking can also cause the adolescent to overreact to criticism and be particularly suscep-
tible to shame and self-doubt. The interviewer should be particularly cognizant of this and
avoid comments that the adolescent will perceive as personal criticism.

Conversely, the personal fable involves the belief that one is special, and that no one
else is capable of experiencing similar events or feelings. This can result in two serious
misconceptions. One is the relatively common "How could you possible understand? You've
never gone through anything like this." In such cases, the interviewer can often facilitate
understanding by describing his experience with a similar event. The following case will
illustrate this.

> **Interviewer:** Sam, you sound really despondent about Marsha refusing to go to the prom
> with you. You seem to think you'll never get a date with anyone.
> **Sam:** What would you know? You just don't understand what it's like to get rejected all the
> time. I might as well just join the Foreign Legion or something.
> **Interviewer:** I can understand wanting to do that. In fact, I remember one time when I was
> a junior in high school. I asked a girl to go to a football game with me. She said yes, and I
> bragged about it to all the guys. But when I went to pick her up, she had changed her mind.
> She went ahead to the game with a bunch of her girlfriends. All the guys found out. They
> kidded me for weeks.
> **Sam:** Oh wow, talk about rejection! That's too cruel. What did you do?
> **Interviewer:** Well, I sulked for days, but I got tired of it. I asked another girl out and we
> went to the next game together. Pretty soon the guys stopped kidding me. But, I'll admit, it
> was pretty tough getting up the courage to try again.
> **Sam:** I bet. I'm not sure I can face it now. What do you think I should do?

In this instance, relating to Sam that others undergo similar experiences had a powerful
impact and prompted him to seek the interviewer's advice actively.

A second misconception associated with the personal fable is the "It can't happen to
me" syndrome. Due to the adolescent's belief that she is special and unique, she readily
assumes that unfortunate consequences will happen to others, but not to her. This is
commonly manifested in such statements as

— "I don't have to use birth control—I won't get pregnant."
— "I can drink and drive—I won't have an accident."
— "I can shoplift with my friends—I'll never get caught."

This type of belief is particularly difficult to dislodge. The interviewer who uncovers
potentially harmful personal fables might consider arranging for the adolescent to interact
with another adolescent who has personally experienced the event in question. For example, the sexually active female might visit with a group of girls from a home for unwed
mothers, or the problem drinker might talk with a youth who has experienced a serious
automobile accident.

The preceding discussion should provide a basis for understanding an adolescent's
cognitive abilities. However, a word of caution is advised. Recent research has suggested
that the advent of formal operations is not as universal as Piaget (1972) suggested. He
believed that by the age of 11 or 12, the majority of adolescents would have reached the
formal operations stage. Several investigators have refuted this; for example, McKinnon
(1976) asserts that 50% of college students are unable to handle abstract thought. Renner

and Stafford (1976) evaluated 588 high school students in grades 7–12 and discovered that a surprising number of students had not yet attained formal operations. Of those evaluated, 443 had reached the concrete operations stage, 87 had reached the transitional stage, and 58 students had reached the formal operations stage. Thus, the interviewer should not automatically assume that an adolescent has developed all the cognitive capacities associated with formal operations. As suggested by Jones (1980), the interviewer who presents abstract concepts should initially include concrete examples that assist the adolescent in making the transition from concrete to abstract thinking. The interviewer should also consider that a dialogue occasionally characterized by questioning, debate, and conflict is not necessarily inappropriate, as these behaviors on the part of the adolescent can encourage higher-level cognitive development.

MORAL DEVELOPMENT

As the adolescent develops his cognitive abilities, so will he progress through stages of moral development. Kohlberg (1971) delineates three levels and six stages of moral development. Young children tend to be very external with their moral judgments; that is, they decide on the rightness or wrongness of an event based on observable consequences (how much damage was done, how angry someone became, whether a set rule was broken). As a child progresses toward adolescence, though, he begins to internalize his judgments, basing decisions on an increasingly more abstract and situational determination of right and wrong. In many instances, the interview with the adolescent will be prompted by a referral from a parent, teacher, or other adult for some infraction of socially determined standards of behaviors (e.g., delinquency, truancy, aggressiveness, involvement with drugs, promiscuity). Thus, when working with adolescents, one should understand how they perceive actions, make judgments, and evaluate consequences of behaviors. A brief description of Kohlberg's later two levels of moral development will illustrate how adolescents may have vastly different perceptions of the appropriateness of their behaviors.

At the conventional level, during stage 3 (the Interpersonal Concordance or Good Boy-Nice Girl Orientation), good behavior is considered that which pleases or helps others or is approved by them. Behavior is frequently judged by intention ("He means well"). One earns approval by being nice.

During stage 4 (the Law and Order Orientation), there is orientation toward authority, fixed rules, and maintaining social order. Right behavior consists of doing one's duty, showing respect for authority, and maintaining the given social order for its own sake.

At the postconventional, autonomous, or principled level, during stage 5 (the Social Contract Legalistic Orientation), right action tends to be defined in terms of general individual rights that have been agreed upon by the whole society. It emphasizes the legal point of view, but with the possibility of changing the law under rational considerations of social utility.

At stage 6 (the Universal Ethical Principle Orientation), right is based on one's conscience in accord with self-determined ethical principles. Important considerations are justice, equality, and a respect for human dignity (Thornburg, 1982, pp. 127–128).

As should be evident, things that might motivate or deter one adolescent may have absolutely no impact on an adolescent in a different stage of moral development. By skillfully probing reactions to a given situation, the interviewer can determine the level of moral development at which the adolescent is probably operating. This should guide the interviewer in making suggestions or interpretations that the adolescent is likely to understand and relate to. The following example illustrates how the interviewer can determine the adolescent's moral development level.

Carl, a 15-year-old black student, was referred to his guidance counselor after physically assaulting the school bus driver (who is white). Carl said he had been riding the bus minding his own business when a youth in the seat in front of him had flicked a still-lit cigarette onto a much younger girl across the aisle. The cigarette had landed on the girl's leg, making an obvious mark on her white skirt. The girl began to cry, while the youth who had thrown the cigarette laughed. Carl picked up the still-lit cigarette and, pinning the youth's arms behind his back, attempted to grind out the cigarette on his cheek. At this point the bus driver noticed the commotion, stopped the bus, and yelled at Carl, "You stupid nigger, get off my bus!" Carl froze, and as the bus driver approached him, still yelling, Carl swung and hit the bus driver in the jaw.

In discussing the event with Carl, suppose the guidance counselor were to pose the following question:

Interviewer: Well, Carl, you know the bus driver is insisting that you never be allowed to ride the bus again. Do you think that's a fair punishment?

Let's further assume three very different, but possible, replies form Carl.

Carl: I guess I should be punished. I know it's a rule that there isn't any fighting allowed on the bus, and I sure broke the rule.

Carl: I don't really think I should have hit the bus driver or messed with the other kid, because I know you're not supposed to fight on the bus, but I really don't think I ought to be kicked off the bus, because someone had to defend that girl. Maybe I could just apologize.

Carl: I don't think I should be punished at all. I'm really being treated unfairly. The bus driver didn't consider the circumstances at all and yelled at me without understanding what was going on. The driver was a bigot and there's no way he was going to give me a fair shot.

By listening to Carl's three responses with Kohlberg's moral stages in mind, the perceptive interviewer should deduce that Carl is in the 4th, 5th or 6th stages of development, respectively. Depending on the response, the interviewer might then proceed with the interview with a better understanding of what types of suggestions Carl is likely to accept.

IDENTITY FORMATION

According to Erikson (1959), one of the primary developmental tasks of adolescence is attaining a solid personal identity. Identity formation integrates all past experiences in an adolescent's life. Erikson maintains that adolescents must resolve three major issues to attain ego identity: accepting their own sexuality, integrating their physical development and accepting their overall appearance, and sensing their future role in society. This section focuses on the last issue, known as identity status. Identity status is a vital part of forming self-identity. It involves a person experiencing diverse social roles, then reaching a firm sense of both who he is and what direction his life will take. Marcia (1980) describes four different categories of identity status:

1. Identity achievement. The adolescent has faced and resolved crises and developed firm commitments to career and personal values. Realistic future goals have been set.
2. Moratorium. The adolescent is currently in crisis but has made no firm commitments. He is unsure of his values and frequently changes jobs or college majors. This adolescent is more likely to "drop out," become rebellious, or experiment with alternative lifestyles.
3. Identity foreclosure. The adolescent has avoided any type of crisis by prematurely settling on a career choice. On the surface this adolescent might appear like the identity achiever; however, he has likely committed himself to future goals without a serious struggle. This adolescent may have decided to follow a career merely because it was what his parents had chosen.
4. Identity diffusion. This adolescent is not actively committed to anything or involved in making a decision.

For the interviewer, knowledge of these stages will be most helpful when working with the older adolescent. The interviewer who is concerned with career and/or vocational counseling will find it particularly helpful to determine how the adolescent is progressing toward identity status. Of course, the more options the adolescent has, the more confusing her choices will be. This seems to be particularly true in today's society, which appears to offer an endless array of career choices and a greater degree of freedom. Thus, part of an effective interview with the older adolescent may need to focus on the adolescent's perceptions of herself, how well this perception may fit with the way others perceive her, her ideas regarding realistic career goals, and the process by which she has settled upon these goals.

In interviewing the adolescent, one should remember concepts related to physical development, cognitive abilities, moral development, and identity formation. Referring back to the analogy of the card game, the interviewer's understanding of these concepts can only enhance her ability to play her cards, knowing that the adolescent may be changing the rules based on his mastery of these different tasks. Thus, the skillful interviewer will realize that the rules will differ depending on the adolescent's current status in these areas. By knowing the rules the adolescent is bringing into the game, the interviewer can conduct a much more empathic interview. Additionally, she can discover areas where the adolescent might be "stuck" at a particular stage or task and where, with the use of challenging questions and perceptive insights, the interviewer can facilitate the adolescent's progression toward mastering developmental tasks.

GENERAL CHARACTERISTICS OF THE ADOLESCENT INTERVIEW

Professionals and paraprofessionals in a wide variety of fields will need skills for effectively interviewing the adolescent. Training programs in teaching, nursing, social work, psychology, vocational counseling, or juvenile justice often ignore communication and problem-solving skills, however.

One problem-solving skill the adolescent needs is the ability to deal with day-to-day reality. This skill can be acquired without the interviewer's probing unconscious processes. Rather, the interviewer needs the basic interviewing skills outlined in Chapter 3: rapport building; role clarification; information seeking; concern identification; and goal setting, implementation, and evaluation. While these skills will be utilized regardless of the interviewee's age, the way they are utilized will vary for the adolescent, depending on his level of development, as described earlier.

The interviewer must first understand some very general characteristics of the adolescent, gradually changing his perceptions as the particular idiosyncracies of this adolescent become apparent. The interviewer will of course be aware that the adolescent is undoubtedly struggling with her sense of autonomy. In early adolescence, youngsters will be making the transition between extreme reliance on their parents to development of social relationships with peers. The adolescent becomes much more dependent on her peer groups to reinforce her attitudes and behaviors, and may depend on their judgment for everything from clothes, to language, to music, to attitudes about drugs and sex. During this important struggle to be accepted by one's peers and attain independence from parents, the adolescent will probably view the adult interviewer as "one of them" and regard her with suspicion. Thus, rapport-building and role-clarification techniques will be vitally important when working with an adolescent. In their dealings with adults, adolescents are quite used to relationships characterized by advice giving, rules, direct orders, and punishment for noncompliance. Many will have been brought involuntarily to the interview and are not likely to perceive the interviewer as someone helpful. At the worst extreme, the interviewer can be prepared for an adolescent who is hostile, arrogant, seductive, negative, nonresponsive, or openly defiant (Nosphitz, 1984). Without proper preparation, the interview can turn into a verbal fencing match that merely confirms the participants' worst views of one another.

On the other hand, the very stresses that have likely brought the adolescent to the interview can aid communication (Rabichow & Sklansky, 1980). Due to his yet-to-be-solidified personality structure, the adolescent will be much more flexible. The adolescent may be going through a very confusing time and may leap at the chance to talk with a sincere, understanding adult. He may be quite surprised that this adult, unlike many he is used to, appears to be nonjudgmental and truly interested in his point of view. The adolescent may be secretly disillusioned with pressures to conform imposed by his peer group and anxious to explore alternatives presented by an obviously well-functioning, confident interviewer. Many adolescents report that they feel more excited, constrained, passive, and weaker when interacting with adults than with peers (Csikszentmihalyi, Larson, & Prescott, 1977). These opposing emotions seem to capture the ambivalence with which an adolescent might approach the interview, alternating between feelings of dependency and anticipation of an exciting interaction on a more mature level. Additional characteristics of the adolescent that make for a more rewarding interview are his rich fantasy life and intense emotions. When conducted properly, the interview can be a stage for novel, creative, and exuberent interactions that leave the interviewer awed by the capacities of the adolescent's developing personality.

TYPICAL PROBLEMS ASSOCIATED WITH ADOLESCENCE

In working with adolescents, the interviewer should be aware of some common difficulties with which the adolescent may need assistance. Although these difficulties are certainly not endemic to teenagers, the professional who frequently works with adolescents will likely encounter one or more of these issues. Thus, it may be helpful to overview the following briefly: academic underachievement, drug or alcohol abuse, suicide, juvenile delinquency, and anorexia.

Academic Underachievement

Underachievement can be caused by a great number of factors, including learning disability, poor study skills, depression or other emotional factors, or a problem with parents involving control or dependency needs. Learning disability or poor study skills would necessitate psychoeducational testing for proper evaluation, but the emotional or interpersonal issues might be noted and explored during an interview. As explained by Weiner (1982), one form of underachievement may be seen in an adolescent who resents parental demands that he feels he cannot or does not want to meet. The adolescent often cannot express his anger or resentment openly to an authoritative parent. Thus, the adolescent expresses his feelings nondirectly in an area over which he does have control—grades.

Drug or Alcohol Abuse

According to a recent survey, 90% of high school seniors report alcohol consumption within the previous year (Johnston, Bachman, & O'Malley, 1980). Given the wide use of alcohol in socially accepted forms among adults, one can easily see why adolescents would want to experiment with this substance as they search for a sense of identity and imitate older role models. Although a large number of students also reported using marijuana or other illicit drugs, the Johnston et al. survey indicates that most teenagers who use drugs do so only occasionally and are not addicts. Thus, the interviewer would want to assess whether the adolescent's drug use involves experimentation, which is quite normal and does not predict lifelong troubles, or whether it is a chronic practice.

Suicide

Suicide is now the third leading cause of death among teenagers in the United States. Although teenagers account for a large number of suicide *attempts,* the number of actual suicides is rather low—between 50:1 and 100:1 (Stengel, 1964). However, no matter how casual a suicide threat may seem, this is *not* a normal part of adolescence and should be taken very seriously. Adolescents who attempt suicide commonly do so after a fight with parents or breakup of an important relationsihp because they feel that "no one cares." Thus, the attempt at suicide may be a cry for help, a desperate plea for someone to listen. If the interviewer suspects that the adolescent may be having suicidal thoughts, it is wise to be very direct and ask the adolescent whether this is the case. He will generally respond very honestly. Important question to pursue are:

— Does the adolescent have a plan?
— Is the plan workable?
— Has the adolescent ever attempted suicide before? (The best predictor of a suicide attempt is a past attempt.)

If the interviewer receives positive responses to these questions, the adolescent should immediately be evaluated by a qualified professional.

Delinquency

Depending on the particular state, a juvenile delinquent may be anyone under 16, 17, or 18 who violates the law. Juvenile delinquents may have committed serious crimes, such as robbery and assault, or status offenses. It is important to distinguish status offenses, which are punishable acts only when committed by juveniles. These include truancy, sexual activity, incorrigibility, or running away from home. Although it is very difficult to predict juvenile delinquency, factors often associated with delinquency are broken homes, child abuse, corporal punishment, and low socioeconomic status. More recently, however, there has been concern about the incidence of delinquency in middle-class and upper middle–class adolescents. It is often helpful to distinguish between the adolescent who commits solitary acts and the adolescent who engages in delinquent acts as part of a group. Delinquency associated with gang membership or peer pressure appears to have a very different etiology and is somewhat less likely to lead to adult sociopathic behaviors than is socially isolated delinquency.

Anorexia Nervosa

Anorexia nervosa is a serious disturbance most common in adolescent females between the ages of 12 and 18. It is characterized by severe weight loss, intense fear of obesity, and a disturbed body image (the emaciated teenager may claim that she is still overweight). This problem is very difficult to treat, since many anorexics refuse to admit they have a problem. Severe cases require hospitalization to prevent extreme weight loss and death.

While the disorders discussed here are not limited to adolescents, the interviewer should have at least a working knowledge of them so that he can recognize them in the adolescent and realize when symptoms are severe enough to warrant referral for more intensive treatment.

STAGES OF THE INTERVIEW

As detailed in Chapter 4, the four stages of interviewing are preparation, initiation, direction, and conclusion. The following section will discuss each of these in turn, with specific suggestions for integrating knowledge of the stages of adolescent development into this interviewing framework.

Preparation

One of the first decisions to make when working with the adolescent involves arranging for the initial contact. A child's initial appointment is almost always made by the child's parent or another adult. Adults, on the other hand, generally schedule their own appointments to fit with their schedules and have had some telephone contact with the interviewer prior to their initial meeting. In dealing with the adolescent, however, one may choose to follow either of these two procedures. The parent or another adult will probably make the initial referral; however, if the interviewee is an older adolescent, the interviewer may want to arrange the first appointment with the adolescent himself. This strategy, in addition to building the initial rapport, has three points to recommend it. First, it reduces the adolescent's fears that the interviewer is already allied with the parents, reducing the likelihood that he will view the interviewer with suspicion as "one of them." Second, making a direct initial contact establishes the adolescent as a person capable of making decisions and reduces the chance that he will take a passive role in the proceedings, allowing others to "fix" his problem for him. Third, this procedure appeals to the adolescent's burgeoning need for autonomy, self-direction, and responsibility. Of course, the interviewer should carefully assess the reason for referral before deciding who to contact first. This would not be appropriate if the adolescent is being referred for a situation in which he already has too much responsibility and pressure to be "grown up." Such circumstances might occur, for example, when a family seeks help for a youngster due to the parents' upcoming divorce, an anorectic girl struggling with parental expectations for achievement, or perhaps a youngster suffering from an obsessive-compulsive disorder.

When the initial appointment is made with parents, the interviewer may need to suggest to the parents ways to explain the upcoming interview to the adolescent. Parents often hide the nature of an upcoming appointment until the moment the youngster actually meets the interviewer. This is especially common when the parents fear that something is seriously wrong with their child, as the following example illustrates.

Mrs. Stevens, a social worker in the pediatrics department of a major cancer hospital, was responsible for the initial interview of all patients admitted to the hospital and their families. With the patients themselves, Stevens generally covered such topics as progress in school, outside activities, friends, and ways in which the diagnosis of cancer was likely to affect these different areas of the adolescent's life. She always tried to determine the adolescent's level of general information regarding the disease as well as any serious misperceptions they might have. Stevens' job became much more difficult on the numerous occasions when the adolescent informed her in the initial stages of the interview, "I'm here to see the doctor because I'm anemic (or have the flu, or an infection). I'm not sure why everyone's making such a big deal of it, and by the way, what's wrong with all these kids in here who don't have any hair?" She then had to decide whether to play along with the parent's charade or to explain to the adolescent the seriousness of the diagnosis.

Stevens could avoid such a predicament by simply asking parents ahead of time how they intended to explain the appointment to the adolescent. Counselors or psychologists frequently experience similar circumstances; They are forewarned by a parent, "We haven't told Ellen who you really are: we don't want her to think she's crazy." Role clarification becomes important in these events. In this particular example, the following discussion with the parent is generally helpful.

Interviewer: Mrs.T..., I know you're worried about upsetting Ellen, but at her age she's probably pretty bright. I'll bet you've found in the past that she figures things out even when you don't tell her things.

Mrs.T: Yes, you're right, she always knows too much for her own good. But I assure you, if she knows we're coming to see you, she won't come.

Interviewer: What makes you think she wouldn't want to come?

Mrs T: She'll be sure that she's got that schizophrenic disease, and that we're going to lock her up in some hospital and never let her out and probably give her electric shocks to her brain.

Interviewer: Well, that's certainly not going to happen, but it sounds like Ellen really has a vivid imagination. I bet she might think that if she senses that you and Mr. T are worried but you won't tell her what's really going on. Usually, adolescents can tell when something's up, and if they can't get a good explanation, they're likely to make something up, and generally what they make up will be a lot scarier than reality. I bet if you told her the truth she'd find that a lot easier to take. How do you think you could explain to her exactly what's going to happen?

Mrs. T: Well, the way you explained it to me, you're going to talk to her for about an hour, and then you'll talk to the whole family and help us decide why she's making such bad grades in school.

Interviewer: That's excellent, Mrs. T. You might also explain to her that she's probably very tired of getting grounded all the time for her grades, and that we're going to discuss as a group, with me helping out, some different things you might try as a family to help her get the kind of grades she'd like.

Mrs. T: I guess I could do that. But what if she still doesn't want to come?

Interviewer: Well, how do you usually get her to do things?

Mrs. T: I bribe her, like with letting her use the car or see a movie.

Interviewer: That probably works really well sometimes, if you reward her for doing things you want her to do. But in this case it might be better if she came to help herself. How do you think she'd react if you explained that you don't know of any other way of dealing with her except to ground her, and this is her chance to change that herself and come up with some suggestions on her own for ways she'd like to be treated?

Mrs. T: She'd probably love that. She always wants to do things her own way.

Several points merit attention here. First, parents may have serious misconceptions about the interview and may need reassurance themselves. Although Mrs. T attributed her fantasy to Ellen, it is likely that she herself had some serious misgivings. Notice that the interviewer did not try to point this out to Mrs. T: rather, she pointed out that this was not the case and reinforced the actual nature of the interview. Second, the interviewer often must give the parents quite explicit instructions, since "just explain to her what's really going to happen" might result in a very different message from what the interviewer intended. Finally, the interviewer can obtain a great deal of important diagnostic information in this initial exchange. She has already learned that this family is secretive and that it has already attempted behavioral interventions as contingencies for Ellen's behaviors.

Initiation

In initiating an interview with the adolescent, the interviewer will have two major concerns: establishing confidentiality and overcoming resistance. Since confidentiality will generally be discussed at the very beginning of the interview, we will deal with it first.

Confidentiality

This tends to be a gray area in adolescent interviews. Most states consider individuals under the age of 18 legal minors; thus, parents would have access to records concerning their treatment. In many states, professionals may provide an initial interview, but counseling cannot continue for more than 24 hours without the parents' or guardian's written consent (Garbarino, 1985). The interviewer is responsible for making clear to all parties the limits of confidentiality and for specifying any general guidelines the interviews will follow in this area. It is best to do this immediately to set the tone for all communication. In interviewing the adolescent, a discussion like the following will probably suffice.

Interviewer: Joe, we're going to be talking about a lot of things today. I'm going to be asking about your likes and dislikes; what sorts of things you do at school, at home, or just for fun; and what your opinions are about a lot of things. Now, some of this will seem pretty personal to you, and I'm sure you might be a little reluctant to share some things with me. So I have a few rules that I always use when I talk with kids like you, and I think it will help if I tell you about them right from the beginning. First, you and I both know that your parents (or teachers) are going to be interested in what goes on in here. Now, while I will tell them in general how you're doing, the specific things we talk about are confidential. That means it's just between you and me. Now, you're free to tell them anything you want, but not me. Okay so far?

Joe: You mean if I was to tell you I skipped school every day, you wouldn't tell my old man?

Interviewer: No, I wouldn't. That's what confidential means. Now there are a few exceptions; let me explain them to you. One, I would tell your parents if I though you were considering doing something to hurt either yourself or someone else. But, even in that case, I'd do everything I could to let you know first. Second, there might be times when we discuss things that I think it would be helpful for your parents to know about, and I'll either try and convince you to talk to them or ask your permission to let me bring it up with them, but I wouldn't do that without your permission. Now, there's one final rule that I have. That is: This confidentiality only works one way. While I won't tell your parents the things *you* tell me, I will let you know what *they* tell me. For instance, if I get a call and they tell me they're upset that you stole some money, I'd let you know about that call and you and I would talk about it.

These guidelines must also be made clear to parents, particularly, the last one. If parents should protest that the last provision is unfair, the interviewer may be able to appease them with the following:

Interviewer: You're right, Mr. R, that's not really fair, but then being an adolescent isn't always fair and parents generally have the upper hand in the relationship. I'm sure you won't mind my evening things up a little and giving Joe the advantage just this once. Besides, my hands would be tied and I couldn't work effectively with your son if I agree to keep secrets from him that really have to do with his behavior. Of course, if you tell me something that really doesn't concern him, I'll respect your desire to keep that private, but you're just going to have to trust my judgment on this one.

The advantages of this approach are obvious. It helps the interviewer avoid parental attempts to collude, and it increases the adolescent's sense of autonomy and trust in the interviewer. Of course, he should also be prepared for the adolescent to "test" the limits of confidentiality; for example, telling him exaggerated tales of misbehavior to determine whether these exploits make their way back to the parents.

Resistance

Although resistance can be a problem in any interview, it seems particularly salient when working with adolescents. Although the notion of resistance has its roots in psychoanalytic theory, we will consider it here to be anything that prevents the adolescent from open and honest disclosure with the interviewer. Thus, the interviewer must change the adolescent's attitude from "I'm here because I have to be" to "I'm here for a reason and I think you can help me if I cooperate." Or, in the less-extreme cases, the interviewer's task will simply be facilitating the transition past initial vulnerability and fears about the interview into the realm of relationships, feelings, and ways of coping with stress (Looff, 1976).

Let's begin with a brief review of why an adolescent is likely to resist in an interview. First, as has been mentioned, adolescents' primary developmental tasks include gradual autonomy and separation from the family, development of strong ties to a peer group and achievement of intimacy on an individual level, and identity formation. The family generally provides clear rules and boundaries, then gradually "lets go" so that the adolescent will gain self-control. An adolescent will probably have a rather fragile self-concept and be in the initial stages of developing a firm self-identity. Thus, requiring adolescents to seek help or submit to an interview will likely seem like a threat to their new-found independence. The adolescent will probably also feel compelled to guard his fragile self-concept, feeling very vulnerable to any suggestion that his present circumstances are less than optimal and that there might be a better way of doing things (McHolland, 1985; Altman, 1985; Looff, 1976). Due to the adolescent's past experiences with adults as authority figures, he may expect that this adult will also teach or give directives. Additionally, the adolescent will be prone to feel that "no one else could possibly understand me" (remember the personal fable?).

The interviewer who has a clear idea of how and why the adolescent might respond to communication can take several steps to develop a more positive relationship. First, she can establish a reason for the interview, using both role clarification and information seeking. This can often be accomplished with the simple question, "Is there anything in particular you'd like to talk about?" This gives the adolescent a chance to describe his perceptions of the interview, which may differ dramatically from what the parents or referral source have told the interviewer. Unfortunately, adolescents commonly answer "I'm here only because my parents brought me!" Cases such as this often need candor from the interviewer, who should not keep the adolescent guessing as to what she knows or has been told. The following example will illustrate how a high school teacher might handle a discussion with a student.

Teacher: It sounds like you're really in the dark about why you're here, so let me start by telling you what I know about the situation. Your parents asked me to talk with you because they know you do well in my class and that you and I get along pretty well. They're concerned that you haven't been yourself lately. They mentioned being worried that you seem angry all the time, they think you've been drinking beer before and during school, and they're concerned that your grades are slipping.

Joe: Well, that's just what they think. You can't believe them. They get all their information from Mrs. Wiley, and she's crazy.

Teacher: Mrs. Wiley? Isn't she your math teacher?

> **Joe:**   Yeah, she calls my parents every week to complain about me.
>
> **Teacher:**   Well, I may not get a chance to talk to Mrs. Wiley. If I were to ask her about you, what would she say?
>
> **Joe:**   She's nuts, I told you. She'd say I don't turn in my homework, and that she thinks I'm drunk in class.
>
> **Teacher:**   But that's not true at all?
>
> **Joe:**   Well, maybe it happens sometimes, but it's not *my* fault.
>
> **Teacher:**   I see. Then it must be someone else's fault?
>
> **Joe:**   Yeah, well, sort of. This is just between you and me, right? I mean everybody drinks before school. They'd think I was a real geek if I didn't. And besides, her class is boring, not at all like your class. I don't see any point in doing the work; I'm never going to use that stuff anyway.

In this situation, Joe's teacher realizes that it will be futile to ask Joe directly to describe his problem, because Joe will deny having one. The teacher merely states what she has been told, establishing that she will not be keeping secrets or colluding with the parents. Then, the teacher asks Joe for someone else's description of him. Joe is more than willing to relate this description, simultaneously denying its validity. The teacher wisely accepts Joe's assertions, but nonetheless elicits Joe's view of the situation by allowing him to frame it as someone else's problem. It would clearly be unwise at this stage to attempt to help Joe achieve insight into his responsibility or effect on others, since the interviewer is still only gathering information. As Rabichow and Sklansky (1980) stress, a very supportive attitude is important initially in an interview to help the adolescent save face. Distortions can be addressed later , if necessary.

In many cases you will find that, after brief reluctance, the adolescent is actually eager to talk with an interested adult. Adolescents may look upon you as someone who has "made it," a person who functions well and can take charge of situations. The adolescent may be anxious to try out his burgeoning self-identity on an admired adult who is obviously not going to lecture or correct. After begin enmeshed for several years in the world of peers—where decisions, attitudes, and beliefs conform rigidly—the adolescent can tentatively admit that some of these behaviors and attitudes are not really all that desirable. That adolescent may desperately need adult approval and confirmation that there is hope.

One of the adolescent's first concerns may be: "Is there really something wrong with me? Am I crazy? Can you help me?" This was apparent in the example with Joe. His immediate denial of having any difficulties and his insistence that other people were "crazy" indicate his anxieties about himself. Let's continue with his interview and examine how these anxieties might be addressed.

> **Teacher:**   You know, Joe, you've mentioned two very important things that seem to be going on. One is drinking with your friends before school and the other is not getting work done in math class. I can't really decide if those two are related to each other or not.
>
> **Joe:**   I never thought about them together, but I guess it is kind of hard to do math when I'm blitzed out.
>
> **Teacher:**   I think you're right about that. What does it feel like to be "blitzed out?"
>
> **Joe:**   Not all that great, actually. It makes me kind of sick to my stomach and my mind just sort of goes mushy. In fact, it's not so hot at all. Am I crazy to do that to myself?

Teacher: Well, you admit it's not such a hot idea, but I don't think it means you're crazy; it sounds like there's a lot of pressure from your friends to drink.

Joe: Yeah, a lot. But if I didn't drink I'd really be out of things. I mean, like, all the guys do it. I don't see how I can *not* go along.

Teacher: Sounds like a tough situation, and one you'd rather not be in if you could just figure a way around it.

Joe: Yeah, but there's no way out of it, and nothing you or anybody else can do will make any difference.

Teacher: Well, if that's the case, there's probably not much point in talking to me; but you know, I've talked to guys before who've gone through things almost exactly like what you're telling me, and they really didn't want to go along with the crowd, either. But between us we managed to come up with some pretty good ideas.

Joe: No kidding? What did you do?

Teacher: Well, we had two or three discussions where we figured out just exactly what got them into their predicament and they tried out some different ways of getting along with their friends. It's not easy, but I'd be willing to try the same with you.

Joe: Guess I might as well, I don't have must to lose.

In this passage you can see the importance of reassuring the adolescent that he is not "crazy." The teacher accomplishes this by pointing out to Joe that he seems to have a very good reason for his maladaptive behavior. Second, the teacher assures the adolescent that others have gone through similar experiences. This can be very beneficial for the adolescent and cause a great deal of curiosity about how others underwent similar circumstances. Finally, it is important to offer some hope, but not promise an instant solution. This gives the adolescent a reason for continuing the interview, yet does not raise unrealistic expectations that the interviewer will be unable to meet.

As the interview progresses through the stage of identifying concerns, the subject may resist again when pressed to express her emotions. Adolescents often have a great deal of difficulty describing their feelings. In many cases, anger and active resistance may be a cover-up for hurt, loneliness, anxiety, or embarrassment (Jones, 1980). Let's progress in our example with Joe, and see how this might be handled in the interview.

Teacher: Joe, we've decided that drinking really makes it hard for you in your classes, particularly math. Are there any other ways drinking makes things hard for you?

Joe: Well, my parents are always on my case. But I don't care about that. I'll be out of there soon. You just wait until I hit 18. I'll be gone and there's nothing they can do about it. I'll show them!

Teacher: Whew! You're pretty angry at them. You really want to make them pay, don't you?

Joe: Well, they deserve it. They're always telling me I can't do anything right. Ah, it won't matter; they probably won't even care when I go. In fact, they'll be glad, because they won't have to get me out of trouble anymore. Man, they will be delighted to see me go. (Pauses.)

Teacher: And how does that make you feel?

Joe: I don't know. I don't care, either. Listen, I gotta tell you about this job I want to get for after school.

Notice that Joe is expressing a great deal of anger; but it appears that underneath he may actually be feeling hurt by his perception of his parents' attitude toward him. In one scenario (after the pause) the teacher could ask Joe directly what his underlying feelings might be. As you can see, this doesn't work very well. Joe cannot describe his emotions, and instead changes the subject in an attempt not to deal with his feelings. Let's examine a way other than the direct "How does that make you feel?" question that Joe's teacher might use here.

> **Joe:** ... Man, they will be delighted to see me go.
>
> **Teacher:** That sounds kind of rough. I think if *I* were a teenager and I really thought my parents wanted to get rid of me, it would make me feel pretty bad. It would probably really hurt my feelings. And sometimes when my feelings get hurt I get really angry.
>
> **Joe:** Yeah, I know what you mean, it makes me feel that way, too.

You can see here that although Joe cannot label his own feelings, he can identify with those feelings when someone else presents them. This then helps him understand his emotions more clearly. It also reduces the likelihood that he will feel so anxious that he needs to change the subject, again reducing the resistance encountered in the interview.

Some final guidelines for avoiding resistance are provided by McHolland (1985).

1. Use friendliness and a sense of humor. You have to like adolescents if you are going to work with them.
2. Start with basic information. Ask questions that can easily be answered, such as "What is your grade, school, favorite TV Show?" Do not expect to discuss a problem until you have established rapport.
3. Avoid silences. This generally makes the adolescent very uncomfortable. He may think you are able to read his mind.
4. Do not interrupt, advise, or judge.
5. Self-disclosure by the interviewer can help promote trust. However, it is important not to try to imitate the adolescent. Adolescents really do not respect adults who try to act much younger. They think this is phony.
6. Avoid taking sides. Be careful not to agree that the parents' perception of the problem is necessarily the only viewpoint.

In the extreme case where the adolescent absolutely refuses to talk, McHolland offers advice on ways for dealing with the silence (p. 358):

1. Relabel the silence. "You are very good at remaining silent. I bet you had this planned, you do it so well."
2. Prescribe the silence. "The best way you can cooperate with me is to remain silent while I discuss your problems with your parents," or "You don't have to say anything. In fact, I don't want you to say anything."
3. Reflect the feelings of "hurt" beneath the defiance.
4. Recognize the inconvenience the interview poses. "Is coming here a hassle? What other hassles do you have?"
5. Schedule a silent discussion. Silence then becomes a cooperative response. It will more likely provoke participation.

As the previous section indicates, the initiation stage of the interview should be spent overcoming any roadblocks preventing effective communication between the adolescent and the interviewer. To summarize, concerns of particular significance to the adolescent will be establishing the boundaries of confidentiality, deciding on how to make the initial contact with the adolescent, defining a reason for the interview, discovering misperceptions the adolescent might have about himself, and helping the adolescent begin to identify some of his feelings about his present situation. Techniques focused on will be rapport building, role clarification, information seeking, and concerns identification. Handling these situations properly should leave the interviewer ready for the next stage of interviewing—direction.

Direction

The direction stage involves getting down to business and directing efforts toward goal setting and problem solving. In this stage it will be particularly important to consider the adolescent's level of cognitive ability. As outlined earlier, knowing the adolescent's facility with hypothetical situations, abstractions, metaphors, perspective taking, and logical consequences will help the interviewer in proceeding through this stage. This will be particularly important in determining how much structure to impose. The adolescent should feel competent as she and the interviewer set goals and solve problems. Too much structure does not allow the adolescent to explore various alternatives and feel she has achieved her objectives. As Jones (1980) cautions, when adults insist on providing answers or attempting to change the environment according to their perception of needs, they are developing a dependent relationship that runs counter to the adolescent's needs for autonomy. Conversely, the professional should not be so nondirective that the adolescent feels confused and frustrated in seeking solutions.

One nondirective approach is mirroring, or reflecting and paraphrasing. Although this will be useful in small doses, the interviewer should avoid excessive use of reflection, since it does not allow for a highly structured interview. In addition, some adolescents seem to find it demeaning, and will object: "Will you stop just saying everything I say?" One way of providing structure without being too directive is to comment on how the adolescent's responses or behaviors make the interviewer feel without commenting on the goodness or badness of those behaviors. This feedback to the adolescent should be very specific and can help him explore other possibilities. Let us continue with the example of Joe to illustrate goal setting and implementation.

> **Teacher:** Well, Joe, I think we've established that your drinking results in some negative outcomes for you. One, it makes it hard for you to do well in class, and two, it creates problems with your parents. Also, it just makes you feel pretty bad. That's all on the negative side. Now what about the positive side. Are there good things about drinking?
>
> **Joe:** Well, like I said, only that it keeps me in good with the guys. I guess that's not really a very good reason, is it?
>
> **Teacher:** Doesn't sound like it to me. What do you think you want to do about it?
>
> **Joe:** Quit, I guess, but I don't see how I can do that.
>
> **Teacher:** Well, I think it's a big step in the right direction to decide that's what you want to do. Now that we've figured out *what* you want, let's think about how you might go about it. Do all your friends drink?
>
> **Joe:** Yeah, everybody.
>
> **Teacher:** So you think they're all getting hassled by their parents and feeling too sick to do much in class?

> **Joe:**   Well, not really.
>
> **Teacher:**   Oh, why not?
>
> **Joe:**   I don't know. Maybe, well, uh, I think I probably drink more than they do.
>
> **Teacher:**   I think I missed something Joe. You say you don't really like drinking, yet you drink more than anyone else? I can't quite figure that one out.
>
> **Joe:**   Well, the guys get on my case more, like they dare me to drink a six pack. I guess that's pretty dumb, isn't it?
>
> **Teacher:**   I think I'd have to agree with you. Can you think of any way not to let them goad you into drinking too much?
>
> **Joe:**   Yeah, I could shake up a beer and spray it in their faces.
>
> **Teacher:**   Well, if someone did that to me I'd probably get pretty mad and do something to get even. How do you think your friends might react?
>
> **Joe:**   Probably the same way. Well, let's see. I guess I could make a joke. I could tell them I'm in training for the Olympics and that beer is bad for my physique.
>
> **Teacher:**   And how do you think that would go over?
>
> **Joe:**   Probably better. The guys are really into having a tough physique, like you know, it turns on the girls and stuff.
>
> **Teacher:**   Well, let's make a deal. Why don't you try that out next week, and then come back and we'll talk about how it works.
>
> **Joe:**   Yeah, sure, I'll give it s try.

Most adolescents, given a little bit of direction, are fairly good at problem solving. Notice how in the beginning of this example Joe's teacher rephrases what they have discussed, summarizing what Joe has said to establish the nature of his problem. Then it is necessary to establish a clear goal, one to which Joe is clearly committed. Notice that the teacher does not merely ask Joe how he might reach that goal. Rather, he asks some leading questions until he thinks Joe is ready to suggest ways to do it. Joe's teacher does not his first suggestion negatively, but tells him how he personally might respond to Joe's intervention. Because adolescents are intensely self-conscious, they tend to take feedback very personally. Thus, it is important that the interviewer clearly separate his feelings about the adolescent from his feelings about his actions. Thus, in this example, the teacher comments on Joe's proposed behaviors, rather than on how these behaviors might reflect on Joe as a person. When Joe provides an alternate intervention, his teacher again asks him to consider the possible consequences of that intervention. Only when it appears that Joe is satisfied with this solution does the teacher suggest implementation. Finally, the teacher provides for feedback regarding the solution the following week.

In summary, probably the most important thing to keep in mind during the direction stage of interviewing is to involve the adolescent as much as possible in decision making. This, of course, will require an appraisal of the adolescent's cognitive abilities. The more the adolescent feels personally responsible for goal setting and problem solving, the greater his motivation will be to follow through with his objectives.

Conclusion

This final stage of the interview involves planning for the future. The interviewer should warn the adolescent when 5–10 minutes are remaining in the session:

> **Teacher:**   Let's stop here and summarize what we've been talking about. I want to make sure we're both clear on what goals we've set and where we plan to go from here.

This evaluation phase gives the adolescent a sense of structure, forewarns him that closure is forthcoming, and gives him a chance to bring up any overlooked issues before the interview ends.

Generally the interviewer should offer her perceptions of the interview first, being very specific about the topics discussed, the issues that seemed to have primary importance, tentative goals, and possible resolutions agreed upon. The interviewer should then determine whether these coincide with the adolescent's view of the proceedings. It also helps to comment on the way in which the adolescent handled the interview. This type of feedback is very useful for adolescents who are refining their self-identity by observing how others perceive their interactions. Observe the following:

> **Teacher:**   You know, Joe, when we began this interview you were pretty reluctant to talk with me, but I noticed you really opening up as you began to understand what was going on in here and got to know me a little better. That's probably a pretty good approach to use with strangers, to be somewhat cautious until you decide whether you can really trust them. I was really impressed with the way you were able to come up with suggestions once you put your mind to it. I feel fairly confident that using all the suggestions we talked about today, you'll be able to make some pretty positive changes.

Note that, in addition to giving the adolescent feedback on his interpersonal skills, the interviewer provided a "prognosis." She should include an opinion of the likely outcome of the session, giving the adolescent a sense of hope regarding his situation.

Finally, the interviewer should promote a sense of closure about what will happen next. Sometimes, the interviewer and the adolescent will meet again. With the case described here, Joe and the teacher agreed that he would return for another discussion with the teacher and that this discussion would center on Joe's attempt at problem resolution. When additional discussions are needed, it is often wise to communicate the expectation that the adolescent will return, rather than ask her permission. Particularly when dealing with an already-resistant adolescent, the interviewer may be setting himself up for refusal when he inquires "Well, would you like to come back again next week and talk to me again?" The teen eager for autonomy may be unable to resist the temptation to wield power over an adult and decline a second interview. An alternate approach gives the adolescent a degree of control:

> **Interviewer:**   This has been a very productive discussion. I think we'll need to meet again two more times. For our next meeting, would you prefer the same time next week, or would a different day be better for you?

Notice that this approach assumes that the adolescent will return. The interviewer should estimate as accurately as possible the number of meetings they will need and give the adolescent a measure of control by allowing her to select the next meeting time.

RESEARCH

Recent research in the area of interviewing adolescents focuses on three main areas. Developmental considerations, as outlined in the beginning of this chapter, continue to be investigated. For many years, textbooks on adolescent development merely extended well-known theories on child development. Recent texts, however, have begun to formulate clearer theories of adolescent development. The second research area involves developmental psychopathology. As the name implies, this field examines specific behavior and personality problems using a developmental perspective. An excellent example of this research is the work of Achenbach and Edelbrock (1983), which found that certain behavior problems occur more often in young children, middle childhood, or adolescence. The third area of research involves specific interviewing techniques, such as ways to deal with resistant adolescents (McHolland, 1985), role-taking interviews (Altman, 1985), and specific counseling techniques (Mills, 1985).

SUMMARY

Interviewing the adolescent can be challenging and rewarding, or it can be quite frustrating and demoralizing, leaving the interviewer with serious doubts about his or her professional skills. The difference may well lie in the interviewer's knowledge of the adolescent's unique characteristics. This chapter has described the adolescent from a developmental perspective, including physical development, cognitive development, moral development, and identity formation. An understanding of these areas is crucial for the successful interview. In addition, the chapter discussed specific difficulties that adolescents are likely to encounter. Finally, specific issues related to various stages of the adolescent interview were discussed, including making the initial contact, preparing the parents for the interview, establishing confidentiality, overcoming resistance, providing an appropriate amount of structure, including the adolescent in decision making, and concluding the interview. This framework can help the interviewer discover the intriguing nature of working with adolescents.

SUGGESTED READINGS

Jones, V. (1980). *Adolescents with behavior problems: Strategies for teaching, counseling, and parent involvement.* Boston: Allyn and Bacon.

Looff, D. (1976). *Getting to know the troubled child.* Knoxville: University of Tennessee Press.

McHolland, J. (1985). Strategies for dealing with resistant adolescents. *Adolescence, 20* (78).

Newman, B., & Newman, P. (1986). *Adolescent development.* Columbus: Merrill.

Rabichow, H., & Sklansky, M. (1980). *Effective counseling of adolescents.* Chicago: Follett.

7

Interviewing Adults

Ronn Johnson
University of Nebraska, Lincoln

Although ineffective communication is costly in every sphere of life, few people every recognize the need to reduce it. Certainly, communication-skills training is often neglected. This is apparent in the generally poor quality of interviews between adults. For example, when two parties are involved in a car accident, a police officer arrives on the scene to collect basic information. The interview requires careful listening to numerous details and facilitating disclosure. It allows the police officer to assess accurately and understand what happened. But consider the officer who fails to gather basic facts (e.g., who, what, when, where, why):

Officer: Did you know your car tags have expired?
Citizen #1: Yes, but I want to tell you what happened.
Officer: Don't try to tell me how to do my job.
Citizen #2: We were driving down Holden Street and this kid on a b . . . (Officer interrupts.)
Officer: I can see you guys don't want to cooperate; I need to write citations for the expired tags.

Different situations require different interviewing skills. Law enforcement calls for a reconstruction of events; business, information for numerous decisions, including hiring and firing; medical settings, pertinent health information. The object of one interview may be merely to gather information. Another may seek the resolution of a conflict. A skilled interviewer obtains salient information and identifies distortions in the interviewee's perceptions (Wachtel & Wachtel, 1986).

This chapter covers the basic skills needed for conducting interviews. A practical guide, it is intended for use in interpersonal skill–training programs for adults. It approaches interviewing as a flexible art that is adaptable to various situations. The chapter is divided into three major sections. The first section explores interviewing of young adults (i.e., ages 21–32). The second section covers midadult (i.e., ages 33–55) interviewing concerns. Examples of interviews will mainly consider adult development issues (e.g., switching jobs or forced retirement). The last section examines interview research issues.

INTERVIEWING ADULTS: AN OVERVIEW

The interviewer uses a variety of general techniques or strategies to provide structure to the information process. An effective interview technique is in practice flexible, systematic, and useful toward some end.

The technique used often depends on the setting. For example, medical emergencies may necessitate foregoing establishing rapport with a patient because precious minutes wasted could be used to save a life. A business executive interviewing an applicant for an office personnel position may need to find out how she would handle difficult clients. For example, the interviewer may decide to assume the role of a tough client and observe how the applicant responds. Similarly, a principal may test the responses of a new teacher interviewing for a position in a tough innercity school. Each setting (business, community, law enforcement, medical, school) enlists a repertoire of techniques to meet specific needs. Most interviews are general, however, regardless of the setting or purpose. Developing an appropriate interview technique requires considering more than a particular setting.

To be effective, an interview technique should be adaptable to a particular setting. Interview techniques that are too rigid will unnecessarily restrict the interaction between the interviewer and the interviewee and this rigidity will restrict the amount and quality of the information collected during the interview. For example, in an emergency medical situation that requires immediate attention, it is inappropriate to collect information about what insurance the patient carries or to insist on completion of the standard hospital admission form.

The interview must be systematic, occurring in a series of stages that allow maximum interaction (see Figure 7–1). That is, the interview has a beginning, middle, and end.

Interviews should serve a useful purpose. On the one hand, the interview must achieve the basic purpose of collecting information. On the other hand, the interview should be adapted to the specific requirements of the setting or situation (Belkin, 1984).

Figure 7–1 Developmental Process–Interviewing Model

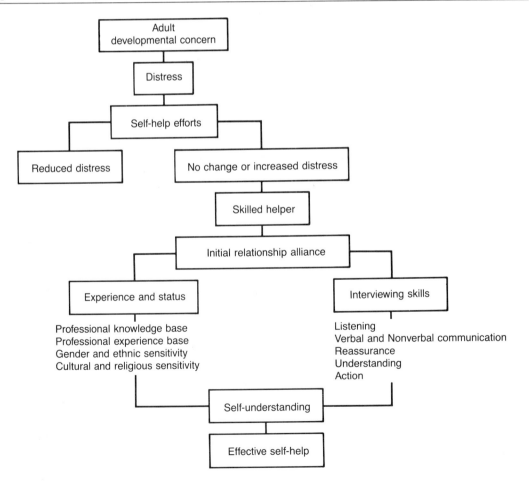

Nonverbal Skills

The ability to listen is fundamental to an interviewer. The interviewer who fails to listen will needlessly inhibit the natural process of collecting information. Certainly, careful listening is important in building an alliance between the interviewer and interviewee. Effective listening occurs in stages. The purposeful use of listening skills begins with a conceptual understanding of the various stages (See Figure 7–2).

The sensing stages include the modalities that allow an interviewer to acquire information: hearing, seeing, smelling, tasting, or touching. An interviewee may deliver a message using any combination of these modalities. For example, an interviewee may indicate the visual or olfactory senses—"It is as clear as a picture to me" or "I can almost smell the bitterness"—or through other senses—"I could hear the tension in his voice" or "She touched me in a meaningful way."

An effective interviewer notes how an interviewee provides information. The choice of sensory language gives additional information that can facilitate an interviewer's understanding. Some interviewees communicate information through one primary modality. At the same time, an interviewer can collect information through one primary modality (Cormier & Cormier, 1985).

At the second stage of listening, the interviewer restructures and interprets the information provided by an interviewee. For example, an interviewee may say "This whole situation smells pretty bad to me." Since it is important to build an alliance, an interviewer might respond by saying "It does smell unusual."

An interviewee will feel he is being listened to when the interviewer makes a conscious effort to understand events as he does. Feedback usually carries more weight when the interviewer matches the interviewee's modality. For example, an interviewer may respond to the statement "I feel that this store is trying to rip me off" with "You feel cheated by the store." Empathizing with the interviewee this way also produces more information.

The interviewer's attention to "how" an interviewee communicates requires the use of a third ear (Reik, 1948). That is, an interviewer listens with a third ear by "associating" along with the interviewee, experiencing her own relevant modality as she speaks. The

Figure 7–2 Listening Stages

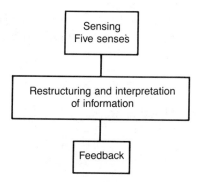

interviewer, naturally, is allowing the interviewee's words to stimulate ideas that he can turn into appropriate feedback. The accuracy of the feedback depends on the extent that an interviewer can correctly mimic the interviewee's communication modality. Listening and mimicking modalities can be better illustrated in a case example of how the listening stages unfold.

Mr. Jones is a 32-year-old store clerk in a large national department store chain. He has worked there for three years and his overall semiannual job ratings have been below average. Specifically, he has been criticized for "tardiness for work," "difficulty in accepting criticism," and "being verbally assaultive when asked to add new assignments." Mr. Jones has come into the employment office to request a transfer.

Mr. Jones: I really can't see how I can get ahead in this store.

Employment officer: Mr. Jones, are you saying you don't see a future in the store?

Mr. Jones: Yes, I can remember several scenes when my supervisor tried to draw negative pictures of my work performance.

Employment officer: Could you explain to me how you see the whole situation?

Mr. Jones: The way I see it (pause) I've got no chance . . . no chance whatsoever . . .

Employment officer: You seem to be painting a real bad picture of the relationship between you and your supervisor.

Mr. Jones: I've been here three years and Don (supervisor) has been constantly on my back. I don't like the way he tries to push me around and give me the assignments that stink or no one else would take.

Employment officer: I can see how getting jobs that stink can make you feel very angry.

Mr. Jones: I am angry, that's for sure.

Employment officer: When you're angry you seem to get louder. I wonder how that affects your relationship with your supervisor.

Mr. Jones: I know he doesn't like it.

This interview clearly demonstrates the stages of listening. The employment officer was trying to understand Jones' complaints. Jones expressed his anger through a visual mode ("can't see," "several scenes"). The officer recognized this visual-anger association and helped Jones make the same connection. This connection represents the second stage of listening (restructuring and interpretation). Jones may not be aware of the anger he is experiencing; the interviewer helps draw the connection. In addition, Jones was sensitized, through feedback, as to how his anger was being perceived. This sensitization process represents the third stage of listening (feedback).

These listening skills allow a natural exploration of relevant issues. The interviewer's listening improves by responding to the modality or sensory language used by interviewees. Furthermore, the whole interview process is significantly enhanced by acknowledging and using nonverbal as well as verbal skills.

Nonverbal Components of Interviews with Adults

The connections between verbal and nonverbal information are revealing. Facial expression, gaze, body movements, vocal cues, and the use of space are all important parts of the complete interview picture (Priestly & McGuire, 1983). For example, happiness, surprise, and frustration may be communicated through the lower face and the eyes. Fear and anger are also communicated by the eyes (Ekman, Friesen, & Tomkins, 1971). Body movements, posture, and gestures modify, amplify, and regulate verbal information collected during an interview. For example, an anxious interviewee will display quick, restless movement of limbs and shaky hands. Vocal (i.e., paralinguistic) cues are less obvious and are conveyed by pitch, vocal intensity, speech pace, pauses, and silences. These cues are used in the interview to facilitate listener or speaker roles. For example, a decrease in pitch may signal a desire to yield the role of speaker.

Another important factor is the physical distance (i.e., proxemics) an interviewee maintains between himself and the interviewer (Hall, 1966; Altman, 1981). For example, young and elderly interviewees may require closer distances. Females may be more tolerant of less space than males. Touch may represent an expression of care in one situation, evaluation in another (Cormier & Cormier, 1985).

Verbal Components of Interviews with Adults

Verbal expressions are important in interviews with adults. The interviewer can gain more accurate information about the interviewee by using various verbal techniques (Hansen, Steric, & Warner, 1982). The six verbal techniques that may be used include minimal encouraging, reflection, clarification, exploring analysis, self-disclosure, and summarizing (see Table 7–1).

Minimal encouragers are verbal cues such as "I see," "yeah," "uh-huh," "mm-mm" that demonstrate the interviewer is actually listening and understanding what the interviewee is reporting (Okun, 1982). For example:

> **Customer:** The clerk just wouldn't refund my money for the bad item.
> **Customer service representative:** I see.

The reflection of feeling or content is a verbal technique that parallels what the interviewee is reporting or experiencing emotionally. For example:

> **Employee:** I have just completed a two-week training course for distributors.
> **Supervisor:** You say you have just completed a two-week training course and you feel frustrated.

It is more useful for interviewers to be selective about what they choose to reflect and avoid a "parrot-like" style. They should not restate everything the interviewee says.

Clarification represents an effort to comprehend the general intention of an interviewee's response. The interviewer should request additional information or express her own misunderstanding to the interviewee. For example:

> **Customer:** I'm having a difficult time understanding you. Could you explain it in a different way.
> **Police officer:** Do you mean? . . . Or do you mean . . . ?
> **Businessperson:** Let me see if I understand you correctly. You're saying . . .

In each of the preceding examples, the interviewer is making an effort to understand or clarify the interviewee's communication.

Table 7–1 Definitions and Intended Purposes of Interviewer Verbal Technique

Technique	Definition	Goal or Technique
Minimum Encouragers	Verbal cues that facilitate interviewee disclosures	1. To elicit continued information from the interviewee 2. To show the interviewer is listening and following what is being said
Reflection	Empathic mirroring of the interviewee's content and feelings	1. To briefly restate what the interviewee has said verbally 2. To offer an indication of how the interviewee feels about whatever she is revealing
Clarification	Gaining a clearer understanding of what the interviewee is stating	1. To illuminate further the information being provided by the interviewee 2. To allow the interviewer to check out his or her perceptions of what the interviewee is stating
Exploring	Encouraging the interviewee	1. To use open-ended questions (i.e., how or what) that extend disclosures 2. To use statements designed to allow the interviewee to elaborate
Analysis	An interviewer's explanation of what is being reported that has the effect of increasing understandings or conclusions	1. To identify inconsistencies in what is being reported 2. To examine other ways of understanding what is being reported by the interviewee
Self-disclosure	An interviewer's attempt to make herself known to the interviewee	1. To reveal personally relevant information 2. To encourage more self-disclosure through the use of disclosure
Summarizing	The condensing of what has been said throughout the interview	1. To highlight the major themes 2. To facilitate clarification or more disclosures

Exploring involves communication techniques designed to extend the information collected. The most frequently used exploring techniques are "how" or "what" questions. These questions require more expanded responses, as in this exchange:

Nurse supervisor: How do you feel about working the weekend shift?
Nurse: I believe it would be fine because I don't do much on the weekends.
Nurse supervisor: What would you normally do on a weekend?
Nurse: Well, I normally go to the movies or watch TV at home.

Exploring techniques include leading questions ("Could you tell me more about that?") or prompters ("um-hmm") that are designed to yield additional interview information.

Analysis is an interview technique whereby an interviewer offers an explanation of what the interviewee is disclosing. This helps the interviewer find out how the interviewee is feeling as they discuss information. For example:

Executive: I have given a great deal of my personal time and effort to completing this project. It's been extremely demanding. I haven't received any recognition for my efforts.
Marketing supervisor: It sounds as though you feel unappreciated.

The interviewer has reflected the essence of the interviewee's feelings.

In self-disclosure, the interviewer makes himself known to the interviewee. For example, after a homicide, police may need to generate important facts very quickly. Stating these facts may create stress in the interview. The police officer can use self-disclosure to reduce anxiety and create an alliance between himself and the interviewee. For example:

Police officer: Could you tell me how all this occurred?
Victim: I saw this guy. . . (Begins to cry and cannot continue.)
Police officer: I know it's really difficult to tell about something like this. I personally don't like asking these questions right now. . . but I really need to, so I would just go at your own pace.

Here the interviewer is using self-disclosure to facilitate disclosure by the interviewee. That is, the interviewer's own self-disclosure rewards the interviewee for disclosing (Hansen, Steric, & Warner, 1982).

In summarizing, the interviewer condenses most of what the interviewee has reported. It is important to highlight major points or central issues. The summary may occur after detailed information is disclosed or toward the end of the interview. It is useful to allow the interviewee to participate or to acknowledge the accuracy of the summary. The examples in the preceding section demonstrated how the techniques could be applied. The next sections examine how interviewing can be used to examine adult developmental concerns.

INTERVIEWING AND ADULT DEVELOPMENT

Interviewers should be aware that adult life is characterized by physical, psychological, and social changes. Adults experience changes in body build (Damon, Seltzer, Stoudt, & Bell, 1972), structural changes in the heart (Gerstenblitz, 1980; Pomerance, 1976; Weisfeldt, 1980), and other changes too obvious to mention. A once-active, vibrant adult may become distressed over a decline in physical prowess. This distress could trigger a depression that could interfere with work and social relationships. Many personal experiences also can alter the course of adult development. A new baby, switching jobs, moving, divorce, changes in health status, or work conflicts are normal developmental experiences for adults.

The effect of some events in adulthood may be more subtle. For example, the birth of a new baby may temporarily reduce the total living space in the home. Other experiences, such as a midcareer change, may directly lead to depression due to lost status or reduced financial power. Some changes in the adult years may result from national political and economic events beyond anyone's control.

Adult experiences interact to produce an effect in the individual. They also affect the interview process. Although many of the experiences can be identified, some are specifically associated with various subgroups. For example, midlife crises are usually observed in the age range of 40–65. Early-adulthood issues occur in 25- to 40-year-olds. Each of these groups functions differently. The relationships of middle-aged adults are characterized by increased marital satisfaction and the importance attached to friends. Early adulthood is typically marked by lower marital satisfaction and fewer new friendships.

If we extend the adult subgroup to include women and ethnic minorities, other unique differences emerge. For example, the birth of a new baby is obviously more of a stress for women than for men (Russell, 1974). Becoming a new parent has a negative impact on marital relationships (Waldron & Routh, 1981). The work patterns of career women necessarily change as a result of the new baby. Finally, some women may be forced to sacrifice career advancement to have a family. Blacks generally have lower social status, lower-paying jobs, and lower incomes than do Whites. In 1983, for example, the average household income of Blacks was $16,531, while that of Whites was $24,455 (Palmore, Burchett, Fillenbaum, George, & Wallman, 1985).

The overall picture shows divergent patterns of development when adults are separated into various subgroups. It is important to remain alert to these variations when conducting adult interviews.

Early-Adulthood Interview Issues

Many events that are associated with adult development can be seen as stressful, especially those that cause dramatic changes (Lowenthal, Thurnher, Chitboga, & Associates, 1975) and require adjustment. Stress can be positive or negative. Regardless of the direction of the stress, it taxes an adults's physical and emotional energy. Adults respond differently to stress and employ various coping strategies that affect the interview directly. In fact, the same individual may respond differently to a particular concern, depending on when it occurs in the developmental process. As Neugarten (1976) describes it:

> Major stresses are caused by events that upset the sequence and rhythm of the life cycle—as when death of a parent comes in childhood rather than in middle age; when marriage does not come at its desired or appropriate time; when occupational achievement is delayed; when the empty nest, grandparenthood, retirement, major illness, or widowhood occur off-time. (p. 20)

The adult developmental process is characterized by tasks that occur as a result of physiological forces and age-specific social or cultural requirements. Resolving these developmental tasks (concerning career, social life, and family) allows one to move on to the next set of tasks. For example, a 25-year-old Hispanic male who has not secured a permanent place in a chosen occupation will have difficulty moving on to the tasks associated with career advancement. An understanding of developmental tasks amounts to a map for identifying problems associated with early adult development (Okun, 1984).

Some theorists identify early adulthood as occurring from ages 20 to 35 or 40. Middle adulthood is identified as occurring from 35 or 40 to 60 or 65. For the purposes of this chapter, early adulthood is defined as occurring between 21 and 35 and middle adulthood between the ages of 36 and 55.

The tasks of adult development interact with numerous life events to produce a variety of adjustment problems that the interviewer should be aware of. Developmental theorists (i.e., Jung, Buhler, and Erikson) identified specific tasks associated with adulthood. Figure 7–3 illustrates adult developmental interactions.

Adults experiencing the stress associated with developmental tasks are predisposed to problems that may be observed as they interact with other systems (e.g., schools, work place, community). Interviewing can help them understand problems associated with career, family, or community.

Early adulthood is a time of numerous problems related to career development. Donald Super has identified various tasks associated with this stage; they are outlined in Table 7–2.

Adult development issues associated with family can also influence career development. Consider, for example, Sam, age 25, who completed a master's program in economics and accepted a position with a New York firm. Sam had ongoing conflicts with his father; he reports that his father always tried to correct him. This overcritical father caused a tendency for Sam to be hypersensitive to evaluation. The job with the New York firm required a six-month training and orientation program. All new employees were also

Figure 7–3 The Interaction of Adult Tasks with Family, Career, and Social Cultural Factors

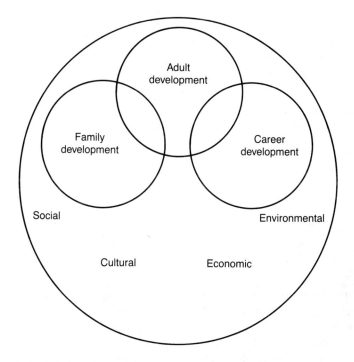

Source: Working with Adults: Individual Family & Career Development (p. 43) by B. F. Okun, 1984, Belmont, CA: Wadsworth. Reprinted with permission.

Table 7–2 Early Adult Career-Development Tasks

Stage	Age	Tasks	General Characteristics
Exploratory	21–24	Implementation through first job	Entering employment of selected occupation
Establishment	25–44	Securing permanent place in chosen occupation	Trying and stabilizing through work experience
	24–35	Stabilization	Confirming a preferred career by actual work experiences and use of talents to demonstrate career choice as appropriate choice

required to work with a senior staff member for six months following orientation. This staff member, directly responsible for supervising and evaluating Sam's work, was a 51-year-old man who had been with the firm for 20 years. He was a knowledgeable mentor who firmly believed in obeying all company policies without questioning. Sam found himself resisting the requirements of his supervisor and ridiculed him behind his back. At the same time, Sam was frustrated and discouraged with his progress in the firm. His supervisor became aware of Sam's disappointment and decided to interview him to resolve the conflict. Sam was able to recognize the good intentions of his supervisor; however, he had difficulty accepting critiques of his work. He could not acknowledge that the evaluations by his supervisor elicited many of the same reactions that his father's criticism had. The following interview excerpt represents the way Sam came to acknowledge the similarities between his responses to his dad and his supervisor:

> **Supervisor:** It seems as though you really can't accept my input.
> **Sam:** What do you mean?
> **Supervisor:** I understand how it must be frustrating being a new employee. I was frustrated my first two years here.
> **Sam:** Well, I (pause) . . . I just want to do a good job.
> **Supervisor:** You say you want to do a good job but I sense you're angry with me.
> **Sam:** I guess I am . . . I don't like to have you or anyone else critique my work.
> **Supervisor:** I see . . . could you tell me more about your concerns with my critiques?
> **Sam:** I've never liked to have people evaluate me . . . my dad did it and I hated it.
> **Supervisor:** So do my critiques sound like your dad's?
> **Sam:** Not always, but I sure get upset whenever you evaluate me.
> **Supervisor:** I wonder how could we change my evaluations to reduce some of your frustrations.

This interview excerpt clearly demonstrates the use of reflection of feeling ("it must be frustrating") and self-disclosure ("I was frustrated"). The interviewer made an effort to explore and identify with the interviewee the source of his job dissatisfaction. In addition to this, the interviewer offered a collaborative problem-solving strategy to the interviewee. That is, "I wonder how we could change. . . ." This interviewer demonstrated a relaxed, supportive listening role that allowed the interviewee the space to explore or vent the emotional distress connected with evaluation. Early adulthood requires the development of occupational and relationship skills and competencies. Those in supervisory or information-gathering/dissemination positions must develop basic interviewing skills to address adult developmental problems.

These interviewing skills will greatly influence the quality of interactions between adults. This is particularly true for early-adult problems associated with the school system. To illustrate, the following interview takes place in the office of the special-education teacher at Fleming Elementary School. The interviewee, Mrs. Henderson, a 27-year-old, has a 3-year-old daughter, Rachell Dellia, and a 7-year-old son, Ross. Her husband is a business executive for IBM. Mrs. Johnson, the special-education teacher, has asked Mrs. Henderson to set up a parent-teacher conference to discuss Ross. Ross has recently been a discipline problem in the classroom; he prevents other students from doing their work. Mrs. Henderson arrives three minutes early for her 4:00 appointment.

Teacher: Good afternoon, Mrs. Henderson; please have a seat. I'll finish grading these papers. If I don't finish now, I'll have to do it tomorrow, which is a very busy day for me.

Parent: I understand. I have a lot of things to do as well and most are already late. (Mrs. Henderson sits and waits patiently for the teacher to finish grading the papers.)

Teacher: As I told you over the phone, Ross has become a discipline problem in my classroom. I was wondering what you could suggest as alternatives for managing him better.

Parent: I generally use time outs at home and they seem to work very well.

Teacher: So time outs work with him at home. I am frustrated because I don't like using time outs. Could you give me examples of behaviors at home where you actually use the time outs?

Parent: Yes, whenever he doesn't comply with my basic requests. For example, he refused to make his bed the other day, so I timed him out.

Teacher: I see. . . .

Parent: I also think he wants to please you because he constantly talks about Mrs. Johnson.

Teacher: I must admit that I really like having Ross in my class. I sometimes treat him differently because he reminds me of a close nephew.

It was clear to the teacher that the basic function of this interview was to collect basic information. She sets the tone of the conference by summarizing a previous phone conversation. This allows her to elicit additional information ("I generally use time outs"). This was coupled with the interviewer's use of self-disclosures ("I am frustrated" and "he reminds me of a close nephew."). The use of the summary and self-disclosure allow the interviewee to provide additional information ("he wants to please you"). The use of basic interview techniques in this situation facilitated a discussion that could have easily been highly stressful. Parent-teacher conferences are one of the various developmental events associated with early adulthood. Some early-adulthood developmental tasks result from social or community-related expectations; for example, starting recreational facilities for youth could create stress for an early adult. Such is the case with Mrs. Morales, a 29-year-old mother of three children, aged 8, 10, and 12. She is concerned about the lack of recreational facilities. These concerns have caused her to challenge the recreation department to develop appropriate facilities. She has requested a meeting with Jim Hastings, who is the community representative for the department. The following dialogue is an excerpt from that interview.

Citizen: It's vital to get something started for our children . . . otherwise they turn to the street and who knows what kind of problems.

Community representative: I understand your concerns, Mrs. Morales. . . . Could you help me understand what you think Parks and Recreation can do to help?

Citizen: You closed the North Park gym and cut the hours at the Northwest gym. Those two actions hurt a lot of the children in this area.

Community representative: Let me see if I understand you. You're upset because we've closed one gym and cut the hours at another.

Citizen: Yes . . . I'm upset because of the closings, but we were told they would begin construction on a new park six months ago.

This excerpt demonstrates how an interviewer can use basic skills to facilitate the collection of basic information. The interviewer uses empathetic responses ("I understand your concerns"). The empathetic responses may be described as the ability to understand Mrs. Morales from her frame of reference rather than the community representative's. The interviewer demonstrates a desire to comprehend and discuss what is important to the interviewee. The interviewee also recognizes the interviewee's feelings ("you're upset because . . .").

Super (1969) identifies various tasks associated with vocational development. The stabilization associated with the establishment phase represents one of these tasks. Employers who provide opportunities for employee stabilization (i.e., advancement) must understand the use of interviewing skills. To illustrate, the Baldwin First National Bank offers a summer internship program designed to provide junior staff members with an opportunity for advancement in the bank. J. R. Henderson, the bank president, started this program, which is very competitive and requires a series of interviews. The interviews assess the motivational level of those applying. In the past, many employees have complained about the disorganized way that the interviews are conducted. Some employees believed the interviews didn't allow them to demonstrate adequately their skills or knowledge.

This year, training was provided for the interviewers. The following case is an excerpt from an interview that occurred after the training. Sally is a 37-year-old accounting officer, an Asian American who has been with the bank for six years. She was rejected for last year's program because of what was identified as a "failure to connect with the interviewer." She did not maintain consistent eye contact. Some of the evaluations suggested she "has a poor self-concept and probably wouldn't benefit from the training because of it." The interviewer, unfortunately, was not sufficiently aware of cross-cultural factors.

For example, some Asian cultures teach a woman never to make eye contact with men outside her immediate family. To do so would be a sign of disrespect. A review of Sally's performance revealed that she was interviewed by three White males. Sexism and limited cross-cultural awareness can interfere with interviewing people with certain handicaps and disabilities; people of limited abilities; and people of different cultures, races, and socioeconomic levels. An effective interviewer has full awareness of cross-cultural and cross-gender factors. These factors play a significant role in understanding the adults interviewed. Okun (1982) identifies age prejudice as another instance where "our beliefs and values about what a person can or should do at different ages" affects how we might interview him. An interviewer may be unaware of her tendencies to stereotype people into groups. Knowledge about gender differences and ethnic and age groups can greatly facilitate the interview process.

Middle-Adulthood

Neugarten (1968) interviewed 100 well-placed men and women in the 40 to 60 age group. Her interviews revealed that these individuals reported an increased awareness of their position in a diverse environment, a desire to examine issues associated with middle age, and a belief that middle age is a time full of potential and ability to manage an extremely complex environment and a fully evolved self.

Bee (1987) reports numerous changes during middle adulthood. Many middle-aged adults (i.e., 34–55) experience a reduction in the importance of a role-dominated life. This contributes to some self-examination. Levinson (1978, 1980) indicates that adults go through a period of distress around 40 that is associated with depression and other reactions. This period of adulthood is often called "midlife crisis."

Despite widespread popular belief in the so-called "midlife crisis," however, there is little research support for such a period. Nevertheless, there are midlife transitions. Middle-aged adults experience transitions in launching children, changing careers, facing the death of a parent, and witnessing their own decline in health. The transition may or may not amount to a "midlife crisis." Distress depends upon how one coped with early developmental tasks.

The career problems of middle adulthood often involve early forced retirement or midcareer change. Thus, an interviewer may be responsible for collecting information to redirect an adult's career. For example, Mr. Jenkins, 45, was a successful executive in a nationally recognized hotel chain. He had worked for one employer for more than 20 years and was extremely pleased with his vocational development and personal life. Mr. Jenkins and his wife of 20 years had invested in a large property about 10 years ago. He planned to retire at age 65 and live on it.

During one summer, Mr. Jenkins began developing serious health problems that resulted in extensive surgery. The health problems forced Mr. Jenkins into early retirement. He became depressed and angry over his situation. Six months after his surgery Mr. Jenkins volunteered to come in for career evaluation under the company's employee assistance program. He was still bitter over his forced retirement but had a strong desire to put his 20 years of experience to work. The following excerpt is from an interview conducted with Mr. Jenkins.

Career specialist: I see where you have been with the company for 20 years. It must be difficult to come here to discuss new career directions.
Mr. Jenkins: Yes . . . I never really expected to be in a situation like this. (Some anger in his voice.) I don't know how much you can actually do.
Career specialist: I can see that you're upset and probably don't want to be here. However, I want to try to understand what your needs are.
Mr. Jenkins: Most of what I'm experiencing you will probably never know. I don't understand it myself.

(Twenty minutes pass.)

> **Career specialist:** You told me how junior staff members used you as a resource consultant. In fact, this seems to be something you really enjoyed.
> **Mr. Jenkins:** Well, yes . . . I have been used in that capacity for quite some time.
> **Career specialist:** How would you like to explore the possibility of using your expertise as a consultant to the firm? You could probably work from home and use the phone for all of your consultations.
> **Mr. Jenkins:** That sounds worth exploring . . . where do we go from here?

This dialogue demonstrates the use of a variety of interview skills. First, the interviewer established rapport by acknowledging Mr. Jenkins' years of service. Then the interviewer used reflection of feeling to identify the interviewee's emotional state ("I can see that you're upset"). Twenty minutes later the interviewer was helping Mr. Jenkins explore alternative career options.

Forced retirement can be a devastating experience for a middle-aged adult because of the loss of status and possible reduction of income. Also, satisfaction with one's work contributes significantly to satisfaction with one's life. The interviewer who is sensitive to these factors can be extremely effective in collecting the information needed to address this adult developmental problem. It is also obvious that an interviewer's sensitivity to cross-cultural and cross-gender issues is useful. This sensitivity is especially crucial in dealing with women because of their frequent reluctance to retire (Streib & Schneider, 1971).

Although forced retirement is an unpleasant experience, some middle-aged adults facing it voluntarily reevaluate their career options. Then an interviewer can help them evaluate occupational choices. Levison (1976) describes this process as a reevaluation of aspirations identified during early adulthood. The reevaluation process itself can be a stressful experience. The stress may be heightened for ethnic minorities and women who seek to change.

For example, Dana, age 55, found that, much as she loved being a mother and housewife, these roles were changing. Her children and spouse were less demanding. Dana found that she was devoting less time to direct family needs. That is, being a housewife and mother, which had been her primary occupational choice and the source of her satisfaction, had shrunk to less than 15% of her time and energies. When she realized that her situation had changed, she decided to take a course in accounting at the university. Her rationale was that she would be able to devote more time and energy to herself and the career reentry process. Thirty-one years ago she had obtained an accounting degree from New York University.

Certainly Dana's reevaluation of her roles in the family allowed her to view herself differently. The following discussion is an excerpt from an interview Dana had at the women's career-information center.

> **Dana:** I guess they (the family) don't need me like they once did.
> **Career specialist:** I sounds as if you're beginning to look at your role in the family.
> **Dana:** Well yes . . . I've given them more than 30 years of my life. But it's hard for me to give up my role as mother and wife.
> **Career specialist:** You're feeling some tension as you think about your future. I would be afraid to think about reentering the traditional work force after being away for 30 years, too.
> **Dana:** Well, I am somewhat nervous . . . I have been out of touch.

Career specialist: Look at it this way... You have more than 30 years of experience in the work force. You've made a significant contribution there and I'm sure that will be true during your reentry.

Dana: I never thought of it that way.

The interviewee indicated some concerns about her occupational role ("they don't need me... it's hard for me to give up my role"). The interviewer was quick to use reflection techniques to identify the interviewee's feelings ("you're feeling some tension"). An individual contemplating a midcareer change or reentry experiences a great deal of stress during the developmental phase. Table 7–3 summarizes the developmental tasks that are relevant to adults in their 50 as observed by Okun (1982).

Knowledge of the aforementioned developmental tasks are especially important to an interviewer. Those in the midcareer change process may need some type of acknowledgment of the work completed and reassurance that their new occupational choices will be successful. The interviewer provided as much to Dana by indicating "you've made a significant contribution there and I'm sure that will be true during your reentry." The interviewer instills hope in the interviewee by using these techniques. Rapport during the interview is one of the by-products of using this approach. The overall quality of interactions is improved by a conscientious effort to critique and rate the interview.

Critiquing the Investigative Interview

It is important to assess all interviews to determine how well the interviewer met basic standards of performance. Table 7-4 shows a brief checklist that may be used as a guide for critiquing an interview.

RESEARCH

Research methods may be regarded as the primary means for establishing cause-effect relations among variables. In this endeavor, the usual research involves comparisons of different values of the dependent variable with different values of the independent variable.

Table 7–3 Developmental Tasks in the Fifties

Developmental Tasks	General Issues	Requisite Skills	Significant Others
Renegotiate relationships	Social and community activities	Self care	Aging parents
Learn new roles regarding in-laws; grandparents	Physical changes	Launching of children	In-laws
Make retirement plans	Health	Interpersonal skills	Grandchildren
Take self-health measures	Sex	Planning	Spouse
	Intellectual functioning	Negotiating	Adult offspring
		Caretaking	Friends
			Colleagues
			Supervisees
			Community

Table 7–4 Checklist for Critiquing an Interview

	Rating				
	Excellent				Poor
The interview had a basic structure or organization.	5	4	3	2	1
The interview had a clear direction or focus.	5	4	3	2	1
The interviewer kept the interviewee on task.	5	4	3	2	1
Questions were direct and to the point.	5	4	3	2	1
Interviewee was made to feel relaxed and comfortable.	5	4	3	2	1
Interviewer set an appropriate pace.	5	4	3	2	1
Interviewer made appropriate use of nonverbal behaviors (e.g., eye contact or body posture).	5	4	3	2	1
Interviewer was nonjudgmental and displayed no distracting mannerisms.	5	4	3	2	1
Interviewer made an accurate and concise summary of information obtained during the interview.	5	4	3	2	1

Both can vary on such components as quantity, quality, and type. The independent variable is usually controlled to produce changes in the dependent variable. Two examples: What effect does certain nonverbal behavior (e.g., eye contact) have on interviewee reports of anxiety? Does the use of reflection result in more information being reported by interviewees? These are a few of many research issues (e.g., ethnicity or gender) that could be examined while using an interview as the independent variable.

SUMMARY

Specific physical, psychological, and social changes are associated with adulthood. These developmental issues include midcareer changes, family conflicts, economic factors, and health issues. Interview techniques help provide a basic understanding of these issues. For example, a summary clarifies the perception of the information provided. It also communicates to the interviewee that he or she has been listened to. During the summary, the interviewer can reassure the interviewee and bring the interview to a close. Closure of the interview is best facilitated by asking the interviewee if the information obtained has been accurately summarized. It is also advisable to ask the interviewee if she has any additional information to share. Once the interviewee responds to any additional information, the interview ends.

Effective interviews incorporate cross-cultural and cross-gender factors. These factors can significantly alter the course of an interview. Most interviews lead to decisions.

Interviewing allows interviewers to generate options available in making a particular decision. The interviewer is constantly making decisions throughout the session. The interviewer may generate questions for herself, and these questions may lead to a particular course of action: "What do I need to know now?" "What can I do to get an idea of how this person responds in certain situations?" "Should I pursue a particular issue or change to a different issue?" and so on. The interviewee's answers to these questions arise from an understanding of the basic purposes of the interview. For example, an executive who works with difficult clients may need to know more about new employees. He or she may be interested in knowing how this person responds under social pressure. Typically, the interview generates information about the potential employee's abilities or previous training experiences. The action allows an interviewer to introduce more realistic situations. Therefore, the decision to hire or not to hire is based on the interviewee's response to real situations.

The interviewer poses questions to himself/herself and the interviewee that are designed to facilitate more active decision making. Interviewing requires an interviewer to be spontaneous and creative in posing various questions. The interview may also require establishing scenarios that have the same requirements. This is particularly true when working with adults.

The interviewer needs to assess the effects of past actions, develop new action plans, predict the possible consequences of various alternatives, and decide how to proceed at any particular moment to have a good interview. The interview involves conscious decisions about how to guide the interview toward the goal of decision making.

Interviewing is designed to communicate information systematically and flexibly. The basic goal is to improve the quality of interaction to achieve a particular result. For example, a design engineer raises a particular set of questions to develop appropriate blueprints for a project. A nurse collects a medical history during an interview to ensure appropriate treatment.

Interviewing has always been a personal, subjective effort to gain information and understanding and it remains the most important tool in adult interactions requiring it. The skilled interviewer continues to use skills in relaxing the interviewee, developing an alliance, knowing how to elicit basic information, asking open-ended questions, attending to verbal and nonverbal behaviors, and bringing the interview to a close. It is important to note that a good interviewer stands the best chance of maximizing the interaction between the interviewer and the interviewee. The skilled interviewer also is knowledgeable about the unique developmental tasks associated with midadult life.

SUGGESTED READINGS

Beer, W. R, (1983). *Househusbands: Men and housework in American families.* New York: J. F. Bergin/Praeger.

Campbell, R. E., & Cellini, J. V. (1980). Adult career development. *Counseling and Human Development, 12,* 1–14.

Dillard, J. M. (1985). *Lifelong career planning.* Columbus: Merrill.

Gerstein, M. (1982). Vocational counseling for adults in varied settings: A comprehensive view. *Vocational Guidance Quarterly, 30,* 315–322.

Lewis, J. A., & Lewis, M. D. (1986). *Counseling programs for employees in the workplace.* Monterey, CA: Brooks/Cole.

Model, S. (1981). Housework by husbands: Determinants and implications. *Journal of Family Issues, 2,* 225–237.

Turner, J. S., & Helms, D. B. (1979). *Contemporary adulthood.* Philadelphia: W. B. Sanders.

Vetter, L. (1978). Career counseling for women. In L. W. Harmon, J. M. Birk, L. E. Fitzgerald, & M. F. Tanney (Eds.), *Counseling women* (pp. 75–78). Monterey, CA: Brooks/Cole.

8

Interviewing Older Adults

Michael Duffy
Texas A & M University

A contemporary book on interviewing skills would be incomplete if it ignored the special circumstances and issues in interviewing older adults. Their perspectives, experiences, and needs certainly affect the approach taken to interviewing. Human beings change in predictable ways throughout their lives, and these changes affect the nature of their relationships and interactions.

We can see these differences vividly if we compare conversations between two children, between an adult and a child, and between two adults. As earlier chapters showed, our conversations, both professional and personal, take on a different character with children, adolescents, and young or middle-aged adults. The same is true of interviewing older adults. One of the most important reasons for including this chapter is that many younger professionals are shy about (or simply avoid) dealing with the elderly. They seem to be overwhelmed by the perceived difference of older persons. So, while differences between age groups exist, one of the worst mistakes an interviewer can make is to assume that the older interviewee is *totally different* and therefore incomprehensible. In fact, the similarities between old and young greatly outnumber the differences. The specific interviewing skills described in Chapter 3—probing, clarifying, confronting, focusing, and so forth—apply to any age group and any kind of interview. Interviewing different groups simply means employing the most fundamental of these interviewing skills—carefully listening, attending, and observing. These techniques will help the interviewer to accommodate even subtle differences between persons as well as groups. This chapter provides some basic understanding and guidelines for communicating effectively with older persons. Talking to—interviewing—older adults is simply unavoidable in today's world.

This chapter will discuss several basic characteristics of older adults and compare them with younger persons. A realistic appraisal of aging should emerge from this discussion to help guide the interviewer successfully through the interview stages and objectives described in Chapter 4. So, when interviewing older clients, the interviewer should have a sensitive approach toward, for example, preparing the physical setting, structuring a comfortable relationship, obtaining personal information, and using certain strategies and tactics. These ideas will then be incorporated into a series of concrete guidelines and examples of interviewing older persons. Since gerontology—the study of aging—is relatively recent and rapidly developing, it may help to begin by outlining recent findings about older adults.

A CHANGING PICTURE

Anyone with "an ear to the ground" concerning the changing profile of society cannot fail to notice the increasing prominence of older persons and their concerns. It is difficult to pick up a newspaper today without finding some article or reference to older persons. There is a growing public sensitivity to the needs and preferences of what is the fastest-growing sector of the population. The contributions and impact of older citizens in politics, business, science, the professions, and the creative arts are becoming clear. The needs of older persons in the areas of health, economics, housing, public affairs, and human services are becoming more pressing. Furthermore, older consumers' preferences are receiving greater attention in the marketplace. Politicians, in turn, can no longer afford to neglect an appeal to the older voter; the content of political platforms at all levels reflects this awareness.

Thus a rapidly changing public image of older Americans has emerged in the last few years. The evidence of their growth as a segment of the population has been clear for the last 20 years. Increases in births over the last 100 years and the proportion of those born surviving into their late years has dramatically increased both the absolute and relative numbers of older persons (Atchley, 1980).

Since 1900, the proportion of older people in the U.S. population has increased at least sevenfold (U.S. Bureau of Census, 1976). This does not involve a change in the human lifespan as such; there have always been individuals who have survived into their 80s and 90s. What has changed is the *proportion* of those who survive into late life. And the greatest increase is among the old-old (75 years plus), the fastest-growing segment of the population. This, in turn, is creating crises in the structure of current social, economic, and health care systems such as Social Security and Medicare, which were based on population projection and policies that are now obsolete. Aging is here to stay. Persons over 65 who represented 4% of the population in 1900 now account for 12% and the projection for the year 2020 is 18% (U.S. Bureau of Census, 1977). This is a trend for the future; these are the people who will affect the conduct of business and professional life—and the process of interviewing.

Interviewing an Older Population

Interviewing skills are required not only by social service professionals but by any person who wants to be interpersonally effective. Business people and professionals are becoming more aware that increasing numbers of their clients are older persons. Again, while this change has been occurring for some time, the full impact has only recently become obvious. Retailers are realizing the need to be attuned to preferences, needs, and tastes of older persons in clothing, household goods, transportation, recreation, and food. Representatives of service industries are learning to change their perception of the "cranky" older person to an intelligent, often assertive consumer. Lawyers and financial consultants are expected to deal increasingly with wills, estates, and trusts. The courts are less willing to award care givers "blanket" powers of attorney that reduce handicapped older persons' decision-making power. Physicians are noticing that more and more of their patients are older persons; and pharmacists recognize older persons as the largest consumers of pharmaceutical products. Acute-care hospitals often derive over 50% of their income from Medicare reimbursements and are having to seriously adapt medical services to meet the needs of older patients. While the current group of older persons underutilizes mental health services, psychologists and mental-health counselors are facing the need to "market" mental health services to older patients who have tended to use the family physician as a surrogate care giver. Architects and urban planners increasingly must consider the special residential needs of impoverished or handicapped elderly people as well as the design preferences of more affluent older people. All these professionals need better skills in interacting with and interviewing older persons. They need at least a basic understanding of the aging process to offer advice and solutions that address the preferences and needs of older persons.

This list is far from exhaustive, but it indicates clearly that the business and professional communities need to be more attuned to the phenomenon of an older consumer. This is a problem, since most professional education and training has been geared to younger adults; it is rare, even today, to find educational curricula that have any substantial reference to older adults. The following section will examine some key issues that help in understanding the experiences of the older person.

Basic Assumptions

Perhaps the most troublesome negative assumption younger people make is that older people are inherently different. They cannot see the older persons they encounter as themselves in a few years. What they don't realize is the similarities between older and younger persons outnumber the differences. Perhaps this lack of understanding between the generations results in part from the older generation's typical reticence in sharing their inner lives and vulnerabilities with their children. This reluctance can deprive children of both a "real" role model and of the opportunity for intimacy with their parents. The net result of this misunderstanding is the younger person's assumption that he cannot deal effectively with them.

Another factor that inhibits conversation between younger and older adults is the role assigned to the older person. For the younger person, it is all too easy to assume a childlike posture, putting the older person in a parental position. This reduces the power and effectiveness of the younger person's role as a professional and often causes her to act with too much deference and too little objectivity. Far from helping, this causes the older person to feel misunderstood and unhelped. As a variation on this theme, the professional artificially reverses these roles and gains power by assuming a parental role. Older persons often complain of being treated like infants by their adult children. Interviewers can be tempted to do the same thing in the attempt to feel adequate in a relationship with an older person. This is simply not effective and usually results in unsatisfactory interaction for both parties.

The interviewee may also trigger these inappropriate roles. He may try to reduce the professional's authority by reducing her status, perhaps to offset the inherent power of her position. The following statements are obvious clues to this type of maneuver:

— "Young lady (young man), there is something I'd like you to tell me. . . ."
— "You probably wouldn't understand this, but. . . ."
— " . . . but that was probably before your time."
— "How long have you been a . . . ?"
— "May I ask how old you are?"

Generally, however, clients or customers come to a professional because they need something—not to score points. They focus on their question or problem, rarely on the interviewer's adequacy or experience. The latter issues will only come into focus if the professional becomes self-conscious about his relative age or experience. Clients will generally assume the interviewer is competent unless she gives them reason to think otherwise!

Of course, the interviewer's helpfulness will be limited by his actual level of skill in his business or profession. While it is important to recognize those limitations, it is rarely helpful to admit them. The trick in dealing with older, perhaps more experienced persons, is neither to oversell nor undersell one's authority, but simply to be oneself. This allows the interviewer to attend to the needs of the older person he is serving and to listen intently.

What can the interviewer do if he does encounter some of the provocative comments illustrated here? While it is reasonable to feel intimidated or discounted, the professional should attempt (often with difficulty) *not* to react to the person on the basis of these feelings. Certainly he should be aware of these feelings, since they often indicate important qualities of the client. To deny them is to fail to learn from the experience. Then, however, the professional must step back from the feelings and avoid reacting to the threat with a childlike (submissive) or dictatorial (controlling) response. Just listen and respond directly.

One background issue may further clarify some of the points mentioned here. Often, a facility for dealing with older interviewees parallels a facility for dealing with one's own parents as authority figures. Many of us, even in our 30s and 40s are still struggling to develop an adult relationship with our own parents. An encounter with an older person may trigger an association with our parental relationship that leads us to react in ways that surprise us—perhaps a timidity or rebelliousness. And, naturally enough, that behavior may in turn trigger the older person to deal with the interviewer as he would with his own children. If the interviewer is aware of these dynamics, then the context of a professional encounter may urge her to remedy this. If she is to succeed as a professional, she cannot afford to react as a child—even in the face of provocation. She may even be able to attain a developmental maturity in her professional work that has eluded her in her family life.

A Realistic Appraisal of Aging

The preceding discussion points up the similarities between older and younger people. The implication of this in older persons is the importance of avoiding the assumption that inherent differences exist. Interviewees must be allowed to act as they wish, rather than as we construe them. Thus, many of the basic interviewing skills discussed elsewhere in this book are relevant to communicating with older persons. The most basic mistake is assuming that little learned elsewhere applies to the elderly—a belief that keeps many professionals from working with older adults. It is also true, however, that the diligent professional will attempt to develop a sophisticated understanding of older persons' experience. As stated earlier, aging is not something that happens to "old people" but is a constant process in our own lives.

Age Differences

Older persons are different from younger partly because of biological, psychological, and social development. Decreased acuity in hearing and vision (McFarland, 1968) and limited mobility seriously affect communication and social interaction. Aging can mean a loss of high-frequency sounds. This hearing loss often causes interviewers to speak at higher volume—with little success. Actually, we need to speak lower, not louder, and perhaps move closer to the older person. When the client must complete paperwork, he may need more light since older persons often require 50% more illumination than younger persons. And if an older person seems to move hesitantly, it is helpful to realize that with age we lose sensitivity to relative intensities of color and light. We can forget how color and shade give important clues to the positioning of objects and levels—like furniture and steps. Increased slowness or caution in older persons is not eccentricity but a response to definable physiological changes.

The best way to respond to these differences is usually not help but patience. If the professional slows down his own pace to match his interviewee's, then these differences will not be important in the interview. An overly solicitous interviewer can appear patronizing and interfere with the purposes of the interview, however. The best guideline is to be sensitive to the interviewee's limitations and offer assistance when and if it seems needed.

Some cognitive changes with age affect the learning process. In an era that stressed the importance of timed tasks, it was assumed that poorer performance in the elderly implied a cognitive decline. Actually, older persons—like many younger persons—generally do better on untimed tasks. This suggests that the real issue is change, rather than decline, in learning and performance. Similarly, manufacturers are beginning to realize that what the older employee lacks in speed of performance is often compensated for by precision and reliability (Welford, 1977).

Experience Differences

Changes in an older person are not merely effected by maturity. Growing older, managing life's problems and challenges, also produces a worldliness that would be impossible at a younger age. Living in a nursing home, for example, with its inherent institutional constraints and loss of so many daily freedoms, presents crises that would defeat a younger person. Older people have learned to survive life's hazards and turn experiences to their advantage. They are survivors. This better-developed perspective, maturity, and judgment ability add an element to formal intellectual ability and learning that is often called wisdom. Traditional academic performance represents only some dimensions of intellectual ability; wisdom results from the maturing and mastery of these abilities. Current research (Willis & Baltes, 1980) supports the ideas that intellectual development continues throughout life and does not stop in the early 20s. The ability to make shrewd judgments about situations and people is an advanced form of intellectual capability.

The old saying "there is no fool like an old fool," however, provides an important counterpoint. We cannot assume that older persons have benefited from experience. If an older client seems to be talking nonsense, the interviewer should not suspend her critical faculties in favor of his assumed greater experience. Many older persons have become "stuck" in their developmental maturity and continue to make poor judgments about life and their situations. We can make mistakes at any point of life, regardless of experience and maturity. This occurs in part because we do not develop evenly in all parts of our lives and we often have blind spots, vulnerabilities, and a lack of specific experience that can handicap us.

Older persons, however, have had opportunities for development unavailable to younger persons. An interviewer in his 20s can realistically expect to find certain personal limitations in dealing with a person in his 60s. A young, unmarried marriage counselor will be probably less effective in resolving an elderly couple's marital problems than an older, married counselor of equal ability. A young architect, realtor, or financial consultant may have trouble understanding the residential needs of an older client who has owned a home for many years. This is the moment to recognize one's limitations and refer to an older colleague whose experience is more comparable to the interviewee's. Unfortunately, recognizing one's limitations and being willing to refer is precisely the fruit of experience. Younger professionals may be tempted to "prove themselves" in situations that overtax their expertise or experience.

Context and Situational Differences

Interviewers should realize that the structure and quality of the older interviewee's life may differ from their own, both past and present. Many differences typically attributed to old age are in fact the result of being born into and living in a different world. When you reach the chronological age of your interviewee you will not view life in the same way, either. It is often assumed, for example, that sexual attitudes become more conservative with age, whereas they are actually more influenced by the social and sexual climate that was prevalent during the person's formative younger days. Further, becoming more mature and circumspect about sex is not the same as becoming conservative. This perspective on the meaning of differences between people at any point of time suggests that our *cohort* (birth group) or *period* (historical experience) often have more influence on behavior than our chronological age.

We must also be sensitive to an important condition of the elderly in our contemporary society. With increased modernization, the social status of older people has tended to decline (Cowgill, 1974). Elderly people today are often at a serious disadvantage. The average income reduction at retirement is 50%, and, while the elderly are proportionally the most frequent health-care consumers, their medical needs are often underserved. Public health-care reimbursement systems are woefully inadequate and private group coverage often vanishes at retirement. In general, the current socioeconomic status of older persons often does not reflect their earlier position. As we deal with older clients and consumers, we frequently need to help them find viable solutions to these problems and needs. These issues very much affect the attitudes older persons bring to the interview situation.

Personality Differences

A popular belief is that people become eccentric as they age—the truth is that they just become more obvious. Most recent research (Neugarten, 1977) and professional experience point to a striking consistency in personality over the life span. Although some aspects of personality functioning are probably biologically determined, personality style generally involves the characteristic ways a person develops and adapts in facing life's challenges and interpersonal struggles. Some of these adaptations are healthy; others are only apparently so. During the young and middle years we tend to moderate our effect on other persons, behaving in socially approved and self-protective ways. As we mature, we gain in self-assurance and are more willing to risk being ourselves with others. Thus, in later life, our traits—positive and negative—become more apparent to others. Very few characteristics or problems (except biologically caused mental illness) have their origins in late life.

Younger people are often surprised by the direct manner of older persons, which they frequently perceive as aggressiveness or crankiness. An interviewer may find their directness and assertiveness disconcerting, but if he can avoid being defensive, the elderly are often more candid than younger clients. Older people have often reached the stage where they know what they want and are less hesitant to say so. A younger client might be reluctant to confront the interviewer, to avoid making the interaction unpleasant; an older client is usually more willing to take the risk.

Being tuned in to an individual's personality style—and trying to avoid being overwhelmed by it—is an important skill for two reasons. First, attending to personality characteristics will help the interviewer better understand the person and avoid some of the pitfalls that could occur in the interaction. Noticing that the older person is, for example, either very deferential or very aggressive will help the professional avoid being reactive to this behavior. Second, understanding the interviewee's personal style will help better meet her needs and fulfill the interview objectives. The client's interpersonal style (often the most important aspect of personality) frequently results in unmet needs and confusion in other parts of his life. Understanding this allows the interviewer to behave differently than the other people in their lives. Human beings will usually continue ineffective behaviors as long as other people in their lives respond in predictable (if ineffective) ways. Unless the interviewer is a therapist, however, confronting the client about his personality is generally counterproductive. But the interviewer should be acutely aware of personality factors to avoid being trapped in nonproductive, confusing interactions.

The best clue to a client's personality style is the interviewer's own feelings and reactions. If she is feeling anger, dislike, enjoyment, affection, pity, boredom, or impatience, this feeling is very likely telling her something important about the client's personality. (On the other hand, if she routinely feels any of these emotions with many clients, she should examine her own personality style and perhaps get some feedback from colleagues.) Using her own feelings as a barometer to understand an interviewee's personality assumes that the interviewer can allow herself to experience negative feelings toward the client. Professional interviewers are often trained to develop positive feelings toward clients to facilitate the relationship. This is a reasonable idea but it sometimes encourages us to neglect or "block" important negative reactions to the interviewee. Certainly a positive attitude is needed to interview a person, but this positive attitude is impossible unless the interviewer is willing to attend to her negative feelings. Failing to do so risks sending a double message that is usually transparent to the person and undermines confidence in the interviewer's sincerity.

Finally, as stated earlier, personality characteristics of the elderly are often more obvious. In addition, younger people tend to make excuses for the behavior of older persons out of a misguided sense of respect. An older person who cuts in at a store line is often excused where a younger person is confronted. To repeat an earlier point, these behaviors rarely originate in old age; this person has probably exploited situations throughout life! Thus, critical judgment is necessary when dealing with the elderly.

This discussion is intended to encourage a sensitive attitude and mindset in approaching the various stages of the interview process as described in Chapter 4. Not only is this information important in preparing for the interview, both physically and psychologically, it is critical to sizing up the situation, targeting relevant issues, and planning realistically for the older interviewee's future. The following guidelines are offered to assist in a variety of typical situations encountered when interviewing older adults.

GUIDELINES FOR INTERVIEWING OLDER ADULTS

This section attempts to distill what has been discussed so far into a series of practical guidelines for the interview. Whenever possible, the guideline will be translated into concrete interview statements and questions as well as illustrations of what to avoid. Chapter 3 described in detail the anatomy of the interview with its various components of building rapport, clarifying roles expectations, setting goals, and implementing strategies and plans. These elements describe *what* the interview is about and are relevant to the interview process, regardless of age. The following guidelines attempt to convey *how* the interview might be conducted with the older client. They focus on some of the qualitative differences in interviewing older persons.

Listen Intently

The basic prerequisite for helping clients is to understand them, and the only way to understand is to develop the capacity for listening intently. Sometimes the hustle and bustle of a busy and often noisy office makes it difficult to slow down and focus completely on the interviewee's needs. At other times, clients are anxious or preoccupied and commanding their attention is difficult. Here is an illustration:

> **Older person:** Thank you for seeing me. I'll try not to take up too much of your time. But I just feel I need some help in making this decision. (Client is feeling apologetic for taking your time—a clue that you may seem preoccupied and insensitive.)
>
> **Interviewer:** That's fine. This is a busy morning but I also think that this is an important decision. Let's take a few minutes to talk about it (closing the door and offering a chair—clear signs you are willing to talk and listen). Let's sit down. Now, what is the most important issue for us to discuss? (Getting down to business and prioritizing, and so making the best use of scarce time.)

Interviewers should try to develop the skill of slowing down internally, shutting out other concerns and focusing on the older client. Sitting down helps, but often interviewers who feel less in control of the conversation fear they will get "trapped" and find it more difficult to terminate the interview if they sit. Another helpful technique is taking a deep breath to slow down—rapid breathing both reflects and maintains a hectic pace and inattention. It is much better to devote a short time willingly and with full attention than a longer time reluctantly and seeming preoccupied. When closing the interview, an approach like the following is appropriate:

Interviewer: I'd like to finish now ("I need to finish" or "I must finish" often sound like excuses and invite disbelief or challenge). Think about what we've discussed and get back to me when you reach a decision or need to discuss it further. Okay?

Ask Simple, Straightforward Questions

What may seem like a reasonable question or comment to us may meet with silence from the client. This can make the interviewer feel stupid, inept, or naive and perhaps think that she lacks the life experience to understand this person. When unsure, an interviewer may overcompensate by asking long, repetitive questions, as the following example demonstrates:

> **Insurance agent:** Well, how do you feel about your current insurance policy? Do you think it adequately meets your needs? Maybe I could show some of our other products? I mean, do we need to talk about a change? Is it adequate?

When this kind of question prompts silence, it may simply indicate that the interviewee does not know where to start. Simple, direct questions are often better: "Are you unhappy with your policy?" for example. Sometimes interviewers will ask a series of different questions, each requiring a separate response:

> **Insurance agent:** How do you feel about our insurance policies? How does your husband feel? Have you looked at any of our other products? I wonder if you have considered a term policy? Or maybe you feel better about a whole life policy?

Often such a barrage will result in silence by the interviewee. Some may answer the least important question, or one that was not asked. Again, a simple question will be more effective: "Would you like me to explain our various policies?"

When the interviewer has asked a straightforward question, he must have confidence in it and not panic at a silence from the interviewee. Asking the question again, or rephrasing it, is usually interruptive. When silence follows a direct question, it frequently indicates that it was a *good* question and requires the respondent to think about it before answering. If the question was unclear, the interviewee—especially an older person—will usually ask for clarification.

Sometimes even a good question will generate an oppositional, almost aggressive response. This can be disconcerting and lead the interviewer to feel unsure, to back off, and even to move on to a safer question:

> **Insurance agent:** Would you like me to explain our various policies?
> **Older person:** I don't think that will be necessary, thank you.
> **Insurance agent:** (Taken aback) Oh, . . . okay. . . well . . . how are you liking living in our community, Mrs. Beeson?
> **Older person:** (Abruptly). . . . Fine, thank you.
> **Insurance agent:** (Puzzled silence.)

A more effective response might be:

> **Insurance agent:** (Recovering and exploring further) Perhaps you don't feel that we have the best product for your needs?

Older person: Well . . . I don't know . . . but, frankly, I wasn't very happy with your secretary's abrupt manner.

Insurance agent: I'm sorry about that. I'll look into it. Thank you for your frankness . . . it helps to have this kind of feedback (pausing to see if client wants to discuss it further). I'll be glad to help you with the information.

Older person: Yes, I think that would be fine.

As we discussed earlier, older persons are more apt to be direct about their dissatisfaction; although it may be difficult, a nondefensive response will usually speed the interview forward.

Be in Control of the Interview

Even seasoned professionals will at times feel intimidated by an interviewee. Usually, upon reflection, some feature of the person's interpersonal style triggers this feeling. As mentioned earlier, an interviewer may feel cowed by an older person's age and authority. She may be overly deferential and think that the subject is more in control than she is. At this point it is important to avoid engaging in a struggle for control, interrupting the person. The interviewer can benefit from an internal dialogue with herself, as in the following example:

Interviewer: (Thinking) Okay . . . slow down. Don't overreact. This person has come for assistance. Just listen carefully for awhile. . . . Notice the way the client is dealing with you. It may help to understand him.

This kind of thinking can help the interviewer regain a sense of control and confidence. Ironically, the way to be in control is not to be preoccupied with controlling the client. Effective control resides in authority, not dominance.

Another situation frequently leads to a loss of perceived control. When the interviewer needs brief answers to a series of structured questions, the older person may digress or reminisce. This slows the interview down, as illustrated here:

Nurse: Have you ever had hay fever or any other allergic disorders?

Older patient: Well, that's an interesting question. I haven't, but as a matter of fact my husband has always suffered from allergies. That's why we moved here. And then, of course, the jobs were better here at that time. I remember our first day in town. . . .

At this point, the interviewer begins to get impatient and looks for an opening or a pause. To simply cut the person off may seem impolite and indicate (correctly) a lack of interest. A more effective response is to keep listening with interest for a moment and look for an opportunity to draw the person naturally into the next question:

Nurse: So, allergies have really had an effect on your life. . . . (Assertively) Now, let me ask you this: Have you ever been subject to migraine headaches?

Older people often enjoy answering questions about themselves—especially about health—and their digressions are usually due to the evocative nature of the material. Their comments are usually interesting, if the interviewer is not too preoccupied with moving along, and even another few seconds of attention will give the professional a connection that can lead to the next question. Another method of structuring the situation is to give advance warning of the nature of the task, as the nurse does here:

> **Nurse:** I need to ask you a series of questions about your health. There are about 170 questions in all. I think you'll find them interesting, but so that we can finish in time you'll probably find me moving along pretty quickly. Okay?

Another issue is relevant here. Interviewers and teachers have over the years decided that the older person's attention span is much shorter than other adults', so interviews must not go beyond 15–20 minutes. This is simply not borne out by experience. Attention is not a problem for older persons if the interview is interesting and engaging. Older persons do often have a lower tolerance for inconsequential material—and they will say so. Older learners are often simultaneously more critical and more engrossed than young learners.

Don't Underestimate Your Ability to Understand

The age and experience of an older interviewee or commonly held myths about old age may lead the interviewer to approach the conversation with hesitancy. Will the person find a suggestion simplistic? Will she disapprove of the interviewer's attitudes? Will she be very conservative? Will she realize how inexperienced the interviewer is? An interviewee of any age comes to an interviewer because she needs something from him; she is not immediately focused on his attitudes or competence. This will rarely be an issue, as explained earlier, unless the professional is so self-conscious that he draws attention to his self-doubts. It can be quite disconcerting for an interviewee to sense a lack of confidence in the professional. Some nurturing persons will assume a protective attitude toward the interviewer. Others will find some excuse to leave. And older persons will generally deal with their doubts directly.

The interviewer should underestimate neither his competence nor his ability to understand an older person's experience. If he listens carefully, he will discover that much about his own life experience is relevant. In other cases he will find that he has managed some aspect of his life better than the interviewee and can be most helpful. Consider the following exchange:

> **Older person:** I really feel pretty unhappy. I realize that I really don't like my husband. I sometimes think I would like to get a divorce, but that seems such a terrible thing. . . . What do you think of this?
>
> **Pastor:** (Stunned that such an old person would be thinking such things.) Surely that would not be necessary? You have lived together for so long . . . What would your children think? I'm sure if you work at it you'll find a solution.

Or consider this response to the same statement.

> **Pastor:** (Feeling like a child being asked to resolve his parent's marital conflicts.) Well . . . that's very difficult. It's really hard to know. . . I wonder if it may not be helpful to talk to Reverend Williams . . . (wanting to escape).

These responses fail to take seriously the older person's request for understanding and help. Both interviewers, overly preoccupied with their own attitudes and feelings, have avoided listening and trying to tune in to the interviewee's feelings. Instead of tolerating their own reactions and putting the interviewee's needs first, they cut the person off. The interviewee probably feels unaccepted, ashamed at such thoughts, or simply misunderstood. These responses fail to recognize that the older interviewee is first a human being—just like the interviewer—with the same need for intimate, satisfactory relationships. The interviewers, thrown off balance, fail to reflect on their own experience as a resource in understanding the person's pain. A more helpful response might be:

Pastor: (Acknowledging the person's strong and mixed feelings.) This must be very sad for you . . . and, I imagine, a little frightening, after so many years devoted to this relationship . . . (affirming the legitimacy of the feelings.) I know it must be hard to admit these feelings to yourself. . . .

Older person: (Relieved at this acceptance.) Yes . . . it's all very confusing. Sometimes I think I must be crazy. . . my husband just acts like he doesn't know what I'm talking about. . . .

Pastor: (Showing further understanding.) . . . You you must have felt very alone in all of this? . . .

Older person: I do! I'm not sure my friends would understand . . . they all seem so settled, I think . . . and I feel they would disapprove.

Pastor: Okay. Well, let's talk about some of the things that are bothering you. . . .

This approach acknowledges the legitimacy of the interviewee's feelings and allows the interview to move forward. Her feelings may not accurately reflect her husband's attitude toward her, but they are very real. Unless an interviewer can accept and discuss them with her, a more objective view will not be reached. Feelings are usually based on accurate perceptions of a situation. They are rarely wrong and can be trusted. The problem is in interpreting the meaning of those perceptions regarding, for example, others' motivations. Our interpretation may or may not be correct, depending on the attitudes and prejudices through which we "screen" our perceptions.

The interviewer should never assume he cannot understand. He may feel confused, certainly. But he should stay there, ask further questions, and listen.

Try Not to Be Preoccupied with Age Differences

Rather than listening to what an older person wants, the interviewer may respond to an assumption of what she thinks the client should want. A salesperson, for example, may have fixed ideas about what is appropriate for an older customer:

Realtor: Yes, Mr. Gardener, how can I help you?

Older customer: Could you give me some details of that property you have listed on Cedar Drive? I'm looking around for a new house at the moment and I rather liked the sound of that one. What is the asking price?

Realtor: (Ignoring the question.) Yes, that's a rather large modern house with a swimming pool. . . . You know, I rather think you might be more satisfied with one of our other properties on Lee Street . . . it's a more traditional design in a very nice, quiet neighborhood. The Cedar Drive area is a much younger family area . . . lots of kids. . . .

Older customer: (With a twinge of annoyance.) Well, I may want to hear about that one later, but right now I'm interested in hearing about the Cedar Drive home. . . .

Realtor: (Still avoiding the direct question, and beginning to wonder about this older client's credit rating.) And I think you might find the Lee Street house more favorable financially. . .

The interviewer should not assume he knows the tastes of older people—this is a sure way to lose a client. And he shouldn't assume that older persons are financially irresponsible—they can still add and subtract! The professional should always start by honoring their expressed desires. At a later point, when the interviewee thinks his needs have been understood, he will be willing to listen to the interviewer's reservations or advice. Well-intentioned interviewers or salespersons often mistakenly force their notions of good taste on older persons in clothing, food, finances, vacations, living choices, and even mates. Family members are notorious for this. Older persons sometimes will date covertly out of embarrassment and fear of their adult children's reactions.

Be Direct

Many of our social interactions are indirect. We make our criticisms oblique, lest we offend. We hint that we want something rather than directly ask for it, so we never have to face being turned down. One of the most important characteristics of a good interviewer is a willingness to deal with situations directly. Even experienced professionals, however, can become cautious and tentative with older interviewees. This is ironic, since older persons are among the first to appreciate directness. Asking a difficult question directly, identifying a problem clearly, naming a previously hidden fear: These may seem impolite and risk hurting the client. But they usually experience a sense of relief when the interviewer is willing to do this. "Beating around the bush" is rarely helpful, as this example demonstrates:

> **Counselor:** (Sensing marital difficulties.) Oh, by the way, how is your husband doing these days?
>
> **Older client:** All right, thanks. . . . sometimes he has a little trouble with his arthritis. . . . Why, have you seen him recently? (Unsure, but a little suspicious now.) He didn't mention talking to you.
>
> **Counselor:** (Backing off.) Well, not really. . . I just wondered how you two are doing these days.
>
> **Older client:** (Wondering if their conflict is obvious, but not feeling free to ask.) Oh, fine . . . thanks. (Changing the subject.) anyway, maybe you can give me some suggestions about dealing with my son. . . .

In this case, the relationship between the parents may have had great relevance to solving the problem with an adult son. But the interviewer did not trust his instincts enough to deal with this directly. Maybe it wasn't his place to raise this issue. Maybe the wife would be offended. Maybe he would be told to mind his own business! With all these doubts, he lost the opportunity to get to a problem. A better approach, especially if the interviewer is in a helping profession, would be to deal with the issue directly, as in this example.

> **Counselor:** (Sensing marital difficulties.) Are there disagreements between you and your husband on this issue?
>
> **Older client:** (Silent for a moment.) Well . . . actually, we have argued about what to do with our son. He feels I'm being too easy on him. He has always felt that way.
>
> **Counselor:** (Inviting further exploration.) Would you like to talk about it?

Older client: (With a sigh.) I think I should.

A good interviewer can free a client from the bonds of social appropriateness by a willingness to raise difficult issues directly. We often feel we are very alone in dealing with our problems and handicaps. We know what they are; we are pretty sure others know what they are. But no one is willing to mention them, and we would be embarrassed to. Direct confrontation can be a relief.

Don't Assume Issues Are Age-related

In talking to an older person, a younger person may assume implicitly that the issues under discussion are somehow related to the interviewee's age. In the interview situation this can lead to misunderstanding and to advice that is insensitive to the person's needs. Consider the following conversation:

Older patient: Doctor, I've been meaning to come in for awhile. I've been feeling embarrassed about this, but in the last few months I have been having more and more difficulty remembering things.
Doctor: (Probing for more detail.) Tell me what kind of things, Mrs. Perkins.
Older patient: Well, it's remembering dates and phone numbers and those kinds of things. I find I have to write everything down or I'll forget. Last week I forgot my dental appointment and awhile ago I even forgot my daughter's birthday. . . . she was very hurt and I was too embarrassed to explain what happened. My husband is not used to having to think about those kinds of things. And he has been telling me that I have changed . . . that I seem irritable and sometimes mean to him. . . .
Doctor: (Registering that Mrs. Perkins is 73 years old and focusing on her memory rather than her mood changes.) Well, you know that when you get a little older (trying to be tactful) memory does tend to fail a little—I'll bet you can still remember things from your early life. . . .
Older patient: Some . . . but even I think I'm not as clear about what happened in the past as I used to be . . .
Doctor: (Ignoring this lack of agreement.) This kind of memory loss in later life is quite normal, but I agree it is very difficult to cope with (assuming her mood change is a reaction to difficulty in remembering).
Older patient: (Unsure.) Well, if you think that is what it is . . .
Doctor: I do, and I think writing things down is a very good way to help your memory.

The physician, while sensitive to the older patient's distress, reached the premature conclusion that failing memory was related to the aging process as such. His patient, while wanting to comply, is left feeling unsure about the accuracy of the diagnosis and whether the physician's suggestions will be adequate. Some degree of memory loss is frequent in later life and often due to normative changes. But it also has other causes unrelated to the aging process. Memory loss, especially with mood changes, can be caused by depression. It can also signal the beginning stages of Alzheimer's disease, which affects both long- and short-term memory. Memory loss can also be a symptom of severe (pernicious) anemia, especially when accompanied by mood and personality changes.

This example shows clearly how even a professional interviewer can be led astray and reach premature conclusions by assuming that the older person's behavior is related to aging itself. Here, the interviewer would have done better to suspend judgement and follow up on other elements of the patient's problem, as follows:

Doctor: Tell me more about your husband's comments about your "meanness."
Older patient: He says I snap at him and I'm not as kind to him as I usually am.
Doctor: Is he right?
Older patient: I don't know. I don't intend to be mean . . . but I suppose he must feel that way. I certainly don't feel very happy these days. I don't seem to have much energy.
Doctor: Let's talk some more about this unhappiness and lack of energy (checking out the possibility that the memory loss may be related to depression).

A further example from health care is the stereotyped view younger people may have about sexuality in older persons. Even health professionals may believe that a lack of sexual activity and interest in an older person is normal and appropriate; some even consider it the "decent" attitude. In fact, research (Verwoerdt, Pfeiffer, & Wang, 1969) indicates that while some decline in the male sexual response may be normal, this is not the case with women. In the following case, the interviewer actively avoids the automatic assumption that sexual difficulties result from aging:

Older person: Since my retirement, my wife and I have had almost no sex life . . . and I thought that when things slowed down we would enjoy having sex even more.
Interviewer: That's very disappointing. . . .
Older person: It really is! I've tried to talk about it, but Jean seems distant and doesn't want to discuss it. This has been nine months now and I felt I had to get some advice.
Interviewer: Yes, that does seem like a long time. . . .
Older person: Do you think Jean's just less interested in sex because she's getting older. Maybe I'm just going to have to accept that (feeling dejected).
Interviewer: Maybe . . . but tell me more about Jean being distant from you (exploring the quality of the relationship). . . .

In this case, sexual performance may not be the real problem. Rather, sexual difficulties may reflect changes in the pattern of their relationship following retirement. Retirement, like other major life changes, can upset as well as improve the style of life and intimate relations. This is not an age change, but rather a change that is merely associated with later life in our society. An ability and willingness to make this kind of distinction is critical for the professional interviewing older persons.

To illustrate this issue, consider this exchange between an architect and an older client concerning the client's wishes for the design of a home:

Architect: Let's start by getting some general ideas of the kinds of things you like in a home.
Older person: Well, first of all we would like to have a quiet, peaceful environment to live in. Another thing, we would like it to be relatively compact—nothing too large. . . .
Architect: I understand. . . . So, really, at this point of your life you don't need anything big, with a lot of work—and you want to be away from noisy kids. . . .
Older person: (Taken aback.) Well, you could put it that way. . . . but really those are just our preferences—always have been. Here, let me show you some pictures of the house we built in San Francisco (attempting to correct the interviewer's impression).

The interviewer would probably never have formed this impression had the person been younger. Because the interviewee was older, the interviewer wrongly assumed that "small" and "quiet" were related to being old rather than representing a consistent preference. The person felt stereotyped because of her age, and misunderstood and the interview was off to a bad start—possibly causing her to lack confidence in the architect's competence.

Again, the message is the same: The interviewer cannot assume that the older interviewee's attitudes, problems, preferences, behaviors, and needs are directly attributable to chronological age. To do so is to risk misunderstanding the person and therefore risk being ineffective.

Listen to the Older Person's Own View of the Situation

Even professional interviewers commonly will listen to everyone's account of the situation—except the older person's! It is as if the older person's views, opinions, decisions, and feelings are judged to be less "reliable" than those of other persons who are "responsible" for them, such as younger relatives, adult children, and other professionals. This is particularly true when the older person is debilitated and therefore dependent on (and vulnerable to) others' assistance. Children are often treated the same way.

Upon admission to a nursing home, for example, a family member—typically an adult daughter—is expected to be responsible for the patient and act as a liaison with the nursing home. The administrative staff will interview her upon admission of the parent and will contact her when problems arise or major decisions must be made. The nursing home interviewer commonly relies greatly on the family members' opinions, judgments and feelings about the situation at hand, and fails to solicit the patient's. This can lead the resident to resist any decisions that have been made affecting him.

Life in an institution and dependence on intensive health care will undoubtedly be constraining, and the older nursing home resident is likely to resist decisions to some extent. If nursing home administrators would take the time to carefully interview the resident and consult him about his wishes and feelings, however, the impact of these decisions could be lessened. In the following example, the administrator is discussing with the resident her wish to go home and live in her own house (a constant theme with many residents):

> **Administrator:** (Closing the door of the resident's room and sitting down.) Mrs. Peters, Nurse Albright tells me that you very much want to go home. Would you like to discuss this?
>
> **Resident:** Yes, I want to go home. I don't feel I need to be here among all these sick people—it makes me feel worse! I could manage fine at home. . . .
>
> **Administrator:** (Avoiding arguing this last point even though valid objections exist.) Well, we certainly don't want to keep you here if it's not needed (conveying an openness to discuss the issue). . . . Why don't you tell me what is most difficult for you about being in the nursing home?
>
> **Resident:** Well, I feel very out of place here—I don't feel part of it. . . . I don't feel there is anyone here I can talk to. . . .
>
> **Administrator:** (Reflecting back her understanding.) I imagine that must make you feel pretty lonely. . . .
>
> **Resident:** Well . . . yes, I do, I suppose. And all those activity programs don't help, either. . . .

The administrator in this case has finally avoided getting into an argument with the resident by not countering her feeling (wanting to go home) with facts (her need for institutional care). If an argument had ensued, the interview would have been essentially finished. Avoiding this conflict allowed the interviewer to explore the resident's feelings further and possibly arrive at a solution that would be more effective than simply "going home." Most importantly, the resident felt listened to and therefore more willing to discuss the issue.

This outcome is very different from a typical ineffective pattern that such exchanges follow—for example:

Administrator: How are you this morning, Mrs. Peters?
Resident: Not too good. . . . I just want to go home.
Administrator: (Feeling a need to oppose this.) Well now, Mrs. Peters, you know that your family only wants the best for you. . . .

Here, the interviewer emphasizes the family's wishes and the resident's medical needs. He makes statements (which provoke argument) rather than asking questions (which help explore the resident's feelings and wishes).

Even when older persons are not institutionalized and are independent, younger persons may feel inclined to take responsibility for them. In the following example an older woman has finally decided that her marital relationship has deteriorated to such an extent that she is considering separation and possibly divorce. An adult daughter accompanies her to an interview with a lawyer. The daughter is feeling both worried and responsible for the outcome, and the lawyer is having difficulty remembering who his client is.

Lawyer: (Addressing older woman.) Please tell me something about your circumstances, Mrs. Atholl (pauses and glances at the woman's daughter). . . .
Mother: Bob and I have become very (hesitates for a moment). . . .
Daughter: (Intervening, feeling invited by the lawyer's glance.) My mother and father are getting on in age—and they really haven't been getting along together . . . we've tried to talk to them. . . .
Mother: (Feeling the situation has been minimized.) Yes, well . . . it really is pretty serious. . . . Bob struck me (visibly distressed). . . .
Lawyer: (Uncomfortable, addressing the daughter, despite being addressed by the mother.) Yes. . . . What were you thinking your mother ought to do?
Daughter: We thought that if a separation could be arranged . . . for a short time, maybe. . . .
Lawyer: (Responding to the daughter's suggestion.) Well, yes, a separation might be the answer. . . .
Mother: (Feeling exasperated and misunderstood.) You don't understand. . . . I don't think I can live with Bob anymore.

Whatever the appropriate decision in this case, clearly the interviewer has failed to take seriously the old woman's distress and has instead paid attention to the daughter's fear that her parents' marriage may be irretrievably disrupted. The message is clear; the interviewer should talk directly to the person whom the situation directly concerns and not others.

RESEARCH

Prior to the last two decades, research on aging processes had been minimal. So, despite current interest and concern, knowledge about aging is far less developed than other topics discussed in this book. And, predictably, the knowledge that does exist is about broad social and physical issues (usefully portrayed in Atchley's 1980 book, *The Social Forces of Later Life*). Only gradually are the professions and disciplines turning specific attention to the older person in research and practice. Members of the fields of business, law, psychology, and medicine, for example, are acutely aware of the knowledge gaps in working with older clients. What information does exist on interviewing older persons comes from the social service context; works by Brink (1986, 1979) and Keller and Hughston (1981) are useful examples of this. See Suggested Readings and References at the end of this chapter for additional sources.

SUMMARY

The ability to communicate effectively with older persons is fast becoming a prerequisite for the business person or professional. While the interviewer must first be aware that older persons are not as different from their younger counterparts as stereotypes may convey, some special qualities of aging must be taken into account. The interviewer must listen intently to the older individual and must avoid any preconceived notions about tastes or needs. Careful listening combined with previous experience and training will help produce a relevant response for the older person. The interviewer need not panic and discount all earlier learning as irrelevent.

SUGGESTED READINGS

Atchley, R. C. (1980) *The social forces in later life*. Belmont, CA: Wadsworth.

Brink, T. L. (1979). *Geratric psychotherapy*. New York: Human Sciences Press.

Brink, T. L. (Ed.). (1986). *Clinical gerontology: A guide to assessment and intervention*. New York: Haworth Press.

Herr, J. J. & Weakland, J. H. (1979). *Counseling elders and their families: Practical guide for applied gerontology*. New York: Springer Publishing.

Keller, J. F. & Hughston, G. A. (1981). *Counseling the elderly: A systems approach*. New York: Harper and Row.

PART THREE

Interviewing Applied to Specific Issues

The subject matter of interviews is as varied as human concerns. Chapters 9–11 examine three sets of issues that are frequent concerns in interviews: marriage and family issues, health-care issues, and employment issues. Family, health, and work are vital concerns for all of us; these chapters focus on effective use of the interview to deal with these issues.

9

Marital, Family, and Sex-related Interviewing

Arthur Roach
Texas A & M University

Until now, this text has discussed similarities and differences in interviewing individuals at various levels on the developmental continuum. In this and the following chapters, the reader should keep in mind the basic concepts discussed early in this text. Interviewing families is different from interviewing individuals or even groups of individuals, however. People in families are involved with one another in a special way—they are not totally separate individuals—and the interviewer must consider this special relationship or bonding. Married couples share a similar bond that makes interviewing a couple distinctly different from interviewing the two members of the couple separately.

Part of this special bonding in married couples and families has to do with emotional and intellectual intimacy as well as shared values and experiences. While some married couples and families might share their thoughts and experiences with one another in the privacy of their homes, most families are not willing to share the private aspects of their family with others. In fact, many families have clear, but often unspoken, rules prohibiting discussion of family matters with anyone outside the family. This tendency to maintain privacy and confidentiality is part of their natural boundary structuring and is also a primary cause of the difficulty found in interviewing them.

If a general reluctance to share information with outsiders exists in families and couples, this reluctance is amplified in matters of sexuality. Families and couples are usually reluctant to discuss not only their own sexual behavior, but are also inclined to prevent others from discussing sexual concerns with them. The opposition to sex education in public schools is related, at least in part, to this hesitancy of many families to deal with sexual material.

Because of families' and couples' difficulty in talking about themselves meaningfully, a prospective interviewer would do well to consider some of the basic principles and techniques for interviewing families. This chapter first looks at interviewing families, then deals with specifics in interviewing couples. Finally, the text addresses human sexuality interviews as a special case of family and couple interviews.

INTERVIEW CONDITIONS

Definition of a Family

At the outset, it would be helpful to ask just what is meant by a family. The traditional view of a family involves two generations—parents and children—with the children most likely having blood ties with at least one of these parents. In today's highly mobile society of divorce and remarriage, however, this traditional view of the family has grown less adequate. This typical traditional family comprises only about 15% of the households in the United States.

Today's world requires a more flexible definition of a family. Experts in interviewing families, such as Carl Whitaker, tend to use the word family in a larger sense. Any group of people who live together and are closely involved in each other's lives over an extended period of time would be considered family by such a broad definition. For purposes of discussion in this chapter, the term "family" will signify this broad group.

Nontherapeutic Purposes

Recent years have seen a revolutionary approach in psychotherapy to include the entire family. This approach has proven to be surprisingly effective. How does family interviewing differ from family therapy? This is an important distinction. Family therapy typically focuses on solving some problem in the family, which involves an attempt to *change* the basic functioning or structure of the family. In the typical nontherapy family interview, on the other hand, the interviewer does not seek therapeutic change in family functioning. Her purpose is to collect information or to inform or persuade the family to take some action.

The nontherapeutic family interviewer may be bent on helping the family to solve a problem it faces, but not a problem involving its organization or structure. Also, interviewing focuses on solutions that can be implemented in one or two sessions and has short-term goals; even brief family therapy often employs 6–20 sessions.

Family Interviews

What kinds of people are likely to interview families? The list seems limitless, and it is constantly growing. We are a nation with a keen interest in the family. Perhaps those who interview families the most are social workers, or those working in various social agencies, such as welfare workers. Case workers in many institutions and organizations such as retirement homes and psychiatric hospitals will do preadmission interviews that generally focus on the family. Police workers such as juvenile officers, probation officers, and detectives will interview families on occasion. Personnel officers in large corporations and family mediators are a few of the others whose jobs involve family interviews.

Other professionals may also involve themselves in less formal family interviewing to be more effective in their services. Some architects will interview families to design a dwelling especially suited to a family's unique living style. Artists and photographers may spend a substantial amount of time with a family before planning group portrait sessions.

Others who are likely to be involved with family interviewing include salespeople in real estate or insurance. Mass media workers such as reporters, commentators, and journalists, as well as professionals such as ministers, lawyers, and some doctors will also find themselves involved in family interviews from time to time.

PREINTERVIEW CONSIDERATIONS: PREPARATION

Just as in working with individuals or groups of people, a small amount of time spent in preparation will yield dividends for the family interviewer. As outlined in Chapter 4, this involves preparing the setting and oneself, learning about the subject (the family), setting tentative goals, and outlining strategies and tactics. Many of the techniques covered in previous chapters also apply to families. Consequently, this chapter addresses only those aspects of preinterview considerations that are more specific to the business of working with families.

Preparing the Setting

To promote optimal family functioning in the interview, the interviewer should provide a suitable environment for the session. In addition to comfort, privacy, and safety (especially for small children), it is important to provide a sufficiently large space for the family. A room that may be adequate for interviewing individuals may be too small and crowded for working with a family. A family crowded into a small room may be fidgety and anxious, preventing them from dealing with the interview objectives.

Small children may need room to move around and play. Also, it is helpful to have a few safe toys appropriate to the child's age for families with small children. When children's needs are ignored, parents will not be able to give sufficient attention to the interview tasks at hand. Drawing materials or coloring books can also keep children occupied.

Family interviewers have differing views on the best seating arrangements for families. Some are careful to provide small-size furniture for children. Others are more concerned about not having a lot of extra chairs in the room, because this tends to spread the family out and also to give the room an uncomfortable, empty look. More important is giving everyone a comfortable place to sit. The more flexible (moveable) the seating arrangements, the better chance the family will have to make itself comfortable.

Some family interviewers prefer to allow family members to select freely where they will sit. This means that the interviewer sits last, in whatever space is left. This procedure allows the interviewer to see who sits next to whom, and which individuals sit furthest apart. One family member may direct traffic and tell others where to sit; the interviewer can learn a great deal about the power structure in the family as members take their places.

Preparing Self

Prior to meeting the family, the interviewer should get in touch with any of his own feelings, attitudes, difficulties, and extraneous concerns that might impede the development of a working relationship with the family. Usually he can dismiss these cares and concerns for the present and plan to deal with them at a more appropriate time. Generally, the interviewer should not attempt the demanding task of family interviewing when dealing with his own pressing problems or deep emotions. A family worker must sometimes decide that due to his present personal frame of mind, the show should not go on! Usually, however, pausing for a few moments and focusing his mind on the task at hand will suffice.

Learning about the Family

Usually the interviewer will have an opportunity to learn something about the group before she actually begins a session with the family. Some record or notes may provide information or clues about the family's size, structure, organization, values, interests, educational level, socioeconomic level, and problems. The occupations of the parents and older children, as well as outside sources of income, are important pieces of information. Religious orientation and societal memberships and activities can provide clues concerning the values, opinions, and attitudes of the family members before the interview actually begins. Sometimes the interviewer can observe the family before the interview process begins. Usually the professional can formulate at least a few ideas about what the family might be like. Even if these hunches prove to be wrong, thinking about them will help focus attention on learning about the family.

Setting Tentative Goals

Before actually beginning the family session, a key part of the interviewer's preparation is clarifying the tentative goals or purposes she wishes to pursue in conducting the interview. Collecting information, understanding family functioning, and making decisions are the three most common purposes. The family worker may have one or more of these goals in mind as she prepares for the forthcoming session.

Collecting Information

The most frequent purpose of family interviewing is simply to collect information about the family. In fact, for many people interviewing is synonymous with asking questions—that and nothing more. For example, a public-health nurse visiting a home might ask the mother a series of questions such as the following:

— Where do you keep your medications?
— Are they out of reach of your children?
— How often have you been getting outdoors?
— Are your children in good health?
— Does your family have sufficient fresh vegetables in its diet?

Such information about the family can usually be obtained from only one member of the family.

Understanding Family Functioning

A second purpose for interviewing the family is to understand family functioning better. Doing this will require observational abilities in addition to asking information-gathering questions. Interviewers for the media such as television reporters may occasionally be interested in this information. Court workers who wish to help a judge determine appropriate custody for the children will also find themselves interviewing various family segments rather than individuals.

Usually one must experience being with the total family to get a genuine feel for the unique way the family group interacts. To interview only the mother and use her experience as the basis for a general view of the family is a bit like asking someone what coffee ice cream tastes like instead of actually tasting the real thing. The full flavor of the family becomes apparent to the interviewer only after she experiences the family members' involvement with each other.

A key to understanding a family is to observe its unique communication pattern. One must observe the entire family firsthand to grasp its special vocabulary and patterns of communicating. Just as an observer cannot determine how an entire football team plays from watching one star player practice, so one cannot understand a family's interaction by conversing with just one family representative. If the professional wants to judge for himself whether a family is functioning as a healthy, interdependent group of people, he will have to interact personally with the whole family.

Aiding Family Decisions

While many interviewers want only to collect information about families, or even to understand the functioning of the entire family, other interviewers are more intent on a third purpose, helping the family reach a decision. A mortician, for example, will find himself trying to help a bereaved family make a decision on appropriate burial arrangements. He will want to help the family make a decision that befits its financial circumstances while also meeting the immediate family's needs, as well as the extended kinship family's. Many people who work successfully with families this way carefully avoid directly influencing the family's decision. The interviewer merely informs the family about its possible choices and accepts the family's choice without pressure. This nonpressuring, neutral approach generally works best for beginning interviewers.

Other interviewers, however, may be more interested in actively persuading or influencing the family. While most professional counselors attempt to remain neutral to help the family reach its own decision without direct influence, other interviewers assume a more encouraging role. Sales personnel most often fit into this category, but other interviewers might find themselves in this position as well. For example, a government agency worker might interview a family intending to prod it to accept the benefits provided by a particular government program that the family has been reluctant to utilize. While some expert interviewers can influence a family merely by their presence and manner of interaction, beginners usually must attempt to persuade or influence much more consciously and carefully.

Of course, whether one remains neutral in assisting a family to make a decision, or attempts to influence the family's decision making, is often an ethical question related to one's respect for the freedom of individuals and families. However, many interviewers comfortably and legitimately try to influence family decisions.

Determining Strategies and Tactics

In preparing for the family session, the interviewer will also want to consider the strategies or approaches that will enable her to achieve her selected goals with a particular family. In family work, the primary strategy decision is who to interview.

If an interviewer wishes to collect information about a family and judges that one person will not offer overly biased opinions, then he could merely interview that one person. However, if the interviewer wants to sample the opinions of various family members it may be best to interview them separately. Opinions elicited while family members are together may be biased. For example, a teenager asked about his opinions on marijuana smoking may say one thing if interviewed alone and quite another if interviewed in the presence of his parents.

Again, as discussed earlier, sometimes there is no substitute for interviewing the entire family. If one wishes to observe family interaction and communication, one must deal with the whole family. If the interviewer wants to sample the opinion of the entire family, then he must interview the entire family. This, of course, is quite different from collecting the separate opinions of various individuals in the family.

Once more, the entire family should also be interviewed if the purpose is to help it as a unit reach some decision that will satisfy all. Not involving everyone in the family in the decision-making process may cause the decision to be later undermined by those who were not in on it.

At times it may be appropriate to interview subgroups rather than an individual or the entire family. Sometimes it helps to interview parents and children separately. Some children tend to be overwhelmed by their parents' presence; they are also overwhelmed if interviewed individually. When the children in a family are seen together as a group, they are much likelier to reveal their real thoughts and feelings. When parents are seen separately as a subgroup, it underscores their authority and control, since the children sitting outside the interview room tend to see this as meeting of a high council of which they are not members. Sometimes in interviews related to human sexuality, it is helpful to see a parent and children of the same sex together if the child is apt to consider this supportive. For example, a mother might be brought into the room while her sexually abused daughter is being interviewed. This is especially true for younger children.

Beginners often ask "Should I include small children in the interview?" Experts often disagree on this topic. Satir (1967) prefers to focus her efforts on the parent couple. She always talks to the parents before dealing with the children. Bell (1961) prefers to exclude children younger than 9 years old. Other authorities insist on seeing all family members who are living together. In general, family interviewers tend to see more than one person at a time, whether it is the total household group or a significant subset of that group. Again, for the beginner, whether to include small children depends on the purpose and on the degree of skill and self-confidence he possesses. This chapter will assume that we are dealing with at least a couple or a significant subset of the family.

Methods

Finally, it is important to recognize from the outset that there is no single best way to go about interviewing families. While some guidelines can be helpful the reader should recognize that interviewing becomes more of an expression of the personality and beliefs of the interviewer as she gains experience.

Some experts prefer a spontaneous encounter with the family, while others, equally expert, prefer a carefully planned strategy. Generally speaking, beginners benefit from a carefully planned strategy until they gain more experience. The guidelines that follow are for the beginner.

Application

Practical suggestions for preinterview preparations for families include (but are not limited to) the following:

1. Arrange for a room that is comfortable and private, and make sure that it will provide a safe environment for small children.
2. If children are to be involved, supply suitable and safe toys and drawing materials.
3. Make sure the room has adequate, comfortable seating for everyone.
4. Pause for a few moments and focus attention and energy on the forthcoming interview, while simultaneously dismissing inappropriate cares and concerns.
5. Use available information sources to learn about the family before the interview.
6. Set a tentative goal for the session. This may be to collect information or to help the family reach a decision.

With these preinterview considerations in mind, we can now proceed to dealing with the various stages of family interviewing. The interview can be seen as having a beginning, a middle, and an end. We will first focus on the beginning stage of the interview.

THE BEGINNING INTERVIEWING STAGE

The first portion of the family interview can be referred to as the social or beginning stage. This phase is similar to "establishing the alliance" discussed in Chapter 4. The important difference here is that, when interviewing a family, the alliance is not with any one person but usually with the entire family. No individual family member should feel left out.

This is the stage in which the interviewer and the family begin to learn about and to understand each other. This process usually involves a certain caution and wariness from the family. The interviewer will have to call on his best social skills in helping them to feel relaxed.

Establishing the Alliance

If the interviewer is perceived as friendly and nonthreatening, as someone who can be trusted, the family will usually relax and settle down to the business at hand. This warm, friendly manner is something that the family looks for in the very earliest contact. Establishing the alliance begins with the first telephone call to set up an appointment.

Joining

Experts in family counseling often refer to this initial phase as joining, while others refer to it as pacing. Joining suggests that the interviewer is fitting in with the family. Minuchin, Montalvo, Guerney, Rosman, and Shumer (1967) emphasize employing the kind of language that the family uses. The interviewer must attend carefully to the language style of the family members and adapt his own style to theirs.

In the following example, Miss Carnegie, a social worker, demonstrates how to join in with the Carson family's style.

Father: I didn't think we would ever get here today. The damned car wouldn't start and then the goddamned engine kept dying at every frigging light.

Mother: Joe, watch your language in front of the children.
Father: Aw, don't be such a prude. The kids aren't hearing anything new.
Carnegie: (To father.) You're pretty angry about all the trouble your doggone car is giving you. (To mother.) You're more upset with Joe than with the car.

Here the interviewer grasps the message that the father's "damns" might occur on rare occasions but that the mother frowns on them, at least in public. The interviewer is quick to fit into the family's public style of not using the father's language, and accommodates by substituting the softer "doggone."

Pacing

Slightly different from the concept of joining is that of pacing. The idea of pacing suggests the action of a pace car at the beginning of an auto race. The pace car goes at a set speed, and the race car drivers match their speed to that of the leading pace car to prepare for an even start when the starting flag is waived. Interviewers similarly match their speed and style of communicating to that of the family.

Some families talk very fast, and ideas and responses bounce around like popcorn in the pan. Others talk slowly and reflect more, and are slow to develop a single topic or idea. For the latter type, the interviewer slows his pace and accommodates his flow of ideas to that of the family. The point is to make the family comfortable by adapting to their style.

Another area to adapt to is the content. If the family indicates that preferred recreations are picnicking and fishing, the interviewer might well work examples of those pursuits into his dialogue rather than referring to visits to an art museum or attendance at a symphony orchestra's latest concert.

Fitting in with the family is very important and must be done early. It takes a conscious effort at first, but it becomes easier with practice. The interviewer must strive to fit in with the *whole* family, not just with one or two individuals. Otherwise, some family members will sense that an exclusive alliance is being formed, and, if they sense they are not part of that alliance, they will become defensive and perhaps withdraw.

Avoiding Collusion

By following these suggestions, the beginning interviewer should find it possible to establish working alliances with the family. He should make every effort to avoid taking one side of any issue, however. Such a disruptive alliance is referred to as collusion. Instead, the interviewer should maintain neutrality. Note that in the example of the Carson family above, if Miss Carnegie had used the father's "damn" and "goddamn," the mother might have felt left out. If the interviewer had sanitized her language completely, the father might have thought that the social worker was taking the mother's side. The interviewer in the example compromises by using a word that suits the family's public policy. Of course alliances formed from a consistent pattern of taking sides with one or more family members, not from any one single behavior, as this example might tend to suggest.

Structuring the Relationship

Once the relationship has begun to take root through joining, pacing, and avoiding collusion, the interviewer begins to structure the relationship further. While many of the steps discussed in previous chapters also pertain to the family, this type of interviewing requires giving attention to dealing with the power structure already existing in the family and to the power balance between the interviewer and the family. Entire books have been written about power in families, but here we want to develop just a few pertinent ideas for the beginner. In any group an astute observer can sense fairly quickly which family member has the major influence over other family members.

Distribution of Power

The skillful observer will notice that no one member usually controls the others in every facet of the group's operation. Thus, in a given family, the mother may have power in determining the dinner menus and organizing the children's care, while the father may control the area of family finances and the care and use of the family car. The teenage daughter may determine which television shows the family will watch between 7:00 and 9:00 p.m., while her younger brother calls the shots regarding television fare from 4:00 to 6:00 p.m.

Cold and Warm Power

To understand power in the family, it is important to realize that power is not always the cold, vicious, or manipulative power that people often think of when this topic is broached. Power need not be only exploitative or negative. In addition to this cold type of power, a warm, benevolent and positive type of power exists. Caring for others and being watchful over their welfare can be a type of power, for example. Influence over another may also provide the opportunity to be concerned, to comfort, to form and reform, as well as to guide. This softer power is most common in healthy families.

Respecting the Family's Power

The interviewer does well to observe the family's particular power balance. If she is to get the job done, the interviewer does not want to oppose or attack any family member's power. To do so would result in a defensive attitude by the member attacked. The resulting power struggle might well prevent the interviewer from achieving her goals. The rule for the beginning interviewer is: *don't fight.* An interviewer rarely achieves her purpose in interviewing a family by confronting or attacking anyone's power.

Maintaining Interviewer Control

When the interviewer enters the scene, the family already has an established power structure. The interviewer is like a newcomer joining an ongoing group. That group (the family) can easily exercise its power over this newcomer if the interviewer allows this. Maintaining control and influence in the interview is essential to family interviewing. Otherwise, the interviewer may not achieve her intended purpose in the session.

If the interviewer fails to take the family power distribution into account, he may not get very far. For example, in a traditional family, in which the father exercises a great deal of control, the interviewer will be unable to function unless the father permits him to proceed. This phenomenon can be very important in certain cultural groups, as illustrated in the example that follows.

A real estate salesman in Texas was attempting to sell a home to a Pakistani couple. In his typical approach, the salesman addressed several questions to the wife, but the questions were answered by the husband. The salesman failed to make the sale. Later he learned from a Pakistani student at the local university that he had made a costly blunder. In their cultural tradition, this foreign couple expected that family business related to arranging living accommodations would be taken care of by the husband. Moreover, a stranger would not speak to the wife without first asking the husband's permission. By failing to consider the husband's authority or power in this particular family, the salesman offended not only the husband, but the family as a whole, because he failed to sense their mutually preferred arrangement.

In some cultures, this can be even more complicated. A Midwestern social worker was attempting to assist several Cambodian refugee families with their needs for food and medical services. Following her usual procedures, she would visit a family and try to befriend the children playing in the yard. Then she would attempt to talk with the mother when she came to open the front door. After several failures with her well-intentioned approach (which had worked with American families), she finally enlisted the aid of a young Cambodian worker who had recently been hired by her social agency.

This young man took her to see the head of the clan to which these Southeast Asian families belonged. After an appropriate tea ceremony and much discussion through the student interpreter of her plans and intentions, she received the clan leader's support. Later, the young man accompanied her and introduced her formally to the eldest person at each home. After she had duly recognized the appropriate authority figure in each home, she was able to interact effectively with the mothers and children in her usual way.

Perceiving the Power Structure

Although power and authority in more typical American families is not quite as unusual as these examples illustrate, the consequences of ignoring power and hierarchical structures can be equally disastrous. An interviewer who is having difficulty dealing with a family would do well to stop and ask herself what the power structure of the family in question is, and remember to keep that particular power structure in mind.

Not all families are male-dominated. Some are maternally controlled. Others are child-controlled. A few may be controlled by a grandparent. On rare occasions families seem chaotic, with no power focus. Whatever the particular power focus is in a given family, the interviewer must learn it at an early point in the session to be effective.

Dealing with the Power Structure

While family therapists may be in the business of attempting to change family power structures, the family interviewer usually has a more immediate goal. Going along with the power structure will facilitate reaching the interviewer's goal more than opposing or ignoring those forces will.

Encouraging Sharing

Just as with the individual (as discussed in Chapter 4) encouragement of sharing is an important early step in the family interview. Encouraging *all* family members to participate according to their interests and ability is important.

At some point children should have a chance to express their opinions and to tell about their pertinent experiences. Doing this emphasizes the idea of a *family* interview, and of all being involved.

An interviewer can sometimes draw silent family members into a discussion by directly asking them for their reaction to an idea or event. When this fails, however, asking another family member what he thinks the silent member might be thinking sometimes ends the silence. If the silent person is a child or adolescent, she will often speak up if only to correct the observation offered by a sibling. Sibling rivalry is a powerful tool here.

Sizing up the Situation

As the interview progresses, the interviewer must evaluate how things are going and may need to modify his initial, tentative plan or strategy. In dealing with families, two important conditions to evaluate are the family's functioning level and the family's goals and interests.

Families are easiest to deal with if they are fully functional. An interviewer can quickly get a rough idea of a family's level of functioning. If the family is adequately providing for its basic physical needs (food, clothing, and shelter), if the marital relationship functions satisfactorily, if the children are progressing appropriately in their education and socialization, if the family can adapt to its circumstances, and if communication in the family is open and direct, then interviewing will proceed fairly easily. The more a family falls below average in one of these categories, the more difficult working with that family might be.

If a given family is not functioning optimally, falling short in several of the areas described, the interviewer may find it resistant and uncooperative. When this occurs, the professional should not try to force the issue, but rather recognize that not all families are easy to interview. An interviewer cannot expect equal success in all cases; some families are simply more difficult.

Sizing up Family Goals and Interests

In the initial stage, the interviewer should develop some idea of what a particular family's goals, desires, and objectives might be. One family in dire circumstances might be concerned with survival, while another, more prosperous family may have set a goal of providing a college education for each of its children. Some families are bent on purchasing a new home in the city, while others are bent on moving to the country. By sensing what the family's major motivation seems to be, the interviewer will be in a better position to relate his efforts to the family's interests and goals.

Sizing up Interviewer-Family Member Relationships

As the interview progresses, the family worker must size up her relationship with each of the family members simultaneously. This requirement adds a level of difficulty not present when interviewing individuals.

For example, Jan, a social worker, notes at the beginning of her visit with the Masters family that Tom, the father, is cold and distant from her and only superficially involved; while Marie, the mother, is warm and animated, displaying an eagerness to answer Jan's questions. Meanwhile, Teresa, the 14-year-old, is aloof and quiet, and Jimmy, age 10, is preoccupied with the sounds of his peers playing outdoors, and would probably rejoice if he were to be dismissed from the interview.

In this example, Jan, the social worker, is simultaneously assessing the kind of working relationship she has with each participant. She is simultaneously aware of each family member's involvement.

Sizing up Interfamily Relationships

In addition to keeping track of her working relationships with each of the family members present, the interviewer will also have to monitor the relationships of each family member to the others. Failure to observe this set of relationships can lead to difficulties in reaching selected goals during the next stage of the interview.

As the interview progresses, it becomes apparent to Jan, the social worker, that the husband and wife, Tom and Marie, are in obvious disagreement concerning their participation in the interview. After a short time it becomes obvious that this couple is in even a great deal more disagreement, and that, in fact, they may well be a couple given to habitual conflict. Jan also notices that Teresa reflects her mother's attitudes and opinions more than her father's and that Teresa is obviously pleased with much that her mother says. The social worker also observes that father and son both show a common tendency to withdraw from the interview. Father and son, then, seem united in their coolness toward the mother and the interviewer. Further observation indicates the usual amount of sibling rivalry and lack of cooperation between the children. This division along the sex boundary (father and son vs. mother and daughter) constitutes a genuine schism in this family. Lack of awareness of this basic family division would be disastrous for the interviewer.

In this example, the social worker notes a number of relationships between family members. This interviewer knows that her work will proceed smoothly only if she keeps these relationships in mind.

The interviewer must also be aware that relationships can shift even during the course of the session. Consequently, she must be alert to any subtle changes in relationships, either between the interviewees and herself or among the family members, as the interview transpires. Relationships, by definition, are always in flux, and a good interviewer will be sensitive to these ongoing changes.

Application

The beginning stage in family interviewing determines how well the rest of the interview will proceed. The most important aspects of this stage—which often occur simultaneously—are outlined in the following list. The interviewer should:

1. Greet each member of the family by the name he prefers. She should attempt to do this in the order the family seems to prefer.
2. Introduce herself and make sure that all members of the family know her name, role, and purpose.
3. Make a favorable, positive statement about the family based on her observations of the family and her experience with it to this point.
4. State the purpose or function of the interview and what she hopes to accomplish.
5. Form an impression of the power structure in the family and decide how she might best deal with it.
6. Determine the family's reaction to this stated purpose. See how this purpose relates to its goals and interests.
7. Form some idea of the level of functioning of the family to determine whether her tentative plans and strategies will be workable with this family.

Returning to Miss Carnegie, the social worker, and the Carson family, provides an example of the beginning interviewing stage.

Carnegie: Hi, I'm Miss Carnegie, and I am a social worker with the department of human services. I need to gather some information from you to help you submit an application for relief funding due to your losses in the recent tornado.

Father: Great! Do we ever need help. I'm out of a job because the plant where I worked suffered a lot of damage.

Mother: And living in the school gymnasium is for the birds! I can't believe our home is just gone.

Carnegie: I'll bet you miss your home too, Bobby. Are you doing okay?

Bobby: Okay, but I do miss my friends and all my toys.

Carnegie: All of you seem to be bearing up well under these difficult circumstances. You seem to be in good spirits. I will need to ask some questions about your income, savings, and other sources of help to complete your application for relief funding. Mr. Carson, you might also want to see about some temporary employment, and I can refer you to an agent of the state employment office right down the hall, if you want.

In meeting the family, the social worker quickly gathers that it is a healthy family group and the members are anxious to take care of themselves. Their attitudes suggest that they are looking for help in a temporary crisis. She gathers that the father is the leader, since he speaks for the group first.

THE MIDDLE INTERVIEWING STAGE

Once the interviewer has joined with the family by establishing rapport and a working alliance, and has begun to know and understand the family, he is ready to begin pursuing the purpose or function of the interview. He can now collect information on a more specific basis or attempt to influence family choices.

This middle stage is usually the longest part of the interview. While the objectives of this stage may vary somewhat in specific interviews, this portion of the work most often includes information getting and giving, problem solving, decision making, and handling resistance and emotional problems. An important first step is targeting issues.

Targeting Issues

An important early part of this middle phase of the interview is targeting issues or setting goals. Here, the interviewer tries to get the family to agree on some common goals or objectives for the remainder of the interview. She may frequently encounter resistance at this point, but it is important to suggest possible goals with the family. If the family does not agree, the interviewer must listen to its disagreement and attempt to reach some sort of a compromise.

> **Interviewer:** I would like to spend the rest of this session collecting information about the kinds of educational goals you have for your children.
> **Father:** That sounds like a good idea. That's what we need to know to decide how much money we need to put into an annuity for the kids' education costs.
> **Mother:** But I don't agree with that. Let's just figure out what it will cost to send both of them to college.
> **Father:** That's absurd! With the difficulty Tom is having in school, it looks like he might not even finish high school, much less go to college.
> **Interviewer:** It seems that we might do better to spend the rest of the session focusing on the educational plans you might have for each child without expecting that both children will have the same goals.
> **Mother:** Okay, let's do that.
> **Interviewer:** Do you like that idea, Tom?
> **Tom:** Yeah. Okay.
> **Interviewer:** Lisa?
> **Lisa:** Sure.

In a way, setting goals for the interview is like a minicontract or an agreement on how to spend the remaining time in the interview. Once a goal is clearly defined, everyone must agree with it, as the interviewer ensures in the preceding example. This is the only way to ensure that everyone will be involved in pursuing the objectives of the interview session.

Obtaining Information

Because most family interviewing is done at least partly to obtain information about the family, many of the information-gathering techniques discussed in previous chapters apply to families. Two key procedures are especially useful, however: effective questioning using either a repeated-question or a circular questioning approach.

Repeated-question Approach

Virginia Satir was one of the earliest family therapists. In her work she preferred to interview members of the family by asking each the same question. This repeated-question approach can be described as a "star" technique, as Figure 9–1 illustrates.

This approach is illustrated in the following interview with the Cummings family.

Interviewer: (To Father.) Mike, what do you like to do in the evening after dinner?
Father: Oh, I like to go down to my basement workshop and do something with my hands. After working all day I find it relaxing to repair something or build something.
Interviewer: (To Mother.) And how about you, Lucille? What do you like to do after dinner?
Mother: Well, I don't get to do what I would like to do. First I have to get the kitchen and dishes cleaned, get the lunches ready for the next day, check on the children's clothes for school, and turn down the beds. If I have time, I like to read some magazines.
Interviewer: (To son.) And, Bobby, what do you like to do after dinner?
Bobby: I like to get outside and play. Whatever the boys in the neighborhood are doing. I just join in.
Interviewer: (To daughter.) Laura?
Laura: I like to call my friends on the telephone.

Circular-questioning Approach

Other experts prefer to use a circular-questioning technique, whereby the interviewer starts out asking one family member a question, and, depending on the answer to that question, follows with a different question to the next family member. The interviewer may go in any order, but eventually asks everyone a question related to the idea or hypothesis he is forming about the family (see Figure 9–2).

An example of this circular questioning approach is seen in the following example with the same Cummings family.

Figure 9–1   Star Questioning Approach

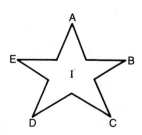

Figure 9–2   Circular Questioning Approach

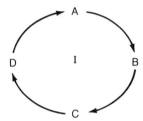

Interviewer: (To father.) Mike, what do you like to do in the evening after dinner?
Father: Oh, I like to go down to my basement workshop and do something with my hands. After working all day I find it relaxing to repair something or build something.
Interviewer: (To mother.) Lucille, what do you think about Mike's going down to the basement in the evening?
Mother: Most of the time I don't mind, but at times when I've had a very hard day, I just wish Mike would offer to help with the kitchen and the dishes.
Interviewer: (To daughter.) Laura, can you tell which are the evenings when your mother wishes your father would help her?
Daughter: Oh yeah! Mom bangs things around and bitches at everyone. You can tell she would like some help.
Interviewer: (To son). Bobby, can you tell when mom wants your father to help her after dinner?
Son: Nope. I leave the table early. I'm gone outside before all that stuff starts.

As these examples illustrate, the outcomes of these two types of questioning reveal quite different things about the family. Which approach to use depends on the interviewer's style. Of course, family interviewers can use the questioning approaches described elsewhere in this book; these are just two approaches.

Giving Information

Although family interviewers are most often involved in collecting information from families, they are also frequently involved in sharing information to inform or persuade the family. Sometimes families require specific information to make appropriate decisions.

Much of what has been touched upon in previous chapters also relates to sharing information with families. With families, however, the interviewer must be certain that all family members concerned understand the information she gives them. Consequently, she may have to repeat important instructions in several versions to give different family members the opportunity to understand and remember.

Stimulating and Handling Responses

Family interviews have a means of promoting responses about personal feelings and beliefs that interviewers in other situations do not have. When one family member hesitates, the interviewer can ask another family member what the hesitant one might be feeling or believing.

Joe Cooper, a mental-health worker, is trying to help a family with an adolescent conflict. He proceeds like this:

Cooper: Mrs. Barkley, what do you think or feel about Samantha's moving out and into her own apartment with a friend?
Barkley: Okay, I guess.
Cooper: You don't sound too sure about your reaction. Samantha, what do you think your mother's reaction is right now?
Samantha: Oh, she is both disappointed and angry with me. She doesn't want me to go, but she's tired of fighting with me about it.
Cooper: How about that, Mrs. Cooper. Is Samantha reading your reaction pretty well?

Solving Problems

An important part of the middle stage of interviewing is dealing with problems that arise as the interview proceeds. In family interviewing, two important problems that frequently arise are resistance and family dissension.

Resistance

Once the interviewer has begun to move toward the interview objective that she and the family have adopted, she may expect some type of resistance from the family. Resistance usually arises out of fear, distrust, or hostility. That is why putting the family at ease early on is so important. In this middle or business stage of the session, the interviewer begins to get feedback on how well she has done during the first phase. If she has done well in that initial stage, she is less likely to encounter strong family resistance in this second stage.

Resistance may be conscious or unconscious. If the family is consciously resisting the interviewer's efforts, he can do little to bring the interview to a successful conclusion, and he is probably better off ending it early. If the family is unaware of its resistance, however, the interviewer can deal with that and continue the interview and achieve the goals of the session.

Resistance most often takes the form of denial. Thus, a family will deny any problem the interviewer may ask about or refer to. Sometimes, instead of denying a problem outright, the family will rationalize the problem, explaining that it is not really a problem or that, even though it exists, it is only very minor and is nothing to be concerned about.

Occasionally a family will resist the interviewer's probes by becoming openly hostile in an attempt to get the interviewer to retreat. At other times the family may simply become sullen and quiet or respond only in monosyllables. A few families will resist by nonstop talking or going on at length about very minor matters. Any of these indications should serve as important warnings for the interviewer.

When signs of resistance appear, the interviewer must not ignore those signs. Resistance is best dealt with by recognition and respect. The interviewer should work with the resistance, taking the family's viewpoint into account and quickly proceeding within that viewpoint without trying to change the family's outlook. For example, an insurance sales-man dealt with resistance in the following manner:

> **Salesman:** After getting to know you as a family this evening, I can see that all of you care a great deal about each other. I imagine that the education of Tom and Lisa is important to all of you, and I would like to show you a way that you can insure that the funds you will need will be there when these children leave high school.
>
> **Father:** Hey, wait a minute, I already have a great deal of insurance, and I don't think we want to talk about insurance.
>
> **Mother:** Yes, I don't want to have to die so that my children can afford to be educated.
>
> **Salesman:** Certainly, I see that you don't want to talk about insurance. Neither do I. You want to accumulate the money for your children's education. That's why I want to review several annuity arrangements with you.

In this brief episode, the salesman picks up the parents' resistance, goes along with it, and switches the focus away from the object of resistance (insurance). He is "reading the resistance." Some might say that he goes around the resistance.

Family Dissension

The other problem, dissension, may actually be simply another form of resistance. When the family members begin to argue among themselves, the interviewer must remain neutral. At the same time, the interviewer may have to act as a peacekeeper for the interview to proceed. Again, the interviewer must avoid minimizing the argument or criticizing the family for its dissension. It is best to suggest ignoring the disagreement for the present so that the interview might continue.

It is, of course, not essential that families agree on everything. A common objective of family interviewing is to find out whether the family agrees or disagrees on a particular topic.

Once in awhile, when a family disagrees too much, or family members become openly hostile, it is best to see only part of the family at one time while the rest of the family members wait in another room. The interviewer should not keep those family members outside the interview room waiting too long. If he does so, they may think that the interviewer is somehow colluding with those who are in the session with him.

Another way to avoid suggesting collusion to those who are waiting their turn is to give each family member or subgroup about the same amount of interview time. If one member or subgroup is seen for considerably more time than the others, it may suggest favoritism. In work with a portion of the family, this "equal time" provision is exceedingly important.

Application

The interviewer should:

1. Work with the family to target goals or issues to deal with during the interview.
2. Use appropriate techniques for gathering information from the family about family functioning.

3. Have family members repeat in their own words any information he has given them.
4. Stimulate sharing of personal feelings and beliefs by asking other family members what they think the nonsharing person's feelings and beliefs might be.
5. Deal with resistance by avoiding direct conflict and working toward the perceived interest or needs of the family.
6. When dissension arises, keep the peace by suggesting that disagreements be ignored for the moment so that the interview objectives might be accomplished.
7. If dissension cannot be circumvented, then it may be necessary to interview family members in separate subgroups. If so, the interviewer should take care to avoid giving the impression that he is in collusion with anyone.

THE ENDING INTERVIEW STAGE

As the interview moves toward its conclusions, the family worker pays attention to the same types of concerns discussed in earlier chapters. The elements in this final stage are similar: verifying communication, planning for the future, rehearsing for action, and terminating the interview. In this section we will emphasize those aspects which are of most concern in family interviewing.

The final stage of the family interview is a winding-down phase in which the session is closed out and the finishing touches added. By this time, the primary purpose of the interview has been accomplished. Because the main business of the session is over, some interviewers might be inclined to end the session abruptly. This would be a mistake. The professional usually wants to leave the door open for another interview should that be necessary. Ending the interview on a positive note is thus advisable. Also, this phase is important for providing closure by bringing the interview to a comfortable, appropriate termination.

Closing

This final stage of the interview focuses on disengagement or strategic withdrawal. In a sense, the interviewer begins to move toward the exit. Often an interviewer plants this suggestion using the words or phrases to which people are fairly accustomed. Here are two common examples:

Interviewer A: Well, that about does it. You've answered all my questions, and I think I can now do my report.

Interviewer B: It has been a pleasure working with you. If you find yourselves in need of any more help I might be able to give you, please call on me.

Verifying Communication

As the session concludes, it often helps to make sure that family members understand and remember important instructions. One technique especially useful in family interviewing is to have family members repeat in their own words the information you have given them.

While many people will feel awkward in parroting back to the interviewer in one-on-one interviewing, family interviewing offers a more natural way of doing this.

Ensuring Understanding

To ensure understanding of the recommendations or actions required by family decisions it is wise to have each person repeat them in some way. For example, the husband may be asked to explain the task to his wife. If mother is then asked to repeat the information to the children, she will often put the recommendation into their language while showing her understanding of it. Having the children repeat the instructions to the father allows them to demonstrate their grasp of the recommendation. Each family member must understand his part in what is to be done. For example, Miss Warner, a public health nurse visiting a home-bound child, enlists the aid of the Westbrook family's mother to convey an important message to the family:

> **Warner:** Now, please understand how important it is for Virginia to get out of bed and start walking for at least 15 minutes three times a day. Once in the morning, once in the afternoon, and once in the evening. Now, Mrs. Westbrook, would you explain that to Virginia in a way that she is sure to understand?
> **Westbrook:** Virginia, the nurse is telling us that it is very important for you to get out of bed and start walking at least three times a day. We'll do it about 10:00 in the morning, about 2:00 in the afternoon after your nap, and in the evening after I finish cleaning up after dinner. Okay?
> **Warner:** Very good. And now, Virginia, tell your father what your plans are for getting out of bed and walking each day.

Planning for the Future

The ending interview stage may require looking ahead beyond the session to see what plans or decisions might be required of the family. Of particular concern is the decision-making process, which should include all pertinent members.

Clarifying Goals

Family interviewers can help with decision making in two ways: Most of the decision-making work of the interviewer consists of helping the family to clarify its goals; at other times the worker will help the family to refocus on already-clarified goals. As the family's goals become clearer, the decision becomes more apparent and easier to make. For example, a marriage counselor worked with a couple, the Devoes, in this way:

> **Interviewer:** Where would you like to go for a family vacation this year?
> **Wife:** Oh, that's easy. I've always wanted to go to Hawaii. With the income tax return we got this year, I think we can finally do it.
> **Husband:** Oh, no. We have to put that money into our savings account. We'll never get ahead spending money every time we get a bit extra. We will just have to settle for going to the coast for a few days.

Interviewer: You really have different ideas about the family's summer vacation. Nancy wants to go to Hawaii and Sam wants to go to the coast. The decision seems to be one of whether or not to spend the tax return money.

Wife: He's a squirrel. Any money we get he wants to save for a rainy day. He never wants to have any fun.

Husband: And she's a spendthrift. She would be happy fiddling around like the cricket in the fable. She wouldn't save a thing. We'll die broke!

Interviewer: You have different attitudes toward saving. One would save nothing. The other everything.

Wife: He exaggerates, as usual. I don't want to spend everything, but I do want to have some fun in life before I get too old to enjoy it. I think we can have some fun and still have money to save.

Husband: She exaggerates, too. I like to have fun just as much as the next guy, but I definitely want to save some money this time. We won't always be young.

Interviewer: You're sounding closer together. At least you both want to do some saving and you both are willing to spend some money on fun. The question, then, is how much you want to spend, and how much you want to save.

In this example, the interviewer begins to bring the Devoe couple from opposite viewpoints toward a compromise. This is a rough example of how a couple or a family begins to clarify its mutual goals, thereby approaching a decision.

Refocusing Goals

Sometimes the interviewer helps the family with its decision making by refocusing on an already-stated decision. In the following example, a couple wants to place its errant son in a boarding school. A probation officer helps the parents refocus on the decision by clarifying their goal:

Interviewer: Dave, you're talking about sending Oscar to boarding school; Mildred, you seem to want to go along with that, but I'm not clear on whether your idea is to punish Oscar or to help him learn to change his behavior by means of a more controlled environment. If it's just punishment, there may be better ways.

Father: Oh, it's not just punishment. It's the controlled environment we want. I'm out of town on my job, and Mildred works. We're not able to supervise him the way a boarding school would.

Mother: Well I certainly believe he deserves some punishment for what he's done. But I agree that punishment is not the main idea.

Interviewer: That clears it up a bit. If you're focusing on control, you may want to think of a particular kind of boarding school. Maybe a military school.

By taking a decision that the parents have already made and clarifying the motive behind that decision, the probation officer helps the parents to refocus on a more specific decision. In this example the decision to send Oscar to boarding school is relabeled as a decision to provide more control rather than punishment. The interviewer can then suggest a military school, introducing the question of how much control. After dealing with this matter of control, the probation officer might help further refocus the decision determining how expensive a school these parents wish to consider. The process continues until the parents have their goals and the means to achieving them clearly in mind.

Collecting information and helping the family to make decisions are the two principal components in most family interviewing. The interviewer often moves from one task to the other as the work of the interview progresses. Eventually, however, the work of the interview is accomplished, and it is time to move on to the final phase of the session.

Recommending Action

When the family has been involved in decision making, the session reaches a point at which recommendations for actions on the decision are needed. These recommendations should be clear and concise. To be clear means using language that all members of the family can understand. These recommendations should also be as concrete and specific as possible, by outlining specific behaviors for the family to undertake. A couple deciding on a vacation can decide who will call the travel agent and by what date, for example. Some right and wrong approaches may help to clarify this idea:

> **Interviewer A (wrong):**   Now I want the two of you to spend some time planning your vacation in the weeks ahead.
>
> **Interviewer B (right):**   Frank, will you take the responsibility for calling the travel agent before next Monday? And Virginia, will you agree to visit the library and check out two books on Hawaii before our next session?

Notice that the first example is vague about who will do what and when. The second example clearly assigns tasks and deadlines.

Rehearsing for Action

Depending on the purpose of the interview, the ending stage calls for various activities. In addition to recommending specific actions, most families benefit from actually doing something to demonstrate a commitment to their goals. One benefit of working with families at this stage is that an older member or older sibling can be called on to model the behavior, then children can be asked to imitate that model.

Teresa, a public-health nurse, has been conducting a home visit involving an aging grandmother. As the session is ending, she begins the rehearsal for action:

> **Teresa:**   Before I go, Mrs. Sanchez, I would like you to demonstrate once more the Heimlich maneuver. Just in case your mother has another choking spell, we want you to be able to do that.

After Mrs. Sanchez demonstrates her ability to carry out the procedure, the nurse asks the 8-year-old daughter to rehearse for action.

> **Teresa:**   And Maria, I would like you to show us all how you have learned to dial the 911 emergency number in case your grandmother has another serious problem.

As Maria dials the number, Teresa explains:

Teresa: Right now I am holding the receiver down as you dial, but in an emergency you will really call. Let me hear you give the person answering your name, address, and a few words about what might be happening to your grandmother.

Terminating the Interview

If the interviewer-family relationship has been an effective one, there is often a natural reluctance to break off from this pleasant experience. But all interviews must close at some point. Once the work proposed for the session has been accomplished and the scheduled time has run out, it is time to close.

Occasionally the interviewer encounters family resistance in ending the interview. Instead of breaking off, someone in the family will ask a question or raise a concern that forces the session to continue beyond its normal limit. In these situations, the interviewer does well to state clearly that the goals of the session (as established in the middle or direction phase) have been accomplished and that it is time to go. Some interviewers like to stand up as a signal that the interview has come to an end. If this does not work, they begin to walk slowly toward the door. If the hint is still not taken, they then open the door. Most families take the hint involved in such signals long before the interviewer gets that far. If these winding down procedures are followed, ending is not usually a problem.

Another occasional problem is unfinished business. If the interviewer does not accomplish her work by the time set for termination, she may need to set up a date and time for completing that work. The interviewer should try to avoid this problem; however, when it must be done, setting a time for resumption should be done soon enough so that the session is not hurried at the end.

Positive Observations

At the close of an interview, sharing an observation or two sometimes helps the family or leaves it with a pleasant feeling. Some experienced interviewers refer to this as "gift giving." Besides leaving a good impression, this also rewards the family's cooperation during the session and conditions it to participate in the interview, thereby increasing the likelihood of cooperation in future interviews.

Some experts prefer to offer a separate compliment or positive observation for each family member; others make a positive observation about the entire family to the whole group. Examples of these styles follow:

Interviewer A: (To the father.) Clyde, it has really been a pleasure working with you. Your involvement with your children is a rare thing these days. This family is lucky to have a father like you. (To the mother.) Laura, you are a wonderful mother. When I see how neat and clean and well-dressed your family is, I know that you have put a great deal of effort into that. (To the son.) Paul, you have certainly been well-behaved. I want to thank you for paying such close attention during our interview. Your parents are fortunate to have a fine son like you.

Interviewer B: (To everyone.) I have enjoyed working with all of you as a family. You work well together. I sense that you have a special quality of unity as a family and I think you will all be happy together for a long time.

Application

In ending the interview, the professional should:

1. Avoid dragging out the interview or allowing it to go overtime.
2. Give signals announcing the approaching end of the session. She should say something like, "We have just about finished our work for today."
3. Make sure the family understands instructions by having members repeat them to one another.
4. Help the family clarify goals by asking specific questions and settling on who will do what by what time.
5. Help the family refine its goal choices by clarifying the motives behind early goal statements.
6. Foster family action by asking each member to accept an appropriate role, function, or task.
7. Help family members rehearse the actions involved in putting decisions into practice. Have them demonstrate skills they have learned.
8. If the family resists the ending of the session, state clearly that it is time to go, stand if necessary, and walk toward the door as a final gesture.
9. End the session by sharing a positive observation with the family as a whole or with each individual.

MARITAL INTERVIEWING

Much of what has been said about family interviewing also applies to marital interviewing, but with several qualifications. Usually marital interviewing is best delayed until the professional has experience with other forms of interviewing. He should pursue some training specifically in the area of marital interviewing before attempting it.

One reason this area demands experience and training is that it can significantly affect the couple's lives. Research indicates that interviewing one person separately about problems in his marriage increases the probability of that marriage ending in divorce (Gurman & Kniskern, 1978). Because marriages are vulnerable and can be harmed by well intentioned, but inept, interviewing, marital interviewing should not be undertaken lightly.

A specific problem of marital interviewing is the tendency of most couples to give socially desirable replies to questions. Most people in our society are bright enough to know what the socially acceptable behavior of married couples is. Few couples are ready to put themselves in a negative light by admitting that their behavior is not acceptable to society. To deal with this problem, the interviewer must spend some time motivating the individual or the couple to participate in the interview. For example, dialogue with an abused wife at a crisis center might go like this:

> **Wife:** I find this whole thing difficult to talk about.
> **Interviewer:** It really is important for you to talk about what has happened to you and your children. We cannot help you to deal with this problem legally unless we know just what has happened without exaggeration or holding back.

Suggestions

In marital interviewing, one can assist the couple to relax and participate by seeing them both together. Most couples will also respond positively if the interviewer spends time exploring the positive aspects of their marriage. People are usually pleased to discuss how they met, what attracted them to each other, how their honeymoon went, and the happy times surrounding the arrival of their first child. Regardless of the interview's purpose, it is worth taking the time to deal with some of these positive aspects first to help put the couple in a positive frame of mind.

Another helpful guideline in dealing with couples is to limit discussion of marital problems. All married couples have some problems, and they are usually prepared to discuss these to some extent if the nature of the interview calls for it. Usually, however, discussing more than two or three such problems in a single interview is not useful.

INTERVIEWS ABOUT SEXUAL MATTERS

As with marital interviewing, several cautions apply to interviews concerning sex. First, no interviewer should undertake such a task without some experience and training. Interviewing about sexual matters requires that the interviewer be comfortable in dealing with topics that many people find embarrassing or unsettling. If the interviewer is not appropriately trained, his own uneasiness may trigger uneasiness in the family or couple he is interviewing. For the same reason, the interviewer's sex education should be well-rounded. A broad background will help him to avoid being shocked by any information in the interview. Should an individual or a couple detect such shock, the remainder of the interview would likely not be effective.

Several specific suggestions can help make sex interviews more successful. Whether the interview is for research purposes or part of the routine in a pregnancy advising service, the interviewer would do well to heed these simple suggestions.

Suggestions

First, it is usually best to approach the interview expecting cooperation. If the interviewer is thinking, "I am going to be asking these people some embarrassing questions, and they will not want to answer them," the person or couple being interviewed will pick up on her uneasiness and fail to cooperate. On the other hand, if the interviewer seems confident and acts like she expects their cooperation, respondents will sense that she knows what she is doing and that the interview has a worthwhile purpose.

Second, directness is always best. A clear outline of the material she is seeking will aid the interviewer here. She should memorize this outline to avoid the hesitancy that referring to a written outline suggests. When asking the prepared questions, the interviewer should utilize eye contact in such a way that the person or couple senses she is not shy or in any way embarrassed by the responses likely to be forthcoming. In the following example the interviewer demonstrates this directness:

Interviewer: (To couple.) How long do you usually engage in foreplay before having intercourse?

Husband: Usually for 5 or 10 minutes.

Interviewer: (To wife.) Is this sufficiently satisfying for you? Would you prefer longer?

Wife: Usually Jack rushes to intercourse. I would prefer longer. Twice as much as usual would be better. At least 15–20 minutes.

Interviewer: (To husband.) Are you aware that women generally prefer more foreplay than men?

Husband: No. I thought I was doing more than a lot of guys would in that department.

In this example the interviewer gets directly to the point in asking about couple foreplay. A written account of this interview does not convey the impression of directness that a videotaped version would clearly show. The interviewer maintains clear eye contact and addresses his questions directly to the couple. Note particularly that he does not rush past the question after the husband's initial answer. The interviewer stays with the question until it is dealt with adequately.

A third related suggestion is to conduct the interview in a business-like manner. This means being serious, but not necessarily grim. Many people feel uneasy or embarrassed when dealing with sexual topics, and they tend to deal with this uneasiness by resorting to humor; however, interviewing about sexual matters requires maintaining a business-like approach and avoiding sexual humor. The interviewer might laugh, but he should not indulge in sexual humor during the interview.

SUMMARY

The major purposes of family interviewing are gathering information and assisting families with decision making. The power distribution in families, resistance, dissension, and goal setting were also explored. For the special cases of marital interviews and interviews about sexual matters as forms of family interviewing, several specific suggestions were made to assist the beginning interviewer.

SUGGESTED READINGS

Beavers, W. R. (1982). Healthy, midrange, and severely dysfunctional families. In F. Walsh (Ed.), *Normal family processes*. New York: Guilford Press.

Bernstein, L., Bernstein, R. S., & Dana, R. (1974). *Interviewing—A guide for health professionals*. New York: Appleton-Century.

Fisher, R., & Ury, W. (1981). *Getting to yes: Negotiating agreement without giving in*. Boston: Houghton Mifflin.

Franklin, P., & Prosky, P. (1973). A standard initial interview in D. A. Bloch (Ed.), *Techniques of family psychotherapy: A primer*. New York: Grune & Stratton.

Golner, J. H. (1971). Home family counseling. *Social Work, 4,* 63–71.

Hartman, W., & Fithian, M. (1972). *Treatment of sexual dysfunction*. Long Beach, CA: Center for Marital and Sexual Studies.

Kantor, D., & Lehr, W. (1975). *Inside the family*. San Francisco: Jossey Bass.

Lewis, J. M., Beavers, W. R., Gossett, J. T., & Phillips, V. A. (1976). *No single thread: Psychological health in family systems.* New York: Brunner/Mazel.

Napier, A. Y., & Whitaker, C. A. (1978). *The family crucible.* New York: Harper & Row.

Paul, N., & Paul, B. (1975) *A marital puzzle.* New York: Norton.

Pomeroy, W. (1972). Interviewing. In W. Pomeroy (Ed.). *Dr. Kinsey and the Institute for Sex Research.* New York: Harold Matson.

Satir, V. (1972). *Peoplemaking.* Palo Alto, CA: Science and Behavior Books.

Satir, V. (1975). "Problems and pitfalls in working with families." In W. Satir, J. Stachowiak, & H. Taschman (Eds.), *Helping families to change.* New York: Jason Aronson.

Walsh, F. (1982). Conceptualizations of normal family functioning. In F. Walsh (Ed.) *Normal family processes.* New York: Guilford Press.

10

Interviewing and Health Care

Robert R. Reilly
Texas A & M University

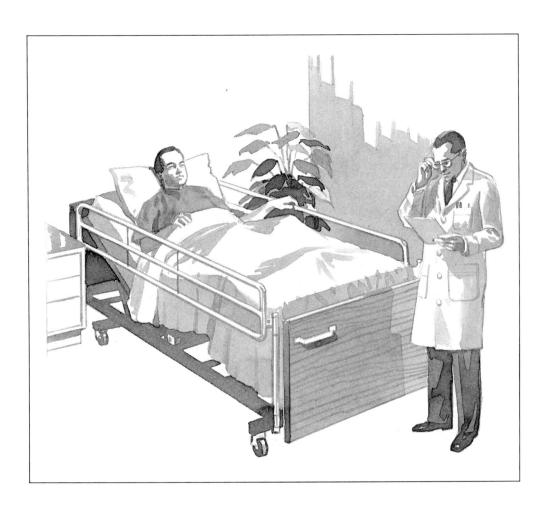

The interview is useful in a variety of settings and issues. It is as flexible and adaptive as the ingenuity of the professional permits. As Chapter 9 showed, interviewing is an indispensable tool in working with marriage and family issues, but special approaches and techniques are required to ensure its effectiveness. Chapter 10 presents another set of issues—related to health care—and discusses the proper use of the interview in dealing with them.

At various times in our lives, nearly all of us experience a health-care interview—as the interviewee. Visits to medical and dental offices, mental-health centers, hospitals, and a variety of other sites often include a health-related interview. The interview may relate to one's own health concerns or those of a loved one. Personal experience with such exchanges may provide an interesting perspective as we discuss the professional's role in these interviews. Since the recipient of health care is customarily referred to as the patient, rather than the client, subject, or interviewee, this chapter will usually follow that practice as well.

HISTORICAL PERSPECTIVE

Concern for our health is so much a part of the human condition that it is difficult to conceive of any time in the history of human awareness void of discussion and inquiry on this topic. At each stage of social development, from the nuclear family to the nation, health has been viewed as a primary need and, therefore, a primary reason for the existence of the social organization. We can easily imagine primitive parents or other elders advising young children and answering their health-related questions. Much later, with specialization and education, certain individuals were designated as health-service providers. In modern America, a wide variety of health professionals specialize in many aspects of health care. Appropriate training, standards, and often certification have been developed to support these specialists.

Over the past century, several important changes in health care have occurred in the more industrialized nations of the western world. The success of medical research and technology has caused the emphasis of health care to shift. The goal of remediation or treatment of seriously ill individuals has increasingly given way to other medical goals. Illness prevention, as exemplified by the public-health movement, has become a major medical consideration. Immunization programs, provision of safe drinking water, and community health-education efforts are examples of the preventive aspect of health. Screening programs to provide early warning of vision, hearing, and dental problems could be added to this list.

During the past few years, a third health goal has emerged: health promotion or enhancement. Unlike remediation and prevention, the goal of health promotion is positive, attempting to move forward from a position of freedom from illness to one of optimum wellness. Rather than being driven by fear of illness, health promotion stresses optimum physical and mental health. The popularity of jogging, aerobics classes, self-improvement seminars, and health clubs attests to the success of this movement.

Changes in the public's attitudes and perceptions have also profoundly altered the nature of medical-care delivery in recent years. The health practitioner—whether physician, optometrist, or dental hygienist—is no longer blindly accepted as an authority figure. For better or worse, democracy has reached the health field. The patient wishes to be a partner in personal medical care; informed individuals want to know the reasons for specific treatments. They wish to be convinced. Additionally, the U.S. consumer movement has added both legal and ethical force to these desires.

The interview provides a particularly effective mechanism to ascertain patients' desires, satisfy the need for information, and solicit patients' help in managing their own health care. To help their patients best, health care professionals must become skilled in interviewing just as they must master the other technologies of their particular field.

DEFINITION AND SCOPE

Health care is used broadly in this chapter to include both mental and physical health for inpatients and outpatients. But it goes further to include many discussions centering on health issues between professionally trained health-care providers (nurse, nutritionist, physical therapist, dentist, and physician) and lay persons intimately involved in the health status of themselves or others. Therefore, conversations both with the patient and the patient's family members are included. (For convenience, however, the term "patient" is usually employed in examples.)

Commonly, health-care interviews have these purposes: (a) assessment or obtaining information, (b) instruction or giving information, and (c) problem solving. Interviews conducted in a health-care setting share certain distinctive features or characteristics, including personal and emotional involvement, trust, ambiguity, and resistance. These features influence the nature and success of the interview. While all of these characteristics may not be found in a particular health-related interview, several are usually present.

People care about their health. Whether it is dental fillings or a new heart valve, the patient and the family are intimately involved and concerned. Because health issues are important to people, they have the capacity to evoke emotion. Therefore, health-related interviews are likely to involve more than the cognitive, objective side of the patient.

We are usually not fully knowledgeable or skilled in health matters. Yet, our health is of vital personal concern. Our lack of expertise requires that we entrust these important matters to others. Only where the trust factor is high can we do this with any feeling of security.

Furthermore, most health-related decisions are not obvious. Frequently, differences of opinion exist even among the experts. This lack of certainty makes health-related decisions and health-related interviewing particularly difficult.

As discussed later in this chapter, people often respond to emotional and personally dangerous situations (such as those regarding their health) with resistance, denial, and reluctance to take any action. The Wall Street gambler who is ready to risk a small fortune on the fate of a stock may be unable to decide about his own operation. Resistance is a common factor when interviewing in a health-care setting.

STAGES AND METHODS

Chapter 4 delineated and discussed four stages of the interviewing process. These same four stages—preparation, initiation, direction, and conclusion—can serve as an outline for the health-related interview. Interviewing skills (see Chapter 3) appropriate to each stage will also be discussed.

Preparation Stage

The preparation stage involves preinterview considerations. Before the interview actually begins, the professional attends to issues and details that could affect the success of the impending meeting: setting, self, knowledge of the subject, goals, and skills.

The optimum setting for any interview is a physically comfortable, pleasing environment that ensures privacy. Further, the social environment guarantees seriousness, attention, and concern for the individuals involved. Such ideals are not always possible in a health related interview.

Malasanos, Barkauskas, Moss, and Stoltenberg-Allen (1977) note that while complete privacy and comfort are often difficult to arrange in a large clinic or multiple-bed ward, some protection—perhaps more psychological than physical—can actually be provided. They stress the importance of ensuring that (a) the conversation is not heard by other patients or individuals unrelated to the case, (b) the health-care practitioner gives complete attention to the patient, and (c) information shared is treated as confidential.

In preparing for the interview, the practitioner should choose a seating arrangement that is conducive to a two-way conversation rather than the authoritarian arrangement where the professional remains behind a desk or, worse yet, stands over the patient (Malasanos et al., 1977). Consideration for the subject's schedule, physical condition, and convenience should help determine the location, time of day, and length of the interview session.

The professional's comfort and preparation is at least as important as the setting. We tend to perform poorly when we are anxious, upset, or otherwise uncomfortable. Often we become very formal, talk louder, and are less sensitive to others' needs. Many health-related interviews have the potential to be emotional and unpleasant. But duty and concern for others requires that we handle them well. Recognizing and dealing with our own feelings in a mature manner is a necessity.

The professional can control her own anxieties somewhat by making plans to handle the anticipated situation. Just as thorough preparation has proven to be an effective aid against test anxiety, learning about the patient, setting goals, and determining methods can help relieve the anxiety associated with an impending meeting.

Initiation Stage

The interview's first phase is the initiation stage. Establishing the alliance, structuring, encouraging sharing, and sizing up the situation are objectives of this stage. But greeting the patient is the first order of business. Cormier, Cormier, and Weisser (1984), in their text on interviewing for the health professions, suggest a brief, concise initial introduction: "Good morning, Mr. Robertson. I am Dr. Johnson, the psychologist here at the clinic, and I will be working with you on a few brief questionnaires we would like you to complete."

Note in this example that the psychologist addresses the patient by name, gives his name, and explains his role in working with the subject. Cormier et al., go on to mention that while children usually prefer to be addressed by their first name, adults may have other preferences. The initial meeting is a good time to clarify this matter. Often, the individual is ready to get down to business once the introduction is complete, but some older adults, particularly members of ethnic minorities, may still be anxious at this point. The skilled interviewer will examine the situation and determine if additional social interchange is advisable before directing the conversation to the purposes of the interview.

The importance of establishing an effective alliance between helper and helpee cannot be overstressed in the health-related interview. Only a joint effort toward mutually understood and acceptable outcomes is likely to be maximally productive. The professional must take the lead in this endeavor, projecting not only concern, empathy, respect, and genuineness but also a promise of aid and assistance. Lazarus' (1981) term "inspiring hope" is particularly appropriate for this stage in the human encounter. Some examples follow:

— Bob, I think there are several possible ways we can deal with this problem.
— I know this has been hard on you and your family. But now that we are working on it together, you should soon be seeing that light at the end of the tunnel.
— This isn't the end of the world! You have a lot of people pulling for you and willing to help.

The patient can be seen as a person in need, with questions, fears, uncertainties, perhaps physical pain and distress. Emotion is to be expected under these conditions. Anxiety, suspicion, and anger are common responses to frightening situations. Conversely, the professional also can be expected to feel considerable emotion in some health-care interviews. We naturally respond negatively to unpleasant situations and unpleasant attitudes. Unfortunately, many health-care professionals have taught themselves to withdraw emotionally from these threatening situations. They believe they "can't get involved." If this withdrawal precludes empathizing with or recognizing the subject's feelings, then these professionals have reduced their usefulness to that of a tape recorder. In these difficult situations, professionals must overcome their own fears.

The effective interviewer can join in with the patient and form an alliance to deal with the situation. She does not remain aloof as an objective observer, nor does she become overwhelmed by emotion. The professional provides hope and leadership by being a caring, understanding person. Of course, she should avoid giving false hopes and unwarranted expectations. The professional helps the patient evaluate the situation realistically so that practical alternatives can be examined.

What is said is certainly a part of interviewing, but nonverbal behavior also plays an important role. Appropriate smiling, eye contact, tone of voice, gestures, and facial expressions all are important in conveying helpful concern. Also, establishing the alliance, like several objectives of the interview, cannot be accomplished once, then forgotten. Once established, the alliance must be maintained.

Interview sessions vary in the amount of structure needed. Often, the patient knows from past experience what is to be expected. Even in these situations, the wise interviewer may wish to provide a brief structuring statement. The interviewer's purpose, time constraints, confidentiality, and the role of each participant should be clarified. Since the interview is a joint endeavor, the parties involved should agree on these important elements. Observe the following illustration:

> **Interviewer:** I should mention to you that we have about 25 minutes and I would like you to give me a pretty complete history of Johnny's health and development up to this point. My notes go into the agency file and will only be available to professionals working with this case, unless, of course, a judge rules that we have to release them. Does this sound all right to you?

Cormier et al. (1984) suggest following structuring by an open-ended question that allows the patient an opportunity to state any particular reasons or expectations for the visit: "What do you have in mind for today's session?" "How have you been feeling since our last meeting?" "What made you decide to come in today?" This type of question can also help encourage sharing. Often the patient needs help recognizing the interview as a mutual undertaking in which he can and should discuss personal matters openly.

As the interviewer works through the initiation stage, she learns a great deal about the patient and the nature of the particular session. This information should be considered in sizing up the situation, that is, judging the appropriateness of tentative plans for the interview and the necessity of any changes. Of course, as with establishing the alliance, structuring, and encouraging sharing, sizing up the situation recurs throughout the interview.

Direction Stage

The professional's skill and attention get their toughest test in the middle interviewing stage. In this stage, usually the longest, the major work of the interview is accomplished. Depending upon the situation, information may be obtained, assessments made, instruction given, or problems solved. The health-service provider must keep objectives in view as appropriate issues are targeted and dealt with. Responses from the subject are stimulated and handled expediently.

Time is always a factor in health-care interviews. In situations involving life or death, it is truly vital. For this reason, the interviewer must keep objectives clearly in mind and guide the discussion toward relevant topics. This targeting or focusing ensures productive use of the time available. It must, however, be balanced by concern for the patient's feelings and wishes, which calls for tact. The following examples demonstrate:

> **Patient:** You know, Doc, I think my hearing is just fine except when I run into one of the young people who mumble. Have you noticed how young people just don't seem to talk up anymore? I blame the schools. They don't teach them right anymore. And. . . .
> **Unskilled interviewer:** Let's get back to my questions.
> **Skilled interviewer:** You might be right there. Am I talking up okay? Let me try this question. . . .

As noted earlier, interviews can be classified by purpose: assessment or obtaining information, instruction or giving information, and problem solving. The following sections provide some specific suggestions for conducting each of these types of interviews.

Assessment or Obtaining Information

The assessment (or diagnostic) interview is probably the most common type in health care. The interviewer's purpose here is to obtain accurate information about the individual's general health status and/or a specific health problem. As with most interviews, the diagnostic interview relies heavily on observation by the professional and on the patients' subjective opinions. Also, as in other interviews, information flows in both directions. Not only does the interviewer learn about the patient, but the patient also can form some impressions about the professional and the agency or institution he represents. Self-understanding and some therapeutic gain from the cathartic effects of unburdening oneself are other possible positive results for the interviewee. These objectives are most likely to be achieved if the professional views the diagnostic interview as a significant encounter between sensing, feeling human beings who have needs and concerns to be considered. The completely "objective" scientist who "just wants the facts" is likely to obtain less useful information and achieve less in the interview than the true professional.

The diagnostic interview usually follows a particular structure: The interviewer has a definite purpose, previously selected content, and a planned procedure to reach the interview's objectives. Central to the interview may be a list of questions or a form to complete. Often, some type of report results from the session. In some cases, structure may be quite rigid to determine whether the patient meets certain diagnostic criteria (e.g., the detailed criteria provided for each mental disorder in the *Diagnostic and statistical manual of mental disorders* (published by the American Psychiatric Association, 1980). Friedman and Powell (1984) also have developed a highly structured videotaped interview procedure to diagnose Type A behavior. Additionally, Turk and Kerns (1985) provide a discussion of the structured interview's role in health psychology. Other diagnostic interviews may be more flexible but still substantive in terms of areas and questions to be covered. But in either case, the effective interviewer must be alert to the patient's special needs and reactions and must individualize the interview in terms of appropriate language level, examples, and time spent on different topics. One would expect the health history interview of a 12-year-old boy and that of his 65-year-old grandmother to be quite different, for instance.

Diagnosis can be considered a special case of scientific problem-solving: you begin with a question, define it carefully, and accept or reject the hypotheses. The following example illustrates these steps:

Joe, a college freshman, reports to the college health center because of a pain in his side. Nurse Jones conducts the pre-examination interview. The question, of course, is the cause of Joe's pain. Careful questioning defines the pain in terms of location, intensity, history, and occurrence. Nurse Jones may develop several theories or hypotheses as to the cause of Joe's pain: a fall, a sports injury, appendicitis, and so on. Each of these hypotheses must be investigated by collecting additional information about Joe's activities, status, or physical condition. Often, some possibilities can be ruled out or supported even before a physical examination or lab test is used.

This example helps illustrate that the interview is an active, dynamic process. Nurse Jones did not just collect information aimlessly. She formed questions based on previously obtained information and her own knowledge of the medical field.

The effective interviewer can form answerable questions, develop hypotheses that in turn lead to useful questions, then direct the interview in response to the patients' answers to these questions. An interviewer should constantly be asking *herself* questions as she progresses through the interview: What condition could explain these facts? How does this new information change the likelihood of my hypothesis being true? What question would help me reach a conclusion?

A word of caution is in order here. The hypothesis is a tool in helping us reach the truth by directing our thoughts and efforts. It must not, however, impede problem solving by blinding us to other possibilities.

A number of suggestions helpful in the assessment interview. First, where possible, the professional should have a plan for the interview—know what he wants to cover and what information he wishes to obtain—but be flexible in executing the plan. Tentative hypothesis based on previous experience or available information may help him develop some questions or activities appropriate to the situation. These can be very useful, but the approach should be individualized based on careful observation of the subject and events in the interview.

Next, patients should be encouraged to tell their story in their own words. The interviewer is likely to learn more if the patient does much of the talking rather than simply responding yes or no to questions. The open-ended question is most helpful here. Also, even though a written report may contain some of the information, it is usually useful to get the patient's point of view. The interviewer should listen carefully to what the patient says rather than allow himself to be distracted thinking of the next question to ask.

The professional should note the patients' reactions—statements, tone of voice, non-verbal responses, coloring, and so forth—to her and to different aspects of the interview. Perhaps these reactions are clues to information that the interviewee is reluctant or even unable to express as shown in the next illustration:

Nurse: I noticed when you were telling me about your family a few minutes ago your voice sort of broke when you mentioned your brother. Was there any reason. . . .
Joe: Well, yes. I guess I was just thinking that my brother Bill had a pain like this a year or so ago, and now he's dead.

The professional should try not to interrupt the patients' responses, but "file away" questions for a few minutes. Interruptions discourage and limit the patients' responses. They may become passive and turn responsibility for obtaining information completely over to the interviewer. Also, the answer to a question may come naturally if the patient is allowed to finish.

The patient should be reinforced or "rewarded" for discussing information the interviewer deems especially important. Showing particular interest, nodding, alert attention, and smiling (if appropriate) are methods of reinforcement. They can help shape or direct the interview without interrupting the patient's flow of information.

A tolerant, accepting atmosphere should be provided. It will help the interviewee to see this situation as safe and accepting and view the interviewer as professional, helpful, and nonjudgmental.

Reassurance should be used carefully. The professional may be tempted—or even encouraged—to reassure the patient in a number of ways: "Maybe I shouldn't have bothered you with this." "Don't you think this is just a growing pain and Johnny will get over it by himself pretty soon?" "This is nothing to worry about, is it, doc?" Generally, it is useful to reassure the patient (or parent) that getting professional advise was the correct thing to do, but avoid implying that the patient's problem is unimportant or trivial.

The professional should ask the hard questions. Often they deal with such topics as sexual behavior, mental disorders, or suicidal intentions. If the information is important to assessing the patient, the professional is obliged to ask the hard questions. A tactful, direct, matter-of-fact (but concerned) approach usually is quite effective. "Have you been sexually active during the last two months?" "In addition to physical health, sometimes people have problems with their mental health—their feelings and ideas." Have you had any problems along this line?" "You mentioned a problem with depression. I was wondering if you ever feel so bad that you consider harming yourself."

Support and a secure alliance between the interviewer and interviewee are vital at these points in the session. Tact and concern for the feelings of the subject will aid in presenting these questions in context rather than "out of the blue."

Avoiding interpretation of the patient's responses is important. If the professional regularly explains to the interviewee what certain feelings or symptoms mean, she will impede the flow of information. Also, the subject is likely to become self-conscious and defensive about saying anything more. The interviewer's job at this point is to encourage response, not to close it off.

Enough structure should be provided so that the patient knows what is expected. Less-able patients may need more structure and more questions. The purpose or need for information about particular topics should be explained and the interviewee informed that this information will be used to his advantage. Occasional questions or comments can indicate interest and provide directions. Reflection ("You first notice the pain on Sunday....") and summary ("So all of the pain has been on the left side and it only hurts when you have recently eaten") can be used to direct the patient's account. Most subjects find an extremely "nondirective" approach by the professional threatening and anxiety provoking.

Questions are extremely important in the health-assessment interview. As discussed earlier in this text, questions can be open-ended ("How are things going for you?" "Anything new I should know?") or closed and objective ("What is your age?" "What is your phone number?") The open-ended question attempts to elicit a longer, more personal statement from the interviewee than the one- or two-word response to the objective question. An open-ended question would be: "Could you tell me a little more about your family and your home?" Its direct counterpart: "Is 1412 Smith Street your correct address?"

Usually, the health interviewer needs both a broad, general view of the subject's status and very specific information regarding symptoms or conditions. A useful strategy is to begin a topic with general questions and then to focus on needed information using specific questions. This allows the open-ended question to establish the outline or the boundaries of the conversation, while the specific questions provide necessary detail, as in this exchange:

Nurse: How have you been feeling since your last visit? (Open-ended.)
Patient: Oh, pretty good. Better. But I have this kind of funny feeling in my chest and a problem with eating.
Nurse: Anything else bothering you besides those two problems that you have noticed? (Open-ended.)
Patient: Nope. I really feel a lot better and that medicine seems to really help.
Nurse: Well, let's see what you can tell me about the feeling in your chest. When did you first notice it? (Specific question.)
Nurse: Show me where it hurts. (Specific question.)

Malasanos et al. (1977) point out both advantages and disadvantages to open-ended questions. In addition to providing the patient's view of their problems in their own words, this type of questioning conveys an interest in the patient and an invitation to take part in the process by presenting any information considered pertinent. Among disadvantages are the inclusion of irrelevant information, the increase in time devoted to the interview, and omission of vital details. Also, these authors point out that patients with limited education and verbal skills may prefer the structure afforded by the brief, factual question.

We generally want the respect and acceptance of other humans, particularly individuals who may be in a position to help or harm us. For this reason, a patient may well tend to give answers that please or satisfy the health professional and avoid socially unacceptable responses. The interviewer can help minimize this type of "response bias" by appearing open and accepting. Any behavior by the interviewer that the patient may interpret as indicating that some responses are not acceptable (bad, "dirty," or ruled out) correspondingly limits the validity of the information collected in the interview. The professional interviewer can encourage the frank exchange of information with a specific question or comment at certain intervals, occasionally by providing a word when the patient's vocabulary falters or simply by avoiding "loaded" questions such as "You haven't been drinking again, have you?"

Giving Information

Providing information about medication, treatment, self-care, or referral sources is a frequent, and often vital, part of the health interview. Usually, because it is extremely important that the patient understands the information correctly, accurate communication is essential.

To give information effectively, the interviewer must attend to the three items essential to any communication: the sender, the receiver, and the message. This division of the communication process can provide a useful framework upon which to present the suggestions for improving information-giving developed by several authors (Bernstein & Bernstein, 1980; Cormier et al., 1984; Egan, 1986).

The professional—the sender—must clearly understand the goals of the communication. Just what objectives are to be achieved? How are these objectives best achieved? How should the information be used? The sender does not wish to give out information simply because it is available. Rather, information should be used as a tool to reach our objectives more effectively. For example, to encourage exercise by a healthy teenager, the physical therapist may mention the city basketball league. But for the middle-aged former athlete who needs to consider slower-paced exercise, golf may be the topic of choice. The sender's goal determines the information to be given.

Understanding the receiver and the receiver's point of reference assists in conveying the information. The receiver is not identical to the sender. Differences in past experience, personal goals, and attitudes are likely to alter the meaning of the message. Appropriate vocabulary, clear examples, and avoidance of technical terminology are useful tactics. Readiness for the information is an important consideration. Information given when the receiver needs it is timely and more likely to be used. The patient's ability or capacity to absorb information is another consideration. Too much information on a variety of topics often confuses the subject. A few brief, related points are more likely to be retained. For example, the occupational therapist just beginning to teach a complicated skill might say, "Let me show you how to do the first couple of steps today. We can add on the others next time."

Some messages are, by nature, more effective in communicating. Consider the American officer's response to the German demand that he surrender at Bostogne ("Nuts!") or Admiral Farragut's answer to his timid subordinates ("Damn the torpedos! Full speed ahead!"). Usually, short, specific statements or directions are more effective than long, complicated, or more general messages.

The message should be considered to have two likely effects: informing and influencing (Cormier et al., 1984). Often we hope the message will both give information to aid the patient in acting and influence or encourage the patient to act in the desired manner. Some examples:

Nurse: You can avoid those blisters on your hands if you just remember to wear work gloves.
Mental-health worker: You know, Bill, often people avoid individuals who seem too eager to make friends and push themselves on others.
Nutritionist: Many canned fruits have a great deal of added sugar. Fresh fruit is usually better for you.

These statements obviously communicate more than information. They attempt to influence and change behavior, to ensure patient compliance.

Understanding the patient and developing a close working relationship of mutual trust and respect go a long way toward improving communication. We are all more likely to follow advice or accept information from a friend rather than someone who seems to have little interest or concern for our welfare.

Part of the process of demonstrating concern and respect is a willingness to discuss. The subject should be encouraged to react, to question, even to disagree, and these responses should be discussed. Giving information is more than simply stating facts.

Problem Solving

The interview in a medical setting frequently involves decisions and problem solving. Patients or family members must deal with problems ranging from how to arrange for care of the family pet to whether to consent to a life-endangering surgical procedure. As noted earlier in this text, the steps in scientific problem solving also apply to making personal decisions. Carefully defining the problem, collecting relevant information, listing alternatives, choosing and trying out a course of action, then evaluating the effectiveness of the tentative solution are all useful steps. Since these procedures are discussed elsewhere in this text and others (Dillard, 1983), this section will concentrate on some barriers to effective decision making in the medical setting.

Some of the characteristics that distinguish health interviewing also make problem solving or decision making in this area particularly difficult. The ambiguity of the situation, emotional involvement, and resistance to change are among these factors.

We find it easier to choose between alternatives that are definite, clear, and certain. But the different alternatives facing the patient or the patient's family are often ambiguous. Differences are, at best, probabilities, and no guarantees are given. Frequently, decisions must be made without adequate information. Waiting until all the facts are available just may not be realistic.

Decisions that involve possible loss of health or life or that concern ourselves or our loved ones are not taken lightly or objectively. The participants, the decision makers or problem solvers, are emotionally involved. And emotion does not promote clear thinking or effective choice.

Perhaps it is a natural characteristic of humans to resist change. Apparently, we revert to resistance when we feel uncertain or threatened, stubbornly refusing to be realistic or to be helped. Egan (1986) states that resistance is a common phenomenon in counseling; it may be present to some degree in all clients. Frequently, the health interviewer will encounter some resistance partly as a result of the two preceding factors, ambiguity and emotional involvement.

These special characteristics of interviewing in the health setting add to the difficulties encountered in helping patients solve problems or make decisions. Some suggestions to aid in problem solving follow:

1. The patient should be given as objective a view of the situation as possible, but the interviewer should admit freely to the inadequacy of the information while pointing out any urgency for the choice to be made.
2. Where possible, the patient should have time to consider the alternative. Often this can be done by anticipating problems and discussing them to avoid a quick choice.
3. Open discussion of fears, anxieties, and any other emotions involved should be encouraged. Emotions are best dealt with in this manner.
4. The professional should explore his own feelings and assumptions about the situation. They may be a cause of some of the patient's uncertainty or resistance.
5. Difficulty in problem solving should be accepted as normal, perhaps even positive (Egan, 1986). The patient may be acting in a normal, predictable manner.

Handling Emotional Responses

As in other stages of the interview, the health-care professional wants to stimulate patient involvement during the direction stage. Often, this involvement is constructive, leading to better understanding and acceptance, or providing valuable information to the interviewer. Emotional responses of anger and fear are also common and may at first seem completely negative. However, considering the steps in the psychological process of handling loss, we should recognize these emotional reactions as necessary and, in the long run, positive (Horowitz, Wilner, Marmar, & Krupnick, 1980).

Denial, anger, depression, and acceptance are expected when an individual faces a loss. Much of the interviewing done by health professionals involves loss—of a loved one, a bodily function, health, time, money, freedom, or life itself. The professional should recognize when emotional expression is appropriate and help the patient express and deal with these feelings. In handling emotional reactions, interviewers should:

1. Encourage appropriate expression of emotion. Cormier et al. (1984) rank respect of the individual's right to react and to feel as the most helpful thing a health professional can do. These authors recognize that encouraging patients to express their feelings in whatever way they wish is extremely important to release pent-up tensions that may prevent patient progress.
   Encouragement can take many forms: establishing a personal, human relationship with the patient; showing interest and concern; nonverbal clues (a touch, an arm around the shoulder) the interviewer accepts the patient's feelings; direct verbal invitation to express feelings. The professional should not react to her own anxieties by trying to force or coerce an emotional response from a patient who is not yet ready to respond. Careful monitoring of her own status along with the patient's should help in this regard.

2. Provide an accepting environment for the patient's emotional response. Once the patient has accepted an invitation to "open up," the experience must be productive. Privacy and time should be provided; the interviewer should remain calm and attentive even in the face of an emotional reaction that could be considered disturbing or threatening.

3. Accept and consider seriously patient complaints that seem trivial or insignificant. Often these complaints are actually symbolic of the patient's anger and fear about death or disability (i.e., to whom do you address a complaint about your brain tumor? The cold mashed potatoes provide a convenient scapegoat). The middle-aged businessman who has come to the hospital to visit his dying father may not be as upset by the parking situation, which he criticizes loudly, as he is regarding his own mortality.

4. Try to allow the patient to have some power. "An ill person surrenders a certain amount of self-control and, with it, self-esteem" (Cormier et al., 1984, p. 233). The frustrations and dehumanizing effects of medical care provide a ready-made source of distress, depression, and hostility. Allowing patients to make some decision about their treatment or routine and to have some power over "the rules" recognizes and reaffirms their humanity.

5. Reinforce positive behavior. Usually even the worse tirade of imagined wrongs, anger, and self-pity contain some positive notes. The individual may mention "the only good thing . . ." or "I guess I'll just have to. . . ." When these positive statements or actions surface, the professional interviewer may wish to reinforce or reward them. Signs of a clearer insight, an acceptance of reality, or a decision to

take positive action can be reinforced and encouraged by a nod, reflection, or statement of agreement.

Conclusion Stage

A number of factors combine to make closing or concluding the health related interview particularly difficult. For the professional, time constraints and other duties pull toward an early closure, and the desire to be of maximum help to the patient pulls in the other direction. The patient, too, may be pressed for time, but he also wants to be sure his questions have been answered and that he knows what to expect or do next.

The conflicting emotions generated in the interview are complicating matters further. Fear, anxiety, dependency, and anger are common patient (or family) responses. Just as the patient's questions must be dealt with effectively, so must these emotional responses. Inappropriately early closure can prevent the patient from gaining what she needs—an opportunity to recognize, express, and discuss these troublesome feelings. While the professional obviously has responsibility for gathering or giving information or helping the patient solve a problem, the interviewer also has responsibility to assist the subject in handling emotions by encouraging her to "talk it out." Where possible, the interviewer also will attempt to encourage hope and point out encouraging aspects of the situation.

The ending stage of the interview obviously requires considerable skill. The professional must achieve several objectives in a brief time. Attention shifts to implementation, the future use of information or solutions gained in the interview. The interviewee must be helped to realize that the session is drawing to an end because its goals have been met, rather than because he is being rejected or dismissed abruptly.

A major objective in the conclusion stage is to ensure that the patient and professional agree on what has been stated or decided. This "checking communication" is usually accomplished by a summary statement by one of the participants, preferably the patient, as in the following example:

Dietitian: So, what does all this information boil down to in terms of your eating habits?
Patient: I have to reduce the salty snack foods, eat more fresh fruits and vegetables, and pay attention to the contents lists on prepared foods, avoiding salt or sodium.

The summary also allows the patient to recognize that time for the session is dwindling and if she wants to present any additional points, now is the time. The experienced interviewer may at times find it advisable to state these points directly: "We have seven or eight minutes to go in this session. We can spend it on making plans, unless you have some other point you wish to discuss."

Just as the summary statement helps the patient see that the session is coming to a natural conclusion, it also leads into the planning phase. What happens next? What should the patient do? How is this information going to be used? What if . . . ? these and other questions can be addressed in "planning for the future." Rehearsing planned behaviors or actions can also be helpful in ensuring that the outcomes of the interview are implemented to the fullest. Rehearsing also instills confidence, provides practice, and uncovers errors in need of correction.

To be most effective, the interview must be terminated professionally and courteously, since the final impression is one that may last in the patient's mind. The impression should not be one of an awkward, abrupt ending, several false starts before a final departure, or a similar unsatisfying termination. The work of the session should be recognized as completed, plans for the future made, and the smooth, natural termination achieved on time. Previous statements by the professional should have ensured that the ending did not come as a surprise. If appropriate, a decision should be made regarding a future meeting.

As noted in Chapter 4, nonverbal clues can be quite helpful in termination: setting forward, preparing to stand, and so on. Thanking patients for their time and wishing them well is usually very appropriate (Hillman, Goodell, Grundy, McArthur, & Moller, 1981; Cormier et al., 1984).

The following examples illustrate many of the points discussed in the previous section.

Mary Swenson, a physical therapist, notes on her calendar that she has an appointment in a few minutes with Jack Robertson. This is their initial meeting, arranged by Robertson's physical, Dr. Jones. Swenson reads the brief referral letter from Dr. Jones and learns that the new patient is a 55-year-old professional man who has a chronic back condition resulting in periodic pain and muscle spasms. The physician gives his diagnosis of Robertson's condition and suggests physical therapy, but is not specific about the patient's history or background.

In preparing for the initial meeting, Mary Swenson checks the consulting room to see that it is in order and that comfortable chairs are conveniently placed; she notes the need to obtain more information about the patient and his condition; and she begins to form tentative hypotheses about its causes and appropriate treatment. Information seeking is her major goal for this session and Swenson's customary informal interview procedure, supplemented by a patient information form, will provide structure. She expects to spend about 15 minutes on the interview and then to begin the physical examination and treatment.

Mary: Good morning, Mr. Robertson. I'm Mary Swenson, the physical therapist Dr. Jones suggested.

Jack: Hi. Yes, I'm Jack Robertson.

Mary: Pleased to meet you. Would you like to come in here and make yourself comfortable so we can talk for a bit. Is that chair okay for you?

Jack: Just fine. No complaints.

Mary: I understand from Dr. Jones that you have been having some back problems.

Jack: Well, it's not too bad right now, but the last week or so, it's been pretty bad.

Mary: Have you seen anyone for physical therapy before?

Jack: No, this is the first time.

Mary: Quite often, physical therapy can be helpful in relieving many backache symptoms, but first I will need to know more about your situation. Perhaps you could fill me in. Then we could work together on developing a program to help you.

Jack: Well, essentially I have a sore back.

Mary: Mr. Robertson, it would really help in planning your treatment if you could feel free to tell me more about yourself and your back problem. I need more detail, and, of course, any information you give me is confidential, just between the two of us.

Jack: Sounds good to me. I certainly want to do anything I can to alleviate this condition. What do you want to know?

As the initiation stage draws to a close, Swenson has established an alliance with Robertson, structured the relationship, and encouraged sharing. As she sizes up the situation, Swenson notes that Robertson tends to give short, partial answers. He is reluctant to expand on these statements or to give much personal information. Yet, she suspects that his attitudes may be an important variable in the treatment of his condition. Mary decides that more encouragement and more open-ended questions are in order.

Mary: How about just telling me about yourself, your work, your daily schedule, and then about the back problem—how it started and how it affects your life? Later on we can get into more technical questions and the examination itself.

Jack: I've lived in this town now for about 20 years; I'm originally from the Midwest. Married, two kids finishing college. I've been an accountant most of my life. Now—for 15 years—I've had my own company. It's doing okay. Daily schedule: let's see. It has changed a lot over the years. I used to be pretty active physically: football and track in high school and college, golf, jogging, tennis, and such. But gradually I've had to give up exercise because of my back. In the last five years, walking to and from my car has been my major exercise. Some days, it's hard even to do that much.

Mary: Your back problem seems to have forced you to change your lifestyle quite a bit—and to give up some things you really enjoyed.

Jack: Yes, I guess you could say that. Also, I'm afraid my general health has suffered. Without exercise I've gained weight, my muscles are weaker, that sort of thing.

Mary: At work, do you spend most of the day at your desk?

Jack: Right. About 90% of the time I am at the desk or the work table behind it. Just spin around in my chair to reach the phone. I don't walk around much at all.

Mary: How about at home or when you are away from work?

Jack: Well, I have this great recliner right in front of the television. That's were you can usually find me. Most of the time I watch television or read. We go to a movie now and then. Also, we eat out or visit friends once every two weeks or so. I mentioned before that I have given up on sports, and my wife and kids do the gardening now.

Mary: It sounds like you spend most of your waking hours sitting and that you get almost no exercise now.

Jack: That's true.

Mary: Could you give me some history of your back problem?

Jack: Well it's like an old friend—not a good one—been around for a long, long time. I guess I got injured in high school, at football practice. It was bad for a few weeks, but seemed to go away. I had backaches on and off during college, but it never seemed to slow me down much. After college, the pattern seemed to be two or three bad "attacks" per year. They would last a couple of weeks, then I would be okay. Usually, I would turn or bend a certain way and that would start it. So I gradually avoided situations where I was likely to make the wrong move, like tennis or golf. As I got older, even the jogging seemed to be a problem. So I stopped a few years ago.

Mary: How about medical treatment?

Jack: Over the years I would see a doctor now and then, but mostly I took care of it myself. They didn't seem to know much more about my back than I did. And when they gave me pills, they seemed to make me sleepy.

Mary: You sound kind of down. Has the problem gotten to you—made you kind of depressed?

Jack: I guess so. It seems to get worse each year and to curtail my actions more. I can't help wondering what comes next.

Mary: I have found that with some injuries, perhaps like yours, the disability is partly physical, but it also affects the person's feelings or attitudes. It certainly is easy to get sort of "ground down" by a chronic health problem. But often the feeling that things are hopeless causes a person to give up and not even do what he can about the condition.

Jack: Well, yes, that could be. I know I have felt that way.

Mary: Our physical therapy program involves some treatment here at the office, but also a great deal of practice or homework. We have had good luck with it, but the patients' motivation to try is very important. Do you think I'm going to be able to talk you into getting off your recliner for an hour or so each day?

Jack: I guess you are giving me a challenge, but I could be the winner if you get me moving. Okay, let's give it a try! But you know I really do have a problem with any kind of an exercise program. What can I do that isn't likely to make me worse? And how do I fit it into my schedule? I can't just forget about work, you know.

Mary: We will have to look at the possibilities once I have had a chance to evaluate your condition more thoroughly. But some types of exercise are low risk yet quite valuable in cases like yours—swimming and walking, to name a couple. And if we look closely at your daily schedule I'm sure we can find some free time.

In the direction stage, Swenson has achieved her major goal of obtaining information by targeting the issues or topics of importance. She gave Robertson some helpful information and made a start at helping him solve his problems regarding the type and scheduling of his exercise. Perhaps of equal importance is her success in helping Jack change his attitude from despair to hope. Some of her hypotheses have been conformed, particularly the one that Robertson's attitudes were significant factors in this case.

Mary: Now, we only have three or four minutes left before we begin the physical examination, and I want to be sure we agree on a few points. Your back problems goes back to your teen years, but has grown worse, particularly the last four or five years, correct?

Jack: Correct.

Mary: Right now you get almost no exercise, partly because of fear that you may irritate your condition?

Jack: That's right. Also, I agree with your point that I have been letting the problem get me down and just not trying to do much about it.

Mary: But I sense that you are ready to make some changes now. Perhaps your attitude of defeat can be reversed. Are you willing to make a real effort to carry through on the program we work out for you?

Jack: Yes, I really do feel more optimistic about it now.

Mary: Good. Now as we develop our plans and start the exercise program, it will be important for you to maintain a positive attitude, even when things don't go well and you have a bad day or two. Improvement may not always be fast and dramatic, but if you keep plugging away, you should see some real change. And I think your new attitude should help a great deal.

Jack: Agreed.

Mary: If you do get down, or if you have any questions or problems, let's spend some time again just talking them out. Now, are there any other points we should discuss? Anything I have missed?

Jack: No, I think that does it—except my medical insurance will cover part of these sessions, won't it?

Mary: Yes, it will. We can take care of the paperwork before you leave today. Now, if you would take off your shirt, we can start the physical exam and then I'll show you a few exercises to start with.

In this final section of the session, Swenson reminds Robertson that the interview will soon end, checks the accuracy of the information she has collected, and helps the patient to begin thinking of the future application of interview results in his daily life. Optimism has been stimulated. The interview is terminated naturally with a routine inquiry about health insurance and the initiation of the physical examination.

In another example, Larry Cole, a mental-health worker on duty at the local psychiatric hospital, has been informed by admissions 30 minutes ago that a new patient is being admitted on an emergency basis. Larry met Bill Langley, the new patient, as he and Mrs. Langley waited in the admissions area. The patient was obviously quite disturbed and irrational and was quickly escorted to his room by Cole and an attendant. After deciding that the patient was unable to provide any background information, Cole decides to conduct the preadmission interview with his wife. As he walks back to the admissions area, Cole takes stock. The Langleys are a young couple, about his own age, and he realizes he must guard against letting his own feelings of distress and sympathy influence the interview. The young mental-health worker is also only too aware of his own inexperience in dealing with cases this serious. He is, however, determined not to let his feelings of insecurity interfere with his job. Fortunately, a private interviewing room is available in the admissions area. Cole has very little information about the Langleys but surmises that they are in their early 20s, recently married, and, perhaps, students at the nearby university. Goals for the interview involve completing an "initial contact" report and attempting to help Mrs. Langley cope with the situation. Because she is quite distressed by her husband's illness, the mental-health worker suspects that he will be forced to take the lead, providing more than the usual structure and direction to the session.

Larry: Hello again, Mrs. Langley. I didn't have a chance to introduce myself earlier. I'm Larry Cole—please call me Larry—and I am the mental-health worker assigned to help your husband.

Mrs. Langley: Hello. Thank you for your help. They told me to fill out these forms, but I don't know half of the information. How is Bill? What's happening to him?

Larry: I left him just a minute ago; he is in bed. They gave him a sedative and he is beginning to calm down now. Let me take the paperwork for now. I'll see just what is really necessary and we can get back to it later. Would you like to come in here where we can talk more easily?

Mrs. Langley: Yes, sure. Thanks.

Larry: Mrs. Langley. . . .

Mrs. Langley: Beth! My name's Beth!

Larry: Beth, I thought that if you feel up to it, we could talk for a bit. I need to get some information about your husband and I'm sure you will have some questions about hospital routine and such.

Beth: Okay. But what is this all about? Why do you have to ask me anything?

Larry: I know it's hard at a time like this, but if you can just give me some help in figuring out what has happened to your husband, it will assist the doctor and the rest of our staff in getting him treated as soon as possible. My job is to collect this information, write a report for his chart and then work with and coordinate the people who will be involved in your husband's treatment.

Beth: Okay, I see. I'll tell you everything I can.

Cole has been fairly successful in starting a difficult interview. The interviewee is emotional, sensitive, and not overly cooperative. Ignoring her occasional rudeness, Cole has been able to gain her cooperation by explaining his role (structuring) and explaining how the information gained can help her husband (encouraging sharing and establishing the alliance). Cole recognizes that he must proceed carefully and tactfully to avoid upsetting her further. Expressions of concern for her situation and allowing her to proceed at her own pace seem appropriate methods.

Larry: Could you tell me just what happened with Bill, what led up to this admission?

Beth: Well, he has been under a lot of stress the last few weeks—at school and at work. I guess I notice it. . . . Is that where I start?

Larry: That would be fine, but are you sure you feel up to this now? Or is there anything I could get you—coffee, a glass of water?

Beth: No thanks. I'm okay. I noticed a problem first about two weeks ago. He got the idea that something was going on at school. Professors had it in for him. He said they were talking about him and asking him hard questions in class, things like that. I told him it was just his imagination, but he didn't believe me. And each day it got worse.

Larry: Go on.

Beth: Well, finally I told him to check with his friends, the ones in his classes, to see if they had noticed anything. They said no and he felt better for a day or so, and then he decided that all his classmates were in on the plot, too! This week he said the same thing had started at work! He delivers for Don's Pizza House and he said they were looking at him funny when he came in and that he got the deliveries that were hard to find. One he never did find and he thought they just made it up to get him out of the building while they plotted something. Yesterday, it got crazy. He told me that the pizzas he delivered were poisoned and that his truck was bugged some way so they could follow him without him seeing them. All kinds of crazy stuff! We didn't sleep much last night and this morning he wouldn't eat anything. When I tried to turn on the television he said no, it was too dangerous. "They" might be watching. I guess he thought people could see us through the television. Well, I was upset, too. I've been calling my mother when Bill was at work and she said to get him to a doctor. Bill wouldn't go to the counseling center on campus. He said they were in with the professors. So we made an appointment with Dr. Davidson, the psychiatrist my girlfriend said was supposed to be good. But the earliest appointment was for next Friday! So when he got real bad this morning I called Dr. Davidson and he said to bring him here. What else do you need to know?

Larry: That was very helpful, Beth. It will help us in working with Bill. Now if you feel up to it, I have a few details to fill in.

Beth: Okay.

Larry: I see here on the form you have Bill's age and address and that he is a student. And you have the job at Don's listed. You wrote that the symptoms first appeared about two weeks ago. I guess that was Bill's ideas about the professors. Do you feel sure that there was no real basis for his suspicions?

Beth: No. No basis. He is in those big sections, 75 or 100 students in class. His professors don't even know him from Adam.

Larry: Has he been doing okay in school?

Beth: Not so well this semester. I guess the job and school together are too much. You know how it is. Tests and papers due every week. He's still getting about average grades, but it's been hard for him.

Larry: Right. It's tough. Beth, it would help to know if Bill has had any problems like this or any similar problem in the past.

Beth: Nothing like this! He is quiet and moody at times. Keeps things to himself. I. . . . (crying).

Larry: I know this is really hard on you, Beth. Maybe another time would be better. . . .

Beth: No. I've got nothing to do now but wait for Dr. Davidson. I need someone to talk to and I want to help as much as I can.

Larry: Okay. You know of no mental health problems that Bill has had?

Beth: Not since I have known him—about two and a half years. We have been married almost a year now. He did mention seeing a counselor for awhile back when he was in high school. But I don't know what it was all about. I thought maybe it was because of his mother.

Larry: His mother?

Beth: Yes, she has had problems, mental problems, off and on for a long time. She seems okay, just sort of distant, and she takes some kind of medicine every day for it.

Larry: Do you happen to know what disorder she has or what medicine she takes?

Beth: No. No one ever talks about it.

Larry: Any other similar problem in their family?

Beth: No. . . . Well, one of his brothers acts kind of strange, but I think he is just different.

Larry: How does he act?

Beth: Well, he's smart enough and finished three years of college, but he works as a trash collector out in the country. Picks up garbage and trash from the farms and takes it to the dump. He lives all alone in a shack and never says anything much when you see him. He dresses real weird, too. But Bill's not like him!

Larry: No, not at all, I'm sure. From what you have told me, Bill has been functioning well at school and work right up to the last few weeks. And you didn't notice any previous problems, anything before two weeks ago or so?

Beth: That's right. Now can you tell me what's wrong with him? What's going to happen?

Larry: I'll tell you as much as I can. But we should know more after Dr. Davidson has had a chance to see him. I think you did the right thing in getting him here this morning. He does need hospitalization at this stage. Fortunately, you have excellent health insurance.

Beth: But will he be alright? When can he come home?

Larry: I think we should plan on at least a few days here, but you will be able to see him regularly. Let me explain our procedures. (He goes on to explain visitation and schedule procedures at the hospital.)

Beth: Okay. That clears up a lot of my questions. And I can call either you or Dr. Davidson to find out what's going on?

Larry: Right. And as I said, you might just as well go on home for now, and check back with me this afternoon.

Beth: God! What am I going to tell his parents? And I think he is scheduled to work tonight. Will he be able to finish his classes this semester?

Larry: Beth, there are just a lot of unanswered questions at this stage. You're just going to have to play it by ear, one day at a time. I guess you can call work later and just tell them he is ill and that he can't make it in. But his parents are a more difficult problem. What do you think your choices are there?

Beth: Well, I could just not say anything, or I could call tonight when his father gets home from work, or wait a few days. . . .

Larry: What do you think would work out best?

Beth: I better call tonight. They have a right to know and would feel bad if I didn't call. I'll just tell them everything I know to that point.

The direction stage is complete. Between the partially completed forms and Langley's responses, necessary information has been supplied for Cole's report. He has given her some information and assistance in coping with the problems that this tragic event has thrust upon her. Note Cole's use of a variety of techniques: direct questioning, indirect questioning, encouragement, reflection, and reassurance. His selective answering of Langley's multiple questions is particularly effective in directing the interview. The mental-health worker has recognized that no clear answer is currently available for many of the interviewee's questions and has chosen to deal with the ones that have some solution.

Larry: I think you have given me all the information I need and I would like to check in on Bill again soon. Maybe in about five minutes we can finish here, for now. Let me just check a few points, and then we'll see if you have any final questions. Bill's condition developed rapidly and was marked by extreme suspiciousness and feelings of persecution. You don't know of any previous mental illness he has had, but his family has had some problems. Bill didn't report any unusual sensory experiences, hearing or seeing things—but he had this strong, irrational belief that people were plotting against him. Does that sound accurate?

Beth: That's right.

Larry: And what did you say your plans are for the rest of today?

Beth: I'll go home for now, make my phone calls, and wait to hear from you.

Larry: We'll be back in touch this afternoon. Either Dr. Davidson will call you once he has seen Bill, or I'll let you know what he thinks when we talk later today.

Beth: Thanks, Larry. That's fine and you really have been helpful.

Larry: I'm glad I could be of help.

Beth: But what's going to happen to us, to Bill and me? Do you think he is going to be okay? Is this the right place for him?

Larry: I know how upsetting this must be for you. Do you need to talk about it some more?

Beth: Thanks, but no, I'll be okay. But did I do the right thing this morning?

Larry: Beth, you have done all the right things, getting Bill in here and contacting Dr. Davidson. He's about the best in town. Of course, I don't know what's going to happen with Bill, but most people who have an acute episode like this are out of the hospital and back home in a matter of days or weeks. Let's hope that's the case with Bill.

Beth: I hope so. Do I need to finish filling out all those papers?

Larry: Just this one. Turn it in at the desk when you leave. Oh, and here is my card with my phone number on it. Goodbye for now.

Cole has now completed a difficult interview. He has met two goals: information for his report and assistance to Langley. She seems less distraught, more able to cope, and appreciative of his efforts. The conclusion stage provided an opportunity to confirm communications, plan for the immediate future, and clear up a few details. Cole was able to give Langley realistic hope that the situation would have an acceptable conclusion.

RESEARCH

While interviewing in health-related settings is certainly not new, interest in the topic has increased greatly in recent years. This interest may in part reflect the attention now being focused on health care generally. The maturing U.S. population, advances in medical technology, and skyrocketing health-care costs have all focused attention on many aspects of the health field. Attention to interviewing in medical settings has also increased as a result of the growing recognition of the importance of psychological and social factors in health. The emerging field of health psychology reflects this trend.

Research and publication on health-related interviewing has originated from several directions. The field of health psychology has produced a number of interview-related publications, some of which are reviewed by Turk and Kerns (1985). The journal *Health Psychology* is another excellent source of current research. Publications directed more at the practitioner that include a review of pertinent interviewing research include Cormier et al. (1984) and Malasanos et al. (1977). Interest in the development of specific interviewing procedures to detect particular disorders has also grown. Friedman and Powell (1984) describe this approach in relation to interviewing for Type A personality.

Professional journals are the usual source of the most recent research in a scientific field. In addition to *Health Psychology,* noted above, these journals frequently carry reports related to health interviewing: *American Journal of Epidemiology, Journal of Behavioral Medicine, Psychosomatic Medicine,* and *Journal of Chronic Diseases.*

SUMMARY

The interview is a common tool in the health-care setting. It is particularly effective in meeting the changing demands of a modern, educated, and sophisticated population. Assessment, instruction, and problem solving are major purposes for health-related interviews.

Certain characteristics make health interviewing distinctive. They include the personal and emotional involvement of patients and family, the need for trusting the professional's judgment in vital matters, the ambiguity and uncertainty of the situation, and the patient's tendency to resist change. Obviously, these characteristics present special problems that must be considered and dealt with.

As with interviews in other settings, four stages of the health-care interview can usually be discerned: preparation, initiation, direction, and conclusion. Instead of being completely separate entities, these stages are best conceptualized as rough divisions that are interdependent and overlapping, and that flow together to make the complete interview.

SUGGESTED READINGS

Cormier, L. S., Cormier, W. H., & Weisser, R. J. (1984). *Interviewing and helping skills for health professionals.* Monterey, CA: Wadsworth Health Sciences Division.

Garrett, A. (1982). *Interviewing: Its principles and methods* (3rd ed.). New York: Family Service Association of America.

Gatchel, R. J., & Baum, A. (1983). An *introduction to health psychology.* Reading, MA: Addison-Wesley.

Karoly, P. (Ed.) (1985). *Measurement strategies in health psychology.* New York: John Wiley & Sons.

MacKinnon, R. A., & Michels, R. (1971). *The psychiatric interview in clinical practice.* Philadelphia: W. B. Saunders.

Malasanos, L., Barkauskas, V., Moss, M., & Stoltenberg-Allen, K. (1977). *Health assessment.* St. Louis: C. V. Mosby.

11

Interviewing in Business and Industry

Ann McDonald
University of Houston, Downtown

The last chapter discussed interviewing as a communications tool in health-care situations. The classic definition of interviewing—a conversation with a purpose—is still appropriate in business and industry, where it has traditionally referred to the personnel or hiring interview. However, the purposes, kinds of information sought, and rules have changed in recent years. Communication in business and industry has taken on new meanings. Yet the interview to select individuals and predict their future performance in a particular work situation continues to be essential. It is a decision-making process that aims to match a job with an employee or potential employee.

This chapter focuses on the personnel interview, reflecting its critical importance. Managers in today's business and industry are expected to have communicative skills for dealing effectively with situations involving interpersonal contact; for example, marketing, supervision, and employee relations. The business interview may be the original hiring interview, or it may be an interview to discuss promotion, demotion, dismissal, or change of responsibility. Interviews often accompany an upward, downward, outward, lateral, or expansion movement of an employee within the business/industry world (Kaye, 1982). Interviewing is also an ongoing communicative technique used to correct, warn, discipline, and evaluate employees. The interview skills presented in Chapter 3 will, therefore, be applied in this chapter to illustrate interviewing in situations for employment, performance evaluation, problem solving, personal assistance, persuasion, and finally discipline and termination. A brief discussion of factors that led to formal interviewing in business and industry will help you appreciate the interview as a significant business activity.

BACKGROUND PERSPECTIVES

As society has changed, so has interviewing in business and industry. When the United States was primarily an agrarian country, a person's physical strength was all that was of interest to an employer. If a person could provide a full day's work, he could receive pay with no questions asked about his training or experience. Performance was all that was necessary. The transition from an agrarian to an industrial world created many changes in the relationship between workers and organizations, ranging from worker abuse, to unionization, to the human-rights legislation passed in the last quarter-century and our current concern for employees as an important resource.

Interviewing is a communicative process that may determine success or failure or maintain the status quo. Employee rights have paralleled human rights with increased expectations and demands for opportunities; these rights have affected the interview. Many legal guidelines govern the business/industry employment interview to guarantee equal opportunity. The 1964 Civil Rights Act, for example, prohibits discrimination in employment based on ethnicity, color, religion, sex, or national origin. Originally, this applied to larger organizations, but in 1972 Congress amended the act to include employers of 15 or more persons. This act also created a federal agency, the Equal Employment Opportunity Commission (EEOC), to enforce these rules.

In addition to the 1964 act and its 1972 amendment, in 1979 enforcement responsibility for the Age Discrimination in Employment Act of 1967 transferred from the Department of Labor to the EEOC. This Act prohibits discrimination in employing or selecting persons 40–70 years of age. In 1973, the Vocational Rehabilitation Act was passed to prevent discrimination against the physically or mentally handicapped for non job-related reasons. This act continues to be enforced by the Department of Labor. Finally, in 1974 the Vietnam-Era Veterans Readjustment Assistance Act was passed to prohibit discrimination against veterans of the Vietnam era and all disabled veterans. Also, two Executive Orders apply to companies that bid or hold government contracts, to ensure equal opportunities. The Office of Federal Contracts Compliance Programs (OFCCP) was established by the Department of Labor to enforce these regulations. Both the EEOC and the OFCCP have published guidelines for employee selection.

The EEOC guidelines apply to tests and other selection procedures that are used as a basis for employment decisions. The employment interview is considered a test under EEOC guidelines for selecting employees, and therefore it must aim to predict job performance. Records and notes containing information used to make employment decisions must be retained. To defend a charge of discrimination in hiring or promotion, the interviewer's notes may be reviewed. Any questions relating to the protected characteristics (sex, ethnicity, color, religion, age, or national origin) must be bona fide occupational qualifications that represent a valid criterion of job performance. The issue is not only of intent, but also of consequences (Megginson, 1981).

The Supreme Court has ruled that an employer does not have to hire anyone who cannot perform the job regardless of background; but neither can an employer blatantly discriminate against any group. This ruling is of crucial importance in the hiring practices of the corporate world. All of this legislation and concern, however, is only an attempt to ensure that the criteria used to make decisions are truly related to the job.

In short, interviewing has changed considerably to reflect changes in American society. The importance of meeting the workers' needs has become more evident. Greater emphasis is placed on individuals than ever before. The importance of workers' attitudes was found to be an important factor in productivity. As individuals' rights have been increasingly recognized in society, laws have been passed to protect the rights of workers.

CONSIDERING THE EMPLOYEE'S NEED FOR SATISFACTION

Clearly, a great deal is at risk in the business interview. The interview may culminate a lengthy relationship, as between a supervisor and an employee retiring after 30 years' service. Or it may be an interview for the first after-school or summer job. Nonetheless, the employment relationship will satisfy certain needs. If it is early on in a career, it is probably satisfying a basic economic or financial need.

It is very helpful to conceptualize job or career development within the model suggested by Maslow (1968). His pyramidal model emphasizes the hierarchical nature of an individual's needs. Basic survival needs form the base of the pyramid; the higher levels are the need for safety and security, the need to belong and be loved, the need for achievement and prestige, and finally, the need for self-fulfillment or self-actualization. An employee will not likely be motivated to achieve great deeds if he is concerned about earning enough pay to purchase groceries or heat his home, for example. Depending on the job and stage in career development, the material and psychological rewards received for performance on the job can be organized to respond to individual needs. Business and industry interviewers should be aware of the range of rewards, aside from salary, and sensitive to the interviewee's varying needs.

Rejection is an important aspect of interviewing in business and industry that is not usually found in other settings. Since the employment goal is to choose individuals who best "fit" the company, some will obviously be accepted and others will be rejected. Interestingly, rejection is not necessarily due to a lack of qualifications; more often the applicant does not exhibit the "accepted" attitudes or personality. Rejection may also occur because some candidates do not meet some subconscious expectations of the interviewer.

Legal guidelines attempt to prevent unnecessary rejections and to focus attention on the critical job-related characteristics presented by the interviewee. The interviewer may find it difficult, however, to withhold judgment when her first impression of an interviewee exceeds the expected range in a visible characteristic such as sex or age. Social factors may preclude serious consideration of a person during the interview process. Before some civil rights legislation passed, an employee could be fired, for example, because of divorce, age, or physical disability. Even today, a man applying for a child-care position or a woman applying for a heavy machinery–operator position is considered outside the norm. It is not surprising for an elderly person or an individual in a wheelchair to report for an employment interview. Shy, unattractive, handicapped, and older interviewees face more than their share of rejections for even the most entry-level positions. Despite legislation, some of these social factors may still surface as managers make selection and promotion decisions. The interviewer should know his own biases and have a clear understanding of the work environment to include the range of acceptable "fit."

The interview setting varies a great deal, from a quiet office in a personnel department to a corner in a manufacturing area. It can be in the work place itself or thousands of miles away. The setting can profoundly affect the outcome of the interview, because it conveys to the interviewee the value of the conversation. The interviewer should be aware of the messages applicants receive through the surroundings.

One of the most organized methods of employment selection takes place on college and university campuses each year when employers, primarily large corporations, interview students for permanent positions following graduation. Although the specifics vary across campuses and employers, the theoretical structure remains relatively the same. A large percentage of the new hires into the corporate world result from this first screening interview, which usually lasts about 30 minutes. Millions of dollars are spent each year planning, training recruiters to make the initial recommendations, promoting college relations, and conducting second interviews at the plant of office site. To hire a new employee from a campus interview is estimated to cost approximately $3,000–$5,000.

Recruiting new hires is very costly, even at the entry level, but the cost of a mistake in hiring or promotion can be much greater. Selection is one of the most critical actions ever taken in business; in fact, McQuaig, McQuaig, and McQuaig (1981) state that "most supervisors and managers spend 50–70% of their time coaching, training, and motivating the problem people in their organization" (p. 3). Many of these "problems" could be eliminated through better initial interviewing.

Considering the seriousness of the decision process in employment selection, great care must be taken to ensure the best possible outcome. Time spent in planning during the preparation stage is usually directly proportional to the responsibilities of the position vacancy. Although all employees should have the benefit of a well-thought-out selection process, if they are to make a successful contribution to the organization, the most planning should probably go into selecting a person who will be making decisions and providing direction for an organization.

In short, human resource management in the business and industry setting requires that the employment interviewer spend more energy in the preparation stage to have self-awareness, get to know the interviewee, and know the specific setting(s) and peculiarities of the job and the organization. Potential candidates must be considered not only for their "technical" skills but for their appropriateness for the organization.

Interviewers are subject to their own personal biases and also to outside influences on their decisions. The interviewee can fall prey to the same influences when making employment decisions. For instance, if the interviewee is meeting a representative of a particular company for the first time, that representative (the interviewer in this case) may profoundly affect the applicant's decision-making process. In fact, the interviewer can affect the perceived desirability of the position (Rynes & Miller, 1983). The interviewer may be the reason why the interviewee does or does not consider the employment opportunity positively.

The interviewer's personal biases may predictably influence her ratings of the interviewee. Contagious bias can carry over to another person who manifests a similar characteristic. For instance, many individuals allow the length of a man's hair to color their perceptions of him, especially in schools and in the work place. In fact, many employment situations have a dress code to reduce discrimination based on appearance. When these requirements are stated in the company's policies, then they are, of course, job related and an applicant would have to make the appropriate changes, if he wished to work in that organization. The contrast between one interviewee and the next interviewee may also influence interviewer ratings. In fact, the degree of difference may account for up to 80% of the variation in the ratings of average applicants when they follow either a poorly qualified or an outstanding candidate (Megginson, 1981).

Since the evaluation of an interviewee often relies on a single individual's subjectivity, it is wise to combine this evaluation with others or with test results. This is especially helpful for positions carrying some authority and increases in importance at the executive and upper-management level. Individuals are apt to choose persons who are most like themselves. There is a strong tendency to associate with individuals who look, act, and espouse similar philosophical, political, or religious ideas. If this occurred in the work place, then organizations would be composed of clones.

When one characteristic colors the individual's entire perception, then it is said to have a halo effect. A person may be easily influenced by certain characteristics of another and yet fit other qualifications around them. This phenomenon is probably the most common evaluation error. Characteristics that fall into this category include dress, speech patterns, demeanor, and general overall presentation. But the interviewer must remember not to be swayed by outward appearances, personality characteristics, social graces, or verbal fluency.

Limited reliability and validity associated with the employment interview were mentioned earlier in this chapter. Some steps can increase the accuracy and predictability of the interview method used in selection and promotion, however. First, as stated earlier, the importance of the preparation stage cannot be emphasized enough. If the organization thoroughly understands its personnel needs, not just in terms of numbers, and the interviewer understands the specific jobs within the organization, then the interview process can be more meaningful to both the candidate and the interviewer.

Second, the likelihood of obtaining useful information on which to base a decision will increase if structure is built into the direction stage of the session itself. It often helps to seek the same information in a variety of methods; for example, asking the same question in different ways at different intervals and combining interview information with other information secured from applications, test results, or references. Information gathered separately from the hiring decision can help limit personal biases that influence an individual's decision.

In summary, many internal and external factors will influence the interviewer's decision-making process. However, if the interviewer is aware of these pitfalls and guards against them, then the process can result in positive interview outcomes. As noted earlier, a clear awareness and understanding of the interviewer, interviewee, setting, and the three component parts of the interview process are central to successful outcomes of the employment interview.

EMPLOYMENT INTERVIEWING

The information sought during the employment interview falls within a specific context so that the facts can be organized within this context and conclusions can be drawn. Specifically, the employment interview is a meeting of individuals face-to-face with a particular purpose; it includes conversation that often encourages a reciprocal relationship between two parties.

The employment interview has three goals: (a) secure information, (b) give information, and (c) establish a friendly relationship. The organization wants to gather information to evaluate the applicant and it also wants to establish goodwill. The interviewee wants to sell her skills, present a positive image, and gather information about the organization. Both parties are attempting to market their positive attributes, minimizing their perceived weaknesses, and seeking evaluation information.

The purpose of the interview, in many other settings, is to gather information from the interviewee so the professional interviewer can provide a service for which the interviewee has sought help and in many cases for which he provides payment. In the employment interview, the interviewer is gathering information to select individuals to provide help to an organization. In the former instance, the interviewer wants to provide a service; in the latter case, the interviewer, or his company, wants some service for which he will pay. This payment takes the form of a salary for a certain job performed, but the job offers payment in much more than just dollars. In fact, this payment is crucial in the complex integration of individuals in our society and one of the fundamental concepts underlying the interrelationships in business and industry. Payment may take the form of extrinsic material rewards, such as benefits to the person and her family; sometimes clothing, shelter, and security; and occasionally even cars, expense accounts, and free services. But more importantly, jobs can provide intrinsic psychological rewards in terms of status, power, title, authority, prestige, and social acceptability, not to mention challenge and opportunities for self-actualization. Communication within this context is, therefore, complicated by the emotional tones associated with one's self-perception as manifested by one's job title.

In many settings, the purpose of the interview is to help the interviewee. In the business and industry setting, both individuals are attempting to solve a problem. The company or organization has a job that needs to be done and the applicant needs a job to collect the rewards.

The success of any organization depends upon its employees' performance. It is critical that the "right" people are hired and supported throughout their careers with the organization. "... The interview is one of the most critical management functions. It literally controls the quality of an organization, by determining the people who work for it" (Jackson, 1976, p. 23). Communication through interviews may also determine how employees develop and grow in their careers.

Considering the attention paid to interviewing in the selection and hiring process, it might be assumed that this technique would have high validity and reliability. Unfortunately, research has documented its limitations. However, few would advocate eliminating the process when fulfilling their own hiring needs (Arvey & Campion, 1982). The employment interview continues to be the most widely used method for selecting employees, despite its reputation as a costly, inefficient, and often invalid procedure. Even when the interview is used in conjunction with other procedures, it is almost always treated as the final hurdle in the selection process (Dunnette & Bass, 1963). Tharp (1983) observes: "Only through the interview process can a manager gather sufficient data to be able to predict whether a candidate will be successful in the position for which he ... is being considered" (p. 636). Although the interview may present many potential problems, the method is quite flexible. It can be used with many types of jobs and applicants and is the only method that provides a two-way exchange of information (Megginson, 1981). The communication exchange in the employment interview has a different significance than in other types of interviews.

Factors Influencing the Employment Interview

Although the employment interview in business and industry is still a face-to-face exchange of information, it is complicated by legal issues added to the usual moral, ethical, and procedural considerations associated with other types of interviews. The communication concepts behind interviewing in the work world are, basically, no different than in other settings discussed in this book. To understand interviewing within the context of business and industry, however, requires comprehension of other fundamental concepts. The issues of emotions, needs, and individual vulnerabilities are compressed into a few crucial minutes that may ultimately determine a person's life course. This is a face-to-face personal encounter in which one person can exert enormous influence on a significant portion of the other person's life. Most interviewing in business and industry, whether in a selection or promotion situation or in less-structured encounters to advise or present information, has an implicit, if not explicit, superior/subordinate relationship rather than a service-provider/consumer-relationship. This and other factors influence the flow of information between the interviewer and interviewee.

The employment interview deals primarily with surface or public information. The employer may want other, more personal or private information, but legal reasons preclude such questions. That information can be volunteered, of course, by the interviewee. It is understood at the start that the information exchanged will concern only some aspects of the interviewee's background. This is an important difference between this interviewing and most other types. Outside the employment arena, the exchange of personal information is expected and often crucial to attaining specific goals.

Adding to the legal constraints are ethical restraints. Despite continual growth in the number of psychologists working in the business world, the interviewer is rarely a professional highly trained to work with the interviewee's personal concerns. Again, the primary purpose of the employment interview within the business/industry context is to hire, select, or help employees perform certain jobs to meet the goals and objectives of both the organization and the interviewee.

Time is also a critical factor to interview effectiveness. Most screening interviews usually last much less than an hour. Outside the business/industry setting, the initial interview usually serves only to develop rapport and establish goals. Generally, within the employment context, the interview is often a one-time assessment with a pre-established goal. For professional-level jobs, the screening interview will be followed by a more in-depth and usually multiple-interviewer situation. The amount of time available will capture only a sample of behavior and the short time must be used carefully to maximize the exchange of useful information. The interviewer is responsible for ensuring that the sample of behavior observed is representative of the interviewee's general behavior.

The critical nature of the interview combined with the time restraints demand that the interviewer organize the environment and plan during the preparation stage to avoid any misuse of time. Effective application of the skills presented in Chapter 3 requires preparation to allow for adequate time to achieve the desired interview outcomes. Time constraints may limit some of the desired and/or expected outcomes for either interviewing party. Whether the desired outcomes are achieved may depend heavily on the professional's interviewing style.

Interviewing Styles

Interviews can be organized in many different ways, but a framework must underlie the interview process. For instance, an unstructured approach can be used in situations to encourage interviewees to express their concerns freely without specific direction from the interviewer. Since one of the interview's goals is to gather relevant information, this approach in its pure form is probably not appropriate for business and industry, especially in light of the usual time restraints. Such an exchange is generally pleasant, emphasizing feelings and emotions; it may fail to attain the necessary information. In fact, this lack of structure may evoke more useless information from the interviewer. The interviewer must assume responsibility for the outcomes and avoid a conversation that turns into idle talk, as the following discussion does:

Interviewer: Mrs. Hampton, perhaps you could tell me a little about yourself.
Mrs. Hampton: Well, I grew up in New York City.

Interviewer: I'm wondering what it is like to grow up in New York.
Mrs. Hampton: Well, since that is all that I ever knew, I wasn't conscious of being different from others my age. But it was great to have so many cultural resources available. One of my favorite things to do was to go to MOMA on Saturdays and look at the new stuff and then sit in the garden.
Interviewer: MOMA?

The purpose of this interview has drifted into a pleasant social exchange and, while it may be interesting, it does not gather job-related information.

At the other end of the continuum is the direct or structured approach. Originally, this structured approach was developed to objectively measure the occupational adjustment of normal people. The procedure is systematic, with little attention to the applicant's feelings or reactions. It emphasizes objective description, testing, and systematic case study. The most obvious example of this approach would be the verbal application form, where the interviewer simply reads written questions and records the applicants' responses. For example, such an interview might continue as follows:

Interviewer: Where did you go to school?
Mrs. Smith: Manhattan High School.
Interviewer: What was your major there?
Mrs. Smith: I was a science major.
Interviewer: What courses did you take?

Much of this type of information can easily be provided by the interviewee prior to the interview to allow a more pertinent exchange of information during the interview itself.

In comparing these two approaches, it is evident that their usefulness depends on the interviewer's temperament and style and the interview's specific goals. Exclusive use of the nondirective method is probably rare. Most employment interviewers use a more direct method, often in combination with unstructured leads or questions.

The third type of interview in this category, the stress interview, should be used with care. Its purpose is to produce anxiety by placing the candidate under stress. Naturally, the amount of stress perceived varies with each individual on both sides, depending on background and experience. For some individuals, especially shy, young candidates, asking "Why should I hire you?" can produce a great deal of anxiety, while for others such a question gives them a cue to present their case. This method is sometimes used in the hiring process for sales personnel to predict their ability to deal with difficult customers. Meriman and McLaughlin (1983, p. 56) provide a list of common stress-inducing questions:

— Why should we hire you?
— Why aren't you earning more at your age?
— How well do you perform under extreme pressure? Give me an example.
— Give us an example of your creative self.
— How long would it take you to make a significant contribution to our organization?
— Why do you feel you possess the skills of top management?
— What types of people seem to rub you the wrong way?
— What factors determine a person's progress in an organization?

Obviously, the same information can be sought in several ways. The wording, tone of voice, and nonverbal cues will influence the response. For example, a simple introductory question might be worded in the following ways:

— Where were you last employed? (Direct.)
— Perhaps you could tell me about your last employment experience, with Company Z? (Nondirect.)
— Why did you leave Company Z? (Stress.)

Also, note the difference in the form in the following examples:

— Do you agree that . . . ?
— Do you feel that . . . ?
— Do you agree with Authority X that . . . ?

Since interviewing is a technique used in business and industry to encourage communication, to gather and provide information, any one of the styles or approaches can be used as a framework. The particular approach will depend on the interviewer's skills and preferences, the physical and philosophical environment in which the interview is to take place, and the dimensions of the particular job vacancy. Also, the constraints of time, space, and resources will always affect this process.

Explicit in each case is the need for the interviewer to "know thyself." Since no one right approach to the interview exchange exists, it is not necessary for the interviewer to follow any particular style; rather, she should understand that her style as an interviewer will influence the interviewee's responses and behaviors. The employment interview itself is a few minutes of time extracted from the behavioral repertoire of both the interviewer and the interviewee. According to Meriman and McLaughlin (1983), "For a brief period, the interviewer and job seeker are under the spotlights on stage and playing parts, whose stake is the career of the individual and the success of the organization" (p. 10). With luck, the exchange will be a representative sample of behavior so that the predictions made will have some worth. The best predictions will be made for the short range, for a situation that is most like the current circumstance; predictions for the distant future may be nothing more than an educated guess.

When thinking of the employment interview, it is helpful to visualize the encounter in its three component parts: the interviewer, the interviewee, and the organization, all within a particular setting. What goes on in any interview is the interaction of those three components at a particular time. However, each of those three parts not only influences the other two, but also brings to the interview history, experience, and knowledge.

Each part is the sum of past experiences, plus the expectations for what will take place in the interview itself and possible outcomes for the future. These expectations can cloud the issues and interfere with the communication process because so much can be at stake. For instance, if this is a first job possibility for a new college graduate, the importance of the interview probably cannot be overemphasized in the interviewee's mind. The emotions and feelings of the interviewee would certainly be heightened by the following question: "John, tell me how you see yourself fitting into my organization with the experience and training you've had."

It is important that the interview style fits the interviewer, while gaining necessary information in a way that communicates a positive image to the interviewee. The style chosen provides the framework for the various techniques and strategies.

Strategies and Techniques

As previously mentioned, the employment interview in business and industry has certain parts and an inherent order, somewhat like the ritual of a dance or a play. But unlike the dance or play, it is a dynamic process, with the characters changing after each performance. The preparation stage is critical for the initiation stage to open on the proper note and for establishing a working relationship. Next comes the direction stage, which is the heart of the session, involving the exchange of information. The conclusion stage allows time for clarification, a closing, and evaluation. Generally speaking, the process should be developmental in structure; above all, it should be flexible.

Because the resulting decision is critical, the interview should be planned during the preparation stage to increase the chances of success. An underlying theme of this book has been the need for the interviewer to have self-awareness and self-understanding—to know her perspective, prejudices, attitudes, defenses, and reactions—and to appreciate the situational factors that influence the interviewer-interviewee relationship. Even the time of day can influence response to the interviewee.

If the interviewer is truly prepared for the encounter, he will know details about the job, working conditions, promotional possibilities, technical qualifications, compensation, and alternative positions (Jackson, 1976). Knowing about the company is simply not enough. Applicants want to know what they will be expected to do and how they will fit into the organization. It is also becoming increasingly important for the interviewer to have some understanding of career possibilities within the organization.

All parts of the interview are important, but the initiation stage sets the tone of the whole encounter. The attitude of the interviewer may be thought of as his orientation (Shouksmith, 1978). It can be formal or informal, structured or unstructured, but it should reflect the organization's setting and philosophy. This stage includes introductions, a brief clarification of the interviewer's role, and a description of what will happen during the interview. For example, the following verbal exchange might begin an interview between a manager and a clerical employee:

Manager: Mrs. Brown, I've asked you to come and talk to me today about some changes that are going to take place in our office soon. Please sit down. Would you like coffee or a soda?

Mrs. Brown: A soda, please.

Manager: As you know, Mrs. Smith is going to be leaving in June and we are going to have to fill her position. I think that you are also aware that our company policy is to promote from within whenever possible. What I hope to do this week is to talk to all of the people in the office who I think might have an interest in her position. Mrs. Brown, you've worked in our office for three years as our secretary, have you ever thought about doing anything else?

Mrs. Brown: Yes, I know my job pretty well now and I've thought it might be fun to do something new.

Manager: How much do you know about Mrs. Smith's job?

Mrs. Brown: Well, I know what she does but I'm not at all sure of the details of how she does it. I've helped with some of her typing on occasion and I transfer calls to her constantly, so I know that she spends a lot of time on the phone.

One of the fundamental goals of the interview, in most settings, is to establish a relationship. Bingham, Moore, and Gustad (1959) maintain that "It is in this relationship between two human beings that things happen. This is the strength of the interview" (p. 270). As discussed in Chapter 3, a few comments about the weather, the latest sports news, or a nonverbal cue such as a smile may be helpful to build rapport. Such exchanges serve two purposes: (a) setting the interviewee at ease and (b) indicating the person's interests. Sometimes this takes only a few minutes; the interviewee's verbal and nonverbal behaviors generally indicate whether the attempts have succeeded. For example, the following exchange might take place between an employment interviewer (Mr. Lewis) and an applicant (Ms. Terry) after the introductions:

Mr. Lewis: Did you have any trouble finding the office?
Ms. Terry: No.
Mr. Lewis: My office is around this way. Have a seat. Did you have any trouble finding a place to park?
Ms. Terry: No, I had a ride.
Mr. Lewis: I haven't been out today. How is the weather?
Ms. Terry: It's raining again.
Mr. Lewis: We certainly have had more than our share this year. Ms. Terry, you are here because of the notice on the bulletin board. Have you ever worked in a lab before?
Ms. Terry: Yes.
Mr. Lewis: Let me tell you a little about what we do down here and then you can tell me a little about yourself. I'm the new lab director for a project called LIRE and I'm looking for people who have had some experience in a lab to help me to set up and then to provide a particular service to our underwater division.

Once the interviewee appears relaxed, the planned exchange of the direction stage can begin. The method used to give and elicit information will depend on the interviewer's background and experience. Earlier sections of this book discussed several approaches and methods, and Chapter 3 detailed communication skills to use here.

The interviewer must listen to the interviewee from her perspective and indicate a willingness to listen more than talk. Interviewing is 80%–90% listening and very hard work (McQuaig et al., 1981). The following exchange might take place between an interviewer (Ms. Thomas) and a potential employee (Mr. Lewis) for a professional-level job following introductions and some casual conversation:

Ms. Thomas: Why don't we go back to my office and talk a little about your background and experience? Have a seat. I understand that you have recently graduated from State U. and that you have a degree in engineering. I'm not familiar with their program; can you tell me about it?
Mr. Lewis: Yes, it's a general degree in engineering with courses in all of the engineering disciplines.
Ms. Thomas: How did you happen to choose such a course?
Mr. Lewis: Well, my father is an engineer and I guess it seemed like the thing to do. I don't know much about anything else.

Ms. Thomas: Is there a particular aspect of engineering that interests you?

Mr. Lewis: No—well, maybe structures.

Ms. Thomas: What is particularly appealing about structures?

Mr. Lewis: Well, I always did like to build things. I've always liked to do physical things. I played ball in high school and college so that I could get in a lot of physical activity.

Ms. Thomas: Did you bring a resume with you?

Mr. Lewis: Yes, here it is.

Ms. Thomas: (Looks it over briefly.) It looks as if you have had some experience in working in an engineering environment. Why don't you tell me a little about yourself and what you want to do and then I'll tell you a little about this department.

Active listening, mirroring or reflecting, clarifying, and probing are all used during the direction stage of interviews. Active listening takes a great deal of concentration. It is not the kind of listening that one usually finds in a social situation. The interviewer must emit both verbal and nonverbal cues indicating that she truly hears what is being said.

Mirroring is used to demonstrate hearing the interviewee's concerns and to communicate that understanding. It also helps to clarify the interviewee's thinking. For instance: "You felt put upon when your boss asked you to type personal correspondence." Clarification helps to sort out conflicting perceptions and inconsistencies and to attain understanding of what the interviewee is saying. It is not interpretation, but it is more than just mirroring what has been said. For example, an interviewer might say to the interviewee: "You seem to be saying that you had a different personal style than your supervisor."

Probing is a skill for seeking additional information, asking the interviewee to embellish what has already been said. A simple open question can often achieve the desired results. For example: "What can you tell me about your volunteer work in the community?" or "Can you describe what your responsibilities were?"

An open, accepting attitude must be maintained while postponing a decision until a representative sample of behavior has been collected. Many people have a strong tendency to make judgments about others in the first few minutes of a face-to-face meeting, especially those who have had a great deal of experience in interviewing. The danger, of course, in drawing conclusions too soon is that it makes the rest of the time unproductive. The best candidates do not always make the best first impression.

The interviewer must attempt to get behind what may be a facade. First impressions can set an unfair expectation level that may be well under or over the performance level. The interviewer's expectations of the interviewee can influence that individual's behavior. If, in the sequence of observations, the first one is positive, the others that follow seem to have less influence. Obviously, the first can also be negative and any positive characteristics may not have the strength to overcome the first. The interviewer can do a great disservice to the applicant and consequently to the organization if she does not guard against quick evaluations.

All employment interviews have time constraints, sometimes severe. In any case, prior to the end of the interview, the professional must begin to bring the conversation to a close. The conclusion stage is the time to review the information exchanged, to clarify any vague points, then to offer additional information and to respond to the interviewee's questions. By this time both parties should have a fairly good idea of the potential matching of skills and characteristics with the demands of the position. The encounter should end on a positive note but avoid false impressions or unrealistic expectations. Continuing with Ms. Minor and Ms. Gonzalo, the closing of their interview might go like this:

> **Ms. Minor:**   Have you given any thought to the new position?
>
> **Ms. Gonzalo:**   Yes, but I'm not sure about my own personal situation. So I'd have to do some serious thinking about my future before I would say yes. I wouldn't want to be considered if I didn't think that I could manage it.
>
> **Ms. Minor:**   Well, Ms. Gonzalo, why don't you give some serious thought to the possibility of a move to this position and then get back to me when you've made a decision?
>
> **Ms. Gonzalo:**   Okay. I'll let you know in a few days.
>
> **Ms. Minor:**   Thank you. If you should have any questions in the meantime, just give me a call. Otherwise I'll expect your call by the end of next week. Is that okay?

Following closure, evaluation should occur immediately, especially if another applicant is scheduled. Memory often distorts over time, particularly with interference. Rating time must be built into the total time allotment. A simple form helps to focus attention on specific qualifications and helps ensure that each candidate is evaluated with the same criteria. Such a form should also provide space for written impressions, comments, or recommendations. This type of information is often difficult to recall over time. Goodale (1982) states: "The greatest tragedy in interviewing is the tendency of human beings to distort, ignore, forget or otherwise waste important information" (p. 33).

INTERVIEWING: MORE THAN AN EMPLOYMENT SELECTION TOOL

So far, this chapter has focused on the selection or employment interview. Interviewing in business and industry, however, is not only used in the selection stage of the relationship, but occurs throughout the relationship. In fact, interviewing is a key tool in the entire career development process. Interviewing is used to assess the work environment, to evaluate employee performance, to gather information when separation occurs between an employee and employer, and to aide in guidance and development of employees. All steps in the career decision-making process involve face-to-face communication to solve problems. Other types of interviewing are found in business and industry: (a) persuasive, (b) performance, (c) problem-solving, (d) termination, and (e) personal helping.

Persuasive Interview

An element of persuasion characterizes almost all interviews conducted in business and industry. In the employment interview, the applicant is attempting to persuade or encourage the interviewer that she is the best person for the job; the interviewer is attempting to persuade the applicant that his is the best company to work for. In the problem-resolution interview, the interviewer is attempting to persuade the employee to make improvements in his work behavior, and in the performance-evaluation interview, the employee is attempting to persuade the evaluator to judge him in a favorable light. In its purest form— sales; negotiations; attempting to persuade others to accept concepts, ideas, and proposals—the persuasive interview moves out of the employee-supervisor format.

Many people prepare for persuasive interviews rather haphazardly. They assume that because they have a great idea, others will naturally see this and go along with any proposals that logically follow. It is unfortunate, but great ideas by themselves are not terribly persuasive unless presented properly. Preparation for the persuasive interview should take into account the setting, for example. Often the place is chosen by others, so the advantages and disadvantages of the setting are not always under the interviewer's control. The interviewer should consider whether the setting is casual or formal, as well as the need to tailor materials such as visual aids and sound equipment. The visual aids appropriate for a small meeting area could prove to be totally inadequate in a larger room, while a powerful sound system used in a small area could irritate the audience. A common mistake in preparing a persuasive interview is to explore only one's own position. It can be more effective if alternative positions are explored and criticisms sought before the interview; this allows for logical changes in position where appropriate. It also allows the interviewer to formulate carefully thought-out responses to likely questions. Part of preparation should include establishing clear goals for the final interview outcome. It is also wise to consider backup positions should compromise be indicated.

In the initiation stage of the persuasive interview it is appropriate to use the skills discussed in Chapter 3 to put the audience at ease, whether that audience is one person or a group of individuals. Small talk and even an appropriate joke often help, although jokes are not obligatory. Many people are simply not very good at telling jokes. A person who typically has little success with "set up" jokes will do well to avoid the "that reminds me of" sort of joke or a little story to begin the presentation. In the initiation stage, the interviewer should clarify his role, letting the audience know that this is indeed a persuasive interview, that he has some points he wants to make. At the same time, he will want the audience to know that he will listen to their views and opinion.

In the direction stage, the interviewer should present her position clearly and without pressure. Having explored the alternatives, she should be able to compare the advantages and disadvantages of her position with alternatives. While believing in one's own position and showing enthusiasm are good selling points for a position, the hard sale should be avoided. In persuasive interviews within one's own company, the audience is probably at least as sophisticated as the interviewer. Pressuring them will most likely lead to resistance. That can affect not only the persuasive interview itself, but also future interactions. The listening skills discussed in Chapter 3 will help in responding appropriately to questions and comments. With proper preparation, questions and comments will be less likely to catch the interviewer off guard. If someone does bring up a new, valid argument, the ramifications of that argument should be explored. For example:

Mrs. Richmond: Mr. Peters, in your proposal will we put computer terminals in each sales rep's office? Aren't they rather expensive? And won't they have very little time to use the computers?

Mr. Peters: The point about the expenses is well taken. There will be a considerable expense to start the system up. Perhaps you could tell me a little more about what you see the problems will be with time.

Mrs. Richmond: Well, Mr. Peters, our sales reps are supposed to spend most of their time out of the office and so I'm not sure they would spend enough time at the computer to warrant the expense of the system.

Mr. Peters: You may be right, Mrs. Richmond. That is a key question. Can computers help sales reps increase their efficiency enough to offset the cost of the system. I put together some figures on how I believe the computer system will help them make better use of their time.

These listening skills, as outlined in Chapter 3, will help involve the audience in the persuasive interview as active participants. This makes any conclusions reached in the persuasive interview more acceptable to the audience.

The conclusion stage of the persuasive interview should recap the major point made during the interview. It should also summarize the next steps to be taken, if any were decided upon. If no decisions were made, then it should summarize any questions that remain. That way, follow-up steps can be taken to address those questions.

Performance Interview

Despite the almost-universal recognition of the need for performance interviews, widespread dissatisfaction with the process exists. Performance interviews often lack clear criteria, goals, and conclusions that can be systematically defended (Donaghy, 1984). Often, performance interviews are seen as unpleasant or punishment for all involved. Several steps can prevent performance interviews from becoming annual or semiannual exercises in frustration and anxiety.

The preparation stage is especially important if the performance interview is to be constructive for all involved. Preparation for the performance-evaluation interview is an ongoing process. It occurs continually throughout the period between interviews. Documentation is critical to this procedure. It is important to document both positive and negative events that will form the basis of the evaluation. This not only provides concrete examples of behavior the company may wish to encourage, it also provides clear examples and dates of incidents that may cause an employee to be passed over for promotion or even terminated. If an employee thinks her legal rights have been violated or she has been treated unfairly, she may challenge the evaluation through legal action. Performance evaluation will also be less stressful if the events that are documented come as no surprise to the employee. Any incident significant enough to influence the evaluation negatively should be discussed with the employee during a problem-resolution interview prior to the evaluation interview itself.

Standardized evaluation and rating forms are available and provide quick ways to monitor employee performance between interviews. If these forms are used properly, deficiencies can be corrected as they become apparent and positive behavior encouraged. Obviously, all employees should be informed as soon as possible about criteria for evaluation; ideally, this should happen at the time they are hired by the company. Reviewing with the employee the forms used to track employee performance helps ensure a clear understanding of what to expect. Generally, available forms are standardized so everyone is evaluated with the same criteria, and they are readily available. Unfortunately, the criteria that apply to all positions are often too general, and do not speak directly to each employee's specific duties and responsibilities.

One flexible approach is to evaluate an employee's performance on the basis of stated objectives that have been agreed on by the employee and his supervisor. Instituting this approach requires more effort, but it has significant advantages. The supervisor and employee go over objectives when the employee takes a new position or periodically. This allows both to appraise priorities and discuss the practicality of each objective. Both parties are aware of the criteria used to judge success, and the individual demands of each position are recognized and dealt with individually. A major advantage of this system is its flexibility in problem-resolution interviews and occasionally performance evaluations. Priorities can be restated, objectives rethought, and criteria for evaluation altered to satisfy new conditions.

Again, the preparation stage should allow adequate time for the evaluation and ensure a comfortable, private setting. Baker (1984) suggests that the performance-appraisal interview be divided into two parts, one to evaluate and the other to counsel and plan a strategy for improvement. This follows the model proposed in this book; first identifying concerns in the direction stage, then following with goal setting and skills implementation. The initiation stage identifies the interviewer's role and the interview's nature. At this point, the format of the interview can be laid out.

> **Interviewer:** Mrs. Spencer, since this is your first performance-evaluation interview with this company, I would like to let you know what to expect. I will be going over all the material that we looked at in evaluating your job performance. And then we will have time to discuss the evaluation in detail. You will have a chance to ask any questions you like and add any information you feel might be helpful.

As with problem-resolution interviews, it is a good idea to keep records of the performance-evaluation interview. If it is recorded, the employee should be made aware of this. After the evaluation material is presented during the first part of the evaluation stage, the second part will follow the interview procedures in Chapters 3 and 4. Open questions are used to get feedback, review objectives, and determine how to continue what is positive and change what is not. Again, this process is most productive if the situation is viewed as two adults working together to find the best solutions possible. Alternatives can be discussed jointly even though decisions on criteria for job performance ultimately are management's. The focus of the interview should be on the job performance itself. Feedback should be encouraged, but not griping. Should the process lead to important areas worthy of discussion but not truly part of the performance interview, then both parties can consider scheduling a separate interview to deal with those issues.

Finally, the conclusion stage of the performance-evaluation interview consists of clarifying any changes in the objectives that future evaluations will consider. This evaluation also includes summarizing areas in which the employee is doing well, those that need improvement, and how that improvement might occur.

Problem-resolution Interview

The problem-resolution interview, sometimes called the disciplinary interview, is dreaded by most supervisors in business and industry. The very name disciplinary clearly evokes the picture of an upset parent scolding a misbehaving child. It is not surprising that scolding adults is often unproductive or even counterproductive. Resolving problems may not change the circumstances leading to the interview or even the decisions to be made as a result of the interview. Focusing on the problem, however, does transform the interaction into one of two adults attempting to identify and define problems accurately, discover how they came about, and decide how they are to be resolved. In a problem-resolution interview, the employee is expected to provide feedback and take part in the solution. The problem-resolution interview recognizes the possibility that the root of the problem may lie within the organization itself, rather than with the employee. The problems that generally prompt such an interview would be failure to perform work up to standards or disruptive behavior that interferes with others, either through attitude, behavior, or infractions of rules and guidelines.

Preparations for the problem-solving interview depend on how much time is available. When an employee is unsafe or is acting in some other totally unacceptable way, immediate action may be required. If possible, however, time should be taken to prepare for the interview. This gives the interviewer time to cool off, but at the same time keeps things moving forward so that the interview is not put off or forgotten.

Because the problem-resolution interview can be uncomfortable, participants tend to avoid dealing with problems. This produces a situation where relatively minor problems that could have been easily resolved are allowed to accumulate and become larger problems. Employees may get the impression that their behavior is in fact acceptable.

If possible, the situation should be investigated before a problem-resolution interview. If standards have been violated, the interviewer should know before the interview what those standards are and be prepared to specify those shortcomings to the employee. If the problem involves disruptive behavior, documented examples of violations should be available. The interviewer should also have a clear understanding of what the rules are, as well as the consequences that can result from the interview, whether it involves a warning, docking of pay, or even termination.

The setting for the problem-resolution interview should be private. This prevents embarrassment to the employee. Helping him to be less defensive encourages him to work productively and discover solutions to problems. A private setting also allows note-taking or recording of the proceedings. Because of the potential for future legal action, company policy may even require a third party to be present, if the anticipated consequences are severe.

Sufficient time should be provided for the interview. Some recommend scheduling disciplinary interviews at the end of the work day so that the employee need not return to face his coworkers immediately (Donaghy, 1984). Unfortunately, this approach leads to some difficulties. These interviews usually follow some identifiable incident and the employee is very much aware that repercussions are likely. Delaying the interview until the end of the day reinforces the idea that punishment will occur. This allows the employee time to worry about the interview and to become anxious and defensive. By the end of the day, she has already imagined the worst possible consequences and is either extremely nervous or very angry. Neither will contribute to the optimal solution.

The problem-resolution interview is better scheduled when it is convenient, as with any important activity. The interviewer should also prepare to resolve the problem, rather than punish the person.

During the initiation stage, the interviewer should clarify her role, appraise the employee of the problem, and make it clear that the goal of the interview is to determine how the problem occurred and how to resolve it so that it will not occur in the future.

> **Supervisor:** Mr. Ash, there is a problem with your work I would like to discuss with you. Today you handed in a report on the Burk account. It didn't have all the material that we will be needing.
> **Mr. Ash:** I know, I just couldn't seem to get done in time.
> **Supervisor:** Let's talk about it, see what went wrong, and think about how we might be able to prevent it from happening in the future.

The direction stage of the interview should include listening to the person from his frame of reference and asking open-ended questions so that the employee's side can be heard. It is important to find out what has caused the problem. The employee may have been unaware of what was expected of him or that his behavior leads to problems. These problems will be the easiest to resolve with the employee's cooperation. On the other hand, he may have willfully broken rules or not performed up to agreed-upon standards. These will be more difficult to resolve. In such instances, the interviewer should emphasize what behavior is acceptable and what the consequences of inappropriate behavior are. Feedback, even in these situations, is very important. The employee may feel justified when he willfully fails to meet standards, for example. It is important to understand his justification and to clarify to him the company's position.

There may also be an organizational problem that forces the employee to violate either one rule or another. The company's expectations or rules may of course be unrealistic in specific situations; this should be explored. The employee should understand that the encouragement of feedback is not seen with the welcoming of general complaints.

In summary, in the direction stage it is important to stay focused on the problem behavior. A supervisor can expect that employees will become emotional and occasionally defensive. Within limits, it helps to allow employees time to vent their emotions and then to refocus them on the problem. Some employees may never accept that their behavior was inappropriate or unjustified. After clarifying what the problem behavior is and how it came to pass, the supervisor should clarify the consequences of past behavior and future expectations, as well as the implementation procedures for ensuring achievement of goals set in the problem-resolution interview. The problem-resolution interview ends with the interviewer checking communication to verify that he and the employee have the same expectations and understanding of consequences should those expectations not be realized.

Termination Interview

The most uncomfortable task for many persons in business and industry is conducting a termination interview. It may cause discomfort because termination interviews are often done badly. When interviewing employees who are voluntarily leaving their positions, the interviewer must try to find out why they are leaving. Even more uncomfortable is the job of interviewing an employee who does *not* wish to leave the job. Then, the interviewer must be prepared to tell the employee that her source of economic well-being and professional identification is disappearing, then observe a person who may become extremely hurt or angry. Often, the interviewer is tempted to abbreviate the termination interview and simply announce the decision, the reasons for the decision, and offer a quick expression of sympathy before ending the interview.

If done properly, the termination interview can provide valuable information for both parties and leave the employee with the feeling that the organization does, in fact, care about her as an individual. The termination interview is best done by someone other than the employee's direct supervisor, because the supervisor is often involved in the reasons for the termination. The direct supervisor may have more trouble conducting the interview and may very well limit honest feedback. Time is needed to prepare for the termination interview.

The interview itself should be scheduled a few days before the employee is due to leave. This allows the employee to get everything in order prior to leaving. The interviewer will need to review the documentation and notes pertaining to the employee. For an interview with an employee who is being involuntarily terminated, the interviewer must ensure that sufficient documentation exists to warrant termination. The same legal rights discussed in the section on employment interviews apply at the time of termination. If an employee believes he has been terminated from a job because of discrimination, then he can and often does bring legal action against the company. That prospect emphasizes the importance of clarifying the reasons for termination and the documentation supporting that decision for the employee. As with the problem-resolution interview and the performance-appraisal interview, careful records must be kept of the termination interview. Recording the session allows the interviewer to concentrate solely on what the employee is saying and provides an accurate record of the interview.

During the initiation stage it is kindest to move fairly rapidly to the purpose of the interview. The employee being involuntarily terminated is rarely surprised totally. Either he is aware that the company is laying off some personnel or, in the case of termination due to the work performance, he should have already had at least one problem-resolution interview and possibly a performance-evaluation interview. He should have been informed then that termination would result from failure to improve. The employee who is voluntarily terminating a position obviously knows he is leaving.

The interviewer should identify herself and clarify her role. When discussing the general goals of the interview, she should make clear that she wants to offer what information she can and to listen carefully to what the employee has to say. The main goal of the termination interview is the exchange of useful information for both parties.

During the direction stage, the employee who is leaving voluntarily is questioned about why she is leaving her job, not to make her feel guilty or to attempt to change her mind, but rather to discover if the company needs to be doing something differently to retain qualified workers. An attempt to work out differences to retain a particular worker should have been made in a problem-resolution interview.

The direction stage of the interview with an involuntarily terminated employee should move fairly quickly over the reasons for termination. The employee should be made to understand why his job is being terminated. Proper documentation will help the employee to understand that he is being dealt with fairly and legally. When the employee is being terminated because of company furloughs, it should be made clear why he is being laid off while others are being retained. Those being terminated because of failure to perform their jobs adequately can be provided with useful information about behavior they will need to change in their next job.

> **Interviewer:** Mr. White, as you can see, your monthly sales figures have been constantly below the agreed-upon quota. They were set at your last performance evaluation. On three occasions, your supervisor met with you to try to resolve this problem. There doesn't seem to be much improvement.
>
> **Mr. White:** I know that I have been coming in under quota with my sales but it seems like no matter what I tried it didn't work.
>
> **Interviewer:** Your supervisor indicated that she feels that you weren't aggressive enough pursuing contacts.
>
> **Mr. White:** I know; that sort of thing makes me uncomfortable.
>
> **Interviewer:** Maybe you would find better success in a field other than sales.
>
> **Mr. White:** You may be right; I never was very comfortable in sales. Perhaps I should seek a job in a different field.

Employees who are being terminated due to layoffs may benefit from knowing the outlook for their job specialty.

The employee being terminated will often respond emotionally. The interviewer should not try to stifle the employee's emotional response, but rather should attempt to refocus the interview after a short period, recognizing the reasons for the emotions. She can also assist the employee by helping him to explore what his alternatives are and what assistance the company may be able to offer in looking for a new job or seeking training for a new career.

In short, the conclusion of the termination interview is especially important because it will likely be the last opportunity for both sides to communicate effectively. The communication that took place during the interview should be clarified along with any future actions, such as reference letters and job referrals. Serious consideration for providing personal assistance or helping may be needed following an employee's termination.

Personal-helping Interview

A manager or supervisor will be called upon, more often than he might expect, to deal with some employees' personal problems. Employees frequently seek guidance and advice from their supervisors. Supervisors provide guidance and advice on professional matters daily, so some workers will assume that a supervisor is prepared to give guidance and help in nonprofessional matters. In fact, managers and supervisors may be least prepared to conduct the personal-helping interview.

The personal-helping interview may also be initiated by the supervisor. She might feel that something is bothering one of her employees, despite the fact that the employee's work is satisfactory or even better than usual. If the employee is using work to avoid other problems and other aspects of his life, the actual output of work may increase. Problems in other areas of an employee's life tend to have negative long-term effects on work, though. In either case, whether employee-initiated or supervisor-initiated, expression of concern is generally helpful.

As with most interviews, the preparation stage is critical. The most important question to ask at this stage is: "Am I the best person to conduct this interview?" Not all persons are comfortable dealing with personal problems, so all supervisors should not feel totally comfortable in that sort of an interview. Some supervisors provide the best service by recognizing that others are more skilled at this particular task than they. Serious consideration of the interview skills presented in Chapter 3 of this book and an assessment of one's own personality and interviewing skills should help answer this question.

Supervisors should also consider their situational limits. Some supervisors will simply not have the time to explore personal relations. They may not even have an appropriate place that would offer significant privacy.

Another issue is involvement in the employee's problems. Being objective in such situations will be very difficult. Sometimes, employees' problems may elicit strong feelings about one of the supervisor's own problems. An example would be a supervisor who spends additional hours at work to avoid continual fighting with his spouse at home. If it appears that an employee has essentially the same concern, that particular supervisor is probably not well-suited to help the employee.

Supervisors should not think that their position demands an ability to handle all concerns. If the supervisor thinks that she is not the best person for the employee to speak with about personal problems, the preparation stage might include an appropriate referral.

This sort of interview, in some ways, is more difficult to prepare for than others. Often, the concerns that arise are unanticipated and difficult to prepare for. Similarly, it is difficult to anticipate how much time will be required. When the employee initiates the personal interview, the supervisor should still attempt to have some time for preparation as well as arrange the schedule to allow sufficient time to work with the employee. When setting aside time, it is important to recognize that more than one interview may be necessary. Thus it is not necessary to set aside sufficient time to resolve all of the employee's problems in the first interview.

As with other interviews, the setting should be comfortable and above all private. Often employees profit most from a receptive ear and clarification of what they themselves are thinking and feeling rather than suggestions. The initiation stage will often begin with the supervisor expressing concern and clarifying roles.

> **Supervisor:** Mr. Eduardo, I noticed you are spending a lot of extra time here at the office. Your work is fine but I'm wondering how you are doing?
>
> **Mr. Eduardo:** I'm doing okay. It's just that since Faye and I broke up, I have a lot more time to devote to my work.
>
> **Supervisor:** Well, I'm kind of concerned about you lately and I was wondering if sitting down and talking about things would help.
>
> **Mr. Eduardo:** Well, I really haven't talked about it much. Maybe that would help.

In the direction stage, most supervisors would probably do well to use the more interviewee-centered approaches that were discussed in the early chapters of this book and the employment-interview section of this chapter. More aggressive techniques for helping people are available, but they require additional training and skill development. The skills outlined in Chapters 3 and 4 of this book will help the supervisor assist others in identifying their own concerns and finding their own answers. The supervisor often may be tempted to give advice on what he considers the central problem. When tempted to do this he might remember that advice on personal concerns is often not very helpful.

Active listening and information seeking can help interviewees identify their major concerns and explore alternatives. Even though interviewees should not be told what to do in their personal lives, the supervisor can help them explore alternatives—looking at both advantages and disadvantages of each—and can provide honest feedback, as the following illustrations demonstrate:

> **Supervisor:** Mrs. Jones, from what you are saying, it sounds like the problems you are having with your husband are really making you pretty upset.
>
> **Mrs. Jones:** I get so upset sometimes I just don't know what to do. He never listens to what I have to say.
>
> **Supervisor:** Well, is there anything you think might be helpful?
>
> **Mrs. Jones:** I tried everything; I think the best thing to do is just to go ahead and file for divorce.
>
> **Supervisor:** Mrs. Jones, have you tried talking with a marriage counselor?
>
> **Mrs. Jones:** No, I haven't. Do you think that there is anything a marriage counselor can do?
>
> **Supervisor:** I don't know, Mrs. Jones. That might give you a better idea of what can be done.
>
> **Mrs. Jones:** I hadn't thought of that. Maybe I should get in contact with a marriage counselor.

The supervisor does not tell Mrs. Jones that she needs to go to a marriage counselor but does present marriage counseling as one alternative she might consider. Of course, other alternatives can be explored. The important point in this example is that the employee must decide what issues need to be explored.

In the conclusion stage, the interviewer should check to be sure not only that she heard the employee accurately but that the employee heard her as well. At this point, she should check to see if further personal assistance is needed. If referrals have been made, it is a good idea to make sure that the employee knows how to follow through and feels comfortable in doing so.

Finally, following the end of the interview, the supervisor should ask herself: Was the interview helpful to the employee? If so, what was most helpful? To the degree that the interview was not helpful for the employee, it is important to understand clearly why not. If the supervisor realizes that he needs additional training in interview skills, he can then seek help in acquiring these skills before he is once again called upon to engage in a helping interview. A second important question during the evaluation phase: What has been learned that is helpful to the organization itself? Is the employee's problem common to others? Can the organization do something to try to help the employees directly or to help train supervisors as a group to recognize likely problems?

SUMMARY

Interviewing in business and industry requires all of the skills and strategies outlined in the early chapters in this book, plus special knowledge about the problems inherent in this setting. Multiple laws protecting employees' rights and the company's special needs provide more structure to the interview situation than might be the case in other settings. Nevertheless, the basic principles of interviewing remain the same. The interview remains a face-to-face attempt to share information, identify concerns, and establish mutually acceptable goals. As such, interviewing has become an indispensable tool in business and industry.

SUGGESTED READINGS

Baker, H. K. (1984). Two goals in every performance appraisal. *Personnel Journal, 63*(9), 74–78.

Donaghy, W. C. (1984). *The interview: Skills and applications.* Glenview, IL: Scott, Foresman.

Kaye, B. L. (1982). *Up is not the only way: A guide for career development practitioners.* Englewood Cliffs, NJ: Prentice-Hall.

Sherwood, A. (1983). Exit interviews: Don't just say goodbye. *Personnel Journal, 62*(9), 744–750.

References

Achenbach, T., & Edelbrock, C. (1983). *Manual for the child behavior checklist.* Burlington, VT: Queen City Printers.

Altman, K. (1985). The role-taking interview: An assessment technique for adolescents. *Adolescence, 20*(80), 844–851.

American Psychiatric Association. (1980). *Diagnostic and statistical manual of mental disorders* (3rd ed.). Washington, DC: Author.

American Psychological Association. (1985). *Standards for providers of psychological services* (rev. ed.). Washington, DC: Author.

Arvey, R. D., & Campion, J. E. (1982). The employment interview: A summary and review of recent research. *Journal of Personnel Psychology, 35*(2), 281–322.

Atchley, R. C. (1980). *The social forces in later life* (3rd ed.). Belmont, CA: Wadsworth.

Axelson, J. A. (1985). *Counseling and development in a multicultural society.* Monterey, CA: Brooks/Cole.

Baker, H. K. (1984). Two goals in every performance appraisal. *Personnel Journal, 63*(9), 74–78.

Balinsky, B., & Burger, R. (1959). *The executive interview.* New York: Harper & Brothers.

Baruth, L. G., & Huber, C. H. (1985). *Counseling and psychotherapy: Theoretical analyses and skills applications.* Columbus: Merrill.

Beatty, R. H. (1986). *The five-minute interview.* Somerset, NJ: John Wiley & Sons.

Beavers, W. R. (1982). Healthy, midrange, and severely dysfunctional families. In F. Walsh (Ed.), *Normal family processes.* New York: Guilford Press.

Bee, H. L. (1987). *The journey to adulthood.* New York: Macmillan.

Beer, W. R. (1983). *Househusbands: Men and housework in American families.* New York: J. F. Bergin/Praeger.

Belkin, G. S. (1984). *Introduction to counseling* (2nd ed.). New York: Wm. C. Brown.

Bell, J. E. (1961). *Family group therapy.* (Public health monograph No. 64). Washington, DC: U.S. Government Printing Office.

Benjamin, A. (1981). *The helping interview.* Boston, Houghton Mifflin.

Bennett, C. I. (1986). *Comprehensive multicultural education: Theory and Practice.* Boston: Allyn & Bacon.

Berman, J. (1979). Counseling skills used by Black and White male and female counselors. *Journal of Counseling Psychology, 26,* 81–84.

Bernstein, L., & Bernstein, R. S. (1980). *Interviewing: A guide for health professionals* (3rd ed.). New York: Appleton-Century Crofts.

Bingham, W. V. D., Moore, B. V., & Gustad, J. W. (1959). *How to interview* (4th ed.). New York: Harper & Brothers.

Birk, J. M., Fitzgerald, L. E., & Tanney, M. F. (Eds.). *Counseling Women* (pp. 75–78). Monterey, CA: Brooks/Cole.

Blackham, G. J. (1977). *Counseling: Theory, process, and practice.* Belmont, CA: Wadsworth.

Brammer, L. M. (1977). Who can be a helper? *Personnel & Guidance Journal, 55*(6), 303–309.

Brammer, L. M. (1979). *The helping relationship: Process and skills* (2nd ed.). Englewood Cliffs, NJ: Prentice-Hall.

Brammer, L. M. (1985). *The helping relationship: Process and skills* (3rd ed.). Englewood Cliffs, NJ: Prentice-Hall.

Brink, T. L. (1979). *Geriatric psychotherapy.* New York: Human Sciences Press.

Brink, T. L. (Ed.). (1986). *Clinical gerontology: A guide to assessment and intervention.* New York: Haworth Press.

Bull, P. (1983). *Body movement and interpersonal communication.* New York: John Wiley & Sons.

Campbell, R. E., & Cellini, J. V. (1980). Adult career development. *Counseling and Human Development, 12,* 1–14.

Carkhuff, R. R. (1969). *Helping and human relations: A primer for lay and professional helpers* (2 vols.). New York: Holt, Rinehart & Winston.

Carkhuff, R. R. (1972). What's it all about anyway? Some reflections on helping and human resource development models. *Counseling Psychologist, 3*(3), 79–87.

Carkhuff, R. R., & Anthony, W. A. (1979). *The skills of helping: An introduction to counseling.* Amherst, MA: Human Resource Development Press.

Carkhuff, R. R., Pierce, R. M., & Cannon, J. R. (1977). *The art of helping, III.* Amherst, MA: Human Resource Development Press.

Charles, D., Fleetwood-Walker, P., & Luck, M. (1985). Communication skills: Information-seeking interviews. *Journal of the Operational Research Society, 36*(10), 883–890.

Cormier, L. S., Cormier, W. H., & Weisser, R. J. (1984). *Interviewing and helping skills for health professionals.* Monterey, CA: Wadsworth Health Sciences Division.

Cormier, W. H., & Cormier, L. S. (1985). *Interviewing strategies for helpers: Fundamental skills and cognitive behavioral interventions* (2nd ed.). Monterey, CA: Brooks/Cole.

Cort, R. P. (1979). *Communicating with employees.* Waterford, CT: National Foreman's Institute Bureau of Business Practice.

Csikszentmihalyi, M., Larson, R., & Prescott, S. (1977). The ecology of adolescent activity and experience. *Journal of Youth and Adolescence, 6,* 281–294.

Damon, A., Seltzer, C. C., Stoudt, H. W., & Bell, B. C. (1972). Age and physique in healthy white veterans of Boston. *Journal of Gerontology, 27,* 202–208.

D'Augelli, A. R., D'Augelli, J. F., & Danish, S. J. (1981). *Helping others.* Monterey, CA: Brooks/ Cole.

DePaulo, B. M., & Rosenthal, R. (1979). Ambivalence, discrepancy, and deception in nonverbal communication. In R. Rosenthal (Ed.), *Skill in nonverbal communication: Individual differences.* Cambridge, MA: Oelgeschlager, Gunn, & Hain.

DePaulo, B. M., Rosenthal, R., Eisenstat, R. A., Rogers, P. L., & Finkelstein, S. (1978). Decoding discrepant nonverbal cues. *Journal of Personality and Social Psychology, 36,* 313–323.

DeRisi, W. J., & Butz, G. (1979). *Writing behavioral contracts: A case simulation practice manual.* Champaign, IL: Research Press.

Dillard, J. M. (1983). *Multicultural counseling: Toward ethnic and cultural relevance in human encounters.* Chicago: Nelson-Hall.

Dillard, J. M. (1985). *Lifelong career planning.* Columbus: Merrill.

Dinkmeyer, D., & McKay, G. D. (1982). *Systematic steps for effective parenting: Parent's handbook.* Circle Pines, MN: American Guidance Service.

Donaghy, W. C. (1984). *The interview: Skills and applications.* Glenview, IL: Scott Foresman.

Donaldson, M. (1987). *Children's minds.* New York: W. W. Norton & Company.

Downs, C. W., & Tanner, J. E. (1982). Decision-making in the selection interview. *Journal of College Placement, 42,* 59–61.

Dunnette, M. D., & Bass, B. M. (1963). Behavioral scientists and personnel management. *Industrial Relations, 2*(3), 115–130.

Dyer, W. W., & Vriend, J. (1975). *Counseling techniques that work.* Washington, DC: American Personnel and Guidance.

Eakins, B. W., & Eakins, R. G. (1978). *Sex differences in human communication.* Boston: Houghton Mifflin.

Egan, G. (1975). *The skilled helper: A systematic approach to effective helping.* Monterey, CA: Brooks/Cole.

Egan, G. (1982). *The skilled helper: A systematic approach to effective helping* (2nd ed.). Monterey, CA: Brooks/Cole.

Egan, G. (1986). *The skilled helper: A systematic approach to effective helping* (3rd ed.). Monterey, CA: Brooks/Cole.

Eisenberg, S., & Delaney, D. J. (1977). *The counseling process* (2nd ed.). Chicago: Rand McNally.

Ekman, P., Friesen, W. V., & Tomkins, S. S. (1971). Racial affect scoring technique: A face validity study. *Semiotica, 3,* 37–58.

Elkind, E. (1959). Identity and the life cycle. *Psychological Issues, 1,* Monograph 1.

Epstein, L. (1985). *Talking and listening—A guide to the helping interview.* St. Louis: Times Mirror/Mosby; Columbus: Merrill Publishing Company © 1985.

Erikson, E. H. (1959). Identity and the life cycle. *Psychological Issues, 1,* 1–171.

Evans, D. R., Hearn, M. T., Uhlemann, M. R., & Ivey, A. E. (1984). *Essential interviewing: A programmed approach to effective communication* (2nd ed.). Monterey, CA: Brooks/Cole.

Faley, R. H., Kleiman, L. S., & Lengnick-Hall, M. L. (1984). Age discrimination and personnel psychology: A review and synthesis of the legal literature with implications for future research. *Personnel Psychology, 37,* 327–350.

Fear, A. (1984). *The evaluation interview.* New York: McGraw-Hill.

Fisher, R., & Ury, W. (1981). *Getting to yes: Negotiating agreement without giving in.* Boston: Houghton Mifflin.

Flavell, J. H. (1985). *Cognitive development.* Englewood Cliffs, NJ: Prentice-Hall.

Foley, R., & Sharf, B. (1981, February). The five interviewing techniques most frequently overlooked by primary care physicians. *Behavioral Medicine,* 26–31.

Franklin, P., & Prosky, P. (1973). A standard initial interview. In D. A. Bloch (Ed.), *Techniques of family psychotherapy: A primer.* New York: Grune & Stratton.

Freedman, J., Sears, D. O., & Carlsmith, J. M. (1981). *Social psychology* (4th ed.). Englewood Cliffs, NJ: Prentice-Hall.

Friedman, M., & Powell, L. H. (1984). The diagnosis and quantitative assessment of type A behavior: Introduction and description of the videotaped structured interview. *Integrative Psychiatry, 2,* 123–129.

Galassi, M. D., & Galassi, J. P. (1977). *Assert yourself! How to be your own person.* New York: Human Sciences.

Garbarino, J. (1985). *Adolescent development: An ecological perspective.* Columbus: Merrill.

Gardner, R. A. (1983). The talking, feeling, and doing game. In C. E. Schaefer & K. J. O'Connor (Eds.), *Handbook of play therapy* (pp. 259–273). New York: John Wiley & Sons.

Garfield, S. L., & Bergin, A. E. (Eds.). (1978). *Handbook of psychotherapy and behavioral change: An empirical analysis* (2nd ed.). New York: John Wiley & Sons.

Garrett, A. (1982). *Interviewing: Its principles and methods* (3rd ed.). New York: Family Service Association of America.

Gatchel, R. J., & Baum, A. (1983). *An introduction to health psychology.* Reading, MA: Addison-Wesley.

Gazda, G. M., Asbury, F. S., Balzer, F. J., Childers, W. C., & Walters, R. P. (1984). *Human relations: A manual for educators* (3rd ed.). Boston: Allyn & Bacon.

Gazda, G. M., Childers, W. C., & Walters, R. P. (1982). *Interpersonal communication: A handbook for health professionals.* Rockville, MD: Aspen Systems.

Gerstein, M. (1982). Vocational counseling for adults in varied settings: A comprehensive view. *Vocational Guidance Quarterly, 30,* 315–322.

Gerstenblitz, G. (1980). Noninvasive assessment of cardiovascular function in the elderly. In M. L. Weisfeldt (Ed.), *The aging heart: Its function and response to stress.* New York: Raven.

Gibson, R. L., & Mitchell, M. H. (1986). *Introduction to counseling and guidance* (2nd ed.). New York: Macmillan.

Ginott, H. G. (1965). *Between parent and child.* New York: Macmillan.

Gollnick, D. M., & Chinn, P. C. (1986). *Multicultural education in a pluralistic society* (2nd ed.). Columbus: Merrill.

Golner, J. H. (1971). Home family counseling. *Social Work, 4,* 63–71.

Goodale, J. G. (1982). *The fine art of interviewing.* Englewood Cliffs, NJ: Prentice-Hall.

Goodall, D. B., & Goodall, H. L. (1982). The employment interview: A selective review of the literature with implications for communication research. *Communication Quarterly, 30,* 116–123.

Goodyear, R. K., & Bradley, F. O. (1980). The helping process as contractual. *Personnel and Guidance Journal, 58,* 512–515.

Gorden, R. L. (1980). *Interviewing: Strategy, techniques, and tactics* (3rd ed.). Homewood, IL: The Dorsey Press.

Greenspan, S. (1981). *The clinical interview of the child.* New York: McGraw-Hill.

Gurman, A. S., & Kniskern, D. P. (1978). Research on marital and family therapy: Progress, perspective and prospect. In S. L. Garfield & A. E. Bergin (Eds.), *Handbook of psychotherapy and behavior change: An empirical analysis* (2nd ed.). New York: John Wiley & Sons.

Hall, E. T. (1966). *The hidden dimension.* Garden City, NY: Doubleday.

Hall, J. A. (1984). *Nonverbal sex differences: Communication accuracy and expressive style.* Baltimore: Johns Hopkins University Press.

Hansen, J. C., Stevic, R. R., & Warner, Jr., R. W. (1982). *Counseling: Theory and process* (3rd ed.). Boston: Allyn & Bacon.

Hansen, J. C., Stevic, R. R., & Warner, Jr., R. W. (1986). *Counseling: Theory and process* (4th ed.). Boston: Allyn & Bacon.

Harper, R. G., Wiens, A. N., & Matarazzo, J. D. (1978). *Nonverbal communication: The state of the art.* New York: Wiley.

Hartman, W., & Fithian, M. (1972). *Treatment of sexual dysfunction.* Long Beach, CA: Center for Marital and Sexual Studies.

Havighurst, R. (1952). *Developmental tasks and education.* New York: Longmans and Green.

Hayakawa, S. I. (1979). *Through the communication barrier: On speaking, listening, and understanding.* New York: Harper and Row.

Hayness, S. N., & Jensen, B. J. (1979). The interview as a behavioral assessment instrument. *Behavioral Assessment, 1,* 97–106.

Herr, J. J., & Weakland, J. H. (1979). *Counseling elders and their families: Practical guide for applied gerontology.* New York: Springer Publishing.

Hillman, R., Goodell, B., Grundy, S., McArthur, L., & Moller, J. (1981). *Clinic skills: Interviewing, history taking, and physical diagnosis.* New York: McGraw-Hill.

Horowitz, M. J., Wilner, N., Marmar, C., & Krupnick, J. (1980). Pathological grief and the activation of latent self-images. *American Journal of Psychiatry, 137*(10), 1157–1162.

Hudson, J., & Danish, S. (1980). The acquisition of information: An important life skill. *Personnel and Guidance Journal, 59,* 164–167.

Hutchins, D. E., & Cole, C. G. (1986). *Helping relationships and strategies.* Monterey, CA: Brooks/Cole.

Irwin, E. C. (1983). The diagnostic and therapeutic use of pretend play. In C. E. Schaefer & K. J. O'Connor (Eds.), *Handbook of play therapy* (pp. 148–173). New York: John Wiley & Sons.

Ivey, A. E. (1983). *Intentional interviewing and counseling.* Monterey, CA: Brooks/Cole.

Ivey, A. E., & Gluckstern, N. (1974). *Basic attending skills.* North Amherst, MA: Microtraining Associates.

Ivey, A. E., & Gluckstern, N. (1987). *Basic influencing skills* (2nd ed.). North Amherst, MA: Microtraining Associates.

Jablin, F. M., & McComb, K. B. (1984). The employment screening interview: An organizational assimilation and communication perspective. In R. H. Bostrom & B. H. Westley (Eds.). *Communication Yearbook, 8.* Beverly Hills, CA: Sage.

Jackson, T. (1976). *Interviewing women: Avoiding charges of discrimination.* New York: Executive Enterprises Publications.

Jahn, D. L., & Lichstein, K. L. (1980). The resistive client. *Behavior Modification, 4,* 303–320.

Johnson, D. W. (1981). *Reaching out: Interpersonal effectiveness and self-actualization.* Englewood Cliffs, NJ: Prentice-Hall.

Johnston, L., Bachman, J., & O'Malley, P. (1980). *Student drug use in America, 1975–1980.* National Institute on Drug Abuse (DHHS Publication No. ADM 81–1066). Washington, DC: U.S. Government Printing Office.

Jones, M., & Bayley, N. (1950). Physical maturing among boys as related to behavior. *Journal of Educational Psychology, 41,* 129–148.

Jones, V. (1980). *Adolescents with behavior problems: Strategies for teaching, counseling, and parent involvement.* Boston: Allyn & Bacon.

Kagan, N. (1975). *Influencing human interaction.* Washington, DC: American Personnel and Guidance.

Kantor, D., & Lehr, W. (1975). *Inside the family.* San Francisco: Jossey-Bass.

Karoly, P. (Ed.). (1985). *Measurement strategies in health psychology.* New York: John Wiley & Sons.

Kaye, B. L. (1982). *Up is not the only way: A guide for career development practitioners.* Englewood Cliffs, NJ: Prentice Hall.

Keane, T. M., Black, J. L., Collins, F. L., Jr., & Venson, M. C. (1982). A skills training program for teaching the behavior interview. *Behavioral Assessment, 4,* 53–62.

Keller, J. F., & Hughston, G. A. (1981). *Counseling the elderly: A systems approach.* New York: Harper and Row.

King, M., Novik, L., & Citrenbaum, C. (1983). *Irresistible communication: Creative skills for the health professional.* Philadelphia: Saunders.

Kirouac, G., & Doré, F. Y. (1983). Accuracy and latency of judgment of facial expressions of emotions. *Perceptual and Motor Skills, 57,* 683–686.

Knapp, M. L., & Miller, G. R. (1985). *Handbook of interpersonal communication.* Beverly Hills, CA: Sage.

Kohlberg, L. (1969). *Stages in the development of moral thought and action.* New York: Holt, Rinehart & Winston.

Krumboltz, J. D. (1966). Behavioral goals for counseling. *Journal of Counseling Psychology, 13,* 153–159.

Lazarus, A. S. (1981). *The practice of multimodal therapy.* New York: McGraw-Hill.

Levinson, D. J. (1978). *The seasons of a man's life.* New York: Knopf.

Levinson, D. J. (1980). Toward a conception of the adult life course. In N. J. Smelser & E. H. Erikson (Eds.), *Themes of work and love in childhood.* Cambridge, MA: Harvard University.

Levison, F. (1976). Patterns of personality development in middle-aged women: A longitudinal study. *International Journal of Aging & Human Development, 7,* 107–115.

Lewis, J. A., & Lewis, M. D. (1986). *Counseling programs for employees in the workplace.* Monterey, CA: Brooks/Cole.

Lewis, J. M., Beavers, W. R., Gossett, J. T., & Phillips, V. A. (1976). *No single thread: Psychological health in family systems.* New York: Brunner/Mazel.

Long, L. (1978). *Listening/responding: Human-relations training for teachers.* Monterey, CA: Brooks/Cole.

Looff, D. (1976). *Getting to know the troubled child.* Knoxville: University of Tennessee Press.

Lowenthol, M. F., Thurnher, M., Chitboga, D., & Associates. (1975). *Four stages of life: A comparative study of women and men facing transitions.* San Francisco: Jossey-Bass.

Lowgill, D. O. (1974). The aging of populations and societies. In F. R. Eisele (Ed.). *Political consequences of aging.* Philadelphia: American Academy of Political and Social Sciences.

MacKinnon, R. A., Michels, R. (1971). *The psychiatric interview in clinical practice.* Philadelphia: W. B. Saunders.

Malandro, L. A., & Barker, L. L. (1983). *Nonverbal communication.* Reading, MA: Addison-Wesley.

Malasanos, L., Barkauskas, V., Moss, M., & Stoltenberg-Allen, K. (1977). *Health assessment.* St. Louis: C. V. Mosby.

Manos, J. A. (1979). Nonverbal communication: The unworded message. *Business Education Forum, 33*(6), 27–29.

Marcia, J. (1980). Identity in adolescence. In J. Adelson (Ed.), *Handbook of adolescent psychology.* New York: John Wiley & Sons.

Marsella, A. J., & Pedersen, P. B. (1981). *Cross-cultural counseling and psychotherapy.* New York: Pergamon.

Marshall, E., Charping, J. W., & Bell, W. J. (1979). Interpersonal skills training: A review of research. *Social Work Research and Abstracts, 15,* 10–16.

Maslow, A. H. (1968). *Toward a psychology of being.* New York: Van Nostrand Reinhold.

McFarland, R. A. (1968). The sensory and perceptual processes of aging. In K. W. Schaie (Ed.) *Theory and methods of research on aging.* Morgantown: West Virginia University Press.

McGann, M. (1980). *Coping with language: Talk your way to success.* New York: Richards Rosen Press.

McHolland, J. (1985). Strategies for dealing with resistant adolescents. *Adolescence, 20*(78).

McKinnon, J. (1976). The college student and formal operations. In J. Renner, D. Stafford, A. Lawson, J. McKinnon, F. Frior, & D. Kellog (Eds.), *Research, teaching, and learning with the Piaget model.* Norman: University of Oklahoma Press.

McQuaig, J. H., McQuaig, P. L., & McQuaig, D. H. (1981). *How to interview and hire productive people.* New York: Frederick Fell.

Megginson, L. C. (1981). *Personnel management: A human resources approach* (4th ed.). Homewood, IL: Richard D. Irwin.

Mehrabian, A. (1972). *Nonverbal communication.* New York: Aldine-Atherton.

Meriman, S. K., & McLaughlin, J. E. (1983). *Out-interviewing the interviewer: A job winner's script for success.* Englewood Cliffs, NJ: Prentice-Hall.

Mills, M. C. (1985). Adolescents' reactions to counseling interviews. *Adolescence. 20*(77), 83–95.

Minuchin, S., Montalvo, B., Guerney, B. G., Rosman, B. L., & Shumer, F. (1967). *Families of the slums.* New York: Basic Books.

Model, S. (1981). Housework by husbands: Determinants and implications. *Journal of Family Issues, 2,* 225–237.

Myers, G. E., & Myers, M. T. (1980). *The dynamics of human communication: A laboratory approach* (3rd ed.). New York: McGraw-Hill.

Napier, A. Y., & Whitaker, C. A. (1978). *The family crucible.* New York: Harper & Row.

Neugarten, B. L. (1968). Adult personality: Toward a psychology of the life cycle. In B. L. Neugarten (Ed.), *Middle age and aging.* Chicago: University of Chicago.

Neugarten, B. L. (1976). Adaptation and the life cycle. *Counseling Psychologist, 6*(1), 16–20.

Neugarten, B. L. (1977). Personality and aging. In J. E. Birren & K. W. Schaie (Eds.), *Handbook of the psychology of aging.* New York: Van Nostrand Reinhold.

Newman, B., & Newman, P. (1986). *Adolescent development.* Columbus: Merrill.

Nosphitz, J. (1984). Consultation for adolescents. In N. Bernstein, & J. Sussex (Eds.), *Handbook of psychiatric consultation with children and youth* (pp. 85–104). New York: Spectrum.

Okun, B. F. (1976). *Effective helping: Interviewing and counseling techniques.* North Scituate, MA: Duxbury Press.

Okun, B. F. (1982). *Effective helping: Interviewing and counseling techniques* (2nd ed.). Monterey, CA: Brooks/Cole.

Okun, B. F. (1984). *Working with adults: Individual, family, and career development.* Belmont, CA: Wadsworth.

Okun, B. F. (1987). *Effective helping: Interviewing and counseling techniques* (3rd ed.). Monterey, CA: Brooks/Cole.

Oldfield, R. C. (1947). *The psychology of the interview* (3rd ed.). London: Methuen.

Paget, K. D. (1984). The structured assessment interview: A psychometric review. *Journal of School Psychology, 22,* 415–427.

Palmore, E. B., George, L. K., & Fillenbaum, G. G. (1982). Predictors of retirement. *Journal of Gerontology, 37,* 733–742.

Palmore, E. B., Durchett, B. M., Fillenbaum, G. G., George, L. K., & Wallman, L. M. (1985). *Retirement: Causes and consequences.* New York: Springer.

Parsons, C. K., & Liden, R. C. (1984). Interviewer perceptions of applicant qualifications: A multivariate field study of demographic characteristics and nonverbal cues. *Journal of Applied Psychology, 69*(4), 557–568.

Paul, N., & Paul, B. (1975). *A marital puzzle.* New York: Norton.

Piaget, J. (1972). Intellectual evolution from adolescence to adulthood. *Human Development, 15,* 1–12.

Pietrofesa, J. J., Leonard, G. E., & Van Hoose, W. (1978). *The authentic counselor.* Chicago: Rand McNally.

Pomerance, A. (1976). Pathology of myocardium and valves. In F. T. Caird, J. L. C. Doll, & R. D. Kennedy (Eds.), *Cardiology in old age.* New York: Plenum.

Pomeroy, W. (1972). Interviewing. In W. Pomeroy (Ed.). *Dr. Kinsey and the Institute for Sex Research.* New York: Harold Matson.

Priestly, P., & McGuire, J. (1983). *Learning to help: Basic skills exercises.* London: Tavistock.

Rabichow, H., & Sklansky, M. (1980). *Effective counseling of adolescents.* Chicago: Follett.

Renner, J., & Stafford, D. (1976). The operational levels of secondary school students. In J. Renner, D. Stafford, A. Lawson, J. McKinnon, F. Frior, & D. Kellog (Eds.), *Research, teaching, and learning with the Piaget model.* Norman: University of Oklahoma Press.

Reik, T. (1972). *Listening with the third ear.* New York: Farrar, Straus, & Sons.

Ridley, C. R. (1978). Cross-cultural counseling: A multivariate analysis. *Viewpoints in Teaching and Learning, 54,* 43–50.

Rogers, C. R. (1951). *Client-centered therapy.* Boston: Houghton Mifflin.

Rogers, C. R. (1961). *On becoming a person: A therapist's view of psychotherapy.* Boston: Houghton Mifflin.

Rogers, C. R., & Roethlisberger, F. J. (1942). Barriers and gateways to communication. *Harvard Business Review, 30*(4), 46–52.

Ross, R. S., & Ross, M. G. (1979). *Relating and interacting: An introduction to interpersonal communication.* Englewood Cliffs, NJ: Prentice-Hall.

Rusell, C. S. (1974). Transition to parenthood: Problems and gratifications. *Journal of Marriage and the Family, 36,* 294–302.

Rynes, S. L., & Miller, H. E. (1983). Recruiter and job influences on candidates for employment. *Journal of Applied Psychology, 68*(1), 147–154.

Samovar, L. A., Porter, R. E., & Jain, N. C. (1981). *Understanding intercultural communication: A reader.* Belmont, CA: Wadsworth.

Sathré, F. S., Olson, R. W., & Whitney, S. I. (1977). *Let's talk—An introduction to interpersonal communication* (2nd ed.). Glenview, IL: Scott, Foresman.

Satir, V. (1967). *Conjoint family therapy.* Palo Alto, CA: Science and Behavior Books.

Satir, V. (1972). *Peoplemaking.* Palo Alto, CA: Science and Behavior Books.

Satir, V. (1975). Problems and pitfalls in working with families. In V. Satir, J. Stachowiak, & H. Taschman (Eds.), *Helping families to change.* New York: Jason Aronson.

Schulman, E. D. (1982). *Intervention in human services: A guide to skills and knowledge* (3rd ed.). St. Louis: C. V. Mosby; Columbus: Merrill Publishing Company © 1985.

Shertzer, B., & Stone, S. C. (1981). *Fundamentals of Guidance* (4th ed.). Boston: Houghton Mifflin.

Sherwood, A. (1983). Exit interviews: Don't just say goodbye. *Personnel Journal, 62*(9), 744–750.

Shouksmith, G. (1978). *Assessment through interviewing* (2nd ed.). Oxford, England: Pergamon Press.

Sincoff, Z., & Goyer. S. (1984). *Interviewing.* New York: Macmillan.

Stengel, E. (1964). *Suicide and attempted suicide.* Baltimore: Penguin.

Stewart, C. J., & Cash, Jr., W. B. (1978). *Interviewing—Principles and practices* (2nd ed.). Dubuque, IA: William C. Brown.

Stillman, P. L., Burpeu-Di Gregorio, M. Y., Nicholson, G. I., Sabers, D. L., & Stillman, A. E. (1983). Six years of experience using patient instructors to teach interviewing skills. *Journal of Medical Education, 58,* 941–946.

Streibt, G. F., & Schneider, C. J. (1971). *Retirement in American society.* Ithaca: Cornell.

Strong, S. R., & Claiborn, C. (1982). *Change through interaction: Social psychological processes of counseling and psychotherapy.* New York: Wiley-Interscience.

Sue, D. W. (1978). World views and counseling. *Personnel & Guidance Journal, 56*(8), 458–463.

Super, D. E. (1969) The natural history of a study of lives and vocations. *Perspectives in Education, 2,* 13–22.

Tapia, F. (1972). Teaching medical interviewing: A practical technique. *British Journal of Medical Education, 6,* 133–136.

Tengler, C. D., & Jablin, F. M. (1983). Effects of question type, orientation, and sequencing in the employment screening interview. *Communication Monographs, 50,* 245–263.

Tharp, C. G. (1983). A manager's guide to selection interviewing. *Personnel Journal, 62*(8), 636–639.

Thornburg, H. (1982). *Development in adolescence* (2nd ed.). Monterey, CA: Brooks/Cole.

Turk, D. C., & Kerns, R. D. (1985). Assessment in health psychology: A cognitive-behavioral perspective. In P. Karoly (Ed.), *Measurement strategies in health psychology* (pp. 335–372). New York: John Wiley & Sons.

Turner, J. S., & Helms, D. B. (1979). *Contemporary adulthood.* Philadelphia: W. B. Sanders.

Uhlemann, M., Hearn, M., & Evans, D. (1980). Programmed learning the microtraining paradigm with hotline workers. *American Journal of Community Psychology, 8,* 603–612.

United States Bureau of the Census (1976). Demographic aspects of aging and the older population in the United States. *Current Population Reports,* Series P. 23, No. 59. Washington, DC: U.S. Government Printing Office.

United States Bureau of the Census (1977). Projections of the population of the United States: 1977 to 2050. *Current Population Reports,* Series P. 25, No. 704. Washington, DC: U.S. Government Printing Office.

Vetter, L. (1978). Career counseling for women. In L. W. Harmon, et al. (eds.), *Counseling Women.* Monterey, CA: Brooks/Cole, 75–78.

Verwoerdt, A., Pfeiffer, E., & Wang, H. S. (1969). Sexual behavior in senescence. II. Pattern of sexual activity and interest. *Geriatrics, 24,* 137–154.

Wachtel, E. F., & Wachtel, P. L. (1986). *Family dynamics in individual psychotherapy: A guide to clinical strategies.* New York: Guilford.

Waldron, H., & Routh, D. K. (1981). The effect of the first child on the marital relationship. *Journal of Marriage and the Family, 43,* 785–798.

Walsh, F. (1982). Conceptualizations of normal family functioning. In F. Walsh (Ed.) *Normal family processes.* New York: Guilford Press.

Weiner, I. (1982). *Child and adolescent psychopathology.* New York: Wiley.

Weisfeldt, S. F. (1980). Left ventricular function. In M. L. Weisfeldt (Ed.), *The aging heart: Its function and response to stress.* New York: Raven.

Welford, A. T. (1977). Motor Performance. In J. E. Birren and K. W. Schaie (Eds.), *Handbook of the psychology of aging.* New York: Van Nostrand Reinhold.

Willis, S. L., and Baltes, P. B. (1980). Intelligence in adulthood and aging: Contemporary issues. In L. W. Poon (Ed.), *Aging in the 1980s: Psychological issues.* Washington, DC: American Psychological Association.

Yarrow, L. J. (1960). Interviewing children. In P. H. Mussen (Ed.), *Handbook of research methods in child development* (pp. 561–602). New York: J. Wiley & Sons.

Appendices

Code of Ethics
National Association of Social Workers

Preamble

This code is intended to serve as a guide to the everyday conduct of members of the social work profession and as a basis for the adjudication of issues in ethics when the conduct of social workers is alleged to deviate from the standards expressed or implied in this code. It represents standards of ethical behavior for social workers in professional relationships with those served, with colleagues, with employers, with other individuals and professions, and with the community and society as a whole. It also embodies standards of ethical behavior governing individual conduct to the extent that such conduct is associated with an individual's status and identity as a social worker.

This code is based on the fundamental values of the social work profession that include the worth, dignity, and uniqueness of all persons as well as their rights and opportunities. It is also based on the nature of social work, which fosters conditions that promote these values.

In subscribing to and abiding by this code, the social worker is expected to view ethical responsibility in as inclusive a context as each situation demands and within which ethical judgement is required. The social worker is expected to take into consideration all the principles in this code that have a bearing upon any situation in which ethical judgement is to be exercised and professional intervention or conduct is planned. The course of action that the social worker chooses is expected to be consistent with the spirit as well as the letter of this code.

In itself, this code does not represent a set of rules that will prescribe all the behaviors of social workers in all the complexities of professional life. Rather, it offers general principles to guide conduct, and the judicious appraisal of conduct, in situations that have ethical implications. It provides the basis for making judgements about ethical actions before and after they occur. Frequently, the particular situation determines the ethical principles that apply and the manner of their application. In such cases, not only the particular ethical principles are taken into immediate consideration, but also the entire code and its spirit. Specific applications of ethical principles must be judged within the context in which they are being considered. Ethical behavior in a given situation must satisfy not only the judgement of the individual social worker, but also the judgement of an unbiased jury of professional peers.

This code should not be used as an instrument to deprive any social worker of the opportunity or freedom to practice with complete professional integrity; nor should any disciplinary action be taken on the basis of this code without maximum provision for safeguarding the rights of the social worker affected.

The ethical behavior of social workers results not from edict, but from a personal commitment of the individual. This code is offered to affirm the will and zeal of all social workers to be ethical and to act ethically in all that they do as social workers.

The following codified ethical principles should guide social workers in the various roles and relationships and at the various levels of responsibility in which they function professionally. These principles also serve as a basis for the adjudication by the National Association of Social Workers of issues in ethics.

In subscribing to this code, social workers are required to cooperate in its implementation and abide by any disciplinary rulings based on it. They should also take adequate measures to discourage, prevent, expose, and correct the unethical conduct of colleagues. Finally, social workers should be equally ready to defend and assist colleagues unjustly charged with unethical conduct.

Summary of Major Principles

I. The Social Worker's Conduct and Comportment as a Social Worker

    A. **Propriety.** The Social worker should maintain high standards of personal conduct in the capacity or identity as social worker.

    B. **Competence and Professional Development.** The social worker should strive to become and remain proficient in professional practice and the performance of professional functions.

    C. **Service.** The social worker should regard as primary the service obligation of the social work profession.

    D. **Integrity.** The social worker should act in accordance with the highest standards of professional integrity.

    E. **Scholarship and Research.** The social worker engaged in study and research should be guided by the conventions of scholarly inquiry.

II. The Social Worker's Ethical Responsibility to Clients

    F. **Primacy of Clients' Interests.** The social worker's primary responsibility is to clients.

    G. **Rights and Prerogatives of Clients.** The social worker should make every effort to foster maximum self-determination on the part of clients.

    H. **Confidentiality and Privacy.** The social worker should respect the privacy of clients and hold in confidence all information obtained in the course of professional service.

I. **Fees.** When setting fees, the social worker should ensure that they are fair, reasonable, considerate, and commensurate with the service performed and with due regard for the clients' ability to pay.

III. The Social Worker's Ethical Responsibility to Colleagues

J. **Respect, Fairness, and Courtesy.** The social worker should treat colleagues with respect, courtesy, fairness, and good faith.

K. **Dealing with Colleagues' Clients.** The social worker has the responsibility to relate to the clients of colleagues with full professional consideration.

IV. The Social Worker's Ethical Responsibility to Employers and Employing Organizations

L. **Commitments to Employing Organizations.** The social worker should adhere to commitments made to the employing organizations.

V. The Social Worker's Ethical Responsibility to the Social Work Profession

M. **Maintaining the Integrity of the Profession.** The social worker should uphold and advance the values, ethics, knowledge, and mission of the profession.

N. **Community Service.** The social worker should assist the profession in making social services available to the general public.

O. **Development of Knowledge.** The social worker should take responsibility for identifying, developing, and fully utilizing knowledge for professional practice.

VI. The Social Worker's Ethical Responsibility to Society

P. **Promoting the General Welfare.** The social worker should promote the general welfare of society.

The NASW Code of Ethics

I. The Social Worker's Conduct and Comportment as a Social Worker

A. **Propriety**—The Social worker should maintain high standards of personal conduct in the capacity or identity as social worker.

1. The private conduct of the social worker is a personal matter to the same degree as is any other person's, except when such conduct compromises the fulfillment of professional responsibilities.

2. The social worker should not participate in, condone, or be associated with dishonesty, fraud, deceit, or misrepresentation.

3. The social worker should distinguish clearly between statements and actions made as a private individual and as a representative of the social work profession or an organization or group.

B. **Competence and Professional Development**—The social worker should strive to become and remain proficient in professional practice and the performance of professional functions.

The social worker should accept responsibility or employment only on the basis of existing competence or the intention to acquire the necessary competence.

2. The social worker should not misrepresent professional qualifications, education, experience, or affiliations.

C. **Service**—The social worker should regard as primary the service obligation of the social work profession.

1. The social worker should retain ultimate responsibility for the quality and extent of the service that individual assumes, assigns, or performs.

2. The social worker should act to prevent practices that are inhumane or discriminatory against any person or group of persons.

D. **Integrity**—The social worker should act in accordance with the highest standards of professional integrity and impartiality.

1. The social worker should be alert to and resist the influences and pressures that interfere with the exercise of professional discretion and impartial judgement required for the performance of professional functions.

2. The social worker should not exploit professional relationships for personal gain.

E. **Scholarship and Research**—The social worker engaged in study and research should be guided by the conventions of scholarly inquiry.

1. The social worker engaged in research should consider carefully its possible consequences for human beings.

2. The social worker engaged in research should ascertain that the consent of participants in the research is voluntary and informed, without any implied deprivation or penalty for refusal to participate, and with due regard for participants' privacy and dignity.

3. The social worker engaged in research should protect participants from unwarranted physical or mental discomfort, distress, harm, danger, or deprivation.

4. The social worker who engages in the evaluation of services or cases should discuss them only for the professional purposes and only with persons directly and professionally concerned with them.
5. Information obtained about participants in research should be treated as confidential.
6. The social worker should take credit only for work actually done in connection with scholarly and research endeavors and credit contributions made by others.

II. The Social Worker's Ethical Responsibility to Clients

F. **Primacy of Clients' Interests—The social worker's primary responsibility is to clients.**
1. The social worker should serve clients with devotion, loyalty, determination, and the maximum application of professional skill and competence.
2. The social worker should not exploit relationships with clients for personal advantage, or solicit the clients of one's agency for private practice.
3. The social worker should not practice, condone, facilitate or collaborate with any form of discrimination on the basis of race, color, sex, sexual orientation, age, religion, national origin, marital status, political belief, mental or physical handicap, or any other preference or personal characteristic, condition or status.
4. The social worker should avoid relationships or commitments that conflict with the interests of clients.
5. The social worker should under no circumstances engage in sexual activities with clients.
6. The social worker should provide clients with accurate and complete information regarding the extent and nature of the services available to them.
7. The social worker should apprise clients of their risks, rights, opportunities, and obligations associated with social service to them.
8. The social worker should seek advice and counsel of colleagues and supervisors whenever such consultation is in the best interest of clients.
9. The social worker should terminate service to clients, and professional relationships with them, when such service and relationships are no longer required or no longer serve the clients' needs or interests.
10. The social worker should withdraw services precipitously only under unusual circumstances, giving careful consideration to all factors in the situation and taking care to minimize possible adverse effects.

11. The social worker who anticipates the termination or interruption of service to clients should notify clients promptly and seek the transfer, referral, or continuation of service in relation to the clients' needs and preferences.

G. **Rights and Prerogatives of Clients—The social worker should make every effort to foster maximum self-determination on the part of clients.**
1. When the social worker must act on behalf of a client who has been adjudged legally incompetent, the social worker should safeguard the interests and rights of that client.
2. When another individual has been legally authorized to act in behalf of a client, the social worker should deal with that person always with the client's best interest in mind.
3. The social worker should not engage in any action that violates or diminishes the civil or legal rights of clients.

H. **Confidentiality and Privacy —The social worker should respect the privacy of clients and hold in confidence all information obtained in the course of professional service.**
1. The social worker should share with others confidences revealed by clients, without their consent, only for compelling professional reasons.
2. The social worker should inform clients fully about the limits of confidentiality in a given situation, the purposes for which information is obtained, and how it may be used.
3. The social worker should afford clients reasonable access to any official social work records concerning them.
4. When providing clients with access to records, the social worker should take due care to protect the confidences of others contained in those records.
5. The social worker should obtain informed consent of clients before taping, recording, or permitting third party observation of their activities.

I. **Fees —When setting fees, the social worker should ensure that they are fair, reasonable, considerate, and commensurate with the service performed and with due regard for the clients' ability to pay.**
1. The social worker should not divide a fee or accept or give anything of value for receiving or making a referral.

III. The Social Worker's Ethical Responsibility to Colleagues

J. **Respect, Fairness, and Courtesy** —The social worker should treat colleagues with respect courtesy, fairness, and good faith.
1. The social worker should cooperate with colleagues to promote professional interests and concerns.
2. The social worker should respect confidences shared by colleagues in the course of their professional relationships and transactions.
3. The social worker should create and maintain conditions of practice that facilitate ethical and competent professional performance by colleagues.
4. The social worker should treat with respect, and represent accurately and fairly, the qualifications, views, and findings of colleagues and use appropriate channels to express judgements on these matters.
5. The social worker who replaces or is replaced by a colleague in professional practice should act with consideration for the interest, character, and reputation of that colleague.
6. The social worker should not exploit a dispute between a colleague and employers to obtain a position or otherwise advance the social worker's interest.
7. The social worker should seek arbitration or mediation when conflicts with colleagues require resolution for compelling professional reasons.
8. The social worker should extend to colleagues of other professions the same respect and cooperation that is extended to social work colleagues.
9. The social worker who serves as an employer, supervisor, or mentor to colleagues should make orderly and explicit arrangements regarding the conditions of their continuing professional relationship.
10. The social worker who has the responsibility for employing and evaluating the performance of other staff members, should fulfill such responsibility in a fair, considerate, and equitable manner, on the basis of clearly enunciated criteria.
11. The social worker who has the responsibility for evaluating the performance of employees, supervisees, or students should share evaluations with them.

K. **Dealing with Colleagues' Clients** —The social worker has the responsibility to relate to the clients of colleagues with full professional consideration.
1. The social worker should not solicit the clients of colleagues.
2. The social worker should not assume professional responsibility for the clients of another agency or a colleague without appropriate communication with that agency or colleague.
3. The social worker who serves the clients of colleagues, during a temporary absence or emergency, should serve those clients with the same consideration as that afforded any client.

IV. The Social Worker's Ethical Responsibility to Employers and Employing Organizations

L. **Commitments to Employing Organization** —The social worker should adhere to commitments made to the employing organization.
1. The social worker should work to improve the employing agency's policies and procedures, and the efficiency and effectiveness of its services.
2. The social worker should not accept employment or arrange student field placements in an organization which is currently under public sanction by NASW for violating personnel standards, or imposing limitations on or penalties for professional actions on behalf of clients.
3. The social worker should act to prevent and eliminate discrimination in the employing organization's work assignments and in its employment policies and practices.
4. The social worker should use with scrupulous regard, and only for the purpose for which they are intended, the resources of the employing organization.

V. The Social Worker's Ethical Responsibility to the Social Work Profession

M. **Maintaining the Integrity of the Profession**—The social worker should uphold and advance the values, ethics, knowledge, and mission of the profession.
1. The social worker should protect and enhance the dignity and integrity of the profession and should be responsible and vigorous in discussion and criticism of the profession.
2. The social worker should take action through appropriate channels against unethical conduct by any other member of the profession.
3. The social worker should act to prevent the unauthorized and unqualified practice of social work.
4. The social worker should make no misrepresentation in advertising as to qualifications, competence, service, or results to be achieved.

N. Community Service—The social worker should assist the profession in making social services available to the general public.

1. The social worker should contribute time and professional expertise to activities that promote respect for the utility, the integrity, and the competence of the social work profession.
2. The social worker should support the formulation, development, enactment and implementation of social policies of concern to the profession.

O. Development of Knowledge—The social worker should take responsibility for identifying, developing, and fully utilizing knowledge for professional practice.

1. The social worker should base practice upon recognized knowledge relevant to social work.
2. The social worker should critically examine, and keep current with emerging knowledge relevant to social work.
3. The social worker should contribute to the knowledge base of social work and share research knowledge and practice wisdom with colleagues.

VI. The Social Worker's Ethical Responsibility to Society

P. Promoting the General Welfare—The social worker should promote the general welfare of society.

1. The social worker should act to prevent and eliminate discrimination against any person or group on the basis of race, color, sex, sexual orientation, age, religion, national origin, marital status, political belief, mental or physical handicap, or any other preference or personal characteristic, condition, or status.
2. The social worker should act to ensure that all persons have access to the resources, services, and opportunities which they require.
3. The social worker should act to expand choice and opportunity for all persons, with special regard for disadvantaged or oppressed groups and persons.
4. The social worker should promote conditions that encourage respect for the diversity of cultures which constitute American society.
5. The social worker should provide appropriate professional services in public emergencies.
6. The social worker should advocate changes in policy and legislation to improve social conditions and to promote social justice.
7. The social worker should encourage informed participation by the public in shaping social policies and institutions.

Ethical Principles of Psychologists
American Psychological Association

PREAMBLE

The Association is an educational, scientific, and professional organization whose members are dedicated to the enhancement of the worth, dignity, potential, and uniqueness of each individual and thus to the service of society.

The Association recognizes that the role definitions and work settings of its

(Approved by Executive Committee upon referral of the Board of Directors, January 17, 1981).

members include a wide variety of academic disciplines, levels of academic preparation and agency services. This diversity reflects the breadth of the Association's interest and influence. It also poses challenging complexities in efforts to set standards for the performance of members, desired requisite preparation or practice, and supporting social, legal, and ethical controls.

The specification of ethical standards enables the Association to clarify to present and future members and to those served by members, the nature of ethical responsibilities held in common by its members.

The existence of such standards serves to stimulate greater concern by members for their own professional functioning and for the conduct of fellow professionals such as counselors, guidance and student personnel workers, and others in the helping professions. As the ethical code of the Association, this document establishes principles that define the ethical behavior of Association members.

Section A:
General

1. The member influences the development of the profession by continuous efforts to improve professional practices, teaching, services, and research. Professional growth is continuous throughout the member's career and is exemplified by the development of a philosophy that explains why and how a member functions in the helping relationship. Members must gather data on their effectiveness and be guided by the findings.

2. The member has a responsibility ooth to the individual who is served and to the institution within which the service is performed to maintain high standards of professional conduct. The member strives to maintain the highest levels of professional services offered to the individuals to be served. The member also strives to assist the agency, organization, or institution in providing the highest caliber of professional services. The acceptance of employment in an institution implies that the member is in agreement with the general policies and principles of the institution. Therefore the professional activities of the member are also in accord with the objectives of the institution. If, despite concerted efforts, the member cannot reach agreement with the employer as to acceptable standards of conduct that allow for changes in institutional policy conducive to the positive growth and development of clients, then terminating the affiliation should be seriously considered.

3. Ethical behavior among professional associates, both members and nonmembers, must be expected at all times. When information is possessed that raises doubt as to the ethical behavior of professional colleagues, whether Association members or not, the member must take action to attempt to rectify such a condition. Such action shall use the institution's channels first and then use procedures established by the state Branch, Division, or Association.

4. The member neither claims nor implies professional qualifications exceeding those possessed and is responsible for correcting any misrepresentations of these qualifications by others.

5. In establishing fees for professional counseling services, members must consider the financial status of clients and locality. In the event that the established fee structure is inappropriate for a client, assistance must be provided in finding comparable services of acceptable cost.

6. When members provide information to the public or to subordinates, peers or supervisors, they have a responsibility to ensure that the content is general, unidentified client information that is accurate, unbiased, and consists of objective, factual data.

7. With regard to the delivery of professional services, members should accept only those positions for which they are professionally qualified.

8. In the counseling relationship the counselor is aware of the intimacy of the relationship and maintains respect for the client and avoids engaging in activities that seek to meet the counselor's personal needs at the expense of that client. Through awareness of the negative impact of both racial and sexual stereotyping and discrimination, the counselor guards the individual rights and personal dignity of the client in the counseling relationship.

Section B:
Counseling Relationship

This section refers to practices and procedures of individual and/or group counseling relationships.

The member must recognize the need for client freedom of choice. Under those circumstances where this is not possible, the member must apprise clients of restrictions that may limit their freedom of choice.

1. The member's *primary* obligation is to respect the integrity and promote the welfare of the client(s), whether the client(s) is (are) assisted individually or in a group relationship. In a group setting, the member is also responsible for taking reasonable precautions to protect individuals from physical and/or psychological trauma resulting from interaction within the group.

2. The counseling relationship and information resulting therefrom be kept confidential, consistent with the obligations of the member as a professional person. In a group

counseling setting, the counselor must set a norm of confidentiality regarding all group participants' disclosures.

3. If an individual is already in a counseling relationship with another professional person, the member does not enter into a counseling relationship without first contacting and receiving the approval of that other professional. If the member discovers that the client is in another counseling relationship after the counseling relationship begins, the member must gain the consent of the other professional or terminate the relationship, unless the client elects to terminate the other relationship.

4. When the client's condition indicates that there is clear and imminent danger to the client or others, the member must take reasonable personal action or inform responsible authorities. Consulation with other professionals must be used where possible. The assumption of responsibility for the client(s) behavior must be taken only after careful deliberation. The client must be involved in the resumption of responsibility as quickly as possible.

5. Records of the counseling relationship, including interview notes, test data, correspondence, tape recordings, and other documents, are to be considered professional information for use in counseling and they should not be considered a part of the records of the institution or agency in which the counselor is employed unless specified by state statute or regulation. Revelation to others of counseling material must occur only upon the expressed consent of the client.

6. Use of data derived from a counseling relationship for purposes of counselor training or research shall be confined to content that can be disguised to ensure full protection of the identity of the subject client.

7. The member must inform the client of the purposes, goals, techniques, rules of procedure and limitations that may affect the relationship at or before the time that the counseling relationship is entered.

8. The member must screen prospective group participants, especially when the emphasis is on self-understanding and growth through self-disclosure. The member must maintain an awareness of the group participants' compatibility throughout the life of the group.

9. The member may choose to consult with any other professionally competent person about a client. In choosing a consultant, the member must avoid placing the consultant in a conflict of interest situation that would preclude the consultant's being a proper party to the member's efforts to help the client.

10. If the member determines an inability to be of professional assistance to the client, the member must either avoid initiating the counseling relationship or immediately terminate that relationship. In either event, the member must suggest appropriate alternatives. (The member must be knowledgeable about referral resources so that a satisfactory referral can be initiated). In the event the client declines the suggested referral, the member is not obligated to continue the relationship.

11. When the member has other relationships, particularly of an administrative, supervisory and/or evaluative nature with an individual seeking counseling services, the member must not serve as the counselor but should refer the individual to another professional. Only in instances where such an alternative is unavailable and where the individual's situation warrants counseling intervention should the member enter into and/or maintain a counseling relationship. Dual relationships with clients that might impair the member's objectivity and professional judgment (e.g., as with close friends or relatives, sexual intimacies with any client) must be avoided and/or the counseling relationship terminated through referral to another competent professional.

12. All experimental methods of treatment must be clearly indicated to prospective recipients and safety precautions are to be adhered to by the member.

13. When the member is engaged in short-term group treatment/training programs (e.g., marathons and other encounter-type or growth groups), the member ensures that there is professional assistance available during and following the group experience.

14. Should the member be engaged in a work setting that calls for any variation from the above statements, the member is obligated to consult with other professionals whenever possible to consider justifiable alternatives.

Section C: Measurement and Evaluation

The primary purpose of educational and psychological testing is to provide descriptive measures that are objective and interpretable in either comparative or absolute terms. The member must recognize the need to interpret the statements that follow as applying to the whole range of appraisal techniques including test and nontest data. Test results constitute only one of a variety of pertinent sources of information for personnel, guidance, and counseling decisions.

1. The member must provide specific orientation or information to the examinee(s) prior to and following the test administration so that the results of testing may be placed in proper perspective with other relevant factors. In so doing, the member must recognize the effects of socioeconomic, ethnic and cultural factors on test scores. It is the member's professional responsibility to use additional unvalidated information carefully in modifying interpretation of the test results.

2. In selecting tests for use in a given situation or with a particular client, the member must consider carefully the specific validity, reliability, and appropriateness of the test(s). *General* validity, reliability and the like may be questioned legally as well as ethically when tests are used for vocational and educational selection, placement, or counseling.

3. When making any statements to the public about tests and testing, the member must give accurate information and avoid false claims or misconceptions. Special efforts are often required to avoid unwarranted connotations of such terms as *IQ* and *grade equivalent scores*.

4. Different tests demand different levels of competence for administration, scoring, and interpretation. Members must recognize the limits of their competence and perform only those functions for which they are prepared.

5. Tests must be administered under the same conditions that were established in their standardization. When tests are not administered under standard conditions or when unusual behavior or irregularities occur during the testing session, those conditions must be noted and the results designated as invalid or of questionable validity. Unsupervised or inadequately supervised test-taking, such as the use of tests through the mails, is considered unethical. On the other hand, the use of instruments that are so designed or standardized to be self-administered and self-scored, such as interest inventories, is to be encouraged.

6. The meaningfulness of test results used in personnel, guidance, and counseling functions generally depends on the examinee's unfamiliarity with the specific items on the test. Any prior coaching or dissemination of the test materials can invalidate test results. Therefore, test security is one of the professional obligations of the member. Conditions that produce most favorable test results must be made known to the examinee.

7. The purpose of testing and the explicit use of the results must be made known to the examinee prior to testing. The counselor must ensure that instrument limitations are not exceeded and that periodic review and/or retesting are made to prevent client stereotyping.

8. The examinee's welfare and explicit prior understanding must be the criteria for determining the recipients of the test results. The member must see that specific interpretation accompanies any release of individual or group test data. The interpretation of test data must be related to the examinee's particular concerns.

9. The member must be cautious when interpreting the results of research instruments possessing insufficient technical data. The specific purposes for the use of such instruments must be stated explicitly to examinees.

10. The member must proceed with caution when attempting to evaluate and interpret the performance of minority group members or other persons who are not represented in the norm group on which the instrument was standardized.

11. The member must guard against the appropriation, reproduction, or modifications of published tests or parts thereof without acknowledgment and permission from the previous publisher.

12. Regarding the preparation, publication and distribution of tests, reference should be made to:

a. *Standards for Educational and Psychological Tests and Manuals,* revised edition, 1974, published by the American Psychological Association on behalf of itself, the American Educational Research Association and the National Council on Measurement in Education.

b. The responsible use of tests: A position paper of AMEG, APGA, and NCME. *Measurement and Evaluation in Guidance,* 1972, 5, 385-388.

c. "Responsibilities of Users of Standardized Tests," APGA, *Guidepost,* October 5, 1978, pp. 5-8.

Section D:
Research and Publication

1. Guidelines on research with human subjects shall be adhered to, such as:

a. *Ethical Principles in the Conduct of Research with Human Participants,* Washington, D.C.: American Psychological Association, Inc., 1973.

b. Code of Federal Regulations, Title 45, Subtitle A, Part 46, as currently issued.

2. In planning any research activity dealing with human subjects, the member must be aware of and responsive to all pertinent ethical principles and ensure that the research problem, design, and execution are in full compliance with them.

3. Responsibility for ethical research practice lies with the principal researcher, while others involved in the research activities share ethical obligation and full responsibility for their own actions.

4. In research with human subjects, researchers are responsible for the subjects' welfare throughout the experiment and they must take all reasonable precautions to avoid causing injurious psychological, physical, or social effects on their subjects.

5. All research subjects must be informed of the purpose of the study except when withholding information or providing misinformation to them is essential to the investigation. In such research the member must be responsible for corrective action as soon as possible following completion of the research.

6. Participation in research must be voluntary. Involuntary participation is appropriate only when it can be demonstrated that participation will have no harmful effects on subjects and is essential to the investigation.

7. When reporting research results, explicit mention must be made of all variables and conditions known to the investigator that might affect the outcome of the investigation or the interpretation of the data.

8. The member must be responsible for conducting and reporting investigations in a manner that minimizes the possibility that results will be misleading.

9. The member has an obligation to make available sufficient original research data to qualified others who may wish to replicate the study.

10. When supplying data, aiding in the research of another person, reporting research results, or in making original data available, due care must be taken to disguise the identity of the subjects in the absence of specific authorization from such subjects to do otherwise.

11. When conducting and reporting research, the member must be familiar with, and give recognition to, previous work on the topic, as well as to observe all copyright laws and follow the principles of giving full credit to all to whom credit is due.

12. The member must give due credit through joint authorship, acknowledgment, footnote statements, or other appropriate means to those who have contributed significantly to the research and/or publication, in accordance with such contributions.

13. The member must communicate to other members the results of any research judged to be of professional or scientific value. Results reflecting unfavorably on institutions, programs, services, or vested interests must not be withheld for such reasons.

14. If members agree to cooperate with another individual in research and/or publication, they incur an obligation to cooperate as promised in terms of punctuality of performance and with full regard to the completeness and accuracy of the information required.

15. Ethical practice requires that authors not submit the same manuscript or one essentially similar in content, for simultaneous publication consideration by two or more journals. In addition, manuscripts published in whole or in substantial part, in another journal or published work should not be submitted for publication without acknowledgment and permission from the previous publication.

Section E:
Consulting

Consultation refers to a voluntary relationship between a professional helper and help-needing individual, group or social unit in which the consultant is providing help to the client(s) in defining and solving a work-related problem or potential problem with a client or client system. (This definition is adapted from Kurpius, DeWayne. Consultation theory and process: An integrated model. *Personnel and Guidance Journal,* 1978, 56.

1. The member acting as consultant must have a high degree of self-awareness of his-her own values, knowledge, skills, limitations, and needs in entering a helping relationship that involves human and-or organizational change and that the focus of the relationship be on the issues to be resolved and not on the person(s) presenting the problem.

2. There must be understanding and agreement between member and client for the problem definition, change goals, and predicated consequences of interventions selected.

3. The member must be reasonably certain that she/he or the organization represented has the necessary competencies and resources for giving the kind of help that is needed now or may develop later and that appropriate referral resources are available to the consultant.

4. The consulting relationship must be one in which client adaptability and growth toward self-direction are encouraged and cultivated. The member must maintain this role consistently and not become a decision maker for the client or create a future dependency on the consultant.

5 When announcing consultant availability for services, the member conscientiously adheres to the Association's *Ethical Standards*.

6. The member must refuse a private fee or other remuneration for consultation with persons who are entitled to these services through the member's employing institution or agency. The policies of a particular agency may make explicit provisions for private practice with agency clients by members of its staff. In such instances, the clients must be apprised of other options open to them should they seek private counseling services.

Section F:

Private Practice

1. The member should assist the profession by facilitating the availability of counseling services in private as well as public settings.

2. In advertising services as a private practitioner, the member must advertise the services in such a manner so as to accurately inform the public as to services, expertise, profession, and techniques of counseling in a professional manner. A member who assumes an executive leadership role in the organization shall not permit his/her name to be used in professional notices during periods when not actively engaged in the private practice of counseling.

The member may list the following: highest relevant degree, type and level of certification or license, type and/or description of services, and other relevant information, Such information must not contain false, inaccurate, misleading, partial, out-of-context, or deceptive material or statements.

3. Members may join in partnership/corporation with other members and/or other professionals provided that each member of the partnership or corporation makes clear the separate specialties by name in compliance with the regulations of the locality.

4. A member has an obligation to withdraw from a counseling relationship if it is believed that employment will result in violation of the *Ethical Standards*. If the mental or physical condition of the member renders it difficult to carry out an effective

professional relationship or if the member is discharged by the client because the counseling relationship is no longer productive for the client, then the member is obligated to terminate the counseling relationship.

5. A member must adhere to the regulations for private practice of the locality where the services are offered.

6. It is unethical to use one's institutional affiliation to recruit clients for one's private practice.

Section G:

Personnel Administration

It is recognized that most members are employed in public or quasi-public institutions. The functioning of a member within an institution must contribute to the goals of the institution and vice versa if either is to accomplish their respective goals or objectives. It is therefore essential that the member and the institution function in ways to (a) make the institution's goals explicit and public; (b) make the member's contribution to institutional goals specific; and (c) foster mutual accountability for goal achievement.

To accomplish these objectives, it is recognized that the member and the employer must share responsibilities in the formulation and implementation of personnel policies.

1. Members must define and describe the parameters and levels of their professional competency.

2. Members must establish interpersonal relations and working agreements with supervisors and subordinates regarding counseling or clinical relationships, confidentiality, distinction between public and private material, maintenance, and dissemination of recorded information, work load and accountability. Working agreements in each instance must be specified and made known to those concerned.

3. Members must alert their employers to conditions that may be potentially disruptive or damaging.

4. Members must inform employers of conditions that may limit their effectiveness.

5. Members must submit regularly to professional review and evaluation.

6. Members must be responsible for inservice development of self and-or staff.

7. Members must inform their staff of goals and programs.

8. Members must provide personnel practices that guarantee and enhance the rights and welfare of each recipient of their service.

9. Members must select competent persons and assign responsibilities compatible with their skills and experiences.

Section H:

Preparation Standards

Members who are responsible for training others must be guided by the preparation standards of the Association and relevant Division(s). The member who functions in the capacity of trainer assumes unique ethical responsibilities that frequently go beyond that of the member who does not function in a training capacity. These ethical responsibilities are outlined as follows:

1. Members must orient students to program expectations, basic skills development, and employment prospects prior to admission to the program.

2. Members in charge of learning experiences must establish programs that integrate academic study and supervised practice.

3. Members must establish a program directed toward developing students' skills, knowledge, and self-understanding, stated whenever possible in competency or performance terms.

4. Members must identify the levels of competencies of their students in compliance with relevant Division standards. These competencies must accommodate the para-professional as well as the professional.

5. Members, through continual student evaluation and appraisal, must be aware of the personal limitations of the learner that might impede future performance. The instructor must not only assist the learner in securing remedial assistance but also screen from the program those individuals who are unable to provide competent services.

6. Members must provide a program that includes training in research commensurate with levels of role functioning. Para-professional and technician-level personnel must be trained as consumers of research. In addition, these personnel must learn how to evaluate their own and their program's effectiveness. Graduate training, especially at the doctoral level, would include preparation for original research by the member.

7. Members must make students aware of the ethical responsibilities and standards of the profession.

8. Preparatory programs must encourage students to value the ideals of service to individuals and to society. In this regard, direct financial remuneration or lack thereof must not influence the quality of service rendered. Monetary considerations must not be allowed to overshadow professional and humanitarian needs.

9. Members responsible for educational programs must be skilled as teachers and practitioners.

10. Members must present thoroughly varied theoretical positions so that students may make comparisons and have the opportunity to select a position.

11. Members must develop clear policies within their educational institutions regarding field placement and the roles of the student and the instructor in such placements.

12. **Members must ensure that forms of learning focusing on self-understanding or growth are voluntary, or if required as part of the education program, are made known to prospective students prior to entering the program. When the education program offers a growth experience with an emphasis on self-disclosure or other relatively intimate or personal involvement, the member must have no administrative, supervisory, or evaluating authority regarding the participant.**

13. Members must conduct an educational program in keeping with the current relevant guidelines of the Association and its Divisions.

Ethical Standards
American Association for Counseling and Development

PREAMBLE

Psychologists respect the dignity and worth of the individual and strive for the preservation and protection of fundamental human rights. They are committed to increasing knowledge of human behavior and of people's understanding of themselves and others and to the utilization of such knowledge for the promotion of human welfare. While pursuing these objectives, they make every effort to protect the welfare of those who seek their services and of the research participants that may be the object of study. They use their skills only for purposes consistent with these values and do not knowingly permit their misuse by others. While demanding for themselves freedom of inquiry and communication, psychologists accept the responsibility this freedom requires: competence, objectivity in the application of skills, and concern for the best interests of clients, colleagues, students, research participants, and society. In the pursuit of these ideals, psychologists subscribe to principles in the following areas: 1. Responsibility, 2. Competence, 3. Moral and Legal Standards, 4. Public Statements, 5. Confidentiality, 6. Welfare of the Consumer, 7. Professional Relationships, 8. Assessment Techniques, 9. Research With Human Participants, and 10. Care and Use of Animals.

Acceptance of membership in the American Psychological Association commits the member to adherence to these principles.

Psychologists cooperate with duly constituted committees of the American Psychological Association, in particular, the Committee on Scientific and Professional Ethics and Conduct, by responding to inquiries promptly and completely. Members also respond promptly and completely to inquiries from duly constituted state association ethics committees and professional standards review committees.

This version of the Ethical Principles of Psychologists (formerly entitled Ethical Standards of Psychologists) was adopted by the American Psychological Association's Council of Representatives on January 24, 1981. The revised Ethical Principles contain both substantive and grammatical changes in each of the nine ethical principles constituting the Ethical Standards of Psychologists previously adopted by the Council of Representatives in 1979, plus a new tenth principle entitled Care and Use of Animals. Inquiries concerning the Ethical Principles of Psychologists should be addressed to the Administrative Officer for Ethics, American Psychological Association, 1200 Seventeenth Street, N.W., Washington, D.C. 20036.

These revised Ethical Principles apply to psychologists, to students of psychology, and to others who do work of a psychological nature under the supervision of a psychologist. They are also intended for the guidance of nonmembers of the Association who are engaged in psychological research or practice.

Any complaints of unethical conduct filed after January 24, 1981, shall be governed by this 1981 revision. However, conduct (a) complained about after January 24, 1981, but which occurred prior to that date, and (b) not considered unethical under prior versions of the principles but considered unethical under the 1981 revision, shall not be deemed a violation of ethical principles. Any complaints pending as of January 24, 1981, shall be governed either by the 1979 or by the 1981 version of the Ethical Principles, at the sound discretion of the Committee on Scientific and Professional Ethics and Conduct.

Principle 1
RESPONSIBILITY

In providing services, psychologists maintain the highest standards of their profession. They accept responsibility for the consequences of their acts and make every effort to ensure that their services are used appropriately.

a. As scientists, psychologists accept responsibility for the selection of their research topics and the methods used in investigation, analysis, and reporting. They plan their research in ways to minimize the possibility that their findings will be misleading. They provide thorough discussion of the limitations of their data, especially where their work touches on social policy or might be construed to the detriment of persons in specific age, sex, ethnic, socioeconomic, or other social groups. In publishing reports of their work, they never suppress disconfirming data, and they acknowledge the existence of alternative hypotheses and explanations of their findings. Psychologists take credit only for work they have actually done.

b. Psychologists clarify in advance with all appropriate persons and agencies the expectations for sharing and utilizing research data. They avoid relationships that may limit their objectivity or create a conflict of interest. Interference with the milieu in which data are collected is kept to a minimum.

c. Psychologists have the responsibility to attempt to prevent distortion, misuse, or suppression of psychological findings by the institution or agency of which they are employees.

d. As members of governmental or other organizational bodies, psychologists remain accountable as individuals to the highest standards of their profession.

e. As teachers, psychologists recognize their primary obligation to help others acquire knowledge and skill. They maintain high standards of scholarship by presenting psychological information objectively, fully, and accurately.

f. As practitioners, psychologists know that they bear a heavy social responsibility because their recommendations and professional actions may alter the lives of others. They are alert to personal, social, organizational, financial, or political situations and pressures that might lead to misuse of their influence.

Principle 2
COMPETENCE

*The maintenance of high standards of competence is a responsibility shared by all psychologists in the in-*terest of the public and the profession as a whole. Psychologists recognize the boundaries of their competence and the limitations of their techniques. They only provide services and only use techniques for which they are qualified by training and experience. In those areas in which recognized standards do not yet exist, psychologists take whatever precautions are necessary to protect the welfare of their clients. They maintain knowledge of current scientific and professional information related to the services they render.*

a. Psychologists accurately represent their competence, education, training, and experience. They claim as evidence of educational qualifications only those degrees obtained from institutions acceptable under the Bylaws and Rules of Council of the American Psychological Association.

b. As teachers, psychologists perform their duties on the basis of careful preparation so that their instruction is accurate, current, and scholarly.

c. Psychologists recognize the need for continuing education and are open to new procedures and changes in expectations and values over time.

d. Psychologists recognize differences among people, such as those that may be associated with age, sex, socioeconomic, and ethnic backgrounds. When necessary, they obtain training, experience, or counsel to assure competent service or research relating to such persons.

e. Psychologists responsible for decisions involving individuals or policies based on test results have an understanding of psychological or educational measurement, validation problems, and test research.

f. Psychologists recognize that personal problems and conflicts may interfere with professional effectiveness. Accordingly, they refrain from undertaking any activity in which their personal problems are likely to lead to inadequate performance or harm to a client, colleague, student, or research participant. If engaged in such activity when they become aware of their personal problems, they seek competent professional assistance to determine whether they should suspend, terminate, or limit the scope of their professional and/or scientific activities.

Principle 3
MORAL AND LEGAL STANDARDS

Psychologists' moral and ethical standards of behavior are a personal matter to the same degree as they are for any other citizen, except as these may compromise the fulfillment of their professional responsibilities or reduce the public trust in psychology and psychologists. Regarding their own behavior, psychologists are sensitive to prevailing community standards and to the pos-

sible impact that conformity to or deviation from these standards may have upon the quality of their performance as psychologists. Psychologists are also aware of the possible impact of their public behavior upon the ability of colleagues to perform their professional duties.

a. As teachers, psychologists are aware of the fact that their personal values may affect the selection and presentation of instructional materials. When dealing with topics that may give offense, they recognize and respect the diverse attitudes that students may have toward such materials.

b. As employees or employers, psychologists do not engage in or condone practices that are inhumane or that result in illegal or unjustifiable actions. Such practices include, but are not limited to, those based on considerations of race, handicap, age, gender, sexual preference, religion, or national origin in hiring, promotion, or training.

c. In their professional roles, psychologists avoid any action that will violate or diminish the legal and civil rights of clients or of others who may be affected by their actions.

d. As practitioners and researchers, psychologists act in accord with Association standards and guidelines related to practice and to the conduct of research with human beings and animals. In the ordinary course of events, psychologists adhere to relevant governmental laws and institutional regulations. When federal, state, provincial, organizational, or institutional laws, regulations, or practices are in conflict with Association standards and guidelines, psychologists make known their commitment to Association standards and guidelines and, wherever possible, work toward a resolution of the conflict. Both practitioners and researchers are concerned with the development of such legal and quasi-legal regulations as best serve the public interest, and they work toward changing existing regulations that are not beneficial to the public interest.

Principle 4
PUBLIC STATEMENTS

Public statements, announcements of services, advertising, and promotional activities of psychologists serve the purpose of helping the public make informed judgments and choices. Psychologists represent accurately and objectively their professional qualifications, affiliations, and functions, as well as those of the institutions or organizations with which they or the statements may be associated. In public statements providing psychological information or professional opinions or provid-

ing information about the availability of psychological products, publications, and services, psychologists base their statements on scientifically acceptable psychological findings and techniques with full recognition of the limits and uncertainties of such evidence.

a. When announcing or advertising professional services, psychologists may list the following information to describe the provider and services provided: name, highest relevant academic degree earned from a regionally accredited institution, date, type, and level of certification or licensure, diplomate status, APA membership status, address, telephone number, office hours, a brief listing of the type of psychological services offered, an appropriate presentation of fee information, foreign languages spoken, and policy with regard to third-party payments. Additional relevant or important consumer information may be included if not prohibited by other sections of these Ethical Principles.

b. In announcing or advertising the availability of psychological products, publications, or services, psychologists do not present their affiliation with any organization in a manner that falsely implies sponsorship or certification by that organization. In particular and for example, psychologists do not state APA membership or fellow status in a way to suggest that such status implies specialized professional competence or qualifications. Public statements include, but are not limited to, communication by means of periodical, book, list, directory, television, radio, or motion picture. They do not contain (i) a false, fraudulent, misleading, deceptive, or unfair statement; (ii) a misinterpretation of fact or a statement likely to mislead or deceive because in context it makes only a partial disclosure of relevant facts; (iii) a testimonial from a patient regarding the quality of a psychologists' services or products; (iv) a statement intended or likely to create false or unjustified expectations of favorable results; (v) a statement implying unusual, unique, or one-of-a-kind abilities; (vi) a statement intended or likely to appeal to a client's fears, anxieties, or emotions concerning the possible results of failure to obtain the offered services; (vii) a statement concerning the comparative desirability of offered services; (viii) a statement of direct solicitation of individual clients.

c. Psychologists do not compensate or give anything of value to a representative of the press, radio, television, or other communication medium in anticipation of or in return for professional publicity in a news item. A paid advertisement must be identified as such, unless it is apparent from the context that it is a paid advertisement. If communicated to the public by use of radio or television, an advertisement is prerecorded and approved for broadcast by the psychologist, and a recording of the actual transmission is retained by the psychologist.

d. Announcements or advertisements of "personal growth groups," clinics, and agencies give a clear statement of purpose and a clear description of the experiences to be provided. The education, training, and experience of the staff members are appropriately specified.

e. Psychologists associated with the development or promotion of psychological devices, books, or other products offered for commercial sale make reasonable efforts to ensure that announcements and advertisements are presented in a professional, scientifically acceptable, and factually informative manner.

f. Psychologists do not participate for personal gain in commercial announcements or advertisements recommending to the public the purchase or use of proprietary or single-source products or services when that participation is based solely upon their identification as psychologists.

g. Psychologists present the science of psychology and offer their services, products, and publications fairly and accurately, avoiding misrepresentation through sensationalism, exaggeration, or superficiality. Psychologists are guided by the primary obligation to aid the public in developing informed judgments, opinions, and choices.

h. As teachers, psychologists ensure that statements in catalogs and course outlines are accurate and not misleading, particularly in terms of subject matter to be covered, bases for evaluating progress, and the nature of course experiences. Announcements, brochures, or advertisements describing workshops, seminars, or other educational programs accurately describe the audience for which the program is intended as well as eligibility requirements, educational objectives, and nature of the materials to be covered. These announcements also accurately represent the education, training, and experience of the psychologists presenting the programs and any fees involved.

i. Public announcements or advertisements soliciting research participants in which clinical services or other professional services are offered as an inducement make clear the nature of the services as well as the costs and other obligations to be accepted by participants in the research.

j. A psychologist accepts the obligation to correct others who represent the psychologist's professional qualifications, or associations with products or services, in a manner incompatible with these guidelines.

k. Individual diagnostic and therapeutic services are provided only in the context of a professional psychological relationship. When personal advice is given by means of public lectures or demonstrations, newspaper or magazine articles, radio or television programs, mail, or similar media, the psychologist utilizes the most current relevant data and exercises the highest level of professional judgment.

l. Products that are described or presented by means of public lectures or demonstrations, newspaper or magazine articles, radio or television programs, or similar media meet the same recognized standards as exist for products used in the context of a professional relationship.

Principle 5
CONFIDENTIALITY

Psychologists have a primary obligation to respect the confidentiality of information obtained from persons in the course of their work as psychologists. They reveal such information to others only with the consent of the person or the person's legal representative, except in those unusual circumstances in which not to do so would result in clear danger to the person or to others. Where appropriate, psychologists inform their clients of the legal limits of confidentiality.

a. Information obtained in clinical or consulting relationships, or evaluative data concerning children, students, employees, and others, is discussed only for professional purposes and only with persons clearly concerned with the case. Written and oral reports present only data germane to the purposes of the evaluation, and every effort is made to avoid undue invasion of privacy.

b. Psychologists who present personal information obtained during the course of professional work in writings, lectures, or other public forums either obtain adequate prior consent to do so or adequately disguise all identifying information.

c. Psychologists make provisions for maintaining confidentiality in the storage and disposal of records.

d. When working with minors or other persons who are unable to give voluntary, informed consent, psychologists take special care to protect these persons' best interests.

Principle 6
WELFARE OF THE CONSUMER

Psychologists respect the integrity and protect the welfare of the people and groups with whom they work. When conflicts of interest arise between clients and psychologists' employing institutions, psychologists clarify the nature and direction of their loyalties and responsibilities and keep all parties informed of their commitments. Psychologists fully inform consumers as to the purpose and nature of an evaluative, treatment, educational, or training procedure, and they freely acknowledge that clients, students, or participants in research have freedom of choice with regard to participation.

a. Psychologists are continually cognizant of their own needs and of their potentially influential position vis-à-vis persons such as clients, students, and subordinates. They avoid exploiting the trust and dependency of such persons. Psychologists make every effort to avoid dual relationships that could impair their professional judgment or increase the risk of exploitation. Examples of such dual relationships include, but are not limited to, research with and treatment of employees, students, supervisees, close friends, or relatives. Sexual intimacies with clients are unethical.

b. When a psychologist agrees to provide services to a client at the request of a third party, the psychologist assumes the responsibility of clarifying the nature of the relationships to all parties concerned.

c. Where the demands of an organization require psychologists to violate these Ethical Principles, psychologists clarify the nature of the conflict between the demands and these principles. They inform all parties of psychologists' ethical responsibilities and take appropriate action.

d. Psychologists make advance financial arrangements that safeguard the best interests of and are clearly understood by their clients. They neither give nor receive any remuneration for referring clients for professional services. They contribute a portion of their services to work for which they receive little or no financial return.

e. Psychologists terminate a clinical or consulting relationship when it is reasonably clear that the consumer is not benefiting from it. They offer to help the consumer locate alternative sources of assistance.

Principle 7
PROFESSIONAL RELATIONSHIPS

Psychologists act with due regard for the needs, special competencies, and obligations of their colleagues in psychology and other professions. They respect the prerogatives and obligations of the institutions or organizations with which these other colleagues are associated.

a. Psychologists understand the areas of competence of related professions. They make full use of all the professional, technical, and administrative resources that serve the best interests of consumers. The absence of formal relationships with other professional workers does not relieve psychologists of the responsibility of securing for their clients the best possible professional service, nor does it relieve them of the obligation to exercise foresight, diligence, and tact in obtaining the complementary or alternative assistance needed by clients.

b. Psychologists know and take into account the traditions and practices of other professional groups with whom they work and cooperate fully with such groups. If a person is receiving similar services from another professional, psychologists do not offer their own services directly to such a person. If a psychologist is contacted by a person who is already receiving similar services from another professional, the psychologist carefully considers that professional relationship and proceeds with caution and sensitivity to the therapeutic issues as well as the client's welfare. The psychologist discusses these issues with the client so as to minimize the risk of confusion and conflict.

c. Psychologists who employ or supervise other professionals or professionals in training accept the obligation to facilitate the further professional development of these individuals. They provide appropriate working conditions, timely evaluations, constructive consultation, and experience opportunities.

d. Psychologists do not exploit their professional relationships with clients, supervisees, students, employees, or research participants sexually or otherwise. Psychologists do not condone or engage in sexual harassment. Sexual harassment is defined as deliberate or repeated comments, gestures, or physical contacts of a sexual nature that are unwanted by the recipient.

e. In conducting research in institutions or organizations, psychologists secure appropriate authorization to conduct such research. They are aware of their obligations to future research workers and ensure that host institutions receive adequate information about the research and proper acknowledgment of their contributions.

f. Publication credit is assigned to those who have contributed to a publication in proportion to their professional contributions. Major contributions of a professional character made by several persons to a common project are recognized by joint authorship, with the individual who made the principal contribution listed first. Minor contributions of a professional character and extensive clerical or similar nonprofessional assistance may be acknowledged in footnotes or in an introductory statement. Acknowledgment through specific citations is made for unpublished as well as published material that has directly influenced the research or writing. Psychologists who compile and edit material of others for publication publish the material in the name of the originating group, if appropriate, with their own name appearing as chairperson or editor. All contributors are to be acknowledged and named.

g. When psychologists know of an ethical violation by another psychologist, and it seems appropriate, they informally attempt to resolve the issue by bringing the behavior to the attention of the psychologist. If the misconduct is of a minor nature and/or appears to be due to lack of sensitivity, knowledge, or experience, such an informal solution is usually appropriate. Such informal corrective efforts are made with sensitivity to any rights to confidentiality involved. If the violation does not seem amenable to an informal solution, or is of a more serious nature, psychologists bring it to the attention of the appropriate local, state, and/or national committee on professional ethics and conduct.

Principle 8
ASSESSMENT TECHNIQUES

In the development, publication, and utilization of psychological assessment techniques, psychologists make every effort to promote the welfare and best interests of the client. They guard against the misuse of assessment results. They respect the client's right to know the results, the interpretations made, and the bases for their conclusions and recommendations. Psychologists make every effort to maintain the security of tests and other assessment techniques within limits of legal mandates. They strive to ensure the appropriate use of assessment techniques by others.

a. In using assessment techniques, psychologists respect the right of clients to have full explanations of the nature and purpose of the techniques in language the clients can understand, unless an explicit exception to this right has been agreed upon in advance. When the explanations are to be provided by others, psychologists establish procedures for ensuring the adequacy of these explanations.

b. Psychologists responsible for the development and standardization of psychological tests and other assessment techniques utilize established scientific procedures and observe the relevant APA standards.

c. In reporting assessment results, psychologists indicate any reservations that exist regarding validity or reliability because of the circumstances of the assessment or the inappropriateness of the norms for the person tested. Psychologists strive to ensure that the results of assessments and their interpretations are not misused by others.

d. Psychologists recognize that assessment results may become obsolete. They make every effort to avoid and prevent the misuse of obsolete measures.

e. Psychologists offering scoring and interpretation services are able to produce appropriate evidence for the validity of the programs and procedures used in arriving at interpretations. The public offering of an automated interpretation service is considered a professional-to-professional consultation. Psychologists make every effort to avoid misuse of assessment reports.

f. Psychologists do not encourage or promote the use of psychological assessment techniques by inappropriately trained or otherwise unqualified persons through teaching, sponsorship, or supervision.

Principle 9
RESEARCH WITH HUMAN PARTICIPANTS

The decision to undertake research rests upon a considered judgment by the individual psychologist about how best to contribute to psychological science and human welfare. Having made the decision to conduct research, the psychologist considers alternative directions in which research energies and resources might be invested. On the basis of this consideration, the psychologist carries out the investigation with respect and concern for the dignity and welfare of the people who participate and with cognizance of federal and state regulations and professional standards governing the conduct of research with human participants.

a. In planning a study, the investigator has the responsibility to make a careful evaluation of its ethical acceptability. To the extent that the weighing of scientific and human values suggests a compromise of any principle, the investigator incurs a correspondingly serious obligation to seek ethical advice and to observe stringent safeguards to protect the rights of human participants.

b. Considering whether a participant in a planned study will be a "subject at risk" or a "subject at minimal risk," according to recognized standards, is of primary ethical concern to the investigator.

c. The investigator always retains the responsibility for ensuring ethical practice in research. The investigator is also responsible for the ethical treatment of research participants by collaborators, assistants, students, and employees, all of whom, however, incur similar obligations.

d. Except in minimal-risk research, the investigator establishes a clear and fair agreement with research participants, prior to their participation, that clarifies the obligations and responsibilities of each. The investigator has the obligation to honor all promises and commitments included in that agreement. The investigator informs the participants of all aspects of the research that might reasonably be expected to influence willingness to participate and explains all other aspects of the research about which the participants inquire. Failure to make full disclosure prior to obtaining informed consent requires additional safeguards to protect the welfare and dignity of the research participants. Research with children or with participants who have impairments that would limit understanding and/or communication requires special safeguarding procedures.

e. Methodological requirements of a study may make the use of concealment or deception necessary. Before conducting such a study, the investigator has a special responsibility to (i) determine whether the use of such techniques is justified by the study's prospective scientific, educational, or applied value; (ii) determine whether alternative procedures are available that do not use concealment or deception; and (iii) ensure that the participants are provided with sufficient explanation as soon as possible.

f. The investigator respects the individual's freedom to decline to participate in or to withdraw from the research at any time. The obligation to protect this freedom requires careful thought and consideration when the investigator is in a position of authority or influence over the participant. Such positions of authority include, but are not limited to, situations in which research participation is required as part of employment or in which the participant is a student, client, or employee of the investigator.

g. The investigator protects the participant from physical and mental discomfort, harm, and danger that may arise from research procedures. If risks of such consequences exist, the investigator informs the participant of that fact. Research procedures likely to cause serious or lasting harm to a participant are not used unless the failure to use these procedures might expose the participant to risk of greater harm, or unless the research has great potential benefit and fully informed and voluntary consent is obtained from each participant. The participant should be informed of procedures for contacting the investigator within a reasonable time period following participation should stress, potential harm, or related questions or concerns arise.

h. After the data are collected, the investigator provides the participant with information about the nature of the study and attempts to remove any misconceptions that may have arisen. Where scientific or humane values justify delaying or withholding this information, the investigator incurs a special responsibility to monitor the research and to ensure that there are no damaging consequences for the participant.

i. Where research procedures result in undesirable consequences for the individual participant, the investigator has the responsibility to detect and remove or correct these consequences, including long-term effects.

j. Information obtained about a research participant during the course of an investigation is confidential unless otherwise agreed upon in advance. When the possibility exists that others may obtain access to such information, this possibility, together with the plans for protecting confidentiality, is explained to the participant as part of the procedure for obtaining informed consent.

Principle 10
CARE AND USE OF ANIMALS

An investigator of animal behavior strives to advance understanding of basic behavioral principles and/or to contribute to the improvement of human health and welfare. In seeking these ends, the investigator ensures the welfare of animals and treats them humanely. Laws and regulations notwithstanding, an animal's immediate protection depends upon the scientist's own conscience.

a. The acquisition, care, use, and disposal of all animals are in compliance with current federal, state or provincial, and local laws and regulations.

b. A psychologist trained in research methods and experienced in the care of laboratory animals closely supervises all procedures involving animals and is responsible for ensuring appropriate consideration of their comfort, health, and humane treatment.

c. Psychologists ensure that all individuals using animals under their supervision have received explicit instruction in experimental methods and in the care, maintenance, and handling of the species being used. Responsibilities and activities of individuals participating in a research project are consistent with their respective competencies.

d. Psychologists make every effort to minimize discomfort, illness, and pain of animals. A procedure subjecting animals to pain, stress, or privation is used only when an alternative procedure is unavailable and the goal is justified by its prospective scientific, educational, or applied value. Surgical procedures are performed under appropriate anesthesia; techniques to avoid infection and minimize pain are followed during and after surgery.

e. When it is appropriate that the animal's life be terminated, it is done rapidly and painlessly.

Name Index

Achenbach, T. & Edelbrock, C., child research by, 138
Altman, K.
  on adolescent resistance, 131
  on proxemics, 145
  on role-taking interviews, 138
Arvey, R.D. & Campion, J.E., on hiring interviews, 11, 240
Atchley, R.C.
  on older adults, 162
  research on aging by, 178

Baker, H.K., on performance-appraisal interviews, 250
Baruth, L.G. & Huber, C.H., on interviewer attitudes and behavior, 19
Bee, H.L., on middle-adulthood changes, 153
Belkin, G.S., on adapting interviews to settings, 142
Bell, J.E., on family interviews, 188
Benjamin, A.
  on advice-giving, 57
  on multiple questions, 45
Bennett, C.I., on interviewee attitudes and values, 22
Berman, J., on interviewing skills, 61
Bernstein, L. & Bernstein, R.S., on division of communication process, 219
Bingham, W.V.D., Moore, B.V., and Gustad, J.W., on relationships in business interviews, 245

Blackham, G.J.
  on goal setting, 55
  on paraphrasing, 48
  on summarizing, 50
Brammer, L.M.
  on goal-setting contracts, 58
  on human-services professions, 15–16
  on "why" questions, 45
Brink, T.L., information on interviewing older persons by, 178
Bull, P.
  on body language, 29
  on decoding nonverbal cues, 33–34

Carkhuff, R.R.
  on alliances, 77
  on interviewing training, 63
  systemized interviewing by, 86
Carkhuff, R.R. & Anthony, W.A., on interviewing skills, 62
Carkhuff, R.R., Pierce, R.M., and Cannon, J.R., on interviewer behavior, 19
Charles, D., Fleetwood-Walker, P., & Luck, M., on questions, 42
Claiborn, C., social influence theory by, 68
Cormier, L.S. & Cormier, W.H.
  on clarification, 47
  on goal statements, 56
  interviewing stages by, 86
  on stages in therapeutic process, 68–69

Subject Index

Academic underachievement by adolescents, 126
Action
  plans of, 7, 59–60
  rehearsing for, 84, 204–205
Active listening, 45–46
  in employment interviews, 246
  in personal-helping interviews, 256
Adolescents, interviewing, 115–116
  characteristics of, 124–125
  and cognitive development, 118–122
  conclusion stage in, 136–137
  direction stage in, 135–136
  and identity formation, 123–124
  initiation stage in, 129–135
  and moral development, 122–123
  and physical development, 117–118
  preparation stage in, 128–129
  problem areas present in, 126–127
Adults, interviewing
  compared to children, 93–94, 96–97
  developmental considerations in, 147–155
  nonverbal components of, 143–145
  setting for, 141–142
  verbal components of, 145–147
  See also Older adults
Advice-giving, 56–57
Age Discrimination in Employment Act, 235
Age norms and interviewing adolescents, 116
Aging and age differences
  dealing with, 172–176

effect of, in interviewing older adults, 164–168
Alcohol abuse by adolescents, 126
Alliances, 76–77
  with children, 103
  in family interviews, 189–190
  in health care interviews, 214
All-or-nothing thinking in children, 97
Alzheimer's disease, 174
American Journal of Epidemiology, 231
Analysis in interviewing, 146–147
Anemia in older adults, 174
Anorexia nervosa and adolescents, 127
Appearance and physical attractiveness
  and adolescents, 117–118
  and interviewee expectations, 24
Appointment scheduling by adolescents, 128
Approval of interviewee actions, 59–60
Arm gestures, nonverbal communication through, 30
Attention span of older adults, 171
Attitudes
  interviewee, 22
  interviewer, 19

Biases
  of interviewers, 17
  response, 219
Body language, 28–32, 144–145

Skills, interviewing
  clarification, 42–43
  and communication, 4–5
  concerns identification, 48–53
  evaluation and followup, 60–62
  goal setting, 54–59
  implementation of plans, 59–60
  information seeking, 43–48
  model of, 38–40
  rapport building, 40–42
  research on, 62–63
  sequence of, 5
Skin, nonverbal communication through, 31
Small talk, 42
Social cognition in children, 97–98, 100
Social environment, 72
Social Forces of Later Life, The, 178
Spatial distance. *See* Proxemics
Speech
  and older adults, 164–165
  rate of, 25–26, 31
Stabilization and career development, 152
Stages, interview, 5, 67–69. *See also*
  Conclusion stage; Direction stage;
  Initiation stage; Preparation stage
"Standards for Providers of Psychological Services," 72
Star questioning approach in family interviews, 197
Stated objectives and performance interviews, 249–250
Story completion with children, 97, 107
Strategies, determination of, 74–76
  in employment interviews, 244–245
  in family interviews, 187–188
Strengths of interviewers, 18
Stress in adult development, 148–149
Stress interview, 242–243
Structured approach
  with children, 101–103
  in employment interviews, 242
Suicide and adolescents, 126–127
Summarization of interview ideas, 50–53
  in adult interviews, 146–147
  in health care interviews, 223
Support giving, 57–58
Symbolic representation and children, 95

Tactics, determination of, 74–76
  in employment interviews, 245–247
  in family interviews, 188
Talking, Feeling, and Doing Game (Gardner), 109
Targeting concerns, 49–50
  in direction stage, 79–81
  in family interviews, 196
Terminating interviews, 84–85
  in family interviews, 205–206
  in health care interviews, 227
Termination of employment interviews, 252–254
Therapy, family, compared to family interviewing, 184
"Third ear" listening, 45, 143
Threat, reduction of, with children, 107
Time and time constraints, 6
  cultural attitudes towards, 30, 33
  in employment interviews, 241, 246
  for health care interviews, 215–216
  in problem-resolution interviews, 251
Tone of voice
  cultural differences in, 26
  nonverbal communication through, 31
Touching, 28, 30
Training, skills, research on, 62–63
Translation of words, cultural differences in, 27

Underachievement, academic, by adolescents, 126
Underestimating abilities, interviewer tendency of, 171–172
Universities, job recruitment at, 237
Unstructured approach in employment interviews, 241–242

Values
  interviewee, 22–23
  interviewer, 17, 20–21
Verification of communication, 83–84
  in family interviews, 201–202
  in health care interviews, 223
Vietnam-Era Readjustment Assistance Act, 236
Vocational Rehabilitation Act, 236
Voice, tone of
  cultural differences in, 26
  nonverbal communication through, 31

WE VALUE YOUR OPINION—PLEASE SHARE IT WITH US

Merrill Publishing and our authors are most interested in your reactions to this textbook. Did it serve you well in the course? If it did, what aspects of the text were most helpful? If not, what didn't you like about it? Your comments will help us to write and develop better textbooks. We value your opinions and thank you for your help.

Text Title _____ Edition _____

Author(s) _____

Your Name (optional) _____

Address _____

City _____ State _____ Zip _____

School _____

Course Title _____

Instructor's Name _____

Your Major _____

Your Class Rank _____ Freshman _____ Sophomore _____ Junior _____ Senior

_____ Graduate Student

Were you required to take this course? _____ Required _____ Elective

Length of Course? _____ Quarter _____ Semester

1. Overall, how does this text compare to other texts you've used?

_____ Superior _____ Better Than Most _____ Average _____ Poor

2. Please rate the text in the following areas:

	Superior	Better Than Most	Average	Poor
Author's Writing Style	_____	_____	_____	_____
Readability	_____	_____	_____	_____
Organization	_____	_____	_____	_____
Accuracy	_____	_____	_____	_____
Layout and Design	_____	_____	_____	_____
Illustrations/Photos/Tables	_____	_____	_____	_____
Examples	_____	_____	_____	_____
Problems/Exercises	_____	_____	_____	_____
Topic Selection	_____	_____	_____	_____
Currentness of Coverage	_____	_____	_____	_____
Explanation of Difficult Concepts	_____	_____	_____	_____
Match-up with Course Coverage	_____	_____	_____	_____
Applications to Real Life	_____	_____	_____	_____

3. Circle those chapters you especially liked:
   1   2   3   4   5   6   7   8   9   10   11   12   13   14   15   16   17   18   19   20
   What was your favorite chapter? _____
   Comments:

4. Circle those chapters you liked least:
   1   2   3   4   5   6   7   8   9   10   11   12   13   14   15   16   17   18   19   20
   What was your least favorite chapter? _____
   Comments:

5. List any chapters your instructor did not assign. _____

6. What topics did your instructor discuss that were not covered in the text?_____

   _____

7. Were you required to buy this book? _____ Yes _____ No

   Did you buy this book new or used? _____ New _____ Used

   If used, how much did you pay? _____

   Do you plan to keep or sell this book? _____ Keep _____ Sell

   If you plan to sell the book, how much do you expect to receive? _____

   Should the instructor continue to assign this book? _____ Yes _____ No

8. Please list any other learning materials you purchased to help you in this course (e.g., study guide, lab manual).

   _____

9. What did you like most about this text? _____

   _____

10. What did you like least about this text? _____

    _____

11. General comments:

    May we quote you in our advertising? _____ Yes _____ No

    Please mail to: Boyd Lane
                      College Division, Research Department
                      Box 508
                      1300 Alum Creek Drive
                      Columbus, Ohio 43216

    Thank you!